# Voices of Italian America

# Voices of Italian America

A History of Early
Italian American Literature
with a Critical Anthology

Martino Marazzi

Translated by Ann Goldstein

Madison • Teaneck
Fairleigh Dickinson University Press

Associated University Presses
2010 Eastpark Boulevard
Cranbury, NJ 08512

The paper used in this publication meets the requirements of the American National Standard for Permanence of Paper for Printed Library Materials Z39.48-1984.

Library of Congress Cataloging-in-Publication Data

Marazzi, Martino, 1963–
Voices of Italian America : a history of early Italian American literature / Martino Marazzi with a critical anthology translated by Ann Goldstein.
    p. cm.
Includes bibliographical references and index.
ISBN 0-8386-4016-8 (alk. paper)
1. Italian American literature—History and criticism 2. Italian literature—20th century—History and criticism. 3. American literature—Italian American authors—History and criticism. 4. Italians—United States—Intellectual life. 5. Italian Americans—Intellectual life. 6. Italian-Americans in literature. 7. United States—In literature. I. Goldstein, Ann, 1949– II. Title.
PQ5981.M3733 2004
850.8'0973—dc22

                                                    2003021431

*To Pia*

# Contents

# Acknowledgments

Parts of this volume are the translation, with a few minor additions and corrections, of a book that I published in Italy in 2001 while living in New York. Now that I've come home to roost, it seems fitting that many of the literary texts that I have focused on are being presented, in English, by an American publisher. The American version of this work is therefore much larger than the original: in fact, it constitutes a new book, which has involved further research and a painstaking effort of adjustment, in many senses. All through these months, I have had the privilege to work side by side, half a world away, with Ann Goldstein, who has shown me the endurance and the zeal of the most professional translator, and has been an invaluable source of help. Harry Keyishian, at Fairleigh Dickinson University Press, has followed with patience and a similar positive spirit the development of the project in all its various phases. I also wish to acknowledge the support of the National Italian American Foundation in Washington and of the Italian Ministry of Foreign Affairs, which awarded two grants for the translation from the Italian.

Introducing *Misteri di Little Italy*, I expressed my gratitude to a number of individuals and institutions, and to them I am still deeply indebted. Three years later, I wish to renew my warmest thanks to Francesco Durante, whose pioneering trail I have tried to follow, without being able to equal his expertise and generosity; to Giorgio Bertellini, a beacon of scholarship and friendship; and to David Freedberg, at Columbia's Italian Academy, who provided an extraordinary environment for this research, in the right place and at the right time. Once again, Teddy Jefferson, Elaine Charnov, Meg McLagan, and Brian Larkin have opened their hearts, minds, and houses when I most needed them. The writing of many of these pages has benefited from conversations with intellectuals and writers who are masters in this field: Fred Gardaphé, Jim Periconi, John Paul Russo, Bill Tonelli, Joseph Tusiani, and Bob Viscusi. A first draft of Ciambelli's *Arrival* appeared in *VIA—Voices in Italian Americana* 12,

11

no. 1 (spring 2001). I thank the editors for permission to reprint it. I owe the first of my two favorite quotations to Mario Rossi, from Fornelli, whose family has always been so gracious to me; the second, sharp as an arrow, to Flora, my radioactive daughter, sweet and cool.

To the friends in Brooklyn, Manhattan, and elsewhere in the U.S., and to my *frère* Nicola, after many years I wish to extend the hope that finally some of this, if not its author, might make sense.

# Voices of Italian America

# Introduction

(I believe more and more in geographical reasons, these *funda-mental* truths)

—Alberto Savinio

Perhaps . . . ultimately, the United States is more Italian than Dutch, German, Russian, Spanish, and even more Italian than Wasp.

—Paul Virilio

THIS BOOK HAS THE GOOD FORTUNE, SO TO SPEAK, TO TELL A STORY that is over; that is to say, a story that has, with reliable approximation, both a beginning and an end. Italian Americans are still present in the United States, even in the literary sense—in fact, more than ever. But the Italian America that speaks and writes in Italian and its dialects, above all in the literary sense, has disappeared forever. Giuseppe Prezzolini, following Handlin's classic vision of the "uprooted American," saw the situation of the "transplanted" in the United States as a *failure:* a tragic failure both in its human implications (the "schizophrenia" of the immigrant, divided between two worlds) and in the historical-cultural sense (the "low" humanity of the Italian Americans contradicted every possible idea of Italian national "primacy"). It was a vision in its way grandiose, but with a negative bias. In place of the notion and the image of the *fall* I would substitute that of *loss,* which is no less problematic for those who experienced it but is limited to certain aspects of the complex cultural dynamic set in motion by the collective, traumatic uprooting that was the Great Migration. Assimilation, adjustment, and generational conflict begin during and after the loss: a whole world and a series of problems that follow separation but, although intimately connected, are distinct from it. This study does not deal with those, except in passing.

Anyone who decides to examine the traces of this story, teeming with lives, events, names, and titles, does so therefore with the knowledge that he is revealing a finite world. The moral, if there is one, lies

15

in the desire to understand *what* and *who* have been lost. The *whys*, or, rather, the historical, social, economic, and ideological reasons, that led to emigration are not hard to understand, and several scholars have in the past undertaken to explain them. Studying the literature, or, if you will, the writing, of the Italian immigrants allows, or at least feeds, the illusion of being able to enter more directly into the heart of the matter: to report, within the limits of the possible, what one has been able to hear. Tragedies and comedies abound in the texts: there is no need for the scholar to add any of his own. It is important, rather, that he be able to provide a means of facilitating readers' comprehension. Such a task is less neutral than one might think, since, in spite of the widespread work undertaken in recent decades, the study of the literature of emigration continues to represent, in Italy, one of the great taboos of research. In fact, before the publication of the great Mondadori anthology edited by Francesco Durante,[1] the very existence of this territory was unknown to the nonspecialist public.

A work on the "mysteries" of Little Italy could begin only with the intention, the mirage, in a sense, of being able to get to know them gradually, moving closer and closer until one arrived at a solution, at least a provisional one. Various references suggested that behind the composition of serialized novels in Italian, in New York between the end of the nineteenth century and the first decades of the twentieth, there was a wide, unexplored world that had given life to a multifarious literary culture in large part unknown until now. The "mysteries," therefore, of Bernardino Ciambelli's titles expanded to define the very atmosphere in which the work took place. But the heuristic hypothesis was supported from the start by a series of encouraging facts and discoveries, whose meaning can ultimately be summarized in the clear evidence of the vitality that characterized nearly every aspect of Italian American culture. To begin with the chronological trajectory, there is at one end the contemporaneous testimony of journalists and social workers, who described in detail the society of the new immigrants, and, at the other, studies of Italian American literature in English, which began to proliferate in the seventies, and—even if one is not eager to give in to a crude evolutionary biology—certainly invite one to ask where the richness of this literature originated or, more simply and in American terms, if indeed, given the results of the second generation, what preceded it could be considered a tabula rasa. In the middle is an increasing number of serious scholarly studies, especially in the fields of history, socioanthropology, and linguistics, which have provided knowledge of, to give some examples and names, the complex story of Fascism in

Little Italy, including politics, social activities, and journalism (the broad, classic works of John Diggins and Philip Cannistraro); the worship of saints and the electoral machine in Italian East Harlem (Robert Orsi and Gerald Meyer); the harsh daily life, and its rare entertainments, lived a few miles south, in the tenements of the Lower East Side (Mario Maffi); the acute divisions within the political and union activism of the immigrants (Elisabetta Vezzosi); the lexicon, morphology, and syntax of the language of the "giobba" (Hermann Haller); and the fashioning of an ethnic identity during the course of the twentieth century in Philadelphia (Stefano Luconi) and, again, in Italian Harlem, seen through the thick "lenses" of the local immigrant food (Simone Cinotto).[2] And leading up to these and other works there have been long periods of research, as well as bibliographical tables that are gradually becoming more complete. Not only that: many of those works were the result of a familiarity with research centers, Italian and American, which, with different objectives and styles, have advocated, then as now, a better understanding of immigrant culture. Because the fruits of emigration, and not only its sufferings, have come to be acknowledged, the historical and literary legacy has in recent years been described and discussed with greater authority.[3]

As the saying goes, there was enough. There was enough, that is, to justify a more strictly literary inquiry. What was needed was the archeological and investigative work of retrieving the texts and documents that might allow us to answer the many unresolved questions. In this phase an aspect emerged whose importance, I think, goes beyond the simple personal satisfaction of the individual researcher. The slow but steady establishment of a "close circle" of similarly engaged colleagues in neighboring areas seemed to me, beyond the implications of usefulness and encouragement, the sign of the development of a widely shared need for knowledge. This sort of "collectivization" of immigrant studies implies, further, that the exploration of the Atlantis that was Little Italy must be carried out in a spirit of collaboration precisely because what is emerging is a broad continent, an entire world originating in the Italian diaspora. In a certain sense, the modalities of scholarly work reproduce mimetically the profound character of the "object" that is meant to be analyzed. The variety of approaches serves to "cover up" the extensive dimensions of the territory to be explored.

Meanwhile, some small signs invited us to advance. For instance, there was the progressive elucidation of biographical details about many of the practitioners of this literature, including, to cite a favorable case, the father, Ciambelli, a mystery man par excellence: not only were his writings being discovered and collected but the principal events and stages of his life were uncovered, as if one were scraping away a palimpsest. The metaphor of the "mystery" therefore assumed, in time, a more concrete significance. Fieldwork added a different flavor to the erudite antiquarian effort: the pleasure of penetrating the unknown was accompanied by that of going deeper into a world that had been until just the other day alive and articulate, and that now offers signs of continuity (even if these are, as I said, "fossils," or, rather, in the case of the more short-lived, folkloric-oleographic traces).

But at this point some considerations of another nature must be introduced. The *ethnic renaissance*, which is one aspect of the rise of multiculturalism, at times gives the impression—above all when it is used deliberately by ethnic groups—of furnishing the pretext for activities of self-promotion and self-gratification. This may be legitimate, of course, in a militant perspective that is taking account of, among other things, a long history of oppression. But precisely because one is approaching a culture, such as Italian American culture, that is articulate and complex, a work of research conscious of ethnic diversity must be sure to indicate the fractures, the contradictions, the failures, especially in the area of artistic production. Something that I found interesting was the study of the rich "derivative" tradition that distinguishes Italian American poetry in Italian. This is a slightly pompous way of noting the fascination of verses that are irremediably "ugly." It is not, however, a question merely of aesthetic judgment: Italian American literature, which is in large part a popular literature, cannot be surveyed out of context, because its aim, in part, thanks to its abundance, is to entertain and amuse by constructing at opportune moments useful occasions of self-reflection for its audience; the real problem, if one can call it that, is that often it includes elements and attitudes that are hardly desirable. It is an immigrant literature as well in the measure to which it depicts its audience's uneasiness with other minorities: that is, it contains notable expressions of anti-Semitism, of anti-Chinese racism, of disdain toward blacks. It is a literature that certainly has to be read with a keen awareness of its relationship to the Italian tradition that it starts from (especially the popular realism and patriotic Carduccian tradition of the late nineteenth century), which guarantees its specificity in the context of the United States; yet this Italian character quite naturally often leads to results that are saturated in nationalism and Fascism (we should recall that there was an Italian American left, both political and cultural, but with the warning that it was a minority, and was bitterly divided internally).

It was an ethnic production, then, but one whose engagement in defense of its own difference has to be realistically recognized as being both confused and aggressive, since the discourse on "identity"—and one still finds this in the historical and critical work—often ends by wrapping itself in a vindication of its own successes: what certain thinkers of the nineteenth century called "primacy" and their late-twentieth-century imitators embellish with the term "achievement."

One example that we can evaluate practically without immediately rejecting it catalyzes some of these tensions: the "sketch" *L'Imperatore Selassiè* [The Emperor Selassie], written in the fatal year of the Empire, 1936, by the prince of the colonial theater, the great Eduardo Migliaccio, whose stage name was Farfariello. Employing his usual sharp alternation of sung and spoken verses, Migliaccio (who only six years later, in *Suldate Americane* [American Soldiers], encouraged the mothers of Little Italy by singing the praises of patriotism to the Stars and Stripes) here sinks into an "amusing" parody of the Negus's arrogance. The linguistic base is the usual clever mixture of Neapolitan, *Italglish*, and Italian, but what is striking is the unconventional and more absorbing mixture of doses of anti-African racism (with the fallout that can be imagined on the black audience of the neighboring ghettoes) and Fascist chauvinism.

Thus nostalgia for the homeland takes on not only innocent and romantic connotations; it is also expressed acerbically in this way, through the mouth of the most popular "entertainer" of the early generations. An official reproof is out of place; yet this example warns us not to make a naïve fetish of Italian American ethnicity, here observed in its literary manifestation. Still less is it an instrument for the use of a rhetoric of "opposition" that with the magic wand of Gramscism transforms into potential revolutionaries those who are, with all their painful contradictions, "postcolonial subjects," rejected and expelled from the harsh mother country the day after the Pyrrhic victory over brigandism, marked as inferior and therefore in large part "negated" (here a truer Gramsci helps out) by the collective consciousness of the Italians, including scholars.

Further, a literary perspective can provide information not only about the tastes and moods of the immigrants. It can, for example, help delineate characteristics of this "subordinate" culture by clarifying ambiguities and identifying the real terms of the dialectic taking place in the immigrant communities, between the extremes of total continuity with the past or total rupture with it, of ethnic insularity or assimilation. In such cases, literature could be interpreted as one of the forms that converge to determine the web of complex "social

networks" (Ramella)[4] whose functioning, far from being casual—
rather, one could say, animated by that "implicit 'rationality'" which
Ercole Sori spoke of years ago in a classic work on emigration—
involves, obviously, not only the area of work, which up to now was
the center of scholarly interest.[5] For example, the relationship between the prevalence of illiteracy, a macroscopic social fact, and the
persistent vitality among Italian Americans of a great variety of institutions of writing needs to be reconsidered. Illiteracy should be
seen not as an immovable rock but as a reality that is continuously
attacked, worn down, overcome; on the other hand, the crushing
statistical evidence, along with a theme, evoked in strong dramatic
colors, that is present in many Italian American autobiographies, has
contributed to giving that constantly changing fact the status of a
generalized myth. Yet even the myth requires precise definition and
clarification, because this literature of the "mysteries" is not in fact a
marginal, bizarre production of a literate minority. Rather, it allows
us to observe a grand transposition-transformation in America of
habits, expressions, and cultural components (written but obviously
not that alone) of the Old World. Narrative, poetry, essays, journalism, and theater flourish and branch out, with varied outcomes and
results, yet almost always displaying a direct kinship with the "popular" and mass forms of the late nineteenth century. The literary stra-
tum of this subordinate culture is thus working out, in a language for
the most part already tested, a collectively traumatic experience
(with absolute precision Prezzolini singled out hunger as the "principal character" in the best Italian American fiction in English).

Whether one likes it or not, the authentic opposition to which
these Italian American writers gave life includes, in short, taking into
account what the contemporary poet Dana Gioia has indicated as the
"central experiences" of first- and second-generation poetry. Having
recourse to an obsolete term, we could say that the literature of Little
Italy has in a broad sense reference to a poetics of the "humble": it is
written by "social and economic outsiders" whose works originate in a
base of real poverty, shared with their audience, often accepted (but
not passively) in the name of a strong work ethic and a mentality
saturated in Catholicism.[6] Think of the narrative masterpieces of the
thirties, composed by second-generation writers such as Garibaldi
Lapolla, John Fante, and Pietro di Donato. But these are, already,
Anglophone writers, on whom the Italian literary tradition exercised
by now a completely exterior pull.

Still, the evident artistic success of the sons with respect, often, to
the dusty dilettantism of the Italophone fathers should not lead us to
relegate the latter to an area of presumed backwardness: from what-

ever point of view one approaches the literary works composed in the United States in the wake of the Great Migration—from that of the Italian America of the post–Second World War, or that of the variegated American mosaic, or even that of a contemporary Italian—it emerges as a historically relevant reality, whose documents and actors deserve to be saved from oblivion and, finally, read and known, with the awareness of their roots and of the networks and relationships that they initiated in the New World. I hope to succeed here in transforming the long silence into an occasion marked by the emotion of a first-time hearing.

# 1

# The Novel of the Italian in America

I forgot Italian and I didn't learn English.
—M. R., Philadelphia

## Narrative and Press: The Ventura "Case"

Let's listen to an authoritative prophet:

> Basically, I believe that the great, true book: novel, epic poem, or whatever it might be, of the Italian in America, if it has not been written up to now, never will be. And it couldn't have been written, except in dialect: in one of those harsh, barbaric, unheard-of dialects that came into existence in our enormous, suffering communities on American soil. In a new language: just as the reality of which our immigrants were in part the creators and victims was new.
>
> Or to be more exact: this book, this poem has been written, but in letters of stone; it was carved into the rock of Manhattan, into the docks in the harbors and the railroad tracks. In the caverns and on the walls of the mine shafts, in the furrows of endless fields.[1]

Thus Emilio Cecchi wrote at the height of the most American period of the Italian twentieth century, introducing sympathetically, but cautiously and with a certain skepticism, two young Italian American novelists: John Fante and Pietro di Donato. Vittorini's *Americana* (1941) had been published and then withdrawn and finally brought out again with Cecchi's introduction (1942), and the first offerings in Italian of the literature of emigration were appearing in bookstores: Fante's *Il cammino nella polvere* [Ask the Dust], in a Mondadori Medusa edition, translated by Vittorini (1941) and di Donato's *Cristo fra i muratori* [Christ in Concrete], in a boldly vernacular version by Eva Amendola, brought out by Bompiani, the publisher of Vittorini's anthology (also 1941). And as if to confirm, in wartime, the assertion of di Donato's proletarian neorealism, a note from the publisher—in all probability attributable to Vittorini—went so far as to declare that "intimately, spiritually, as the reader will clearly see, this is an Italian

22

book as few books in Italian are." It was a statement between the opportunistic and the propagandistic, intended to feed the casual myth of a categorical Italianness operating outside historical, cultural, and linguistic boundaries. It was a mistake that was quickly spotted and returned to the sender by Cecchi in the above-mentioned review: called into question in the name of a nationalism with, if anything, even narrower, coarser, and angrier features, and of a more experienced and aesthetically shrewd sense of the literature of the United States.

Today, however, the reading of that prophecy raises rather different considerations. Above all, it seems to us that we can say that the "great and true book" was in fact written, although outside the time frame: that is, the autobiographical trilogy of Joseph Tusiani, which flowered slowly and brilliantly from the roots of that dried-up and dying agave represented by the Italian language in the United States (that is to say, from a literary point of view; in the sociolinguistic area, as Haller's studies demonstrate, it should be considered anything but dead). Tusiani's work is a triptych composed in prose of classical elegance, behind which decades of literary mastery can be felt; it is a work in which an explicit theme is the affectionate and at the same time unmistakable detachment of the author from the by now self-referential milieu of the immigrant community's last literary circles, whose principal points of reference in the fifties were the socialist periodical *La Parola del Popolo* in Chicago, the weekly *Divagando* in New York, and the Union Square Club in downtown Manhattan. Apart from the strictly biographical aspects, Tusiani's "new word" marks the nearly, if not fully, complete achievement of a different identity, constantly in search of a fruitful relationship between the two *nationes*.

Rather than denying Cecchi's prophecy, Tusiani's work invites us to undertake an excavation back into the fertile soil deposited by more than a century of immigration, to discover the literary culture of the immigrant communities. Even if we wished to narrow our focus to narrative, a context emerges immediately in which theater and cinema, journalism and publishing, social and political activism intermingle daily, delineating a cultural dimension that for a full half century (from the 1880s to the end of the 1930s) is, in its complex variety, organic and unitary. The dialect of immigration is expressed with comic force in the theater: in its highest form, by Eduardo Migliaccio (stage name Farfariello), with a clever mixing of Italian, Neapolitan, and American. In short, already in Cecchi's time a dialect literature was being produced, and would continue to be; but the real "new language," after a series of notable early attempts (the uneven and "post-*Voce*" Emanuel Carnevali, the proletarian Pascal D'Angelo, Constantine Panunzio, and Louis Forgione), came into existence in the thirties as the young literary practitioners of the second generation became fully and convincingly acclimatized to the American language.[2] And so in words, or, rather, in deeds, they made concrete the separation—which, if not traumatic, was certainly profound and visible—from the America of their fathers (literate fathers, of course), who in all those years had continued to read and write, to express themselves, in Italian.

Consider, as a point of departure, the persistent vitality of the press, which flourished wherever a significant number of immigrants had settled. To give an idea: not long ago Pietro Russo prepared a *Catalogue of Italo-American Periodical Publications* that, covering the period 1836–1980, enumerates at least 2,344 titles. It is a rich patrimony (and a trial for the researcher) that is quickly seen to be fundamental, once we have understood the dependency—aesthetic and material—of a great part of Italian American literature on the press. In fact, the consistent presence of "serial" works in the overwhelming majority of the periodicals allows us to grasp the connection between the means of literary production, the orientation of the public, and the choices of the writers. Dominating the shelves of the shops, of the newsstands, of the bookstores and libraries as well as the columns of the press is a form of popular literature prepared on the spot by a squad of wildly prolific writers.[3] Over the decades it moves from a realistic sentimental sketch like *Il Piccolo Genovese* [The Kid from Genoa] (unsigned, in *L'Eco d'Italia,* New York, 14 May 1869) to the hardboiled memoirs of a tough guy like Detective Michele Fiaschetti (in *Corriere d'America,* in the late twenties). In the middle, the serial novel and the short story flourish, taking advantage of the simple, easily understood structures and themes that, in the same period, can be found in the productions of a Neapolitan–New York film company, Elvira Notari's Dora Film.

The drama of immigration—not yet distorted by the assimilationist ideology of more or less forced "Americanization"—is repeated and reformulated, following some basic variants: the hard-won love that unites and divides an immigrant man and an American woman (or vice versa), with, in the last lines, the ray of light of a wedding; the loss of dignity in the humiliations of the ghetto, in the mechanized, ethnic jumble of the metropolis, in the exhausting routine of a job that is almost always synonymous with exploitation; the impassive and cruel face of a justice that too often becomes a repressive machine, the penitentiary Moloch leading to the electric chair; the social redemption that arises unexpectedly from the diffuse, tangled plots. In the background, amid crimes, flights, disappearances and reappearances, deflorations and the Black Hand, is a world irremediably divided between a mother country that is for the most part lost, and is evoked with nostalgia, and the land of arrival, which is harsh and unrelenting but also the scene of hard-earned victories.

Once we have acquired an overall view of this world, fragmented and dispersed in the newspaper columns, we can more reliably make a list of the important names. Among the journals, those which were deeply engaged in promoting an indigenous Italian American literature were: *La Follia di New York* (still active, founded in 1893 by Francesco Sisca and his sons Marziale and Alessandro—the latter, under the pseudonym Riccardo Cordiferro, was a central figure in the immigrant scene, especially in theater and poetry); *Il Carroccio*, edited by Agostino De Biasi (1915–35), a nationalist-Fascist monthly that was not always well thought of by official representatives of the regime;[4] *L'Italia*, in San Francisco (founded in 1886, in circulation until around 1945); *Il Corriere d'America* (1922–43), especially in the first period, when it was edited by its founder, Barzini Sr. Two of the most popular and long-lived follow an editorial policy that is less relevant here but cannot be ignored: *Il Progresso Italo-Americano* (1880–1988), through whose editorial staff passed quite a number of writers from Little Italy; and the already mentioned *La Parola del Popolo* (which originated as *La Parola dei Socialisti* in 1908 and was still going at the end of the seventies), with its enduring predilection for an engaged and effusive lyricism. It is no accident that the principal names among the writers discussed in the following pages coincide with those of some of the most influential journalists.

The relative variety of the genres (the novel of urban "mysteries," a rudimentary form of the thriller, the novel that is sentimental when not an actual "romance," the diary of denunciation, etc.) indicates, among other things, the attention paid to the successful Italian literature of the time. The intellectuals of the Little Italies were quite open to and aware of the news coming in a continuous and regular stream from the mother country, as is further confirmed by the biographies and the journalistic activities of the protagonists of this story.

To start off with an eccentric "father," let's take the "strange case" (Maffi) of Luigi Donato Ventura (1845–1912), the author of an early work of Italian American fiction entitled *Peppino* (published in French in 1885 and, the following year, in English by the prestigious Ticknor of Boston, to open the collection *Misfits and Remnants*).[5] The long tale centers on the story of the tenderly paternalistic relationship between the eponymous protagonist—a twelve-year-old shoeshine boy from the Lucanian village of Viggiano, "his dark skin made even darker by the sun,"[6] with his heart of gold and his empty pockets—and a Mr. Fortuna (from the name, a transparent alter ego of the author), in search of better times. But Ventura was also a translator and editor of, among others, De Amicis, Mantegazza, and the memoirs of Adelaide Ristori. His task as a cultural mediator and benevolent chronicler of the first wave of immigration is further revealed in his contributions to the Italian press: we can read, for example, his articles in *Cuore e Critica,* Arcangelo Ghisleri's review, which in its brief life (1887–90) promoted political and social debates, together with ethnographic and economic inquiries, uniting broad horizons and realistic reformism. Notable among Ventura's contributions, between 1888 and 1889, are a muddled and rather disconcerting article on the racial question,[7] an introduction to Mantegazza's *Testa,* and a review of Italian women writers. The more properly "immigrant" writing, in short, is accompanied by a view, however questionable, of the literary and social activity of the two countries.

It is the sign of an attitude that, in different forms, recurs in the following decades: for the more visible exponents of this literary world, contact with the Italian public proves to be a determining factor in confirming the (relative) prominence of their role within the immigrant community. For Paolo Pallavicini, the inclusion of his novels in the successful illustrated series published by Sonzogno is invaluable; similarly for Eugenio Camillo Branchi, who—after youthful contributions to the *Corriere della Sera*—distinguished himself both in *Il Carroccio* and, later, in volumes published by Cappelli, Vallardi, and Garzanti. The bard of immigrant workers, the union rhetorician Arturo Giovannitti, became a cause célèbre in 1912, when, at the same time as he was among the defendants in a trial resulting from his union activities, his high-flown language—indebted to Stecchetti, Rapisardi, and Whitman at once—appeared in the columns of the socialist daily *Avanti!;* for the memoirist Camillo Cianfarra, the dynamic yet risky character of the decision to emigrate is reflected in a career in which he was, first, inspector of the office of employment in New York (financed by the Roman authorities), and as such the author of valuable descriptive reports, and later the Italian bureau correspondent for the American press. And as for Corrado Altavilla, apart from his years at *Il Progresso* and the novel *Gente lontana* [Faraway People] (1938, published in Milan)—his sole work, but of great interest—his contributions to *Corriere della Sera* should be recalled, particularly in 1938, the same year in which Cecchi was sending the livid and astute letters that were later collected in *America amara* [Bitter America].

## Mysteries in Little Italy:
## The Serial Novels of Ciambelli and Stanco

Having noted that these literary practitioners had a twofold vocation, we can turn more easily to an examination of the works, beginning with those of a figure who is almost perfect of the type: the Lucchese Bernardino Ciambelli (1862?–1931), the little Sue of Little Italy (Bernabei). Although Ciambelli was both a novelist and a playwright, he was above all a journalist (he was also an actor and a well-known personage, an authentic "character" of Italian America, from New York to Colorado). He was a major contributor to many journals and papers, from the *Bollettino della Sera,* which he founded in 1898, after the outbreak of the Spanish-American War (on the initiative of his publishers, Frugone and Balletto), and edited, to the *Corriere d'America,* where he was working when, one foggy July morning, he collapsed, with a theatricality worthy of one of his own novelistic extravaganzas. But although his work is chaotic, vast, widely dispersed, and difficult to reconstruct in its entirety, its meaning has remained, through four decades, easily comprehensible. Ciambelli's chief goal—the entertainment of the reader—was in plain sight, so that even the anonymous author of his obituary in *Il Progresso* could allude to it with warm and sympathetic candor:

> In his novels . . . one gets a picture of the Italian colony of a half-century ago [that is, in the 1880s and 90s], a canvas painted by an Impressionist, who does not care to perfect his work, who is not worried about creating a masterpiece or even something lasting.
> He writes in a rush, like a "reporter," as if assailed by the need to take notes instantly on what is happening, so that nothing may be forgotten or distorted. . . . The trials [of his characters] . . . more than as literary constructions, serve to give us a faithful impression of the feelings of our great immigrant masses, in a period of confusion, before they settled into a new and in a certain sense hostile country.[8]

Impressionism, yes, but what material! The literature of the "mysteries" was widespread both in the United States—in English and also in the other languages of emigration—and in the countries of South America where the emigrants ended up.[9] In 1903, for example, *I misteri di New York* [The Mysteries of New York], by a writer named Menotti Pellegrino, was published. It was a muddled, extremely incoherent work; for one thing, Pellegrino was, to put it mildly, shameless in his total neglect of grammar (this sort of amateurism was in fact rare in the immigrant literature). And yet even Pellegrino (who later undertook an immense cloak-and-dagger novel set in Sicily) displays the clichés of the genre, including descriptions of the slums, an equivocal view of other ethnic immigrants (Jews and Chinese in particular), attraction and repulsion toward the judiciary system. We read, in succession, of Ellis Island, the slum ghettos, the halls of justice, the prisons (the infamous New York Tombs). For the good characters, recognitions and reunions are in store; for the bad there is the specter of the electric chair.

Bernardino Ciambelli, on the other hand, handles the same material with assurance. His power, his specificity, if you like, resides in the freedom, the boldness with which he constantly presents the most improbable absurdities, serving them up in a lurching but always readable prose. This unabashed stylistic poverty guarantees a naïve reading and the superfluity of interpretation; it can be explained in part by the circumstances of publication, in serial form in newspapers or in weekly booklets, but also—and it is a false paradox, characteristic of this type of mass creation—points to his rich use of narrative devices.

Another result of the fact that Ciambelli's novels were published serially, and that, further, they make up a cycle, is that the plots are inevitably unwieldy, though this is mitigated by the author's admirable if ineffectual talent as a master planner. Especially in the works of the nineties, a whole series of characters moves through the different "mysteries," imposing a covert continuity; in addition, the onerous propensity for these multiple, complex plots is coupled with a use of characters that tends to be caricatural. On the one hand, there is the joint effort of the "good" detectives and policemen, Italians and Americans, to untangle the knots of evil: Inspector Byrnes (a character taken from real life) and Cavalier Boni (a sort of alter ego of the narrator), who in *I misteri di Mulberry Street* [The Mysteries of Mulberry Street] and *I drammi dell'emigrazione* [The Trials of Emigration] hunt down the elusive Ruiz and the noble Genoese patricide Carlo Rialto. On the other, there are women who are either corrupted and wanton or pure, madams in brothels or orphans, and who not only reappear but often "link"—through improbable plot twists, reunions, and coincidences—one story line and novel to another. In *I misteri di Bleecker Street* [The Mysteries of Bleecker Street] and *La Trovatella di Mulberry Street* [The Foundling of Mulberry Street], as in the more linear and fast-paced *I misteri della Polizia di New York* [The Mysteries of the New York Police] and the more diffuse international entanglements of *I sotterranei di New York* [The Underworld of New York], many of the names change, but not the functions of the characters. There are thefts, abortions, obscure births and recognitions; jewels, gambling dens, opium; prison escapes and mid-ocean shipwrecks. That the novels truly form a cycle can be seen more in the taste for excess and the uniform tone in which it is expressed through the decades than in the innumerable accretions of the plots. The jumpy progress of the prose serves to neutralize, so to speak, the excesses of the story line.

Another constant is a pre–melting pot point of view, situated in the tentacular and dangerous life of the new metropolis. The standard, strongly colored figures of the more facile serials are given a twist of sex and violence (the latter often attributed to the American police and judicial system) and act in a context of unmediated realism, amid multiracialism, chases in the depths of the subway, orgies, and crimes on ships and in the shadows of the docks: the temptation, barely avoided on many occasions, is to sink into Grand Guignol and pornography. In sum, it is the extravagance and the coups de théâtre, in essence formulaic, which predominate, deftly transposed onto a map familiar in outline to the readers of Little Italy. Thus the assured entertainment and suspense of these "contemporary novels"—keeping readers' attention broadly focused, from one installment to the next, on the geography (spatial, social, psychological) of immigrant life—establish an "effect of reality," in its own way grandiose, which uses the weapon of documentary in a deliberate and purposeful manner. In the middle of *I drammi dell'emigrazione*, for example, the book that provides the freshest and most vivid consideration of the traumas of emigration, a broad window is opened onto conditions in the mines, with important allusions to the exploitation of workers and union organizing. Thus even in Carlo Tresca's militant autobiography Ciambelli's "mysteries" are cited as an example of historical novels that make social statements.

But their importance does not stop there. Ciambelli proclaims repeatedly that what he is telling is a "true story": he confirms this with a meticulous topographic precision, which illustrates the physical expansion of the city (including addresses); with appearances by real personalities in the guise of characters; with the denunciation of social ills and individual immorality; and with the emphasis he gives to the ethnic babel, not without anti-Irish, anti-Semitic, and anti-Chinese undercurrents. But he is smart enough to temper his moralizing with his promiscuous taste for excess, and to move out of the purely local dimension with recourse to dizzying changes of scene that expand the plot from New York to Paris, from Russia to Italy, from South America to Australia. Ciambelli offers a sort of freewheeling mass entertainment, which plays easily between didacticism and unrestrained fantasy: the result is a narrative sustained at once by authenticity and by a representative, single-minded ambition that we will find less and less in the future.

A second-generation follower of Ciambelli's, who as such offers a greater display of both polish and artifice, is his associate (a colleague at *La Follia di New York* and *Corriere d'America*) and successor Italo Stanco (the pseudonym of Ettore Moffa, who was born in Riccia, in the province of Campobasso, in 1886, arrived in the United States in 1909, after two years in Argentina, and died in 1954). It would be arduous and in a certain sense superfluous to follow the plots and analyze the themes and characters of his various novels, which are often quite long: *I rettili d'oro* [The Golden Serpents] occupied two full years in *La Follia,* in 1915–17, and was reprinted in *Divagando,* in 1952–53; *Le piovre di New York* [The Bloodsuckers of New York], in 115 installments, monopolized *La Follia* from 1944 to 1949.

The materials of the serial novel are treated with obvious premeditation; the most evident reprises from Ciambelli (the corruption or kidnapping of the ingenuous virgin immigrant; the thrilling multiethnic fabric of the city; the crime-news details effectively assembled with a simplistic Manichaeism; deaths, recognitions, and whirlwind encounters) are the trademarks of populist immigrant realism. In any case, Stanco was quick to acquire a greater astuteness, one might almost say a more fastidious style. Over the years, in addition to writing, he was active as a translator (of "serials" from Spanish, French, and English), and as a commentator and ironist—sharp as a commentator, ineffectual as an ironist. Even before setting out for the New World, he displayed, from Naples to Florence, noticeable assurance as a versifier and critic, evincing the brashness of youth but an awareness of his goals as well. His is, in short, a multifaceted and cultivated character, capable of citing Imbriani with critical authority, of alluding to Schopenhauer amid the most tortuous intrigues, of constructing an entire novel—even the title, *Sull'Oceano* [At Sea]— in the form of an homage, very much sui generis, to De Amicis's great work on emigration. Here, too, as in Ciambelli, contempt, denunciations, and abundant pathos originate in an intense participation in the phenomenon of emigration, although it is filtered through a point of view that judges the disinherited masses as the "human herd," "ants," at the mercy of the most elementary instincts. The result is that the prose often strives (awkwardly, we would say) to maintain a tone of respectability. In the berths of the ship *Vespucci* inconveniences of the following type occur: "Suddenly his hair was bathed with a warm viscous matter and a nauseating stench spread around. It was the good Calabrian peasant, 'the tenant on the second floor,' who, wakened by seasickness, was vomiting on the head of his comrade" (*Sull'Oceano,* 10 December 1918; eighth installment).

Not only the vocabulary but the structure of the events reflects a different, more advanced degree of literary culture. The "mysteries" have the distinct quality of detective fiction, not so much because of the police theme (a passage in Ciambelli featuring Jack the Ripper in the setting of low-life New York is notable in this respect) as because of the effort to tie up the plot threads by means of the detective work carried out by the "good" protagonist. Stanco's novels are not, however, circumstantial, rationally laid out: the evidence is, on the one hand, the almost folkloristic use that is made of an Italian American icon like Inspector Petrosino and, on the other, the destructive effect on the detective that the discovery of the truth can have. In *Il diavolo biondo* [The Blond Devil] the hero, James Forley, alias Giacomo Forlì, of the New York police, after solving the crime kills himself, jumping off a bridge in Harlem.

If the "detective" element serves, at least in its intentions, to make the action more compact, the truth is that a grim morality casts its shadow over these novels, which are anything but consoling or reassuring. As is customary in so much writing about Italian American mores and habits, there are skeptical and exculpatory passages on Italian criminality (including a defense of the crime of honor), while, in the background, the presence of spy intrigues and terrorist attacks linked to the turmoil brought on by the Great War projects readers onto an international scene that will soon determine the end of the Great Migration and, in prospect, the decline of Little Italy. Behind Stanco's crimes and plots one can descry, therefore, a dark sense of isolation and defeat, confirmed after the Second World War by his withdrawal into writing gossip columns, with an extremely narrow focus.

### SENTIMENTAL REALISM: PALLAVICINI, BRANCHI, AND THE ROMANCE NOVEL OF *IL CARROCCIO*

In the twenties, the literary climate of the immigrant community was enriched by a cloyingly "worldly" and sentimental streak, thanks to the arrival of Paolo Pallavicini, Eugenio Camillo Branchi, and a handful of women writers. The new centrality of the love theme is anything but an index of disengagement; rather, it allows the social trauma and the family and individual dramas connected to the process of assimilation to be dealt with on a much broader scale. In the abstract, these narrative efforts could be interpreted as the point of contact with the nascent literature of Italian America in English, which was fostered by these traumas: but the voice of the Italophone writers brings a distinctly different note.

Paolo Pallavicini (or Pallavicini-Pirovano, 1886–1938),[10] with his limitations and his verbosity, fully embodies the sort of schizophrenia innate in the immigrant experience. His books alternate between hyperconformist outbursts of exasperated nationalism (*La guerra italo-austriaca, 1915–1919* [The Italo-Austrian War, 1915–1919], a book of popularizing reportage, which exploited the irredentist feelings widespread in the immigrant community) and diatribes against anti-Italian "racial prejudice" on the part of the Wasp majority. His preferred narrative scheme develops, between languorousness and a high tone, in a lower- and middle-class immigrant milieu, situated for the most part in wealthy rural California. The intrigues, passions, and crimes involve young second-generation Italians, torn between loyalty to their roots and the desire for success, between affection for their parents and the temptations presented by the world of the "Americans": the whole is catalyzed by tormented, drawn-out love affairs. The scenes are of ample proportions, and welcome with an unusual generosity the unsentimental theme of the "giobba," of hard work, presented, however, from an optimist's perspective (the Italian workers are occasionally exploited but are successful, from the fields to the mines, from professional offices to the Hollywood studios); and, in keeping with the California ambience and the author's own origins, his Little Italy has a "northern" character that is expressed in delightful interjections of Lombard-English slang (also in Pallavicini's prose the Americanisms, with an involuntary candor, are more pronounced). Bruno Speri, the just and strong hero of the diptych *Per le vie del mondo* [Along the Highways of the World] appearing as a serial also under the title *Il romanzo d'un emigrato* [An Immigrant's Story] and *L'amante delle tre croci* [The Lover of the Three Crosses], will have to bring to a conclusion, together with the rich California heiress Adriana Rosenthal, a "mission . . . for the advantage of our other army that travels periodically along the highways of the world in search of work, because the great common mother is too small and too poor to provide for all."[11]

And in *Carezza divina* [Divine Caress], a posthumous novel dated 1939, which expresses the mood of the majority of Italian Americans, the unresolved duality of the children of the second generation is temporarily mitigated thanks to the appearance of a hero of art (Mascagni) and a hero-demigod of the new Italy ("Him," that is to say, Mussolini, in whose name the interminable romance ends). But, before that, the Italian American identity crisis had had a chance to be tested in remarkably concrete terms, in the course of an American trial and then in the period following the Crash on Wall Street, which had a disastrous effect on the immigrants' savings. Let us recall that this sentimental-realistic version of immigration—an almost unique case—met with reasonable success both in the United States (especially in the serial novels in *L'Italia*, in San Francisco, and in various volumes) and in the far-off homeland, in a series published by Sonzogno.

The prose of the professor and journalist Eugenio Camillo Branchi (1883–1962) takes us to a climate that is fairly similar, at least stylistically. His voice was somewhat less in tune with the world of the immigrant community, as one might expect of such a versatile and wide-ranging character. Branchi worked from the first decade of the century to the late fifties, and his activities included, among other things, a translation of the Koran, maritime adventure books (also for children), and a defense—as erudite as it was uncritical and dilettantish—of the historical victories of the Italian explorers. He lived mainly in North Africa, the United States, and Latin America; in Chile, at the end of his life, he recalled, in a nostalgic, philosophizing tone, his various encounters and world travels over the years ( *Così parlò Mister Nature* [Thus Spoke Mister Nature], 1953, which is perhaps his best book, although by that point he had little connection with the milieus of Little Italy). He is not, strictly, an Italian American author but, rather—especially in the twenties and thirties—an observer transplanted to that world, where he was able to count on, among other things, the esteem of "prominent" figures in the Italian-speaking intelligentsia like the journalist Agostino De Biasi (who welcomed him generously in the pages of *Carroccio*) and the historian Giovanni Schiavo (whose Vigo Press published some of his studies). *"Dagoes": Novelle Transatlantiche* ["Dagoes": Transatlantic Stories], for example, sums up, in its title, the simultaneous presence of populism and high society, of improbable international aristocratic love affairs (consummated preferably in luxurious settings, and ending in suicide or anyway in the lovers' being cut off from each other forever) and dramatic attempts at incorporation into or simply survival within a hostile reality like that of the United States. In the long title story, the dago Michele-Mike, a former soldier in the U.S. Army, is forced by the unjust restrictions of the Johnson law to cross the Mexican border clandestinely (in a fine, affecting crescendo); in *Hold Up!* the protagonist is Tony, an unemployed miner who, forced to leave the coal region of Scranton,[12] is, in spite of himself, transformed by the pitiless machine of production into an armed robber (with predictable remorse and a happy ending). It is fiction supported by a rhythm and a sense of proportion that we do not find elsewhere, but in which one also notes a certain intentionality, a premeditated, almost deliberate plan, of presenting a "strange" and in its way "marvelous" world.

Taking up a valuable remark of Bénédicte Deschamps, one might usefully compare this type of narrative to the more uniform style of certain women writers: not so much the nationalist Maria Moro Gabelli (who in 1918 offered a slender parable of the immigrant adolescent-prodigal son, ready to cross the ocean to become a hero in the trenches on the Grappa) as the more "feminine" Caterina Maria Avella, Dora Colonna (a teacher and longtime resident of the United States), and Clara Vacirca (wife of the exiled socialist deputy Vincenzo Vacirca), whose works have mawkish, sentimental aspects but are not completely banal. The first two, significantly, became known in *Il Carroccio* during a brief period between 1923 and 1926, and were presented in photographs as coquettishly feminine. (That the woman writer, to be accepted, had to be attractive in her femininity is confirmed in the socialist arena by the preface to Vacirca's book, by the poet Arturo Giovannitti, who praises her as "an exemplary wife and mother.") In the work of the women writers published in *Il Carroccio*, the vein of romanticism—which Pallavicini during the same period expanded disproportionately—was modulated in the better passages in an unusual manner, with a particular eye for the glitter of the roaring twenties and the sufferings of the immigrant woman. Caterina Avella, setting her stories in the world of rich, integrated Italian Americans—among yachts, villas, and shiny new automobiles—uses this as the means to introduce the new figure of the flapper, the emancipated woman, master of her own body and her own feelings, including even a divorced young mother. These are stories of the Jazz Age, with flirtations, parties, and the triumph of true affections, prepared for by female cunning. Colonna is more problematic, and even disconcerting in her denouements: an Italian man who has seduced and deceived two fellow countrywomen, forcing them into the hardships of immigration (the one an abandoned mother who works in a factory, the other a solitary commuter), is killed on a freezing, snowy night by one of the two, in a desperate affirmation of freedom. In another story, an immigrant woman, after having had to leave her home following an adulterous relationship, is so overwhelmed by the emotional gap that separates her from her daughter that (despite a renewed relationship with her son) she dies. It is a dilemma of the heart that can clearly be read in a sociological key but which the author does not overburden with didactic purpose.

Thus both writers present "romances" that without pretense place in the foreground the difficult liberation of women in the context of the New World. The setting of Clara Vacirca's novel *Cupido fra le camicie nere* [Cupid Among the Black Shirts] is more conventional, and, although it was composed and published in exile, can be included in the category of Italian American literature only by a stretch. The black shirts and the cruel, fearful, and violent world they represent are the true obstacle to the fulfillment of the love between two young people who are pure of heart: the semi-clandestinity of the relationship and the boy's activities in opposing the regime express an anti-Fascism that is a movement of the spirit rather than a political position. Of course, it is significant that the love story sinks fully into the conventions of the romance novel and, at the same time, flourishes in a climate "of the left." This was one of the forms that political activity in exile could assume—and certainly one of the more neglected, compared with the "serious" work of Borgese, Salvemini, Ascoli, and so on. Moreover, from the twenties on, the serial novels and Sunday supplements, no different than in Italy, offer, in addition to the novels of Invernizio and Misasi, of William Galt and Dumas, a rich selection of new (or almost new) names: Zuccoli and Varaldo, la Marchesa Colombi, Contessa Lara, Neera, Serao's *Castigo*, Anna Vertua Gentile, and later Flavia Steno, Baroness Orczy, and soon also Liala—more or less, and unsurprisingly, the best-sellers and belles-lettres of the twenties. In spite of the protagonists' social isolation, Vacirca's novel could easily enter this literary zone.

## MEMOIR AND COMMITMENT:
## CIANFARRA, CAMINITA, TRESCA, VACIRCA, AND OTHERS

On the imaginary plane of historiographic reconstruction, the axes of chronology and genre are often intertwined, advancing and evolving with accelerations and pauses that the scholar has difficulty keeping track of. Let's go back in time and turn to another area of Italian American prose, which would include—in the name of a common if heterogeneous "critical" engagement—the autobiographical works of Camillo Cianfarra, Ludovico M. Caminita, and Carlo Tresca, and certain attempts at proletarian or, in a broad sense, social novels.

Cianfarra's *Il diario di un emigrato* [The Diary of an Immigrant] of 1904 and Caminita's *Nell'isola delle lagrime: Ellis Island* [On the Island of Tears: Ellis Island] of 1924 display an engagement and immediacy typical of autobiographical writing but are even more valuable in this case, in which testimony from within the immigrant community presented expressly for that community is rare.[13] Both authors can boast an interesting bibliography that reflects the different but comparable arcs of their respective careers. It will suffice to mention here, in the case of the first, a strong involvement in journalism (he was the editor of *Il Proletario* between 1898 and 1901, and contributed to *L'Araldo Italiano, Gli Italiani e l'America, La Follia di New York,* and then to the American press at least until the mid-twenties), and the demanding job of inspector of work, that is, the official charged with supervision of his fellow countrymen.[14] As for the second, Michele Caminita, born in Palermo in 1878 and documented up to 1943 (early in his career he took the name of a brother who had died young and tragically in Canada), he was a prolific contributor to the anarchist newspapers in Paterson, New Jersey—*La Questione Sociale, L'Era Nuova, La Jacquerie*—and a pamphlet writer (on many subjects, including politics, unions, education, anticlericalism), playwright, novelist, poet, and caricaturist, and, from the twenties on, was on the editorial staff of various publications (from *Il Bollettino della Sera* to *Corriere d'America* and the *New York World*); he went on to recant anarchism and, in Scranton, for the coal miners, began publishing *Il Minatore.*[15]

Although at this point there are unfortunately many gaps in our knowledge, these two volumes of memoirs stand out, among so much journalism, as not only more mature and effective from an expressive point of view but also less burdened by circumstantial polemics and transient ideologies. The narrating, autobiographical "I" manages in both cases to construct a convincing character, attractive in its changeableness and human frailty. These two writers avoid both the very American teleological scheme of the "success story" and an equally pacifying populism. Cianfarra effectively documents a white-collar youth's slow and painful assimilation into what at the beginning he calls the "the vulgar, low stage that is called the 'colony,' a putrid swamp where profit and shame stagnate."[16] The need to survive, however, insures that anathema and revulsion do not turn into a paralyzing rejection (furthermore, love for the young niece of the landlady adds a note of uncertain tenderness). Misdeeds, prejudice, difficulties of every sort, divisions within the immigrant community are not the elements of a litany recited by a third-rate intellectual who has not adapted well to proletarian life but the real substance of the diarist's days, as he observes and suffers, full of hard work, pathos, and pity. In fact, the narrator, in spite of himself, goes so far as to collaborate with the exploitation of the bosses and the thieving of the "bankers." Yet it is precisely this involvement that makes him a figure without rhetoric, equidistant from a purely utilitarian interpretation of the emigration and an alienating nostalgic grief. Cianfarra experiences or has immediate knowledge of the underworld, of prostitution, of staggering swindles, but he expresses a dream of, or, rather, the "great faith" in, a dignified assimilation, with an attitude steeped in nationalism and potential racism that can generate some unease even in us, who read at the comfortable distance of a century, in a climate of multiculturalism and political correctness:

> Today they call us "dagos," today they reproach us for not being clean, for the frequent use of the knife. . . . but tomorrow we will be a part of this unity and begin to make our weight felt, the weight of a strong and healthy race, in whose blood aims and inclinations that once made it glorious have been working for infinite generations—aims that today make it sympathetic. . . . The hundreds of dollars put aside rummaging in trunks, or making shoeshines' chairs, or selling fruit from a cart will serve one day to educate the children, to launch them in this American world where we, having arrived too late, will never enter.[17]

There is a landing place, but, consistent with the book's autobiographical realism, it is on the staff of an immigrant newspaper, a further stimulus to knowledge and service in a world that by now the immigrant has entered and become part of.

Caminita's memoir is drier, a sort of first-person report on the effects of the oppression of radicals in the period after the First World War. The attitude of the author, who in 1924 recalls his "odyssey" through the judicial and prison system in the years 1920–21, remains throughout the text somewhat ambiguous: whether for understandable reasons of personal opportunism or through a sincere change of mind, Caminita presents neither a denunciation of the "red scare" (not that he had lacked polemical power in the past: read in particular *Free Country!*) nor the aggrieved complaint of one who has been persecuted. During these years, following the spread of anti-anarchist propaganda (i.e., against Sacco and Vanzetti), the militant Caminita tried to rebuild his credibility without sinking to a public renunciation. In short, we can make out between the lines, not entirely explicit, a political content that could be brought to light by a meticulous investigation into that era of the Italian American anarchist subculture. Still, if the politics is taken on with diffidence, on another level bewilderment, confusion, stupefaction—the emotional state of a man who is suddenly arrested as the leader of a band of dangerous terrorists—are evident. The book's importance lies in rendering this ordeal with a sense of proportion; it immediately becomes an experience shared with others—from the police station on board the ferry boat to confinement as "politicals" at Ellis Island, a limbo of uncertainty (although not comparable to that endured by immigrants in transit) where the true specter is expulsion from the country. Based on personal experience, this autobiographical text maintains a bitter intensity as it succeeds in expressing a human and moral climate of fear and distrust, humility and arrogance.

The work of the major leaders of the socialist, union, and libertarian left who were active in the United States also had a literary character. The harangues, polemics, and articles of Alberico Molinari, Luigi Galleani, and Carlo Tresca, to mention just a few, were always "signed" pieces, unmistakable in their prose and in their animus, and, depending on the cases, rational-positivist, late-romantic Carduccian, expressionistically venomous. None of these pretended to equanimity or a high intellectual profile; on the other hand, they became a point of reference for an anti-capitalist and, soon, anti-Fascist rhetoric of opposition.[18]

The ponderous, unfinished volume of memoirs by Carlo Tresca, however, represents, in its literary specificity, an episode too large to be ignored: an unpublished autobiography, written in English, that covers in thirty-four chapters the period from 1895–96 to 1915 (with some forays into later years). It is a broad canvas that, especially in the first half, has the fresh naturalness of a bildungsroman, deeply marked by an adventurous personality, who is instinctively "against." The work is full of an energy that, supported by a concise, succinct prose, instills blood and concreteness into moments of emotional abandon (the farewell to his mother), accounts of early battles, oratorical outbursts, the major "break" represented by his "rebirth" on American soil. Later on, Tresca often lingers on minor political news, or on partisan militancy, but in the last chapter he completed, on the United States' entry into the war, he regains his verbal charge, displaying an unmistakable power. Because it is unpublished and in English, this monumental autobiography is, strictly speaking, outside the category of early Italian American narrative (although it does not seem to me far-fetched to hypothesize that the typescript was circulated). In any case, it is an exception that cannot be ignored, not only for its intrinsic qualities but also as a touchstone, in its engagement with political and social activism.

It is only natural that in this climate attempts at narrative should be made, such as those of an "Ant." Perotti who in 1922 published in the socialist *Parola del Popolo* a war novel, *Verso l'ideale* [Toward the Ideal]. The serial is notable for its presentation of a collective portrait of a group of workers employed on the construction of a railway line, among whom—after trials that include exploitation, death on the job, being shot at as unarmed strikers—a spark of social and political conscience is ignited. In the same months, to give an idea of the context, the paper advertised books by Zola, Upton Sinclair, and, in contrast, *Opere* [The Complete Works] of Guido da Verona, while among the literary and journalistic contributors were the old radical Paolo Valera (whose books were considered compromising material by the F.B.I.) and the socialist De Amicis.

Another interesting testimonial of literature doubly bound to the bare events of the times is *Ricatto* [Blackmail] (1924), the original reconstruction of a trial, based on the actual proceedings, by the lawyer Ernesto Valentini.[19] Published in Turin, it is identified half a century later, by Joseph-Giuseppe Zappulla—an old lion of Little Italy journalism—as one of the rare titles worthy of consideration. Using documents and lengthy excerpts from the hearings, Valentini recounts a famous trial (thus coming close to a successful subgenre of popular literature) that took place in the Bronx in the early 1910s in which a respected doctor, Nicola Brunori, was accused of belonging to the Mano Nera, or Black Hand.[20] It is a book-container, carefully composed, which is striking for the harsh disparity of its keys: from the narrative rendition of the context, with its presentation of the characters and the background, to the long quotations from the documents, and the lively use of direct discourse from the trial.

Even a slightly later serial novel as different as *Il rogo* [The Pyre] (1927–28), by the socialist deputy in exile and polygraph Vincenzo Vacirca (1888–1956; several sojourns in the United States, in 1913–19, then in 1925–46), moves between the two poles of grieving social denunciation and attention to the changeable outline of private life.[21] Here the small modern world of the more or less well-to-do immigrants returns (artists, professionals, beautiful women of various origins). It is an environment whose more sensitive souls are shaken, in their tranquil and polite routine made up of dinners, walks, and courtships, by contact with the contradictions of the metropolis. The "pyre" is the factory-sweatshop fire in which dozens of poor working women perished, among them Lucia, the proletarian heroine; but the title also refers, figuratively, to the confusion and restlessness of the small middle class of which Vacirca is both exponent and spokesman. The protagonist, Sirio, and the aristocratic Elena assuage that anxiety precisely as a result of their encounter with the girl of the people, whose example of purity and self-denial will blunt their petty selfishness and smooth the road to love.

PARODIES AND THE "BLACK" OF THE END:
SENECA, FIASCHETTI, ALTAVILLA, AND DR. DANIELE

Italian American narrative also reflected the great success of vaudeville, whose major exponents were the Neapolitan (from Cava dei
Tirreni) Eduardo Migliaccio and the Sicilian Giovanni De Rosalia
(stage name Nofrio). They were histrionic performers who in their
"sketches," often accompanied by music, were able to create humorous parodies of the average immigrant's difficulties in adapting;
his basic defensive parochialism is affectionately laid bare and his
minute, daily mishaps are described, from ingenuous rebukes to
lively impulses toward American novelties large and small. A similar
world is conveyed in *Il Presidente Scoppetta,* by Pasquale Seneca (1890–
1952), a professor of languages at the University of Pennsylvania,[22]
which was privately printed in 1927 and appeared the following year
in twelve illustrated chapters in *La Follia di New York*—the equivalent,
within the context of immigrant literature, of a sort of investiture.[23]
Sketches and more or less satirical "vignettes," in Italian but also in
dialect and in the various forms of Italian American slang, were an
established institution of the principal humor weekly of Little Italy
(among the contributors were Ciambelli, Stanco, Cordiferro, Migliaccio).[24] The relative novelty offered by Seneca consists in his
expanding of the animated, informal atmosphere sufficiently to tack
on a thin narrative thread. The whole, as Prezzolini noted, makes one
think of the traditional satire of peasant life: the cultivated element
among the immigrants (Professor Seneca) mimics his ignorant fellow citizens, with a good nature that does not hide either the culture
gap (every chapter is constructed around the juxtaposition between
the Italian of the narrator and the ridiculous language of the protagonist, Scoppetta) or the essentially minor sins that, more through
ingenuousness than through malice, stain the various members of
the community. At the center is one of the distinctive traits of immigrant life: internal animosities and rivalries, stirred up by any social
occasion. In the immigrant community of Brigantello there are two
roosters in the hen house: Francesco Saverio Scoppetta, thirteen
years of prison ("But I came out of it with honor and respect!" [32]),
the owner of the paper *La Calzetta d'Italia* [Italy's Little Sock] and of a
travel agency ("from others' pockets to mine" [8]); and Angelantonio Squaglianzogna. The object of contention is the presidency of
the Our Lady of Peace Mutual Aid Society (10); but more valuable
than the characterization is the parodistic portrait of some typical
forms of immigrant social life: banquets, dancing parties, "pichinic-
chi," weddings, with a broad array of toasts, speeches to the *sorgi*

(members), hoaxes, fistfights, knifings, and shootings. The extended joke ends, after yet another violent episode, with the arrest and trial of almost all the characters: the language of the parody gives voice to a critical view of the community from within, expressed with greater force and conviction than in the numerous "tales" or romances in a more realistic style.

Leading more directly to the contemporaneous world of organized crime is a raw crime novel under the signature of one of the most singular authors of Little Italy: Michele or Michael Fiaschetti. It is likely, in fact, that one must speak of the "signature" rather than of the actual writer. After Petrosino was assassinated, Fiaschetti (born in Rome in 1886; lived in the United States as a child, where he is well documented at least until 1950) succeeded the famous detective as head of the Italian squad of the New York Police Department, a post he occupied until 1924. Later he opened a private investigator's office (widely advertised in the immigrant press) and by 1937 had been appointed by LaGuardia to keep a check on the illegal activities that flourished in the public markets. He was "tough," and was responsible (if we are to believe the rumor reported by Pietro di Donato) for the condemnation of several people to the electric chair.

The figure of Petrosino had fostered a myth with parallel tracks in cinema and popular literature, in English as well as in Italian. We may note, for example, two films, the Italian *I funerali del poliziotto Petrosino* [The Funeral of Lieutenant Petrosino], by Giuseppe Gabrelli (1908) and the American *The Adventures of Lieutenant Petrosino,* of Sidney M. Goldin (1912), along with at least one weekly magazine, *Giuseppe Petrosino: The Sherlock Holmes of Italy.* Even Bernardino Ciambelli, the father of the popular noir of Little Italy, celebrated the figure, in a four-act play: *Il martire del dovere, ovvero Giuseppe Petrosino* [The Martyr to Duty, or Giuseppe Petrosino].[25]

His younger colleague Fiaschetti, whose life was equally crammed with excitement and violence, insisted in his stories, which were avowedly autobiographical, on the more everyday, substantive aspects of the job, in contrast with the over-intellectualized image of Conan Doyle's popular detective. The battle horse of this hard boiled diarist is the indiscriminate use of "stool pigeons," the "spies and informers" who give the Italian version of the book *The Man They Couldn't Escape* its title. (The Italian, *Le spie e i confidenti,* came out in 1929 in *Corriere d'America;* the English version was published in London in 1928, and in New York in 1930 for the Crime Club, by Doubleday, Doran and Company, as *You Gotta Be Rough.*) The stories in English were edited and transcribed by a journalist who specialized in such work, Prosper Buranelli; as for the Italian versions, although they are copyrighted in the policeman's name, we may nevertheless assume that they are translations edited by the staff of Barzini's daily. Fiaschetti, in other words, might be called a nonwriting author. But if the paternity of the writing remains obscure (the first examples, in Italian, date at least from 1926, in the *Corriere d'America*), the energy that flows through these "rough" news reports is incontestable. Fiaschetti's chronicles are often animated by a touch of "evil" that is closely connected to an undercurrent of irony. It is an irony as much in the words as in the deeds, since the outcome of the struggle between the police and the underworld is basically taken for granted: it is the figure of deception that dominates, as expressed in the gangsters' betrayals or in the detective's disguises. Fiaschetti sees himself as the defender of the community's good name; but to deserve the title he has to immerse himself—and he does so eagerly—in the iniquities of the underworld. The contrast between the character of the cop and the portrait that he himself gives us of the tender father and widower is irresistible, like his genuine confession of faith in a romanticism worthy of Little Caesar and Scarface. The "tough guy" Mike sounds weaker, of course, when this authenticity serves to justify the social vision of an upright man of order (with a predictable lecture in praise of the repressive activities of the Mussolini regime); but mostly it is the narrator who prevails over the moralist. The episode of "Treat-'Em-Rough-Mike" is a curious one, and should be reevaluated: ending up in book series and high-circulation newspapers, with a flair for the genre that one might call innate (and practiced in its most successful years), made even more credible by a close relationship to the community it belonged to. It is a non-mannerist anthology of the world of godfathers and goodfellas, the same world on which, with a paradoxical, ambiguous sense of pride, the image of Italian America after the Second World War will base a substantial part of its fortunes. In Fiaschetti, however, lights and shadows are not added for aesthetic reasons but are still part of a world that is absolutely real, and which the sociologists of immigration call deviant: it is an aspect of the immigrant uprooting that cannot be exorcised, and is here entrusted—such is the irony of fate—to the words of a policeman.

The thirties and the early forties represent, from various points of view, the period of passing from a first-generation ethnic culture—deeply marked by its Italian origin—to one more decisively hybrid, hyphenated. One can verify this by looking at the local press, which gives more and more space to English—both on the East Coast and in the heartland, both in the big papers and in those with small circulations. Not only the news and advertisements are printed in the majority language but sometimes the serialized stories as well, and even the early comic strips of some of the popular American cartoons (which appeared in *Il Progresso Italo Americano* in the original, but with the Italian translation at the bottom of the page). Certainly, names like those of Pallavicini and Branchi and, in poetry, Giovannitti and Bartoletti continue to count; but it is clear that they are ever more isolated and anachronistic. There is, however, in this literary scene a remarkable swan song: the first (and in all likelihood the only) novel of Corrado Altavilla, *Gente lontana*.[26]

If we stopped to lay out straightforwardly, one after another, the motivations and characters of this novel, which is limited in its objectives and in its setting but comprehensive and deep within those limits, we would find a sort of catalogue of the imaginary Italian American narrative such as we have up to now described it: there are descriptive tracking shots along the avenues and in the representative neighborhoods of the city; painful and sympathetic pauses on the commuter army of immigrants; and ethnic portrayals that border on caricature, as much among the former *prominenti* (the corrupt Italian American upper crust) observed with pitiless clarity, as among the varied citizen masses—the Irish pimp and gambler, the mulatto prostitutes, the Chinese opium traffickers, the Jewish shopkeepers and loan sharks, and the almost unconscious black murderer. In addition, there is the violent, pernicious face of American justice, with its exhausting, emotionally intense trials, and an uprooted and bewildered youth, unable to manage the formal freedoms guaranteed by the system (excess pushes young men toward crime, while it defiles the sexual purity of girls). The economy is relatively prosperous, the political system is run by the well-oiled mechanisms of the old constitutional democracy; but behind the façade corruption and immorality dictate the law, as the parents and two children of the Sacchi family must painfully discover for themselves. They are the sociologically unexceptionable nucleus of the lower middle class. The father, Stefano, who emigrated from Rome twenty years earlier, has been employed for fifteen years in the advertising department of a soap maker; with his wife, Maria (who soon quits the factory where she works as a seamstress), he leaves the crowded Little Italy of East Harlem to move to the green suburbs, where, thanks to a loan, he is realizing a modest dream of being a property owner (a small house like all the houses in the neighborhood, with a back yard, a garage next to the kitchen). The son and daughter, on the threshold of adulthood, can't wait to get out, to break the suffocating shell of conformity imposed more by society's standardization than by the confusion of the parents (the father, in particular, is effectively drawn as a restless bundle of frustrations, in both his emotions and his work). The children's anxiety to flee in search of change precipitates the drama, when the boy, John-Giovanni (the alternation of names is deliberate), is unjustly accused of the murder of an unhappy young prostitute with whom he had a brief encounter. Through a combination of circumstances, the father—who was the girl's last client—becomes involved in and then overwhelmed by the case, and the novel is quickly transformed into a typical court drama, with prolonged and almost Orwellian interrogations, a forensic report, the choosing of the jury, the trial, the tactics of the defense strategy (entrusted to an Italian American lawyer), outbursts and a pathetic coup de théâtre (the mother's death from exhaustion). Thus, given these strong critical premises, John's acquittal turns out to be a Pyrrhic victory, since it does not prevent the breakdown of the fragile suburban, conformist equilibrium, the only dream within reach of a hardworking and loyal neo-American. Thrown back to the margins of society (the father has lost his job and his wife, and the house and furniture are sold), the Sacchis are forced, in an explicit blackness, to re-embark for Italy. The conclusion is, to put it mildly, depressing, especially since the novel represents one of the artistic peaks in the historical-literary context and also an almost definitive full stop. Yet it is a completely legitimate conclusion, not so much because of the ability of Altavilla, as a New York chronicler of long standing, to portray and typify, as for the uncommon subtlety displayed in the portrait of family psychology, in the orchestration of the simple but incredibly dense plot, in the evocation of an oppressive and neurotic climate that covers equally the irresponsible unruliness of the children and the unnatural senility of the parents. Thus, just at the time when Little Italy was receiving full political legitimacy (LaGuardia was elected mayor of New York in 1933) and was beginning both to open up and to come apart, one of its most serious and solitary writers delivered a funeral ode, in its way nihilistic. (However, the tragedy expressed in the Italian American novels in English of the same period is rather different: *The Grand Gennaro,* by Garibaldi Marto Lapolla [1935], and *Christ in Concrete,* by Pietro di Donato [1939].) The Sacchi family's return to Italy in defeat signals the end of the novel and coincides with the sunset of the Italian American novel in Italian.

Altavilla's novel had some resonance in the immigrant press. Of particular importance was an entire page devoted to it in *La Follia* by a "prominent" exponent of local letters, the lawyer and poet Rosario

Ingargiola, who places the author beside the three other novelists who are "worthy of note: Bernardino Ciambelli, Paolo Pallavicini and Italo Stanco," thereby indicating the existence of a specific tradition. Barely two years later, in a similar review of Italian American literature, in the same weekly, by Edward Corsi, the Italophone line is completely ignored, and the names that recur (beside the "cases" of Carnevali, D'Angelo, Giovannitti) are those of the second, Anglophone generation: John Ciardi and the pair Fante-di Donato. The two worlds are so distinct as to display a complete, reciprocal unconsciousness of the works of the other. Scholars will note, of course, occasional points of contact; and there are some interesting exceptions, but they are of little importance in the long run, and just as exceptional in many senses (Joseph Tusiani and Giose Rimanelli are the obvious examples) is the post–Second World War literature written in Italian in the United States.

Let us turn, in closing, to the culturally and linguistically enlightening case of the doctor F. Michele Daniele (1879–1957),[27] who, from California, successfully sent to Italian publishers two extremely heterogeneous volumes: a collection of *Rime vecchie e nuove* [Rhymes Old and New], published by Zanichelli in 1930 (and introduced as "a precious document of Italianness"), which expresses the strong lure of Hollywood, but also the travails of integration into a new culture (with poems dedicated to the Ku Klux Klan, to Farfariello, to Halloween, and to Thanksgiving); and a detailed and valuable prison diary, *Calvario di guerra* [War's Calvary] (published in 1932 but written in 1923, in Ohio), which is to all intents and purposes a war memoir, and which enjoyed national distribution, thanks to a prominent publisher, Alpes. A mere three years later, Daniele is publishing fiction, but this collection of eleven stories, although in a certain sense it returns to the worldly yet disquieting scenes of the best of *Il Carroccio* (Branchi, Avella, Colonna), marks the passage to English, in the shelter of, among other things, a programmatic title: *Yankee Faith* (1935). His autobiography, *Signor Dottore* (1959), was published posthumously almost a quarter-century later, also in English (its fluency owes much to the editor, a journalist named Victor Rosen). It, too, is a substantial volume, in which the author reviews seriously and intelligently the personal and professional events of his life, providing a consistently interesting document of genuine realism. Daniele gives a reading of his life as an immigrant of the lower middle class (the same scrutinized by Altavilla) that is not, reasonably, either defeated or triumphant ("Mine I am afraid could not be called a 'success story'"). But already these bare notes and the editorial and linguistic circumstances point to a fascinating journey between two worlds and two cultures, experienced, suffered, and even enjoyed. Bilingualism thus becomes an index of a fully matured equilibrium and integration. The thirties represent a watershed that is both chronologically and historically definitive.

## Envoi

These are the approximate coordinates of a "submerged" Italian American narrative literature to be saved from oblivion. The progressive unravelling of the immigrant cultural fabric and, in rapid succession, the caesura introduced by the Second World War invite us, by contrast, to recognize the existence, in the preceding decades, of a sufficiently articulated civilization of emigration, of a "common ground" that allows us to understand both the more repetitious or ingenuous products and the more successful and lasting results. In any event, it is a panorama that belies a supposed backwardness; the clear and swift conclusion of that story can perhaps be attributed, rather, to the extreme compactness of Little Italy. With decades of distance, and even keeping in mind all the obvious differences of individual cases, one cannot help feeling the air of family that circulates among the pages of the press, whether nationalist, Fascist, socialist, anarchist, or simply commercial. There is a homogeneity that is surely a sign of ethnic self-consciousness (and it is easy to read these novels as rich parables of Italian American "identity") but at the same time a synonym of closure with respect to the broader American context.

With the breaking of that protective dike and the opening up to the language of the country of arrival, Italian American literature was abandoned by the "faraway people," and began to speak English. The foundations—with their "mysteries," and the "detectives" and "romances" of their pages—were rapidly submerged by the new wave.

## ▨ ▨
## *Anthology*

### A NINETEENTH-CENTURY ANTECEDENT:
### *THE KID FROM GENOA*

Even before the great wave of immigration at the turn of the century, descriptions of the Italian underworld in the cities of the East Coast were abundant in the American and the "ethnic" press. The beggar seems to be the pitiful counterpart of the more common stereotype of the lawless Italian with a dagger stuck under his waistcoat, and all the more pitiful in the case of the young child standing on a street corner or made to work for practically nothing. Here is one of these sentimental snapshots, thinly fictionalized, from the first Italian American paper of record, *L'Eco d'Italia*.

**The Kid from Genoa**

"For the love of heaven, sir and madam, give me a penny; I'm asking only a penny!"

"Off with you! I am not in the habit of giving alms to street urchins."

And Mrs. Parker, having spoken, sat back on the seat of her carriage. But her husband, Paul Parker, to whom the boy now turned a humble gaze, said:

"Come here, kid. All I've got for you is a fifty-cent piece. I'll be back in a week, at three in the afternoon: will you come and pay me back the money? Mind you, I am merely *lending* it to you. . . . Try to find some work."

"Oh, yes, sir," the boy answered, with effusive gratitude. "Without a doubt, I will not fail you." And grabbing the wheel of the carriage, he took the money that was offered.

"You're mad, Paul Parker," said the wife, in irritation, to her husband. "You're mad, blindly throwing away your money. Do you seriously think you'll ever see that little beggar again?"

"I hope so, my dear," said that elderly gentleman, urging his placid horse to a trot. "I would be sorry to see a good boy fail in his duty. And I wouldn't want to miss a favorable opportunity to test a young and innocent heart."

The burning rays of the August sun struggled to penetrate a tiny hovel, on a dirty, neglected stretch of a street, where that ugly lout Fontana Buona was smoking his black pipe, and two or three boys were lying half asleep on the bare earth. A portable organ was leaning against a wall, a small monkey in a red jacket was prancing near the window, and Nino's organ and his tambourine were beside him: he kept glancing toward the door, as if waiting for a favorable opportunity to slip away unobserved.

There was a strange contrast between the handsome figure of the boy and the rags that covered him. His patched and grimy jacket showed no trace of its original color, his pants, torn in many places, barely covered him, and a pair of worn-out shoes were no longer useful for their job. And yet his eyes were pure and shining like the sky of Italy in spring, and there was a sweetness mixed with unusual spirit in the deep little creases that flanked his mouth. Nino's features recalled the physiognomy of a higher class; you would say a young Apollo, but alas, rags, misery, and abuse had been the inseparable companions of his brief and unlucky existence.

Suddenly, the ugly man laid down his pipe and threw a sidelong glance at the hapless boy.

"So, you had secretly put aside fifty cents? You wanted to cheat me, right?" he asked. "May I know, you pathetic vagabond, what you intended to do with it?"

"It was mine," Nino observed. "I got it singing under windows at night after I'd finished my required hours of work. I have always brought you my daily earnings faithfully, always!"

"Yours?" the man stammered, savagely. "Here nothing is yours. You belong to me, and all that you get is mine; and if I catch you cheating again I'll break your head. Where do you think you're going? Sit down."

"Give me one moment: let me go to the West Landhill Tavern," begged Nino, clasping his hands and glancing anxiously at the sun's rays that slanted in through the door, brightening the squalid place. Those rays were a kind of substitute clock for Nino.

"By Jove! We'll see if you'll do what you want," the man burst out, even angrier. "Back to your place. You will not go out, do you understand me? You will not go."

"I'll be back in ten minutes, I promise you. . . ."

"That's enough!" replied the master, gnashing his teeth.

Then, finding no further resistance in Nino's attitude, he calmed down somewhat and turned to another boy.

"Tito, a light for my pipe."

Nino, taking advantage of the moment, made a move for the door, creeping like a snake: but he was not very lucky in the attempt, for the worn sole of one shoe slipped on the floor, giving the master a chance to grab him roughly by the arm and shove him back like an inert mass. He fell, his forehead hit an iron bar, and there he remained, in a corner, giving no signs of life.

"Well! It looks like Nino is set for good this time," said one of the impassive spectators of the scene, a boy of thirteen, who was also accustomed to such treatment.

"Leave him alone: it's a lesson!"

At that moment the bell in the old square mournfully announced that it was three in the afternoon.

"I told you he wouldn't come," exclaimed Mrs. Parker, exultantly, her gray eyes peering triumphantly into all the corners of the West Landhill House. "I knew it very well. And now what do you think of the honesty of that fine boy of yours?"

Dismay and disappointment were evident on the face of Paul Parker.

"I'm sorry about it, my dear, sorry from the bottom of my heart. This time, I thought I had found a fellow who would stand out from the degraded and abject masses. It's pointless to stay here; it's better. . . . Let's go."

The swift passing of the years had silvered the head of Paul Parker and covered the face of his wife with pitiless wrinkles: they had done much, however, for the graceful figure of their daughter, transforming her into a beautiful young woman.

"I hear my father's footsteps," exclaimed Lucia, flinging herself at the door. "Hello, father, what news?"

"Bad enough," answered her father, shaking a quantity of snow from his overcoat. "Milton is in bed with a fever, and, judging from the obvious poverty of his wife, there is little to hope in that quarter; as for Bruce, he has a headache and finds it impossible to work."

"Will they pay you your money? Oh Paul, what a fool you were to lend it to them," his wife cried. "And what is there left for us to do about the banker Mr. Martin, who writes letter after letter, asking for the sum that we owe him?"

"Nothing, my dear wife."

"We'll sell everything at auction and go and die in the poorhouse. Oh Paul, I have always foreseen a bad end to your mad, kindhearted deeds."

"Not so bad, I hope," said old Paul, attempting to give comfort while the contraction of his lips visibly betrayed his intention.

"Tell me, father, this Mr. Martin, that we owe the money to, is he the same as the banker on Leeds Street?"

"Yes, what do you know about him?"

"Not much; but I have met his son in various places, and I . . . I suppose, if you went to him with me and told him the state of our affairs, or at least wrote to him. . . ."

"Don't fool yourself, Lucia," replied Mrs. Parker, with an air of bitter disappointment. "Not everyone makes a habit of throwing away their money with that lack of consideration so typical of your father."

"That remains to be seen," said old Paul, full of hope. "We'll write to him this very night, and next week we will go to Boston to hear what sort of answer he'll give us."

And Lucia Parker ran to get the address, with timid faith in her plan.

"It's impossible that his father's heart could be so hard," she thought, "and, besides, they are so rich that for them it's a small sum, that five hundred dollars."

◼

The elegant office on Leeds Street had seldom seen a carriage as humble and muddy as Paul Parker's stop at its door; and, for his part, the young banker who was sitting at the desk examining various papers was surprised to see an elderly man and a beautiful girl enter and approach him: sad December and smiling May.

"Lucia!"

"Nino! I thought that your father. . . . I didn't know that. . . ."

"My father," the young man answered, "was detained in the country, and my signature is as good as his. Last week he gave me an active role in your affairs, and this is. . . ."

And as he spoke he nodded toward an individual with a dark face who, sitting modestly in a corner of the office, made a deep bow.

Lucia introduced her father, and painted a picture of her family's affairs with an enchanting grace not unmixed with a slight blush; she could never have imagined meeting her gallant young knight in the office of Mr. John Martin.

"Oh Nino, we are very poor; and my father cannot pay off this debt just now; but I am hoping very soon for a position as a music teacher in Madame Elvain's school, and then we will be saved; so if your father would be so kind as to agree to a brief delay, we . . ."

Lucia stopped suddenly; her voice failed, and only her pride kept the tears from pouring out of her eyes in the presence of Nino Martin. The young man, having listened in silence, searched through his desk, took out some packets of bills and receipts, and, like a man who is trying to find something, said to his visitors:

"It's a matter of a note for five hundred dollars, right?"

"Yes sir," said the elderly man; "five hundred dollars."

"And this is your note?"

"Yes, sir."

Nino Martin coldly tore up the piece of paper and threw the scraps on the fire. Paul and Lucia looked at the young banker in astonishment. He gazed at them with his calm black eyes.

"In this case, Mr. Parker," said Nino, "you may understand that you have received the payment of an old debt. We have balanced our accounts."

"I don't understand, sir," said the old man. "I don't remember. . . ."

"And I, on the other hand, remember very well. It has been almost ten years, Mr. Parker, since you gave money at interest."

"Sir? . . ."

"I will explain," answered the young man, smiling; "perhaps Miss Parker doesn't know that I am only an adopted son of the man to whom I owe more than a father. My real name is Nino Berlani. I am Italian by birth. Ten years ago I was on the streets of Landhill with no money. A kind hand—you know which one, Mr. Parker—reached out to me in my hour of need."

A flash of understanding shone in the old man's face.

"Now I remember. It was a fifty-cent piece; and I told you to come back in a week, and . . ."

"And I didn't. No, I did all I could to get there; but I was prevented by the brutality of the man I served. Afterward, I went to that place every Thursday to wait for you; but in vain."

"No, we left Landhill."

"Well, I ran away to Boston to escape my tyrant. One night, Mr. John Martin found me on the street nearly dying of cold and hunger. He had lost his only son, who was just my age, and he invited me to take his son's place in his house as well as in his heart. Now you know my story; I would never have dreamed that Lucia was the daughter of my benefactor."

At Nino Berlani's smile, Paul Parker could not hide his own emotion, and simply said:

"I thank you, sir; yet we have no right to your generosity. Your father. . . ."

"My father and I form a single will."

"In that case I can only thank you both."

"Do not be so quick to give me your thanks; I may find myself wanting to ask you a much greater favor. . . ."

Paul Parker arrived home with a look of triumph.

"My dear wife, I have always said that I would be vindicated!"

"What do you mean?" asked his skeptical competitor.

"I will explain immediately."

And he recounted the entire adventure, adding:

"My fifty cents paid good dividends, didn't it?"

Mrs. Parker peered in amazement over her glasses.

And then her husband said in a softer tone:

"I know very well that Mr. Nino held back from asking a much more important favor. What do you say, Lucia?"

"I don't know, father!" answered Lucia, covering her face with both hands.

Her blush and her tear-filled eyes announced a deep, ill-concealed joy.

The marriage of Nino and Lucia took place soon afterward.

New York, 5 May 1869.

---

*L'Eco d'Italia* 20, no. 20 (14 May 1869).

## BERNARDINO CIAMBELLI:
## THE FATHER OF THE ITALIAN AMERICAN IMMIGRANT NOVEL

Soon after arriving in America, the immigrants who are at the center of Ciambelli's wild and hefty novels find themselves overwhelmed by a whirlwind of romance, corruption, and crime. Indeed, the lures and snares of the big city consist of sex and violence, in the most varied guises, and are what guarantee the seemingly endless flow of "mysteries" that come from the pen of this prolific and popular writer. The year 1893 was heroic in a way for Ciambelli, who started his career with three huge books, among them *I Misteri di Mulberry Street*, in which the "good" characters, Inspector Byrnes of the New York police and the Italian Mr. Boni, always on the track of the sleazy villain Ruiz, are introduced, along with an array of female victims and victimizers.

### The Mysteries of Mulberry Street

CHAPTER I
*THE ARRIVAL*

That October morning, the large wood-paneled hall of the Barge Office, where the newcomers file past the gaze of the immigration commissioners, was overcrowded; the transatlantic steamboats had brought more than two thousand immigrants from Europe—Germans, Russian Jews, and at least half from the southern regions of Italy.

The Jews, with a timid stare, packed together in their long coats with fur-lined hems, formed a group apart, as if they were afraid of mixing with the crowd that bustled around them.

The Germans, serious but satisfied, like people arriving in a land of conquest, remained close to each other, like soldiers who are about to assault the enemy.

The Italians—happy, carefree, noisy—added a joyous note to the picture, animating it with loud observations in the different dialects of the southern provinces, whose accents range from the barbarous to the soft tones of the Arab tongue.

The immigrants filed past, one by one, walking in front of the commissioners, who carried out their customary interrogations, translated by interpreters of different nationalities.

More than half the immigrants had gone by when, breaking away from the group of Italians, a young and beautiful girl stepped forward. Her clothes and her air had nothing to do with those of her traveling companions.

Indeed, while the Italian immigrant women sported gaudy clothes, shawls, and kerchiefs whose dominant colors were red, yellow, and green, the woman who was about to pass in front of the commissioner was dressed with great simplicity: a black petticoat, not new, but clean, wrapped about her elegant body; her bodice, which was also black, enclosed a supple waist and full and provocative breasts; a little round hat of the same color crowned her head, leaving her beautiful Greek features uncovered, framed by shiny jet-black hair.

The woman's eyes, two wide almond-shaped turquoises, had a sweet and good expression, veiled by long eyelashes. They glanced from here to there, apprehensive, timid, and frightened; but when her eyes rested upon a sweet child, of about five years of age, whose hand she held, she had such a loving expression, demonstrating how much affection and adoration the beautiful immigrant felt for him. He must have been her son, because only a mother could have such an affectionate gaze.

The woman had arrived in front of the commissioner.

The federal official looked at her with surprise, and, abandoning the rough tone he had used with those who had gone before her, he prepared to do his usual interrogation. When he realized that the woman was Italian, he called the interpreter, and made him ask her the usual questions:

"What is your name?"

"Vittoria Ruiz," the woman replied, in a sweet and melodious voice.

"Where are you from?"

"From Naples"

"Is this your child?"

"Yes," she replied, in a tone that was not without a certain fierceness.

"Do you have relatives in New York?"
Vittoria hesitated a moment, and then adamantly replied:
"Yes, my husband!"
"*Basta,* you can go ahead."

---

From *VIA—Voices in Italian Americana* 12, no. 1 (spring 2001): 89–91; translated by Martino Marazzi and Beagan Wilcox.

## CHAPTER VIII
### *LOVE'S MADNESS*

Ruiz, from the moment he saw Clara, had felt his blood boil, and the delightful hours he had spent with the beautiful girl, whom he loved so much, returned to his mind. The memory of the pleasure of that time awoke in him a burning wish to again possess that woman, whom he found more beautiful than ever, and whom the seductions of the stage made even more desirable.

Clara had not been very welcoming, it was true, but that was easily explained: he had some serious faults to be forgiven, and her contempt was natural. Then perhaps that evening Clara had an appointment with a fortunate lover.

With a lover!—this thought enraged Ruiz, but then he calmed himself, gradually, with the thought that women of the theater usually have rich lovers who pay for their bodies but never win their hearts.

Ruiz could not sleep that night, he had a fever, shivers of desire shook him, he had never wanted a woman so desperately.

Tired of lying in bed he got up, put on a luxurious silver-gray bathrobe, lighted a cigar, opened the window, and stood looking out at the stars. It was cold, but Ruiz needed that frigid air to calm the ardor that was consuming him.

He had been at the window for a few minutes when he saw a woman stop at the door of his house, and soon afterward the bell rang.

"Who the devil is looking for me at this hour?" he murmured as he went to open the door, "if the woman is young and beautiful, it is certainly opportune."

The nocturnal visitor was Mama Margherita. Ruiz stepped back in amazement as he recognized her.

"Why have you come here?" he asked brusquely.

"I've come because grave danger is threatening us."

"What sort of danger?"

"Napoleon has been arrested. They must know who he is—he's been at police headquarters for quite a while already, in the clutches of that Byrnes, who keeps far too close a watch on us."

"Where was he arrested?" asked Ruiz, who was extremely agitated by the news.

"In my room at the Ferronis'; he was dead drunk and he walked right into the enemy's hands while the police were occupying my room."

"That miserable drunk!" Ruiz murmured.

"The damage is done now," Margherita continued. "We have to try to repair it. I'm being followed by the police everywhere, I can't move, take a step outside the safe haven I've found for myself, it's up to you to ward off the blow that is about to knock us down, because I know my husband, he'll fall into the trap and tell everything, like a boy."

A flash of anger blazed in Ruiz's sidelong glance.

"All right, I'll take care of it, tomorrow I'll see that Napoleon is reassured and that he'll hold fast and not say anything about the unfortunate occurrence in your house. Is there anything else?"

"I would like to say, that, since I'm being followed by the police, I need . . ."

"I understand, money, always money, you must be rich, Mama Margherita."

"Poor as Job," the woman whined, "business has been terrible for a while . . ."

"Is twenty bucks enough?" Ruiz interrupted. "I don't have anything else in the house."

"It's enough for now," the old hag answered, holding out her hand.

From a drawer in a handsome desk of inlaid ebony he took two ten-dollar bills and handed them to Margherita, who immediately stuck them in her pocket.

"Now then, I'm leaving, look out for my Napoleon, take away the danger that is threatening us—that threatens you above all."

When Ruiz was alone he sank into a dark meditation.

Bad luck had been pursuing him for some time now; he had secret enemies who wanted to ruin him, who made war on him without quarter, enemies who surely knew more than a few things about him.

Now the police had caught a man who with a single word could ruin him, send him to jail.

After long meditation, Ruiz raised his head, his cold gaze harder than usual, with something sinister in it that inspired fear.

"I will get rid of the danger," he said, and then, going to his closet, he quickly dressed himself as a worker, putting on a blue shirt of the kind worn by conductors, and on his head a silk beret, and blackened his face, and thus transformed he left his house and headed downtown.

It was three in the morning, the infrequent passersby hurried their steps, eager to get home.

The great carts of the sanitation department rolled through the streets, raising clouds of dust and dirt; legions of sweepers, for the most part Italians, were busy pushing the debris into piles along the edges of the streets, to be thrown into the appropriate wagons later.

Ruiz walked with his head lowered, thoughtful, frowning.

Arriving at Mott Street, he stopped before a rundown-looking little house, stuck between two buildings inhabited entirely by Chinese immigrants.

Mott Street at that hour was deserted, the children of the celestial empire were sleeping, or delirious, in the grip of the intoxication brought on by opium.

Ruiz knocked loudly three times at equal intervals on the door of the house, and waited.

A good five minutes passed, then he heard a sound of steps, and a tiny window placed at the height of a man opened, and a hoarse voice asked in English:

"Who do you want?"

"Someone who buries secrets."

"Who sends you?"

"No one, I'm the boss."

The door opened immediately and Ruiz went in.

Preceded by the man who had spoken to him, the villain followed a long, totally dark corridor; reaching a door they knocked, and from within came a question.

"What do you bring?"

"Friend."

The door swung open on its hinges and a ray of bright light came from the room, where a table had been laid, loaded with food and wine. Three men and three beautiful young women were dining.

The dinner was almost over and it was clear that the guests had not been sparing with the wine.

When Ruiz entered, the men got up quickly, and murmured: the boss!

"Sit down, sit down," Ruiz said, "I'm happy to find you in good company."

"Need us, boss?" asked one of the guests, speaking in dialect.

"Yes," answered Ruiz, in the same language. "I need to talk to Quick Hand."

One of the three got up and, still in dialect, said to Ruiz: "I'm at your disposal."

"Thank you, friend; but first let's drink a glass to the health of the ladies."

The three ladies smiled graciously and in a single gulp emptied their goblets, filled with champagne.

"And now, if you will allow me," Ruiz said chivalrously, "I must take away one of your fellow-diners, but only for a few minutes."

"Go on, go on," the women cried. "We'll drink while we wait."

Ruiz and Quick Hand retired to a room apart, and stayed there for more than half an hour.

What plot did they hatch? It won't be long before we find out.

When Ruiz and his companion returned to the dining room, the wine had produced its effects: the women were half naked, with their hair down, and were singing lascivious songs, accompanied by obscene gestures and provocative movements.

Ruiz, although he was corrupt and dissolute, was disgusted by the sordid picture before his eyes.

The depravity of these women, who were not yet twenty, was beyond every limit, they were like beasts in the grip of a furious passion; to flaunt themselves they tore off their few remaining garments, and, bathed in champagne, they ran drunkenly, madly, from one man to another.

It was a repulsive spectacle, and Ruiz hurried away.

CHAPTER XXIX
*BRUTE LOVE*

Ruiz devoured Clara with his eyes.

The girl seemed more beautiful than usual that evening. The simple yet elegant pink dress she wore became her marvelously.

There was a long silence, then Ruiz began:

"How beautiful you are, Clara!"

"You think so," the girl answered, with irony.

"Beauty that would damn a saint; when I'm near you I forget all the dangers that surround me, the enemies who pursue me. Past, present, future, you're everything to me.

"Listen, Clara, I'm rich enough, I have a nice nest egg in the bank vault, I can go far away from a city where, from one moment to the next, I may be arrested; if you'll follow me we'll leave tomorrow, I will be your humble slave, you will be my queen.

"To satisfy all your whims, to fulfill all your desires, I will commit any crime, I want you to be envied, rich, powerful."

Ruiz was moving close to Clara, his voice was suffocated, his hot breath burned her neck, and she began to be afraid; preoccupied only with meeting her friends, she had not thought to furnish herself with a weapon, to defend herself; besides, she thought she could dominate Ruiz, prevail over him.

"Answer me," Ruiz continued, growing more and more excited, "answer me: will you agree? Will you be my adored companion? Life is beautiful with the one you love."

As he spoke the villain put his arms around Clara's slender figure, and she rose with a shudder of revulsion.

"Do I frighten you, does my love make you afraid?"

Clara didn't know what to say, she tried to protest with a gesture; for some time she had been making the sacrifice of smiling at her persecutor, but that farce repulsed her, and she could no longer do it.

Ruiz's blood boiled in his veins, his eyes flashed, his hands trembled, a fever of the senses invaded him when he was near that enchanting woman, to whom he had first revealed the mysteries of love.

"Clara, listen to me, I seem to be going mad; give me back my reason, let me press you to my breast, to my thirsty lips, give me the coolness of your kisses."

"No, no, a thousand times no!"

These words were uttered by Clara in a tone of such hatred that Ruiz could not miss it, and he cried:

"Then not only do you not love me, but you despise me, you hate me?"

The girl had betrayed herself, it was a mistake that could not be easily rectified, and she proudly raised her head and answered:

"Yes, yes, I hate you as the victim hates his torturer; do not hope that I will ever be yours, I will die before I belong to such a one as you!"

Ruiz was undone, Clara, forgetful of the danger she ran, continued, implacable:

"Hear me: once I was a chaste, pure girl, he who called himself my father, your accomplice, made me a thief, you, whom I loved, made yourself master of my body, tainted its purity, then threw me into the arms of libertines, who paid you for my caresses. Thanks to your evil work, the joys of a family were denied me, now I am dishonored, the accomplice of thieves and murderers, a merchant of love: my life was to be an uninterrupted series of crimes."

"Why repeat this story of the past? The future will be glorious if you want it to be."

"The future with you? Me! but don't you see that you disgust me, don't you realize that nausea assaiis me just having you near me?"

"Clara, Clara," Ruiz shouted, "think of what you're saying!"

"I'm not afraid of you; I know that you are capable of anything; but you don't frighten me."

"Clara, don't provoke the beast, it could tear you to pieces."

The girl responded to these words with a disdainful smile, her head high, her arms folded on her chest; in the room's semidarkness, Clara looked like a pink marble statue, representing some proud chatelaine.

Ruiz was checked, but it was only a moment; the desire to possess that woman increased with her contempt.

"Listen to me, Clara, I will forget your bitter words, which fell on my heart like burning lava, but tell me that you do not hate me, and that what you said was to put me to the test."

"The test of what? Are you so mad as to think that your love matters to me?"

"Clara, Clara, don't bring me to extremes . . ."

"Do you want to know everything? Let it be, so you will understand the abyss that separates us, you will understand that my heart thirsts not for love but for revenge!

"One day I met a man who mastered my heart, my soul, my whole self . . ."

"You have a lover!" Ruiz shouted.

Clara pretended not to understand and went on.

"That man could not love me, he loved another; a chaste, pure, and wealthy girl. I, the lost, the dishonored, the prostitute of Naples and Rome, the dancer, could not compete with the American virgin, who possessed entire the heart of the man I loved.

"I gave up the struggle, and gradually love changed to another, sweeter feeling, and I devoted myself entirely to insuring the happiness of my friend, my brother."

Ruiz sneered, impossible for him to believe in a fraternal friendship between a young man and a beautiful girl.

"Unfortunately the girl loved by my friend loved another, a wretch, who by means of surprises and betrayals and clever stories, made himself master of her virgin heart.

"Well, I aligned myself with those who wanted to unmask that wretch, that thief, that murderer, I was an energetic, valuable ally, and the mask fell from the face of that criminal, and Fanny Spencer was saved!"

Ruiz, who for some moments had been in the grip of the most intense excitement, at the last words, concerning Fanny, gave a cry that echoed in the room like the roar of a wounded lion.

With a bound, the wretch threw himself on Clara, who felt as though she were being squeezed in the coils of a monstrous serpent.

"You betrayed me, you used my blind, foolish love to sell me to my enemies; now I will take my revenge with a single blow, because you will be mine, the redeemed will once again feel the caresses of the murderer, the thief . . ."

In vain Clara tried to free herself from that furious grip, she wanted to scream, but could not.

Ruiz smiled the way the damned smile, if those miserable creatures exist.

"Mine, mine!" Ruiz continued in a stifled voice. "I will satisfy the burning desire to possess you that overwhelms me, I will break that pride of yours."

And as he spoke the villain dragged the poor girl to the sofa, while she herself desperately tried to fight him off.

Clara's clothes were in shreds. Ruiz, in a bestial fury, was ripping the pink garment, and already the white of her slip could be seen, and the even whiter flesh.

In Ruiz there was no longer anything human, as, nearing his triumph, about to possess the woman he so deeply desired, he was invaded by delirium.

Clara did not call for mercy, she knew that Ruiz would have none; one hope only remained to her, the immediate arrival of the Spencher family.

Ruiz realized that he was lost; Clara's words had revealed the abyss into which he had fallen.

Well: after satisfying his desires, he would joyfully offer his wrists to the handcuffs, to be led off to jail; but first, first the dancer would be his.

To possess her, to bend her to his will, was a desire of the senses bound to the desire for revenge.

The struggle had exhausted Clara's strength; she felt Ruiz's hot breath burning her.

There was nothing human left in him, we repeat, he was like one of those dangerous beasts who, lurking in the forests of the tropics, terrorize travelers.

The girl's clothes were in tatters, the black satin bodice tore under Ruiz's hands, which seemed to have claws.

The unfortunate girl began to realize that for her it was all over if help was delayed any longer.

Meanwhile Ruiz laid Clara on the sofa and placed the full weight of his body on hers. His kisses were the bites of a raging beast, and the face of the victim was here and there stained with blood. Her lovely limbs, half uncovered, appeared to be pure white.

"You betrayed me," Ruiz murmured, "now you're going to tell my enemies that you have been mine, you're going to tell them that the thief, the murderer was delirious in your arms. You'll be mine, and then I will kill you.

"Mine is a strange destiny, which compels me to obtain by force the caresses first of my wife, then of my old lover."

Clara didn't respond, from her dry throat not a word came, her cold eyes, like stone, gazed at the man who was torturing her. In that gaze, in that submissiveness, was an absolute resignation, an immutable decision.

Yes, Clara believed that if Ruiz made himself master of her body, she would kill herself.

An exaggeration, this, of a wretched soul, who did not comprehend in that terrible moment that violence was not her fault.

Ruiz was already enjoying his triumph; but he wanted it complete, he wanted Clara to share in his intoxication; a libertine without conscience, without shame he took Clara's submission for tacit consent to his base desires.

"Clara?" he said. "Love me, love me, even for an hour, and then I will go far away from you. I'll forgive your betrayal, I'll forget everything, but come to me, as in the early days of our love, I love you so much, have pity!"

Clara did not respond, Ruiz's caresses made her shiver as if she felt on her flesh the cold viscous skin of a serpent.

"You won't respond? Do I inspire disgust and fear? Now you will be mine just the same, and I will punish your vile, shameful betrayal. Your lover will now have a fortunate rival."

Ruiz's mouth was on Clara's, the poor girl made a last effort and managed to get up, but he pushed her roughly and she fell, groaning, and did not move.

Ruiz stretched her beautiful motionless body on the sofa, then looked at her for a long time, his bold hands tearing off what remained to cover her nakedness, and then, letting out a cry of triumph, he threw himself on her.

Clara was lost. . . . The door opened violently and Fanny appeared, her eyes sparkling with anger.

She held a revolver, and in an imperious voice cried:

"Ruiz, leave that woman or I will kill you like a mad dog!"

Ruiz let out a terrible curse and detached himself from Clara's body, backing away surprised, frightened, undone, defeated.

Fanny's arrival had saved Clara, and Ruiz would go to the gallows without having possessed her whom he so ardently desired.

*I misteri di Mulberry Street* (New York: Frugone & Balletto, 1893), 1–2, 140–41, 246–48.

**The Underworld of New York**

Despite the title, in this late novel Ciambelli considerably broadens his scenario, introducing a long aside on Ukraine, as the motherland of his fellow immigrants the Jews. However, although Ciambelli's novels display the predictable racial overtones, he speaks clearly against Russian anti-Semitism, and in an interesting passage tries to compare it with American racism against blacks. All this is set forth in the context of an international imbroglio involving kidnappings, lost princesses, and impossible love stories, with the customary happy ending. Italian characters play a lesser role here, while the dutiful hero, Jim, manages to save Sara, the "beautiful Jewess."

CHAPTER XIX

Jim had never traveled; but he was young and intelligent, and he wasn't afraid of going to a foreign country, where the language spoken was unknown to him, and where the habits and customs were utterly different from those of America.

Jim had been provided with credentials that prompted a kind reception from the chief of police of Kiev, who spoke English very well and had a deep hatred of Jews.

When the chief of police found out what Jim's mission was, he declared that there was no way that a supposedly wealthy Jew by the name of Isaac, who had made a hefty fortune, had arrived in Kiev.

"The police," said the gruff General Ivanoff, "do not lose sight of Jews who return from your cities, where their subversive ideas are reinforced. If this Isaac you are looking for were in Kiev we would know it. Our police are not blind. We have very sharp eyes."

The police chief's words did not make a good impression on Jim. It seemed to him that the general was boasting too much, especially since he was not ignorant of the fact that Russia was the classic land of mysterious and powerful associations that the police managed to uncover only with great difficulty.

Naturally Jim contented himself with saying:

"My duty is to find the criminal who fled my country, and I will look for him even if I have to search all of Russia."

The old general gave a loud laugh; then, in an ironic tone:

"Russia is big, very big . . . but perhaps for an American it is small."

Jim felt like telling him where to get off, but he restrained himself; when, however, the general added:

"It seems to me, and don't take offense, that, for such a mission— which may be very hard—you are too young."

With some haughtiness Jim answered:

"In our country the old men take it easy . . . it's the young ones who do the work."

The general understood the barb, but he wasn't upset and with a certain good humor said:

"All right . . . but I will prove to you that old men are still worth something."

"Thank you."

"Besides," the general continued, "in the case of a dog of a Jew, I will do everything possible to enable you to take him back to your country. If we find him there will be no opposition to his being extradited. We do not deal with Jews the way we deal with other citizens."

Jim did not love Jews, but as he listened to the general he felt disgusted and realized how true what he had heard many times was, that in Russia the Jews were treated worse than mad dogs.

When Jim left the police station, he had come to the conclusion that he could expect little from the Russian police and would have to do everything himself.

The prospect did not displease him, because he was anxious to prove he had a good nose for pursuit.

CHAPTER XX

It was already the middle of the night when Jim and Wilhelm left the hotel and went to a café-chantant that was frequented by all the pleasure-seekers of Kiev.

The Russians are mad for the theater, for cafés-chantants, for artists, and for champagne, and those who have money spend it happily.

Jim enjoyed the show, partly because there were some American singers; however, he was not content merely to watch the stage, but also occupied himself with the audience and at a certain point he said to the German:

"They told me that in Kiev there were a lot of Jews, and here I do not see a single one."

"There are Jews," the German answered, "a lot of them; but they do not come to places frequented by Christians, because they would be thrown out."

"Thrown out?"

"Yes. The Jews, although they control the city's commerce, are considered inferior, and a good Russian does not want to have contact with them. The Jews have their own theaters, their own cafés-chantants, and even places where they go to take their walks."

"It's strange."

"It may be strange, but that's how it is. Besides, isn't it the same in your country for Negroes?"

"But Negroes . . ."

"Negroes are much better than Jews, at least that's what the Russians think. If you want, I'll take you to the Jewish clubs."

Jim, who had been expecting this offer, was quick to respond.

"You would be doing me a real favor, because even though I've been here for two weeks, I would like to get to know the life of the city thoroughly."

"It will be a pleasure to be your guide. Would you like to see a Jewish club tonight?"

"Would you mind?"

"Not at all, we'll go right away."

Jim and the German paid for their drinks and left.

They went along the main streets of the city, which were brilliantly lighted, and then they entered the Jewish quarter.

The city did not spend much on street lights in the neighborhoods where the Jews lived, so the streets were sunk in semi-darkness, in harsh contrast with the splendor of the streets that welcomed the true Russian population.

Finally they went into a café-chantant with a big lighted-up sign that was visible from quite far away.

The place was large and elegant, although there was perhaps too much gold, in the ceiling, in the columns, in the balustrades.

It looked as if all that gold might from one moment to the next fall on the heads of the audience.

The show was more or less the same as the show in all the other cafés-chantants, and aside from a play that was performed by Jewish actors in the language of Jacob and the Nazarene, one who merely looked at the stage would not have known he was in a Jewish theater: however, one who, like Jim, observed the audience more closely than the show would realize immediately where he was.

The elegant women, whose elegance was rather ostentatious, possessed that Jewish type of beauty that fades early, but is very attractive in its flower. Almost all the men wore beards.

Some had short full beards, others were brush-cut, and quite a few, generally the older men, had beards like those we have all seen in pictures showing old Simeon.

There was none of the uproar that had reigned in the theater that Jim and the German had visited earlier.

The spectators were quiet, and even when they clapped their hands they did it sparingly.

There was in all of them a sort of resignation: that resignation which always dominates people who are enslaved.

The policeman could not help making, in his own mind, a comparison between the Jews of New York, bold, tumultuous, rebellious, and those of Kiev.

But when the little play was performed, which was inspired by the liberation of the Jews from Egypt, then the quiet and tranquillity disappeared, the bowed heads were raised, the timid eyes were ardent, the faint applause became loud, and when the man who played the part of the grand rabbi announced that the great Jewish family was free, they all rose to their feet, shouting deliriously.

It made a great impression on Jim; he understood that the Jews of Kiev longed for freedom and, for this reason, the Russian authorities could not forgive the people who prayed for an uprising.

---

*I sotterranei di New York* (New York: Libraria Italiana, 1915), 166–67, 170–71.

## MENOTTI PELLEGRINO: SELF-MADE MYSTERY WRITER

Menotti Pellegrino, perhaps a Sicilian living on New York's Lower East Side but in essence a mystery himself, left his name on a novel in which the title stands out as the clearest element in an almost indecipherable hodgepodge. Pellegrino is a minor master of the rough-hewn, blunt opening, especially when he can vent his outrage and denounce the darkest sides of the metropolis. Crime, corruption, and political entanglements within and outside the Italian community eventually result in a long trial and the electric chair for the evil female protagonist.

### The Mysteries of New York

CHAPTER I

NEW YORK! The sigh of every derelict of the old world; the refuge of hearts longed for by the delinquent; the cradle of fortune sought by the disinherited of all peoples.

NEW YORK! Chaos, where hope and disillusion swirl, gold and tin, virtue and vice, wealth and misery; and the greedy hand of every newcomer gropes as it attempts to seize the good part and often ends up grasping only the bad. The enigma, where through the whole gamut of base and shameful acts one sees the insolent boor rise, while the wellborn person who refuses to join in the prevailing corruption falls. The anomaly in which guilt is bowed down; crime, prostitution, promiscuity, and theft are crowned, and shame, honesty, and justice are derided or pitied. The altar of the Almighty Dollar, where everything is traded and measured, from heart to mind; where love and honor, every affection, every feeling, by which everything is inspired, on which everything hinges, at which everything genuflects, are only things with a price.

NEW YORK is the synthetic word, it is America for the majority of the innumerable worshippers of the powerful Almighty Dollar. In fact, among all those thousands of immigrants who from every part of Europe and elsewhere converge on the great metropolis, a considerable number always remain there, even to the detriment of their own capacities, which would find greater opportunities in spreading out into the other states of the American union.

NEW YORK will be the first land on which our eyes, tired of the sight of the sea, rest, said a traveler with an aristocratic air, leaning on the rail of the first-class bridge of an English steamship, to a fair woman with a shapely figure and majestic bearing, whose beautiful eyes, of a bright, enchanting black, along with the evidently unusual pallor of her cheeks, revealed traces of fear, which had caused those eyes to widen.

CHAPTER IX

Just as papal excommunication makes the fields more fertile and inspires the soldiers of liberty to victory, and makes cowardly the hearts of the soldiers who, with bayonets bearing the motto of tyranny, are blessed by the priest, so in New York (where if the unavoidable vices are covered up because of the immense crowds of people, the highest virtues, which honor human creation and move God to a smile of complacency toward his work, blaze with light and overflow in public well-being) many genius scourges, like anathema and plague—as if their wings had been clipped by the cold of the ocean placed between the old world and the regions of free thought— never arrive.

In mother New York, the synthesis of America, merciful and provident mother whose mantle covers so many different sons of the earth, who redeems for them a new, prosperous existence elsewhere denied or precluded; kind new homeland, where the bitterest natures, the most savage characters, the most quarrelsome souls, the most perverse hearts, the most reckless minds are tempered, it seems, by the strong northern cold, while the sloth, the laziness of those who elsewhere were sluggish, becomes, as if kindled by the scorching rays of the burning sun, energy, industry, talent, all the lances of the curse are blunted, all the arrows of malediction.

And all the restless peoples of decaying Europe, of soft, voluptuous Asia, of black, inert Africa, though marked forever by their own characters, adapt to the new regime, without stripping themselves of their racial vices, and form a single people, in the rigid circle of the law: strong, lively, entrepreneurial, rich.

That people which in its flourishing, energetic, hardworking existence denies more than any other that eternal curse pronounced by those who said it came from the lips of crucified love incarnate is the people of Israel: it is the Jews.

The neighborhoods where the people of other nationalities have clustered in New York can be indicated by a name like Little Italy, where there are a large number of Italians, or Germantown or Chinatown, or the Greek, French, Arab, or Turkish city, yet one could not call a ghetto that extensive part of New York where the Jews live, because it includes the whole southern edge of the city, which by itself would be equivalent to a substantial European city, in addition to the fact that Jews are scattered around other points of the immense metropolis, far from the larger community.

However, just as, passing along certain streets in New York, for example Mulberry, Elizabeth, and so on, one has the not-always-pleasant illusion of finding oneself in a poor neighborhood in Naples or Palermo because the customs and language of America are utterly lacking, so, finding oneself passing along certain other streets, in the Jewish neighborhoods—where a swarming population of sweaty and greasy women, ragged, emaciated children, bent old men, all selling something, shouting near carts loaded with rotten fruit, old fish, salted and stale meats, ribbons, iron goods, bread, mended shoes, saints, fruits and vegetables, all in a horrible muddle—one sees that one is in the midst of the ghetto.

That pandemonium of peddlers, amid the garbage piled up along the street, amid arguments, chatter, shouts, din, especially on certain days of the week when it is not easy to get through these parts, makes one's mind run immediately to the mysteries of the ghetto, where great riches lie hidden, where there are diamonds and rags, as you see in the ears and on the bodies of so many women in sandals with the old sleeves of their dresses rolled up to the elbows as they strive to sell their foul wares.

One thinks, it's true, that in the midst of those people, among whom some patriarchal and aristocratic figures move, mixed in with the masses, is the greedy, sharp-eyed serpent usury; that profit, however it may be, would make those who appear to be the best of them new crucifiers, and they deceive, they steal from each other, they betray one another, they bite each other like dogs, they would sell each other for gold. But if they are made to suffer an insult from other people, they forget usury and remember that they are only Jews, alone in this world, bound to one another, and as a single man they assert themselves, struggle, and win.

An example of solidarity in New York, more than the Germans, more than the Irish who will give up their vote for a glass of whiskey, a thousand miles away from the divisions among the Italians, who through lack of agreement and mutual interest, to the shame of their numerical majority, remain out of power, the Jews have officials, magistrates to protect their rights, whom, united, they elevate, with the weapon of civilized peoples: the vote.

CHAPTER XIV

Bowery!

It's not only a street, it's a world in itself.

There exist all the layers of human society.

Surely if one were to seek in the world a city thoroughfare of equal classicism, of equal importance as the Bowery of New York, one would fail in the undertaking.

Broad enough for more than four separate trolley tracks, with shoulders wide enough to be streets themselves, in addition to spacious sidewalks on both sides, surmounted by the high tracks of the elevated trains that run noisily up and down, at intervals of perhaps a minute, it has no repose at night, nor the peace of repose.

In the long line of disparate buildings, in that whole long linked extension, you would not find the habitation of a family.

Hotels, furnished rooms, clubs, theaters, stores, warehouses, factories, schools, credit institutions, banks, and next door to one another countless bars always full of drinkers, shops for every kind of article, workshops for strange objects, antique stores, anatomical museums, displays of mummies, of freaks, of talking machines, instruments that play by themselves, and a crowd of the curious, always new, pressing in to admire, and a rabble of pickpockets, always active, taking from the more intent admirers whatever it can, in spite of the sign, in block letters, in the entryway of every attraction: Watch out for pickpockets.

At all hours of the day, in the deafening noise of the elevated trains, in the continuous rhythmic rolling of the trolleys, a flow of people goes up and down that sidewalk, among them the artisan hurrying to work, the prostitute who seems to follow her shadow and hopes only to be followed, the girl on her way to the factory nibbling an apple or chewing gum, the idler who is looking for a swindle, the street peddler, the newsboy, the junk dealer, the man hurrying by as if he feared to be sullied, the grande dame who avoids looking at the passersby, pulling a small dog with her little finger burdened by a large diamond.

And the drunk, who tacking this way and that cries, threatens, or sings; the cop who is in close conversation with a young woman, while others, pairing up after making an agreement, where is the more and the less, climb the steps of one of the many taverns; two ragged vagabonds having a fistfight who act like athletes in a ring of spectators; the pimp who pretends to be attentively admiring something in a shopwindow, while in fact waiting to make his offering to the first who approaches; the secret policeman who collects his weekly bribe from the peddlers, while his partner, under some pretext or other, arrests any among them who refuse.

Greatness, splendor, wealth, depravity, filth, misery—all find confused yet typical expression on the Bowery.

At night the actors and the scene change, but they are no less characteristic than the figures, the things of the day.

If the number of passersby who are hurrying about their business is less, the noise of trolleys and trains is the same, and the number of women seeking adventure, stationed at every corner, in every doorway, near the pillars of the elevated tracks, is greater, until the dawn hours of the morning, when like bats they go home, as if fleeing the light. They offer themselves to whoever passes by, leading him to a dark area, dragging him to the entrance of a hotel, starting a conversation as they skillfully steal the watch of the fool who's been caught, then leaving him waiting in vain in a room where they've brought him, after cadging the agreed-on price before fulfilling the bargain.

The men who, lacking any sense of honor, strangers to every virtue, live on these women, eat off their flesh, covering themselves to the last abuse, often follow them, and when the inexperienced fellow falls into their hands and is led into a suitable bar, they fall like wolves on a sheep, like falcons on a sparrow, and strip him of everything and beat him, if he resists, and divide the spoils with the owner of the place.

The shouts, the obscene cries of the drunks, the vulgar scenes around the improvised stalls selling fried or boiled food that a crowd of strange customers devours on the sidewalk, the frequent arrival of the ambulance, announced by the ringing of its electric bell, to pick up someone who has been injured—these are all things typical of night on the Bowery.

---

*I misteri di New York* (New York: Tipografia Italiana U. De Luca & Benedetti, 1903), 5–6, 241–42, 358–60.

## ITALO STANCO:
## THE SELF-CONSCIOUS BEGINNING OF A NEW TRADITION

Lucio and Claudio are two minor characters in Stanco's novel, young men trying to making ends meet in Italian Harlem right before the First World War. They could be crooks, involved in the larger story of the kidnapping of the daughter of an Italian American cop who is madly in love with a treacherous femme fatale, the "blond devil" of the title; but, really, their good hearts demand nothing more than a nice dinner and some light fun with local girls. Italo Stanco, who continued in Ciambelli's vein well into the 1950s, is at his best when he manages to deviate from the worn formula of the ethnic thriller to offer a glimpse into the smaller worlds of those who are just trying to get by.

**The Blond Devil**

VII. IN WHICH A LUCULLIAN MENU IS PREPARED

One evening, soon after Lucio Fini had returned to his monklike room on 106th Street, his friend Claudio came in, for once neither cheerful nor talkative. He had, rather, a serious and remorseful expression and appeared unusually preoccupied. He carried a suitcase, and he flung it into a corner.

"Ah, you're here? A little late, if you haven't dined. The servants have already cleared the table and now, as you see, I'm in the smoking room. May I offer you one?"

Thus speaking, the sybarite with comic gravity held out to the sculptor a cigarette butt chosen from the many that he had on a small tray.

"They are Beard of the Sultan, imported expressly for my use and consumption."

Claudio took the cigarette butt, sat down, and let out a melancholy sigh.

"Ah me, so it's an evening for Beard of the Sultan?"

"As you see. But what's happened to you? You look as if you'd just swallowed Aristotle with all his peripatetic treatises."

"A trifle, really. You know I still owed two months' rent to my landlady . . ."

"Well?"

"That old hag, who promised to be patient for a few days, today put all my furniture out on the street."

"Did you say furniture?"

"Don't joke. I found my apartment empty. . . . My poor statues confined in a basement . . . I'm devastated!"

"And now you've come to ask my hospitality?"

"No more nor less."

The sybarite dug a notebook out of his pocket and began to consult it, while he muttered some incomprehensible words.

"Oh, very well!" he said finally. "I am happy to be able to be your host for at least three days, after which we will be forced to leave this place together. My hour strikes at dawn Friday morning."

"You're behind, too?"

"The question is unworthy of you. But we have three days before us and the world is ours. I will immediately have your rooms prepared, and I will put at your service the most beautiful slaves in my harem . . ."

Who were these two friends who were joking about their impecunious circumstances and squeezing wit out of their empty stomachs?

We have already introduced them to the reader: two artists, a sculptor and a painter. The life of young artists, of course, is always that of the classic *Bohème,* and our friends managed to relive the exploits of Murger's heroes even in an intractable society like America.

They had left Italy after early disappointments, and spurred by the spirit of adventure. Claudio Sparta had a well-off family in Naples, and he could have returned to its bosom, if by now his closest friendships and the shame of returning as the prodigal son had not bound him to New York. Lucio Fini had no one, except an ex-fiancée who had cheated on him, and at whom he had hurled his palette, of porcelain, in a burst of insane jealousy, striking her in the forehead. In Italy, therefore, a six-month jail sentence awaited him.

They both had talent, even genius, and they could have earned enough in New York to live comfortably if they had agreed to clip the wings of their art within the walls of a so-called artistic workshop.

They did their best to search out commissions, and often, by producing a noble likeness of some wealthy shopowner or sober housewife, they solved the problem of living. In the meantime, they created some wonderful works, and waited for a patron who would enable them to hold an exhibition.

Young, eager, energetic, equipped with a refined sensitivity and great powers of observation, they enacted, with no goal in mind, a profound study of the cosmopolitan milieu in which they lived.

We have already seen how the spirit of observation sometimes led them to come upon secrets because of which they then undertook—with their astonishing generosity—reckless enterprises.

"By the way," Lucio asked his friend, "will you let me offer you dinner?"

"The truth is I haven't had time to get to a restaurant. They'll wait for me in vain at Martin's tonight."

"Have you any appetite?"

"Several hours ago it yielded its place to its venerable mother, hunger."

"Then we must consult our ledger," added Lucio, turning his pockets inside out. "Among goods movable and not I possess nineteen cents."

"You're a Croesus. I only go as high as three."

"Twenty-two in all, a capital that it will be well to employ judiciously. I will prepare the menu and you will go down to make the purchases."

"Remember to include in the urgent expenses a little wood to throw in that old stove. These days you can't survive. It's as cold as winter."

"And to think that we are barely at the end of January!"

The painter sat down at a table loaded with books, canvases, brushes and boxes, took a piece of paper, and began to reflect.

After ten minutes of serious reflection he gave his friend the following:

Assorted antipasto made up of a salted anchovy. 2 cents.

Chopped beef, 5 cents.

Egg poached in God's mercy, 3 cents.

Vegetable cheese, 2½ cents.

Horsemeat salami, 2½.

Fresh fruit 1 cent.

Sweets, 1 cent.

Bread 2 cents.

Omega cigarettes, 1 cent.

Rosewood to feed the heater, 2 cents.

Total $0.22.

Claudio read the menu and burst out in an enthusiastic exclamation.

"How wonderful! We will dine like two gourmands. Lucullus, Vitellius, Sardanapalus and similar of our predecessors will groan with envy in their respective graves."

"Cleopatra did not offer better to her friend Antony," the painter added gravely. "Now go and spend it. Here is your patrimony and be judicious. At the corner there's a little Italian restaurant that will give you a good portion of boiled beef for 5 cents. I, in the meantime, will prepare the table."

## IX. IN WHICH CLAUDIO GOES FROM ONE SURPRISE TO ANOTHER

Left alone Lucio devoted himself to clearing the room, piling up paintings, palettes, and articles of clothing helter-skelter; then he went to the mirror and gave another quick glance at his outfit.

It was eleven.

"It's time to call the girls," he said to himself. "They must be back from the moving-pictures and the snail must have gone to bed by now."

He went out to the landing, where the doors of all three apartments opened, and knocked discreetly on one of them.

The door opened almost immediately and a pretty young girl appeared in the doorway.

"Were you expecting me, Miss Maria?" asked the artist, greeting her.

"I had a feeling you might come calling on us."

"A real gala. The guests are already crowding the rooms and the dances are warming up. Don't you hear that intoxicating Strauss waltz?"

The girl pretended to listen; then she burst out laughing.

"We'll be right there, Mr. Lucio."

"I'll give you half an hour."

Mary and Luisa Monte were two sisters who had recently arrived in America with their father, a good-for-nothing of the first order, whose golden dream was to live by exploiting his daughters. We don't know what form of exploitation he had in mind; he was content, however, that they, by their own choice, were singers in an Italian vaudeville act.

They did fairly well, and the honest father had enough money to keep himself on intimate terms with the bar across the street and the nearest cigar store.

Since they all lived in the same building, a cordial friendship perforce developed between the two young women and the painter, who had then introduced them to the group of starving artists. There was, however, nothing illicit in that friendship: the two sisters were not exactly nuns but they had solid principles and, even if they spent entire nights in the convivial company of young men, knew how to set up a barrier in the way of their . . . expansiveness.

In the meantime, while Lucio was preparing the room for the guests, Claudio had brought the list of supplies to the nearest restaurant, ordering that everything be sent to the address written on the piece of paper.

He then went back to 106th street, where Betty lived, a model with whom he professed to be a little in love, and urged her to get dressed and go to Lucio's.

The night was dark and foggy, but not too cold. Passersby were rare and some of the shops were already closing.

Claudio was not in the habit of looking behind him, and so was not aware of a man who had been following him since he left the house.

That man was wearing a black overcoat with a collar so wide that, when he raised it, his whole face was covered.

It appeared that he was interested not only in following our young friend but in staying very near him, for he frequently came so close that he grazed him with his elbow.

As Claudio left Betty's house, he turned onto Pleasant Ave., picking up his pace, for the dampness penetrated his very bones.

He was just passing in front of a mean-looking bar when the stick he was carrying under his arm was torn from him, and a commanding voice whispered in his ear:

"Not a word, or you're dead!"

He turned quickly and found himself facing a man of imposing stature, whose face was covered by the broad collar of his overcoat.

In the hands of the attacker a revolver flashed.

Claudio stopped, more surprised than frightened, but, when he saw a few people sitting in the aforementioned bar he paid no attention to the threat and gave a cry that the other shoved back in his throat, grabbing his head and covering his mouth with a hand that felt like lead.

The artist, seeing two men running toward him, took heart.

Logical hope but vain! His surprise was unbounded when the two new arrivals, instead of defending him, grabbed him by the arms and dragged him into the bar, through a doorway above which was written "Family Entrance."

He found himself in a vast room, saturated with smoke and alcohol, and occupied by both men and women. Some were engrossed in a game, others were drinking, and joking crudely with a drunk woman, others were performing a dissolute, obscene dance.

Claudio realized that he had fallen into a den of corruption, and he considered himself done for.

"All this for fifty dollars!" he reflected sadly, for he assumed that his assailants must have known what he had in his wallet.

The three companions pushed the artist into a small semi-dark room, piled with cases of empty bottles. Then the man with the raised collar said to him:

"Put up your arms. Obey! A person of your intelligence knows that in certain situations there's nothing better than to obey."

"You're a man of spirit," answered Claudio, raising his arms, "and you speak like a law graduate from Salamanca."

The fellow looked at him, not knowing if he had given him an insult or a compliment; then he shrugged his shoulders and made a rapid but meticulous search of the young man's pockets. He took possession of the wallet and left quickly.

"You're free," he said, returning after a few minutes, and giving the wallet back to the artist. "Get out and, if you value your life, don't tell anyone about your adventure."

"Sir," said Claudio, straightening the disarray of his clothes as well as he could, "you have ruined our party. In return, you have enabled me to feel the emotions of a millionaire, and I am grateful to you. I do not ask you your name, because official secrecy forbids you to reveal it. I am Claudio Sparta, sculptor, willing to build you a monument, if you become a famous outlaw tomorrow. I am an admirer of Cartouche."

Having said that, he left, humming, as he crossed the hall filled with people drunk on crime, wine, and lust. A beautiful wild-looking girl, with tousled hair and dishevelled clothes, stopped him, jumping on his neck:

"Hello, sweetheart, how did the doctor find you?"

"Fifty dollars' of fever, my girl," the artist replied, without batting an eye. "Ten minutes ago I would have offered you a bottle of champagne; now all I can offer you is a kiss."

"Well, I'll take it at that," the girl replied, presenting her lips, which still had the fresh scent of adolescence.

A drunken voice called the girl:

"Come on, come on! Cut that out!"

Reaching the street, Claudio breathed deeply, hurrying to get away. But it was fated that he was to go from one surprise to another that evening. He had not taken ten steps when, from the shadow cast by a cart, a man jumped out and appeared in front of him.

"Again!" the artist said this time, in astonishment. "I'm not fond of encores. What do you want?"

The unknown man seemed, by his face and clothing, one of those vagrants for whom life passes solely and uniquely in the adoration of whiskey.

"I have nothing, not even a cent!" Claudio added, in English.

"I don't want anything," answered the other, in perfect Italian. "Don't you know me?"

"I don't have that honor, nor am I sorry about it."

The other leaned into his ear.

"I am Sergeant Petrosino and I'm on a trail."

"For Heaven's sake! Made up like that? You'd outdo the greatest actor."

"Are there a lot of people in that bar?" the brave Italian policeman pressed him, for it was indeed he.

"A lot."

"Did anything strike you?"

"Yes; a stink of whiskey that would turn the stomach of a hippopotamus."

"I don't mean that. Was there a meeting going on?"

"I don't think so, at least not in the room where I was taken. Men and women drinking and carousing."

"That's enough; thanks and good night."

"Good night."

Claudio was about to go off, when Petrosino called him back and, with an abrupt gesture, took him by the arm and began to laugh crudely, writhing and now and again punching the young man in the stomach.

"Now what's got into you?" exclaimed our friend, taken aback.

The other, with the skill of a ventriloquist, said, while continuing to laugh raucously:

"We've been spied on. In a loud voice tell me to go home and sleep it off."

"*Yes, dear friend,* she's a fine figure . . .very nice girl," the policeman continued in a tipsy voice. "I want her . . . yes, I want to marry her and when I've married her, *yes, goodbye!* . . ."

"You are dead drunk!" said Claudio, who had understood the game perfectly.

A well-dressed young man had stopped under a street light, five paces away, and appeared intent on lighting a rebellious cigar.

"You call me a drunk? No, dear, I've had only eleven glasses, yes . . . odd, really only eleven . . . She says yes, mama no . . .

"Ah! ah! we need the mother? I'm supposed to marry the old lady too? Ah! Ah! . . ."

While the detective was playing this scene, so artfully that the most brilliant actor would have paled beside him, he found a way to say to Claudio in a low voice:

"Go home and be careful. I don't know why, but you've been followed for several nights, in fact for several days. Meanwhile, speak naturally, treating me like a drunk."

"Go home and sleep!" cried Claudio, laughing, too, and freeing himself from the clasp of the pseudo drunk. "You've got a terrific crush. If the girl saw you like this she wouldn't think about marrying you anymore. *Good night,* John!"

"*Well, good night, dear!* But I tell you what would be nice . . . No . . . no, . . . marry the old lady! Ah! ah! ah! . . .

*In the shade of the old apple tree*
*For the love in your eyes I can see*
*And the paint on your face*
*Is a perfect disgrace.*"

The cop went off, humming the crude song and stopping from time to time to contemplate the stars.

The well-dressed young man had finally lighted the cigar and, passing close by the drunk, without even glancing at him, began tailing Claudio.

The latter proceeded rapidly toward First Avenue, talking to himself with a certain bitterness:

"Here's how man proposes and the Lord God disposes, when he is not truly indisposed! Alas, my poor friends, the banquet will remain a dream . . . But how the devil did those fine fellows guess that I was carrying fifty nice new dollars in my pocket? At least, the attack seemed to have the flavor of robbery. And that wizard Petrosino, who shows up as if by magic and seems to be as ubiquitous as Saint Anthony?

"Here, for example, is a detective who will be very successful if his worthy adversaries do not cut short his life.

"He told me that someone has been following me for several days. I didn't think I was such an important personage. . . . For that matter, I wouldn't like it if my esteemed pickpocket had also stolen Lucio's letter . . . Let's see!"

Claudio stopped near a streetlight and took out his wallet.

The last surprise was the biggest of all: the fifty-dollar bill was there, intact, just as he had stuck it in.

Carefully as he searched, however, he could not find the letter that his friend had given him to mail.

He stood motionless for a moment, like the statue of astonishment; then he shrugged his shoulders and started off again, murmuring:

"Upon my word, I don't understand anything anymore! In this wonderful country the thieves prefer the harmless letter of a lover to a fifty-dollar bill! Bah! Meanwhile our stomachs are safe and tonight we'll party!"

---

*Il diavolo biondo* (New York: Nicoletti Bros. Press, Inc., 1916), 43–47, 55–62.

## CATERINA AVELLA:
## THE ROARING TWENTIES

Flashy new cars (including, not by accident, a Fiat), parties, long weekends, yachts, sailing in the moonlight, flirtations: the Jazz Age as seen by an Italian American woman who clearly identifies herself with the new character of the liberated "flapper." The main plot concerns the love travails of a rich, assimilated youth, tying together literary romance and the point of view of the upper middle class.

### The Flapper

On a foggy evening in August, Amedeo, yearning, waiting, and hoping, received from the woman he believed to be the principal object of his existence a decisive no for an answer.

He had to change. It was essential to forget at all costs; he could find balm for his wounds only in numbness, distance, oblivion.

Thus he decided to abandon the town of his birth, with all its burden of fond, sad memories, which at every evocation burned his soul.

He wished to be far away; what did it matter to him if he ended up east of Suez, in that place which Kipling said was beyond the reach of "the ten commandments," where every restraint on life was absent, every moderating force of civilization, morality, decency? Experience of the most extreme, the wildest emotions would carry him far from his all too recent sufferings! What did it matter to him if he was east of Suez or south of Gehenna? To go away, far away, to the most remote corner of land and sea, isolated, as far from human contact as possible, where he would have no opportunity of seeing other women, any woman; to leave, to flee, was the most indispensable decision.

Distance, time, that great mitigator of all things, would succeed in resolving the tremendous crisis in which he was ensnared; and so, he wished to leave.

Two years passed in the most distant country, deep in the heart of the vast North American continent. Amedeo Villadio, from the porch of his little house, looked at the small port, nearby, where the lights of a steamer shone in the velvet of the night like tropical stars; but his thoughts wandered far from lights and stars; clasped in his hand he held an invitation:

*Mr. and Mrs. Francesco de Roberti request the honor of your presence at the wedding of their daughter Lilla Luisa.*

So she was to be married!

At the bottom of the card he read: *Please, please come.*

The eternal feminine! he thought, with a certain satisfaction. No emotion, however. Whereas once he would have been unable to resist the smallest sign from Lilla, now he had only a slight smile, ending in a murmur: "Always the same! . . ."

In two years of isolation, during which he had not once returned to the North, Amedeo had changed completely, not only temperamentally but also physically: the torrid sun had tanned him, given him that particular coloring that is so attractive in certain men, whose strong features become more marked. His old, habitual talkativeness had also vanished: now he expressed himself briefly and concisely.

And Lilla? Had she changed, too? Who could say what impression he would have if he went to her wedding!

A voice called to him from inside the house, and, shrugging his shoulders, he went in.

Mr. Rocas had come from the main office to check the accounts, hand over everything to his successor, and inform Amedeo that, given his merits acquired through the zealous, irreproachable cooperation in the management of the business, the directors, as a reward and compensation for his merits, were sending him to headquarters, in New York.

"What do you think of that, Mister Amedeo!"

"I would say that such a decision is unexpected as well as sudden; and that I have the right to think it over, doesn't it seem to you?"

"You are fortunate, dear fellow; I, on the other hand, had to languish for five endless years before reaching . . ."

"I must really be fortunate . . . but in a sense I need time to prepare for this repatriation . . ."

"I certainly consider that you will be pleased to see how many changes New York has undergone; both in the streets and in social life, you understand?"

In this moment's hesitation, Amedeo was again thinking that on the 26th he could be present at the event of the invitation.

❖

Upon arriving in New York, he thought that he would be starting work immediately, but he was given a month of vacation before taking on the directorship of the new office.

What to do? Go home, to his town? He had no relatives, no one; there was only his house, with its memories. . . .

Coming out of the station, the first thing he saw was a Fiat with a beautiful young girl in it who looked at him, smiling mischievously. Amedeo approached.

"Do you recognize me, sir?" said the young woman, offering her hand.

"Of course I recognize you, Vera, the little rascal from long ago . . ."

"Yes, right . . ." and since Amedeo was still looking at her, clasping her hand, she said, as if to release herself, "I'm not Lilla in the least, you know—only her little sister. Oh, how you have changed!!" she continued without losing her composure. "Are you coming to the wedding?"

"I don't know; I'm only here for a few days."

"It would please Lilla; she hopes to have quite a number of 'inconsolables.'"

Amedeo recalled the words written on the invitation. Who could say how many others she had written to, but what did it matter to him, anyway?

"Where are you staying?"

"At the Inn," and seeing a taxi he said quickly, "I'm glad to have seen you after all this time. . . ."

"I doubt it," Vera interrupted. "In any case, let the taxi go. I'll take you; I came to meet Grandpa and since he's not here, I'll be your chauffeur, is that all right?"

Amedeo thanked her, his eyes taking in Vera's figure as she prepared to start the car. She wasn't beautiful, like Lilla, but there was something inexplicably attractive about her; she had always been sharp-witted and free in speaking, while Lilla wrapped herself in mystery. He noticed that her hair was short and that she was wearing men's clothes. Although he didn't much like that masculine air, still he thought that if Lilla had had a little less femininity and a little more freedom, maybe at this moment . . . !

In the meantime, Vera raised her eyes and stared at him, asking:

"Do you find me very changed?"

"A little."

"Generally, they say that younger sisters, with their long legs, are more beautiful in the end."

"But you've never had long legs. . . ."

"Lilla inherited all the beauty in our family. . . ." she ended, without rancor.

"Who is she marrying?"

"Luigi Martinis, of Philadelphia, a forty-year-old slowpoke who's madly in love and dripping with money; Lilla will be happy."

"What a blunt way of talking," Amedeo thought; he was amazed to find such frankness in this girl; she represented, in essence, modern society. The very model of the "flapper!"

Vera was talking, but that didn't distract her from maneuvering the car skillfully. Amedeo looked at her sidelong, observing every gesture. She wasn't a true beauty, like Lilla, but her almost flawless profile, her sparkling eyes, brilliant as stars, and the whole of her person, made her sympathetically interesting.

Vera surprised him gazing at her, and: "I think myself that my profile is quite interesting to look at: but it is so hard to always show it off!"

Amedeo gave a start; recovering, he said, with a slight smile:

"I hear it's the style of the new woman, to talk unself-consciously about herself and show off . . ."

"The 'flapper,' right? But you, too, are very different from what I imagined, maybe because you aren't wearing tight pants and big boots, the way you used to when you were . . ."

"How do you know that?"

"Your friend Pio, when he came back from visiting you, brought some snapshots. I got one from him and was immediately in love. For almost a month all I talked about was you, all I thought about was you. Aren't you flattered?"

"Absolutely!" he said, and thought, "What odd behavior!"

"I'm only telling you because Lilla found the picture in my drawer, and I'm sure that she'll tell you at the first opportunity; besides, she thinks I've always been in love with you, that's why Tommy is around constantly."

"And who is Tommy?"

"Tommy is twenty-three years old, he graduated from Harvard, his father is very rich, and. . . ."

In the meantime, it was a pure miracle that the Fiat did not crash into a car that was coming from the opposite direction at full speed; there was a little commotion and then once the danger had been averted, she recovered.

"Their fault, they should have honked," said Vera in self-defense.

"But why didn't you?"

"I was thinking about Tommy. . . . And I was thinking that your appearance is somewhat embarrassing, since Tommy thinks I'm in love with you more than ever."

Amedeo didn't answer. Meanwhile Vera had a sudden inspiration: "Would you mind playing a very simple part in the sentimental comedy that I would like to perform in order to make Tommy more jealous?"

"Slow down," Amedeo interrupted. "It's dangerous to play with fire . . ."

Vera looked at him with a mischievous smile. "Don't be alarmed on my account, or is it yourself you're worried about?" and in a different tone of voice she went on: "I'd like to get engaged to Tommy, especially because my father won't hear of it, and I'm sure that if you show some interest yourself, I'll manage it."

Meanwhile they had arrived at the Inn. A boy came over to take the suitcases and Amedeo could only say: "Thank you, and we'll return to the subject that is so interesting to you as soon as possible."

"It's nothing; in fact it was a real pleasure for me. I'll tell Lilla that you're in town, and I'm sure you'll get a phone call immediately."

In fact, right after lunch Amedeo was called to the telephone. It was Lilla:

"I heard that you had come back. What a nice surprise; are you going to the Rivaldis' dance?"

"No, I just got here and no one knows I'm here."

"Oh, then come to my house. Luigi will be here at nine, and if you'd like to come fifteen minutes earlier, we can talk; I am so eager to hear about your adventures."

Always the same! But sooner or later he'd have to see her. . . . So better a time when there would be only a few minutes.

Precisely at quarter to nine, Amedeo arrived at the entrance of the De Robertis' gracious house. A well-known voice called his name; in the shadowy light Amedeo thought it must be Lilla.

"I'm over here, come here," continued the voice, which was successfully trying to imitate the inflections of Ethel Barrymore. For a second Amedeo was confused, but the other, without pausing, went on: "You've been very lucky, I hear you've done very well. . . ."

"But don't say that . . ."

"After all, you should be a little grateful to me. . . ." She went on, resting her hand on his arm. "If it hadn't been for me. . . ."

Amedeo made a gesture of surprise; this he had not expected.

"At least, you should be." And since Amedeo gave no sign of response, she continued: "Besides, I think it's better this way, because if you had stayed, perhaps, who knows. . . ."

"Of course," Amedeo thought, she would have to allude to that night in August.

A car turned onto the street and approached the driveway, and the headlights illuminated the darkness for a moment.

"Vera!" Amedeo exclaimed, amazed.

"Oh well, I almost succeeded. I'd be a good artist if I were better-looking. I'm a good mimic. I imitated you often in the past, and if you had seen how Lilla laughed. Seriously, you should be grateful to me, because otherwise she would have married you. . . ."

"So it was you who telephoned me?"

"No, Lilla. But I heard her and I'm sure that she would have said what I've said; besides you'll see her in a moment and you can convince yourself. . . . Tommy is impatient," she added, because the horn of the automobile that had stopped in front of the house had honked twice. "If he meets you, he'll ask me so many questions and he'll be a beast all night. He certainly won't imagine that I was imitating Lilla." And with a "Good night and have fun" she left him there.

Just then a servant announced to Amedeo that Miss Lilla was expecting him in the library.

"You're late," said Lilla as she held out her hand. "But I forgive you, since you came from so far away for my wedding."

Amedeo was about to contradict her, but Lilla went on:

"I hoped you would come, if only to be sure that you had forgiven me."

Amedeo found himself annoyed for a moment. It seemed that her sister's words were to be proved true, and he was pleased; but at that moment her fiancé came in, and he was spared having to respond.

Lilla introduced them, and picking up her shawl said: "So, you're not coming with us?"

"No, thank you."

"I'm glad you came at least for a short visit, and I hope you'll come again soon," Lilla said as they parted.

Alone again, Amedeo could not help reflecting on what was happening. Two such different types of women: Vera more modern and unconstrained, Lilla always the same. After all, he had to admit, Lilla wasn't such a great loss.

The next day Amedeo went to the Club to play golf and on the steps of the veranda he ran into Vera.

"Hello, have you come for a game?"

"If I find someone who will give me an invitation, since my membership lapsed when I went away."

"I'll give you one, right now, if you'll play a round with me."

Amedeo hesitated for a moment. He was beginning to be afraid of Vera, insecure, never knowing what she would say or do from one moment to the next.

"I'm out of practice. I didn't have much chance down there to play golf."

"It doesn't matter; besides, Tommy needs a lesson: he promised to meet me at ten and it's already five after; I accept no excuses for these hitches."

"Don't be too hard on Tommy!"

"On the contrary, I'll make him pay for yesterday evening. Funny, how men become ridiculous when they're jealous, and Tommy gets terrible every time I mention your name. And therefore I mention you often."

"I would be very flattered, if. . . ."

"Oh, there's nothing to worry about. Tommy thinks that everyone wants to carry me off, kidnap me, or something like that. And the odd thing is that only last week he said to me that it was a real relief to meet a girl one could be friends with and not have a lot of nonsense."

"And is that why you treat him so badly?"

"I swear! You are intelligent. Certainly it's no fun to hear that you're harmless, and are admired only for your intelligence."

"What did he say to you?"

"Yes, I have the honor of being the only one who can understand him, in that heady atmosphere he moves in; he told me, too, that he's not a marrying man, and I bet that he'll swallow those words."

Tommy showed up when Amedeo and Vera were already on their second game. He greeted them from a distance. He wanted to give an impression of indifference, but he wasn't very successful.

"I bet he'll invite Emilia," said Vera. "And to think that only yesterday he told me she bored him. Maybe he thinks I'll be jealous"—and, carelessly, she began to hum a popular song as she prepared to set up her tee.

"You're good," Amedeo complimented her.

"I know. A lot of men don't like to play with me. They prefer girls who dissolve in silly sentimentality and banal compliments. Oh yes, that's what you men want."

"I have no intention of contradicting you," Amedeo interjected. "Since I'm sure I would never succeed."

So Vera won the game.

"You won't forgive me so easily for this?" she said as they returned to the Club House.

"Do you also manage to beat Tommy?"

"Absolutely never," Vera exclaimed.

Amedeo smiled.

"Heavens, there's Lilla," Vera exclaimed again, and with a slight toss of her head left him.

Once he would have thanked her for this, but now Amedeo felt himself abandoned. Lilla confessed that she had come for lunch and not for golf. Luigi, she said, was somewhere in the neighborhood, and when Amedeo offered to look for him she burst into a provocative laugh.

"Once upon a time you wouldn't have been so eager to leave me. . . ."

Although the woman spoke with ostentatious indifference, Amedeo had to make a great effort to extricate himself from her spell, until Luigi came to free him.

"Emma told me that she sent you an invitation for her dance tonight," said Lilla as she said goodbye. "I'm sure I'll see you there, because I'm sure you won't miss it," and taking Luigi's arm she went off.

"Phew!" murmured Amedeo. "I prefer Vera's direct methods after all—at least you can defend yourself."

That night, Emma telephoned and begged him to promise not to miss her dance, and Amedeo had to accept.

As soon as he entered the room, Vera came up to him. She wore a lovely dress, and at her waist a magnificent bunch of purple violets.

"Thank you for your gift," she said, nodding graciously, and smiling.

"For what?" asked Amedeo.

"For these." She touched the flowers. "It was really thoughtful of you, after my beating you in golf."

Amedeo didn't understand; he was about to stammer something, but a look from Vera silenced him. He looked around and nearby saw Tommy, who was looking at them with a tragic expression.

"You're welcome, you are most kind," and he bowed.

Vera didn't answer but looked at him, smiling, and glancing around said in a whisper, in English, "*You're a duck*. Tommy looks as though he'd like to attack someone. If you will insist on at least five dances, I'll see him capitulate."

Amedeo still didn't know if he was enjoying this or not. Only when his last dance ended did he realize that he was sorry not to have asked for more. In fact it annoyed him to think that Vera would be dancing with Tommy. And yet wasn't it perhaps for Tommy that Vera was dancing with him? But after all, why did he care so much? He was certainly not in love with Vera, he had known her for barely two days. Yet he was happy when he seemed to read in her eyes a certain disappointment as she realized that it was their last dance. And without reflecting too deeply he asked her for two more. Vera looked at him oddly; for a moment Amedeo was sorry, but her words reassured him.

"So I'm a good dancer?"

"Perfect; but that's not why I asked you." Big imbecile that I am, he meanwhile contradicted himself; "Why did I say that? Vera will be within her rights to make fun of me." And he waited for that sarcastic laugh; she, however, looked at him with a happiness so sincere that Amedeo was almost consoled.

It seemed to him that as they danced she pressed herself closer to him, making herself smaller in his arms; in fact, in one turn Vera's head seemed to touch his shoulder, her hair grazing his cheeks. Amedeo gave a shiver at this, a sudden movement out of time with the music, and Vera looked at him.

It was a flash. Amedeo was amazed that that fleeting touch should make such an impression and not wanting Vera to realize it he said, "You do dance delightfully."

"Thank you," she said, ingenuously. "I'm sorry if I look at you with . . . adoration? Tommy says that the way I look at you exasperates him."

Amedeo smiled, and as Vera lowered her head for a moment he touched her hair with a kiss.

When the music ended, Tommy came up to Vera and reminded her that she was engaged to him for the next dance.

Meanwhile, it was time that Amedeo danced with Lilla.

She showed him that her card was full, but Amedeo, glancing at it, crossed out a "Luigi" and replaced it with his name.

"Oh well, Luigi won't be too upset; I know he is a perfect and proper gentleman."

Luckily the dance was short and Amedeo was again with Vera.

"Well, how did you manage?"

"Oh, he begged my pardon for having been late this morning and for staying with Emilia, in fact he wanted to invite me for tomorrow, but I said no."

"Why?"

"Have you forgotten that you invited me?" and she looked at him with such sincerity that Amedeo was confused. She was extraordinary, this Vera!

"I'm sorry," he said.

"My fault . . ." she assured him and continued: "I told him that I can't even go canoeing in the afternoon, because you already asked me. Of course he won't know that you're asking me now." And she looked at him again.

Amedeo was stuck. "Of course," he said finally. "I'm happy to invite you and I'm flattered by it."

"It seems, rather, that you're having trouble accepting. I promise you not to be too dull, and then I will protect you from Lilla, who can't get used to the idea that you've forgotten her so quickly; in fact I warn you that she is looking for the first opportunity to draw you in again. Oh, it's pointless to put Luigi in the middle. Lilla is Lilla."

And again Vera's words were proved true. On a simple pretext, Lilla refused to dance with Amedeo, and asked him instead to follow her into the garden.

After a while they sat down on a bench, and although Amedeo tried to steer the conversation to the day's events, Lilla at the first opportunity interrupted him, and, in her Ethel Barrymore voice, said: "Seriously, are you 'cured'? And yet I hoped . . ."

And as usual her thought remained uncertain, suspended. And here again Luigi appeared, and, unwittingly, once again relieved him of embarrassment.

It was clear that, from now on, he had to avoid any encounter with Lilla. But by pure chance a few days later they ran into each other again on the veranda at the Club.

"Are you waiting for Vera? I left her just now with Tommy," said Lilla, slightly maliciously. "But I think she'll be here very soon."

Amedeo bowed, simply to avoid prolonging the conversation, but Lilla continued, "What are you trying to do with Vera, I'd like to know?" and she smiled lightly.

"Say, rather, what is she trying to do with me . . ." but he repented as soon as he had spoken.

"Undoubtedly, Vera is trying to amuse herself and is doing it behind your back."

This doubt had surfaced often in his own mind in recent days.

"Furthermore, you can't blame her, you make such an easy target; even in the past she never lost a chance to make fun of you," Lilla continued.

"At that time, yes. I realize that I was very foolish then."

Lilla smiled. "You were, but not so much as now. Don't you see that Vera wants to use you to make Tommy jealous?"

"I know, she told me and I find it amusing."

"Really?" Lilla couldn't keep herself from exclaiming. "But there she is," and saying goodbye she went off.

"I'm sorry to be late, but Tommy . . ." Vera excused herself.

"Don't you think it's time now to stop this and have a little compassion for him? You're treating him pretty badly."

Vera looked at him with surprise.

"It seems to me I recall that the treatment Lilla gave you was even worse . . ."

"What you say corresponds perfectly to the truth; but my psyche at the time was very different."

Vera didn't answer, her eyes were lost, staring into space, while Amedeo, enraptured, admired the delicate, beautifully modeled profile of her face. "Meanwhile," Amedeo added, "I'm sorry to tell you that I have to leave tomorrow."

In fact Amedeo had no idea of leaving; it was simply a little test. But when he realized that Vera, at this sudden announcement, was nearly distraught, he had to insist on his almost immediate departure. Meanwhile Vera's gaze darkened like the sky before a storm bursts.

"It's business, duty calls me to my office."

"If your departure is settled, at least agree to come to the picnic tonight."

"Picnic?"

"We're going to Captain Kidd's Island in Tommy's yacht, with Emma and another friend, we'll have dinner there. It's a full moon tonight and the evening promises to be lovely."

"Thank you, but I have to pack . . ."

The other was about to insist, but she changed her mind. When the game was over, she offered to take him to the hotel in her car.

Vera was silent and Amedeo took advantage of this to admire her. She was a beautiful girl, he thought; but it was her eyes that bewitched him; they shone with a splendid brightness, reflecting a brilliant light. . . . Her strange but likable behavior had made inroads in his heart.

They were approaching the Inn when Amedeo said, "Goodbye, then. It may be that we'll never see each other again . . ."

Vera looked at him for a moment, then, as if she had come to a decision: "No! this can't be; you have to come with me tonight at any cost!"

Amedeo made a gesture as if to rebel, but, seeing that he was powerless in the speeding car, remained silent, and, as if he had been led by a voice that came from her heart, pleased by and proud of the sight of this unexpected, intimate tenderness, was content to let it be.

But an instant later, he thought with terror of the danger of falling into another trap.

"Don't be unkind to Tommy. And although I told him that you might not come, he insists on thinking that you are in love with me and so you will. It's the last time I'll bother you, because it's my last chance."

Amedeo was about to protest, but he seemed to see Vera's eyes grow wet. He accepted silently.

It was thus that he found himself with two couples on Tommy's yacht, which, gliding swiftly over the water, brought them to the Island just as the sun's last crimson rays of the day were setting.

And yet Amedeo felt a restlessness that he couldn't explain. "Why did you come?" he wondered. "Why did you let yourself be carried to this slippery slope?" At times he seemed to be outside of himself; Vera, after all, was completely interested in Tommy—and yet how to explain the riddle of this modern sphinx?

Meanwhile, the conversation of Emma and her friend drew his

attention. He could not help noticing the novel behavior of these modern young people. Emma said: "I am so sorry I didn't bring my bathing suit, it would be lovely to take a dip in the moonlight."

"Why trouble yourself about a bathing suit?" answered her companion.

Such boldness, in other times, would have shocked anyone; now, however, though it might be surprising, it went by without even the favor of a comment.

Meanwhile Amedeo grew more and more restless, and he decided to go to the beach; the fresh sea breeze might distract him, revive him, pull him out of the great lethargy that had come over him.

He thought of Vera with regret, now that, having followed her whim, he would have to endure abandonment! And as if in reaction he began to hate that stupid Tommy.

Suddenly he heard a whisper:

"Now we've gone as far as we can, and you have to come to a decision, Vera, tell me frankly if you love me; it's time I knew!"

"Sh-h-h," Vera warned.

Tommy and Vera were sitting behind a parapet, protected by a faint shadow.

Amedeo, who had come upon them purely by chance, approached, saying, "I didn't mean to disturb you, but since I have, I must tell you that I want to go back alone. I'll walk."

"But it's impossible to walk," said Vera. "The way is much too long."

"A little exercise will certainly do me good. Good night." And he went off, just like that.

The moon's brightness lighted his way; the stars were points of different colored sparkling light; it was an enchanted evening, but Amedeo felt discouragement, unease, an infinite solitude around him.

So he quickened his pace, not without thinking that after such a long period of a serene and tranquil life he had fallen again, rashly, into the whirlwind of love.

At one point, Amedeo saw that Tommy's boat had also left the beach, and was moving rapidly. He stopped and watched it grow smaller, then continued on his way.

From time to time the headlights of a car assailed him and he moved aside to let it pass. He was almost halfway home, when, puffing rapidly, a car stopped practically beside him.

"I made it my business to come and find you." It was Vera.

"Thank you, but I prefer to walk."

Without a word, Vera turned off the motor and got out. "All right. I'll walk, too."

Amedeo stopped decisively, like one who has something to say, but he couldn't find the right words and stood there looking at her. Vera had placed herself in front of him and she was gazing at him, too. Her face was as if surrounded by an aureole; to Amedeo it was like a divine image.

"Why are you angry with me?" said Vera.

"I'm not at all, I assure you."

"You've been sulking because I haven't talked to you all night, isn't that true?"

Amedeo couldn't contain himself any longer, he would have liked to shout at the top of his lungs that he loved her. . . . He loved her so much . . . but he still had the strength to suppress the explosion in his heart; and, nearly trembling, his face pale, he managed to murmur: "Why are you tempting me?"

Vera was downcast; she stared at him a long time with a penetrating look, then she said, "Thanks," and was about to go off.

It was then that Amedeo, repenting, restrained her, grabbing her by the hand.

"Tell me frankly, Vera, what would you like to do with me? You wanted to make Tommy jealous, and now that you've succeeded, what do you want?"

"Do you think I'd go to so much trouble for Tommy? Oh, Tommy makes me sick."

"What?"

"No," she went on heatedly; "it was certainly not for Tommy that I worked so hard two years ago to keep Lilla from marrying you. . . . And it wasn't for Tommy that I stole that invitation that Lilla was sending you and wrote in my own hand 'Please, please come,' and. . . ."

"You . . . you . . . wrote . . ." Amedeo stammered.

In the moonlight he made out a strange expression on Vera's face, which became more and more interesting and fascinated him.

"Yes! I hoped that you would come and at the same time I wished for the opposite, because you would have thought the invitation came from Lilla. Then . . . then I did what you know and it wasn't to make Tommy jealous but you . . . this evening was my last chance and . . ." She couldn't finish and for the first time she lowered her eyes.

"Vera . . ."

"I know perfectly well what you think of me; you probably think I'm a little bold, but what could I do? I'm not beautiful . . ."

"What do you mean, not beautiful?" Amedeo almost shouted. "You, you are . . . he couldn't continue, he was afraid. . . .

"Well, go on, quick, say it!"

"You are simply an adorable creature!"

"*Great Scott*," cried Vera with satisfaction. "So you love me more than I thought!"

Amedeo, in an incomprehensible torment, seemed to be dreaming with his eyes open.

She came closer to him, so that she touched his face with her hair. Amedeo no longer . . . and. . . .

The man in the moon for a moment found his face hidden by a kindly cloud, but soon freed himself and . . .

"Vera, my dear little Vera! Do you really love me?"

Vera hugged him closer and hiding her head in his arms said, with a laugh:

"*Men are so funny . . .*"

---

"La 'Flapper,'" *Il Carroccio* 18, no. 2 (August 1923): 159–69.

## DORA COLONNA:
### IMMIGRATION FROM A WOMAN'S PERSPECTIVE

A revealing tale of abandonment, emigration, and solidarity, with a bold dénouement that leaves us with a desire to know more about the author, a teacher, who is little more than a byline in the nationalist monthly *Il Carroccio*. The themes of independent life and single motherhood, of betrayal and female bonding, of old-world decadence and suburban loneliness are treated with an emotional self-assurance and a fictional intensity that indicate a rare maturity in the field of early Italian Americana.

### The Two Friends

They had met by chance one evening on the elevated train that goes out to Long Island from New York. At that hour the train was crowded, and since Nora, the older, was standing and was thrown off balance at every jolt, Amalia had risen and with great courtesy had offered her the seat.

It happened that the two young women got off at the same station, and, once on the street, as they walked along beside one another in the late evening, they could not help talking.

"Are you Italian, too?" observed Nora, who was small and elegant, with the face of a Madonna. "Who would have thought, so fair and with those blue eyes!"

Amalia smiled and said nothing.

The way was quite long and Nora felt like talking.

Had Amalia been in America for many years? Did she speak the language well? Did she like it here? Oh! Amalia had been in America for about three years, and the language, she spoke, so—not that well, and—as for how she liked it, oh—*well.* . . .

The responses had been evasive, disjointed: they seemed fragments of a hidden thought that did not want to be caught unaware. Only in speaking of a daughter did Amalia's toneless voice acquire a sudden vivacity.

"A daughter?" said the other, incredulous. "Who would have thought? So young, and already married and a mother?"

Yes, Amalia was married and a mother. Edith, as the child was called, was a cherub of about three, this tall, lively, a real elf, with curly black hair.

Nora's inquisitive glance flew to the other's face.

"And yet, you are as blond as ripe grain!"

"Edith looks like . . . her father."

There was a brief hesitation between the two words.

"Where is she now?"

"Oh, at a private teacher's."

"Oh!"

"Otherwise, how would I manage to go to the factory?"

"*Oh, I see!* . . ."

"How I love her, and how I fear for that child!" Amalia added with a sigh.

"Fear? Why?"

"You have to be a mother to understand certain anxieties and fears," said the first with an adorable modesty. "And you understand, don't you?"

"Oh, well," said Nora with a melancholy smile.

"You're not a mother?"

"No . . ."

"*Oh, that's different . . .*"

Nora coughed and looked for a handkerchief in her purse.

"Tell me about yourself," Amalia added.

The other shrugged her shoulders. She had come from Italy about three years earlier, and didn't know the language, except for a few idioms, nor did she care about knowing it. For doing the "finishing work" at the factory you didn't have to be educated! And here came a harsh laugh with a slight tinge of irony. That was how she thought, plainly. And then . . . Nora was a spinster, which for her was of the greatest importance; she had no one, she had no bonds, no responsibilities, nor did she intend to have any.

The husky voice of the other interrupted her: "You wouldn't get married?"

"Married? Never!"

But surely she might change her mind later; love is subtle and you never know when it might arrive.

Nora had not answered. Her pale Madonna-like face had contracted in anguish as if at the memory of a great sorrow. Amalia realized that she had been indiscreet and repented it.

"You haven't yet told me how you find New York," she said then, just to say something.

"Better than I imagined," Nora answered with sudden animation. "I hated this country before I knew it; not anymore. New York is a whirlpool. If you carry with you a memory from home that overwhelms you, throw it in that vortex and you will be sure of having got rid of an enemy . . ."

"*It is wonderful!*" exclaimed Amalia.

As they made their way, talking, along the road through the barren countryside, the two women discovered that they came from the same province, which pleased them greatly, but they didn't say from what town, they didn't take the trouble to ask each other, they didn't care to know: the confidences that had expanded, retreated at that point, remained suspended in the air like a veil drawn to cover an empty space.

It was perhaps this peculiarity that bound the two women in a harmonious accord of thoughts and feelings.

Every morning the same meeting in the village square, the same walk along the path to the station, the same talk of things abstract and light, the same exchange of courtesies in the crowded train, until, heading in opposite directions, the two friends were swallowed up into the whirlwind of the metropolis.

They met again in the evening, usually at Amalia's.

Some evenings, Nora spent happily playing with the child, whom she loved, while Amalia read the newspaper sitting before the broad Japanese lampshade.

Other evenings Nora sat at the piano and Amalia sang in a quiet voice, sitting in the rocking chair with Edith half asleep in her arms. And when the piano stopped and the voice was silent, the two friends sat there in silence, stiff and unmoving, heads bowed, thoughtful.

Confidences: none, ever.

Between the two friends there was an unconscious but watchful and persistent reserve, which put them on guard against any expansiveness, as if in attempting to delve into each other they would be violating a sacred prohibition.

But one evening that reserve broke down.

Nora had entered her friend's house with her heart beating rapidly. She had been called in a hurry, and not having been told what the matter was, had had a strange apprehension that the child was sick. In fact, for some days a harsh wind had been blowing, and several cases of influenza had been reported in the village.

But it was not the flu.

Amalia was a little nervous, and, as usual, she needed company, *that's all.*

"You made me imagine so many things," said Nora. "I was especially worried about Edith. The cold is intense, and one never knows. If you saw how it's snowing!"

"It's snowing?" asked Amalia, as if the news irritated her.

"*Yes,* it's snowing *to beat the band!*" her friend assured her, smiling in triumph for having been vouchsafed the luxury of an idiomatic phrase.

Amalia went to the window, looked out, and withdrew sighing.

"Where is Edith?" asked Nora, blowing on her numbed fingers.

"She's sleeping. My little one was tired."

They both went to the bed where the child was sleeping.

"Oh, how I wish I were you," Amalia let slip.

"Me, why?"

"To live without ties and without responsibilities is a privilege, isn't it?"

Without replying, Nora leaned over to gaze at the sleeping child.

"She looks like a cherub," she said, finally, raising her head, after a pause. "If . . . I were a mother I would choose the moment when my child was sleeping to look at her. I don't think that for a woman there can be a greater satisfaction, a joy more intense."

Her eyes glittered with tears. Amalia didn't notice, and she had nothing to add. Her thoughts were far away.

As they were about to move away from the bed, she said:

"How I suffer! . . ."

"Why?"

"I don't know."

Passing by the piano, Nora ran her agile fingers over the keyboard.

"*No, please, no,*" Amalia begged her.

They approached the blazing hearth.

"Sometimes, you know? . . . I'm afraid of losing her."

"Losing whom?"

"Her, my daughter!"

"Why such odd ideas?"

"Oh, my poor head! . . ." exclaimed Amalia, beating her forehead. "My poor head . . ." And again she wrapped herself in silence.

"Tell me, please," Nora implored, putting an arm around her waist. "Are we friends or not?"

With a gesture Amalia invited the other to sit beside her before the hearth. For a few moments neither spoke. Both seemed intent on the monotonous crackling of the wood on the andirons.

Nora said, "You have some memory that's killing you."

Her friend raised her head as if to protest, then lowered it again.

"To cling to the relics of a past sorrow," the other continued, "is the same as letting oneself sink with them into the swamp. Forget. And if you can't forget, and my words can be helpful, speak, I beg you, so that I may understand you . . ."

The voice that was questioning the mystery had never been sweeter, never more coaxing and soulful.

Amalia was shaken by it.

"It's something more than a memory, my dear friend . . ." Although she was calm, Amalia's hands trembled. In her slender little fingers vibrated a desire to strangle, crush, destroy. Nora saw this. With a gesture full of pity she placed her delicate hand on Amalia's.

"Tell me, Amalia."

"You haven't known life, Nora. You won't understand . . ."

There was an instant of silence. Nora's face kindled with a sudden flame.

"I have seen how one can suffer and . . . die," she offered quietly but with biting emphasis.

"It's not everything, it's not everything," Amalia sighed. "One has to be a mother to understand certain things . . ."

Her friend didn't answer. A convulsive tremor agitated her lips. After an instant she said: "Speak."

"Something terrible is happening to me," said Amalia, panting.

"Yes?"

"They are threatening to take my child."

"Ah?"

"Do you understand?"

"Criminals?"

"No . . ."

"But then?"

"Her father . . . the child's father!"

※

A story of passion and its consequences followed.

Amalia had gambled on life and had lost.

The only daughter of a wealthy family from the mountains, she had been brought up in the city among the young daughters of the aristocracy, and on her return to the mountains had found the life exasperatingly dull. The mountain air, which should have calmed the tumult of her eighteen years, filled her with lethargy, brought her obscure temptations, left her empty and sad. She became sullen, rebellious. She despised the tender ministrations of her parents, often making her gentle, good mama cry, and threatening to run away.

It was then that she met the man of her dreams.

Oh what a day! Amalia would never forget it. It was May. She had taken the path up the mountain. She went there often. The peak drew her with infinite promises. And it was on that peak that she first saw her Adonis in his hunting outfit, the gun under his arm, his hair waving in the wind, tall, slender as a cedar of Lebanon.

So love was born.

But at home the news of this meeting aroused serious apprehensions.

No one knew the young mountaineer. He was an adventurer, up to no good, said her father, a fortune hunter.

Amalia would not be convinced.

Her father shifted from warnings to threats: he would shut her up in a monastery where she would comb St. Catherine's hair for the rest of her life.

Vain words.

One day Amalia ran away from home, took the path up the mountain, where her lover was expecting her, and without even waiting for the young man to make the usual promise of marriage, offered herself to him with total devotion.

"We have to go, we have to flee this place," the girl said, fearing her father's anger.

He hesitated before answering. There was urgent business to take care of. Later they would leave; they would go to America.

The idea of living in another country pleased the girl. But when? Maybe in the winter. Anyway, they could not stay long in the village. What would they do? The young hunter was ardent and full of plans.

He proposed to his lover that they spend their honeymoon in the countryside, in the mountains, on the opposite slope.

To Amalia the adventure was of an unparalleled daring. They would take their love, already mature, to the mountain peaks where it had begun. But the idyll didn't last.

Winter arrived. The mountain wind began to blow in violent gusts. The two lovers were forced to take shelter in the village, while they waited for the time of departure as for a liberation.

Until the night of their flight arrived. A night of pandemonium with driving snow and howling winds. He was crushed by sadness, and Amalia, not knowing the reason, was silent and gazed at him in wonder.

Never had the young man been more handsome. That air of thoughtful sadness gave him a new grace: something noble and spiritual that hadn't been there before.

On the steamer she found out what it was.

She found out that on the other side of the mountains another woman and a child had the right to the man she thought was hers!

It was a terrible revelation.

For the first time in her eighteen years Amalia looked at life with horror, as one looks into an abyss.

Something deep inside her rebelled, but she didn't dare protest. It was too late. Love had opened in her heart a fatal breach, and then . . . she was to be a mother.

The first days in America were not happy ones. The formidable shadow of New York intimidated the two young people, embittered them, made them hostile to one another. Then came the child, and things were more complicated. The necessities of life became even more urgent. He became deceitful. He was reluctant to find work. He said bluntly that he would never become part of the herd that killed itself to make rich men richer. So began the reproaches, the arguments, the days without bread, without peace . . . until one of those days he disappeared, just as he had appeared . . .

And so three years had passed without a word from him: three years of work and humiliation for a young woman who had never worked or suffered, until . . .

Here Amalia interrupted her story.

※

Her friend had listened to that long account without batting an eyelash, motionless, absorbed. Her pale face had acquired an ashen color and in places was furrowed by deep creases.

Before speaking, she held out her hands to the flame to warm herself.

"Well?"

The other didn't answer.

"What is the name of this man?" There was a certain bitterness on her lips, almost a sneer.

"Marco."

A long pause.

In the silence a suffocated sound could be heard, as of repressed sighs.

With a mechanical gesture Nora patted the shoulder of her friend, who was crying, and said: "Come, come, these are things of the past."

The other dried her eyes:

"There's more, dear friend."

"Ah!"

"In the past month he has been giving signs of life. He won't leave me alone; all he does is ask for money, ask the impossible."

"This too?"

"This and other things. He wants me to take him back or . . . he will take away the child. The villainy! Here, read . . ."

Nora held out her hand, slightly hesitant. She read:

My Dear! *Whatever you do to escape the dilemma, you will not succeed. Either you consider me yours, giving me the place that is my due beside you, or . . . you will lose the child. How and when that happens there is no need for you to know. Tonight therefore your final answer, and . . . watch out because I will go to extremes if you should continue to be unreasonable.* Marco.

"I don't understand that 'going to extremes,'" said Nora, giving her back the letter.

Nora appeared to reflect.

"What do you intend to do, Amalia?"

"I don't know. It has been impossible for me to come to a decision. For two days I have been shut up in the house guarding the door, *that's all.*"

"You think, then, that he's serious?"

"I think he's capable of any madness."

Neither spoke. In the silence the ticking of the clock could be heard. Amalia looked at the time. Eight o'clock.

"Why didn't you tell me before?" asked Nora, a slight harshness in her voice. "Locking yourself up in the house gets you nowhere, you know!"

"It's true," the other said with a sigh, and looked at the clock again. The incessant ticking was a torment to her.

"You . . . no longer love him?" her friend asked suddenly.

Their gazes met.

"Well?" she asked, since the other hesitated.

Amalia shook her head and lowered her gaze, disturbed by that insistence.

"Don't you think I would already have agreed to his demands if . . . I loved him?" she said all in one breath.

"Then it would be too great a sacrifice on your part to yield?" asked Nora.

"Horror!"

They fell silent. Amalia was agitated.

"To take him back after that brute left me at the lowest depths of misery and despair! After the neighbors think I'm a widow. Terrible!"

Nora said nothing.

"And then . . . and then . . . I hate him, I abhor him! . . ."

"You wouldn't do it for Edith?"

"For Edith? I would rather see her dead than in his arms."

Again they were silent. Nora got up. A slight faded pink color suffused the noble paleness of her face, which suffered without tears. Seeing her go toward the door with her head bent, Amalia went to her, and seized her hands impulsively.

"Nora, dear friend. I have been too rude in speaking to you of my trouble, isn't that true? . . . You, you are suffering . . ."

"It causes me suffering to know that you are unhappy!" Her lips were white, but she was calm. There was a pause. Nora said:

"Do you really think that he is capable of coming here tonight to trouble you?"

Amalia clasped her hands in an attitude of prayer:

"I don't know, I don't know! It's not the first time he has made these threats; and yet tonight I am strangely fearful." She glanced at one of the windows, and added: "That window frightens me."

"Why?"

"I don't know."

"You're a child," said her friend, forcing a jovial tone. "Maybe he's doing it just to test you. If he finds it as hard as he has found it up to now he'll get tired of it."

"Ah no, Marco's not a man to give up."

"Listen," said Nora after a brief reflection, "I'm surprised that you haven't thought of moving, you've had plenty of time."

"I have thought about it and I'm sorry about it. But you will understand. I liked it so much here. In New York, life is expensive, *you know,* and then I was enjoying my reputation."

"Yet you should have foreseen . . ."

"If I get through tonight safely, I'll do it tomorrow. I'll leave everything that belongs to me to the landlords and . . ."

"That wouldn't save your reputation," her friend interrupted. "You would only be complicating things, and giving him the opportunity to become even more insolent."

"Then what would you advise me to do?"

"Confront him."

"Are you mad?"

"Yes, confront him!" cried Nora, vehemently. "Ask him to meet you, and tell him just what you think of him."

"You imagine that then he'll leave me alone?"

"I don't see why he would persist!"

"Nora! Your simplicity is exasperating! If I told you that Marco is a dangerous man?"

"I don't understand."

"He belongs to the 'gang,'" cried Amalia, covering her face with her hands: "he is a derelict who lives by extortion."

Nora closed her eyes for a moment as if in the grip of vertigo. A little afterward, patting her friend's shoulder, she said:

"Come, come . . . you'll end up making yourself sick."

"I'll end up driving myself mad."

"Don't be afraid. Tomorrow we'll make the proper provisions," said Nora, going toward the door.

"But tonight . . . suppose . . ." exclaimed Amalia, trying to hold her back. "Oh I am a coward, a coward . . ."

"Your fears may be unfounded, Amalia."

"It may be; yet I can't deny that I have an intense fear. It's especially from there that I'm afraid of an attack, from the window that opens onto the 'yard.' Oh, this place on the ground floor is a disaster! . . ."

"Even an extraordinarily tall man couldn't reach that window with the tips of his finger," Nora observed, with a sad smile.

"Marco has wings . . ." said Amalia, her head lowered.

"You, you love him still!!" Nora burst out, and her eyes flashed.

"I tell you I hate him!" cried the other furiously.

At the door they embraced and kissed as usual.

◼

When she got to her room on the third floor, Nora closed the door and heaved a sigh. She was breathing hard. She felt an unbearable weight on her heart. There was a moment when she could have cried out, that weight oppressed her so. She wanted to weep, but she could not. Her eyes were dry, burning. Her hat in one hand, her gloves in the other, she walked around the room a couple of times; she stopped for a moment in front of a painting on the wall, and then started again. Weary, she threw her hat and gloves on the bed and fell heavily into a chair where she sat without moving for some time, hunched over as if bent by a yoke.

Marco was his name. And on the other side of the mountain another woman and a child had the right to the man whom Amalia believed to be hers!

Nora restrained a cry. Her heart was even heavier, her eyes were burning in agony.

A vain and empty man, Marco! He had broken two lives and had not had to pay. He had returned to the attack again; he waited at the threshold like a bird of prey. A gentleman he had never been, but so cruel . . . criminal! Oh God, oh God!

Nora rose in agitation. That memory burned. The memory she believed that she had drowned in the whirlpool of New York had come back to the surface more vivid than ever, he laughed at her with his harsh laugh, kindling in her heart a flame of revenge.

She went to the window, opened it, looked out.

It was still snowing. The silence lay heavy as a tombstone over the world. On the elevated tracks the train went by, screeching, and disappeared shrieking as if it were in pain.

Nora shuddered, drew back, closed the window. She was again in the dark, isolated, with her memories . . . the child—her child—who was dying in his cradle, and Marco, the unfaithful husband, who couldn't wait to escape . . . Her vain attempts to restrain him, her tears, the entreaties that would have moved a stone; the hand-to-hand struggle between him and her up to the final moment before he went out the door. Marco! But he had already fled, and she after him! An agonizing rush into the dark night, against snow and wind, onward, always onward, until, exhausted, she had fallen to the ground. And on returning to the desolate house, Nora had found that the child, even her child, had gone, never to return! . . .

Amalia, left alone, had tried in vain to calm her fears and go to sleep. She had thrown herself on the bed without undressing, and just as she was about to fall asleep, the clock struck ten and she jumped to her feet like a fury. Edith woke at the sound and asked for some water. When she had gone to sleep, Amalia ran to the door to make sure that it was locked. She turned out the night light, went to the window that overlooked the yard, pushed aside the curtains slightly and gazed out into the night.

It was from there that she feared the ambush; and why she should expect to be attacked from there and not the front door she could not have said; yet that presentiment tortured her.

The yard belonged to the landlords, who lived next door; it was fairly spacious, full of wood and other things, and surrounded by a tumbledown fence. Behind the yard was an alley leading to the main street.

Amalia kept watch with a vigilant eye. The snow persisted. A street lamp at the corner cast a sidelong light. A short distance from the entrance to a dance hall a group of young people were shouting and laughing. A woman came out of the alley, light as a shadow, paused for a moment and disappeared. Amalia reflected: she thought of her broken life; she thought of that tomorrow which was so uncertain. No! tomorrow would not be any better than today! She had either to flee or to hide. Marco would pursue her to the ends of the earth.

Confront him? Oh yes! How easy to say it! what would she not do if not for the child? Oh, to be a mother is a curse!

Amalia shook her head. This time she would confront him, she would tear out his flesh with her nails.

A woman—the same as before?—emerged, carefully skirting the fence, and went off at the same hurried pace.

"Oh," exclaimed Amalia, and moved aside the curtain to get a better look. Strange; how that feminine shadow had, in the uniform whiteness of the street, seemed to form the silhouette of Nora.

The thought of her friend gave her courage. The clock struck eleven. A train whistled in the distance. The child cried in her bed and immediately fell asleep again. Amalia felt tired and even sleepy. Oh, to sleep; she wanted only to sleep, to forget!

She withdrew for a moment to close the curtains, throwing a last glance outside. She stood there, peering out more carefully. She had descried a shadow, a man under the street light. Who was it? how long had he been there? The snow was falling more slowly. Someone went by singing. The noisy young people were gone, the windows of the dance hall dark. The man at the lamppost crossed the street and disappeared in the entranceway of a building under construction. Amalia felt faint, but didn't move. She would stay all night watching from behind that curtain. The man reappeared. He seemed wary and undecided, like someone who is afraid of being followed. Amalia sharpened her gaze. The uncertainty tormented her. She couldn't hear a sound. The night was silent, threatening. The man took a few steps toward the window, stopped, appeared in the light. Marco! The same Marco of the mountain, fearless, his hair flying in the wind, tall, slender as a cedar of Lebanon.

Amalia felt dizzy and she leaned against the windowsill to keep from falling.

But the vision drew her as it had that first day, and, curious, she pushed aside the curtain, showing her pale face through the bare glass.

Marco saw the raising of the blind, looked, recognized his lover. And, absorbed in that contemplation, he was unaware of the enemy who had been following him for two hours—Nora, the wife, who was just behind him.

A sudden explosion tore the silence—a cry—and Marco fell heavily, on his back, his arms crossed on his chest.

---

"Le due amiche," *Il Carroccio* 23, no. 4 (April 1926): 429–37.

## Eugenio Camillo Branchi, or the Well-Crafted Story

Although Branchi was both biographically and intellectually a sort of outsider, he addressed the plight of the immigrants. Characteristically, his best stories, while full of energy and inventiveness, do not reach satisfactory endings; it is as if too much malignity, too much anxiety, hovered, as in this tale of crime and immediate repentance which juxtaposes wealth and grim poverty, the glitter of millionaires and the honest desperation of a destitute father. It is not by chance that the hero, Tony, has just arrived from Scranton, Pennsylvania, one of the main centers for Italian miners.

### Hold Up!

The public knew it by reputation but did not know precisely where it was situated, since the Fifth Avenue Literary Circle was not on Fifth Avenue. It was called "the millionaires' club," because it was said that no one could belong to it who did not have an income of at least fifty thousand dollars.

In fact the name of the club was to its social purpose as an expensive *toilette* is to the beautiful body of an unchaste young woman. Literature was a flag that waved by day in the grand and aristocratic salons, where an élite group of intellectual ladies met to hear the words of a fashionable poet or the reading of the latest novel by a decadent writer. At night the beautiful body was stripped, and the same salons received the depraved husbands who usually have wealthy intellectual wives. Then the only thing literary about them was a profanation of names: Shakespeare became synonymous with baccarat, Dickens with twenty-one, and Longfellow with poker.

The Fifth Avenue Literary Circle was organized in an ideal way. One could perceive the imprint of some clever Wall Street banker. "Fixed" and elaborate games had been abolished and only games of chance were allowed, so-called "instant" games, based on ready cash. No telephones, no bells, no gossiping servants. The employees had to be mute from birth, and orders were given according to different-colored electric lights, which replaced acoustic signals. When the normal light turned blue that was the alarm; and then all the players concealed their cards and banknotes and assumed the dignified pose of readers immersed in old illuminated manuscripts and American journals. The nighttime "entrances" allowed daytime "exits." If the light of the sun increased the literary prestige of the club, the nocturnal shadows increased its passion. For gambling is not a vice but, rather, a luxury and a passion: a passion that surpasses love in that it is more pathological, more feverish, more constant, more costly; a luxury because only millionaires can participate with impunity.

But the virtuous ladies, in expiation, had decreed two annual donations that the husbands regularly paid, and which formed the Metropolitan Foundations: the first to encourage young authors and the second to intensify the struggle against vice. With Machiavellian intuition, they preferred the venial sin that does good to the virtue that remains passive.

※

That night William Ross, the club's treasurer, was in luck.

At eleven, the hour of opening, he had begun to play as usual, without missing a round of baccarat, and he had accumulated a pile of banknotes that already nagged him with the thought that he had to pocket them. Because Mr. Ross was, yes, a fan of the game, but he played to enjoy himself, not to win. Just as all things, even pleasurable ones, become boring through constant repetition, the luck that pursued him—while at first it had lured him—had later become tedious. Those always favorable cards, that continual raking in of winnings, that invariable pileup of bills, along with the irritating exclamations of his less fortunate companions, made him nervous. He had intended to lose a hundred dollars every night, and he followed that plan with the nonchalance of one who every night pays a little money in order to enjoy a theater spectacle. The winnings, from time to time, had served merely to make the game more interesting and, one way or another, to balance his losses. But now it was too much. He was no longer enjoying himself.

His fellow players looked at him in surprise.

"You're in the flow, my dear Ross," exclaimed Sam Morgenthau with some envy. "Your luck has finally turned."

"If you were at Montecarlo you would have broken the bank at the roulette table!" added Jack Monroe, the son of the well-known millionaire.

In response Ross merely murmured:

"Sincerely, I would prefer to lose."

"Oh, don't say that. It's obvious that you don't have the soul of a gambler. One should never protest against success."

"Ross isn't a gambler; he's an artist."

Another round of baccarat had ended, and Ross, who held the bank, picked up off the table another half dozen bills.

"How could I lose?" he asked, feeling in himself the mathematical certainty of winning, of winning yet again.

"The only way is to abandon the game and leave," Morgenthau hinted to him.

A bald and obese gentleman, the fortunate owner of the majority of the Texas Oil Company's shares, proposed:

"Would you like me to ally myself with your luck? I always lose!"

"Take it!" answered Ross throwing him the still new pack of cards. "You're right, Sam. I'm leaving. I can't stand it anymore."

And availing himself of a player's right to abandon the game at whatever moment he desired—a right that was often taken advantage of at the club—he got up resolutely, trying to find in his various pockets places large enough to hide the thick rolls of banknotes. In an ugly humor he said goodbye and, passing through the other rooms, headed for the door. In fact it wasn't his usual time, but he preferred to search elsewhere for amusement, immersing himself in the night life of the metropolis.

He was a man of about forty, of small stature, with a chubby face. His beautiful smooth hands, his slightly plump body, the placid expression of his features, and a premature baldness denoted in him the habits of a sedentary life. And in fact for fifteen years he had managed a well-reputed real-estate office downtown, which, it was said, was a real gold mine. He was not a hero. He was a gentle and generous soul who loved novels and as a young man had made a stab at one with little luck. He had devoted himself body and soul to gambling because in it he had found that emotion which was lacking in his tranquil existence. He feared one thing above all others: the robberies that were plaguing New York. He had a presentiment that some day or other that adventure would happen even to him. Yet if the "hold-up" was not bloody he wouldn't mind it, because such an adventure would be a diversion that, for once, was enjoyable. But . . .

He crossed several rooms in which some gentlemen in evening dress were playing in silence. He exchanged greetings with two of them. He remained deaf to the appeal of a friend who called on him to complete a foursome for bridge. He made sure that the husband of the beautiful Lolette—a blonde from across the ocean who had entered his life like a meteor—was involved in a game, and entered the lobby through a thick door that opened at the touch of a button. As soon as the pink light appeared in the new room, one of the attendants handed him his fur coat and derby.

He went out.

The night was dark. Veils of fog hovered over the street lights, shrouding them in a yellowish aureole. The cold was intense. The great night life of the city seemed to be suspended. It must have been two o'clock. He headed for his car, a few steps away, and ordered his chauffeur, half-asleep, to go home. He would get home by himself that night. He thought of Lolette.

The subway entrance was just two blocks away. He walked toward it, impelled by a hidden desire. All his winnings that evening were not worth the kiss of a well-known mouth. He was in search of a reward for his outrageous luck.

He walked quickly, skirting the wall of buildings. The sidewalk was deserted. Cars passed like shadows sliding on the pavement. Suddenly he heard, behind him, a heavy step and a voice—a voice with a foreign accent made him stop.

"What time is it, please?"

He turned, looking instinctively at his watch, and as his pupils perceived the form of a wretched-looking man, his heart sent jets of blood violently through his veins. He had a terrible presentiment. Before he had time to say a word the man was on him, shoving him into the empty doorway of a shop.

An energetic voice, strange, commanding, whispered to him:

"Hold up! if you make a sound I'll shoot."

And he could see, from the gleam, that the barrel of a revolver was pointed in the direction of his heart.

❈

New York.

That night, too, the American Urbs—in which sovereigns without crowns and slaves without chains live in the most fantastic splendor and the blackest misery, which offers to the light the virtue of its marvelous works and to the shadows the mad frenzy of sin—on that foggy night, too, into the hundred thousand meanderings of its greedy heart, New York inserted the viscous tentacles of desire and greed, of pleasure and crime.

New York, the modern Babylon.

New York, the tentacular city with suckers of human flesh.

❈

The East Side of Manhattan is the refuge of the wretched.

In a squalid room at the end of a Hundred and Tenth street, Tony couldn't sleep. He had lain down that night in the one bed that held Maria and feverish little Joe, in the middle. He felt the intense heat of that poor sick flesh that had barely entered into life and felt a sharp remorse for a situation that in his despair he had no solution for. For five months the mines of Scranton had been closed. He had knocked on every door, in vain. For a week he had been looking for a way out. Where to go in two days, when the eviction notice would be served on the only refuge that now remained to him? Discouragement had become desperation in the silent night of his brain. He could not resign himself to destiny because of his duty to those two creatures who depended on him and who represented his entire world.

The whisper of his wife reciting prayers had been quiet for a while. He felt, obsessively, the touch of Joe's feverish limbs. He had to—had to—find a solution to the insoluble problem.

Every day the big daily papers of the metropolis presented the grim events of the news. His mind took them in and ruminated on them in his forced idleness. Two things, especially, had become fixed in his brain: robbery and suicide. All he had to do was turn on the gas and they would all go to sleep forever, without pain, without sorrow. . . . In that way, every day, the shipwrecked of life, like him, died in the great city. But the vision of his innocent creatures, lying stiff on a table in the morgue, revolted him. It was cowardly, too cowardly for a father, for a husband who would have given his life for them.

Hold up? and why not? It was now a common event, daily. If the attempt went well he could keep them going while he searched for honest work . . . if he failed, his pitiful case would interest public charity in his innocent family. If the deed was unworthy and immoral, it was not cowardly, for it had as its stake his life, his only life. His conscience was silent. Day by day in the slow agony of poverty, a small edge of it was obscured. Imperious necessity crossed over the barrier of a morality conceived by men with full stomachs. His situation required the extreme attempt. . . .

Then, having come to a decision, he got up and dressed quickly in the frigid cold. The pale reflection of a street lamp outside illuminated the room. He tried not to make noise, in order not to wake his wife, but as he picked up his cap he didn't notice that lying on it was one of those fake guns that are sold as children's toys. It was Joe's, Joe's only plaything. The thud that it made on the floor woke Maria, and she rose, frightened.

"Where are you going at this hour, Tony?"

"I'm going to get medicine and milk for the child," he exclaimed in a whisper, trying to avoid her gaze.

Maria stared at him, with a premonition.

"You won't do anything bad? Tell me, Tony? . . . You'll do nothing wrong? . . . rather death. . . . God will watch over us. . . ."

"Don't worry," he lied as he pulled on a soft hat. "Don't worry. I'm going to the docks to see if I can find work."

"But how will you be able to work there if you don't belong to the Union?"

"I'll try again."

He left his old overcoat on the bed, whose main covering it was, kissed little sleeping Joe on his half-open mouth, hid the toy gun and the cap in his pocket; then, again avoiding the questioning gaze of his wife, he quickly left.

So he had decided. Let happen that which had to happen.

He reached Fifth Avenue at Central Park and walked along the sidewalk that passes by the wealthy residences of Fortune's privileged. The frigid temperature was accompanied by a veil of fog. Through the gates of the park, he glimpsed the milky stain of unshoveled snow.

The way was long, and he had to walk, for he didn't have the five cents for the subway. He had miles to go. Because he had a goal. He had a plan. The next-door neighbor, a Polish woman, in chatting with Maria had said that her husband—who had been mute from birth—earned thirty dollars a week as a servant in a nighttime gentlemen's club where every night money was thrown about profusely. The address had impressed itself in his memory. There he would find his victim. What was a few dollars to a millionaire, finally? He would wait for one of them to come out alone and would confront him. Yet he was afraid of the crucial moment. He counted on the terror that a holdup would inspire to easily get the upper hand over his victim. He felt certain, however, that he would not resort to violence, because he would be the victim himself if the victim should rebel. And then how to shoot? And what if the victim did not have the money on him? It might turn out to be a gambler who had left all he possessed on the green baize. Oh! A few dollars would be enough to silence the landlord and buy medicine for his baby. Who knows if fortune would not help him in that situation, the fortune that had up to then been so bitter an enemy? He had eighty chances out of a hundred to succeed.

He walked quickly, with his hands in his pockets to warm them. The avenue was empty of pedestrians. Only, from time to time a car sped by. Something struck his imagination. Half closing his eyes he saw against his eyelids a black spot, whirling, whirling. He noticed that it always came upon him at the most intense, critical moments of life.

In front of the Plaza Hotel he saw the place where a week before he had shoveled snow with other unemployed men. There, just there, he had earned his last dollars. And through an association of ideas he remembered the little restaurant on the East Side where the owner, an Italian, had given him leftovers out of charity. That was how they lived now. . . .

He was downtown. The profusion of lights accentuated its liveliness. The thin fog formed luminous halos around the big signs. There were more people: couples, mostly. It was happiness, the joy of others, that moved him. So happiness still existed?

He reached the Tenderloin: the gay heart of the city of theaters and grand hotels. Memories flowed through his brain. He remembered the sleepless nights spent near luxurious haunts, hoping to find some object lost at the entrance to a show. In New York there are people who live on such proceeds. But his search had been fruitless: two dollars knotted in a handkerchief, a pair of gloves, a few packs of cigarettes.

So there were people who were still enjoying themselves while his child was at the threshold of death. And he thought of the strange contrast, that it is the richest city which contains the direst poverty: opposite the gold, blood.

He passed a building where a charitable society had promised him a subsidy a month ago, but because of a practical complication that he didn't understand he had never been able to obtain it. He smiled. But his smile was no more than a contraction of the muscles of his face.

At the intersection of Forty-second Street he stopped because of a milling crowd. A policeman was arresting a drunk. He wasn't curious, so he started on his way again, pushing through the crush. Someone observed, surprised, this wretched person unprotected from the cold of the night. He still had a few more blocks to go.

Finally he arrived. The address corresponded to a graceful three-story building with lighted windows. Up there they must be gambling. Curiously he observed that the unknown victim would be led to his encounter by destiny. Was destiny not already written in the great book of life? He approached the entrance but there was no sign. He hesitated. Yet the number could not lie. Several cars were parked in front, including some taxis.

He stepped back to look around the neighborhood. The subway station was two blocks away and had four entrances, one of which came out on Broadway, after a complicated underground passage through the basement of a large department store. He could not hope for anything better. It seemed to him that fortune, good fortune, had given him a hand. And coldly he made his plan.

In order not to attract the attention of the chauffeurs he stationed himself around the corner, so that he could see without being seen. A long, anxious time went by. His freezing blood thawed in the nervousness of the wait. He would have liked to be already past that terrible moment. And he sought resignation in the thought that in an hour all would be over.

A group of three men had come out of the club and begun walking, heading up Broadway. From time to time, an automobile left and others arrived. He was afraid that the victim would escape, but with that fear he felt a certain contentment in the depths of his silent conscience. He wished that the tragic moment would appear like a lightning bolt or move indefinitely into the distance. . . .

Finally he saw a small plump man, wearing a derby and bundled in fur, approach an automobile and, after pausing for a moment, proceed toward him. He rejoiced to see the man's obvious physical weakness, while he stayed hidden around the corner of the deserted street. The gentleman, who appeared to be rich, passed at a rapid pace, without noticing him.

Here was the victim. He roused his courage murmuring: "Necessity!"—like an order he was giving himself and could not escape. He followed the man to the middle of the second block. Then he confronted him from behind by asking for the time. The unknown man stopped, hesitant, and he, with an energy that he barely recognized, pointing the revolver shoved him into the doorway of a shop.

"Hold up! If you make a sound I'll shoot."

Some unknown force made him act. He didn't remember what he said or what he did while the pale and trembling victim leaned against the shop window with his hands up. He found himself running to the subway entrance with a roll of bills in his pants pocket. Danger gave him mastery over himself. He went down the deserted stairs, threw away the soft hat, pulled his cap down over his forehead, and passed the ticket window without going in the gate. He mingled with a current of people who, having just got off the train, were going up the opposite steps and turning into the underground passage that came out on Broadway.

When he was in the free air he let out a deep sigh, as if a great weight had been taken from his heart. He was safe. Fortune had finally helped him.

At first he felt relief. He was overflowing with joy.

Sinking his right hand deep in his pocket, he closed his fist around the roll of bills. It seemed to him that the world had become his again. Now he looked at the people passing under the fantastic lights of the signs as an equal, smiling, as if he did not feel the cold that pressed around him. He would be able to live, buy, enjoy his family who for a few hours still would be moaning in a miserable bed. How, how, how beautiful life was! And he would become honest again. . . .

His excited mind was now focused on one desire: to know the amount. What was the amount? Fifty . . .a hundred . . . a hundred and fifty dollars? His nervous fingers rubbed the bills. The paper, rough to the touch, was precisely that of American banknotes. Oh, how well he knew it!

In Times Square an idea flashed on him. And immediately he descended into the labyrinth of the subway to find in the solitude of a toilet stall a refuge safe from the inquisitive eyes of the public. He did not abandon his prudence. When he had locked himself in the weakly illuminated private stall, he took out his stolen treasure. And saw wrapped in three ten-dollar bills seven more bills, unknown to him, which bore on the sides the figure 5 followed by two zeroes. He looked at them in surprise, as if they had no value. Were they counterfeit? He mentally added up the numbers: 3530 dollars. Was it possible that he had so much money in his hands? He felt lost. Then his attention was attracted by the papers: an envelope and a visiting card. They both bore a name and address: William Ross, 214 Riverside Drive.

The robbed gentleman? Yes! Destiny wished him to know the name of his victim. Strange. And so?

His nervous tension increased when he was outside again, on Broadway. The restaurants, the drugstores, all open at that morning hour, seemed to invite him in: "Come and buy for your little Joe, for your wife." His reason repeated with a musical fascination: "Two years, two years, two years of lovely, gay, peaceful life." But his conscience, reawakened, cried out:

"Thief!"

Ten times he was on the point of going into those stores that in windows radiant with light offered him every good on God's earth, but ten times he held back. Now reaction to his insane act had set in. Little by little, as if at the lifting of a veil, he realized the gravity of what he had done. No more joy but fear; no more fear but dismay. Conscience, straight as an arrow, struck.

He had stolen. The bills that he clutched in his fist burned him. He had stolen. A contempt for that other self who had acted seized him. He had stolen. He felt that a profound abyss now separated him from the *other*—from the thief—as if a new personality had entered into his being. He had stolen out of necessity but he had s-t-o-l-e-n! he recalled his father's last words, in his native town: "You must be proud of only one thing: of holding your head high!"

He felt a tear descend from his eye. He was moved. His temples beat as if with fever: his throat seemed constricted by a lump.

He stopped at the corner of Fifty-fourth Street. All his thoughts bore traces of distant memories. Right down there at that dock five years earlier, he had deserted from his ship . . . a morning in August, hazy . . . He started uptown again. He passed Columbus Circle.

Everything now seemed to him a dream—more than a dream, a nightmare. But the nightmare was unbearable. He wished he could become again the man of two hours earlier. But was it not a dream, a truly terrible dream? And he wished to wake up so that all that "reality" would vanish.

Where to go? Throw himself into the Hudson? And Joe? And Maria? the innocent creatures who had been entrusted to his manly conscience. . . .

Oh, no! there was a street and a number: Riverside Drive, No. 214.

And he walked. And the spot, the famous black spot of his nightmare, was whirling, whirling, in the center of his half-closed eyelids.

He did not have long to wait on the cold steps of the great apartment house that launched its pallid mass against a leaden sky.

After a quarter of an hour a taxicab stopped and the small familiar man, with the rich fur and the hard hat, got out. He paid the fare, and then, as the car drove off, he crossed the courtyard toward the door.

Tony, trembling, drew himself up, and, extending the hand that clutched the roll of bills, said with a broken voice and in his foreigner's English:

"Mr. Ross . . . I beg your pardon . . . I have brought back to you the sum that I took a little while ago. . . ."

The gentleman stopped, dismayed, fearful.

"I am honest!" the man said, to reassure him. "I am a miner from Scranton. For five months I have been without work, for two I have been searching in vain in the great city, offering myself everywhere. At home I have a child and a wife who are dying of hunger and cold. I beg your pardon!"

The gentleman came closer.

"You are the man who robbed me?" he said in low voice, staring at him. "But don't you know that I reported you an hour ago to the Police?"

"I am in your hands, ready to pay in person, but . . . save my family. Here is your money."

Ross took the roll of bills, closely observing the lost face of the miner.

"What nationality are you?"

"My act has no nationality. I am a man of the crowd: a wretch who, for you, comes from the unknown."

"How did you find out my address?"

"From your papers."

There was a brief pause while the gentleman gazed at him. He had now regained mastery of himself.

"You have given me the greatest proof of honesty a man can offer. No, I don't want to know your name or who you are. I believe you at your word. One single thing I would like from you, something precious that for me will represent the memory of the most exciting day of my life: your revolver. In exchange I will give you as much as you need to get out of your difficulties."

Tony took from his pants pocket the toy belonging to his little Joe and held it out.

"With this?" the gentleman said, astonished, when he had looked at it carefully.

"With this!" repeated the miner.

In response the millionaire put back in his hand the pack of bank bills and said to him:

"I think your revolver is worth more!"

"Oh, no!" Tony burst out, restraining his emotion. "My act deserves to be punished. Let me have only the three ten-dollar bills!"—and taking from the outstretched hand the small bills that were wrapped around the roll, he fled, running, determined.

The millionaire, newly surprised, watched him as he grew distant, and then, in an impulse of generosity, cried after him:

"I forgive you! I forgive you!"

But Tony had already disappeared into the soft veil of the fog.

---

"Hold Up!," *Il Carroccio* 24, no. 8 (August 1926): 169–76.

## AN IMMIGRANT'S MEMOIR: CAMILLO CIANFARRA

Although there was clearly a pressing need for autobiographical accounts of the traumatic immigrant experience, written evidence and firsthand memoirs in Italian were scarce during the peak of the exodus. All the more significant, then, was the carefully constructed "diary" of Camillo Cianfarra. The author weaves together painful emotion and shrewd observation of the world of the immigrant community, chronicling failures, disappointments, and, especially, the difficulty of adjustment for young professionals. He describes a journey that is at once intimate and collective, providing clear, first-rate testimony of daily life.

**The Diary of an Immigrant**

VI

Ah, if only my old friends and schoolfellows could see me, those who link America to all their dreams of fortune and glory and look with an envious eye at all whom destiny forces to depart! Fortune? Wealth? Yes, precisely these: a pot of glue, a brush, a pile of deceitful labels, and six dollars a week that, once I've paid my room and board, leaves me two dollars and twenty-five cents that I could save if I didn't smoke and were happy to give up collars and starched cuffs. And how long will this life last? Two, four, six months, a year? And who knows? The boss, who after a conversation with Giovanni is kinder to me than to the others, often tells me to learn English quickly so that I will be able to earn more: twelve, fifteen dollars a week—he says—it's easy to get that here. Learn English, yes, but when?

Every night I go home tired, done in, and everywhere all I see is labels, white, red, gilded, the labels that I have begun to feel a mortal hatred for. Books, that once I loved, now lie dusty on the table, and the old eagerness to read is fast asleep. To learn English means to study night and day, and to study one needs that tranquillity of mind where one can concentrate with the certainty that no other thought can disturb. Instead! Look: the glue pot is always before me and the thought that I have not been able to find something better keeps me from sleeping. How many people who have not gone beyond third grade, who have never seen the cover of a book by Loria or Spenser, live better than me, and work less! Giovanni, for example, in two or three hours earns from three to five dollars, and some days, when he's lucky, he even earns twenty or thirty. He works for a company that imports oil, and tells me that, on average, the company that imports ten thousand *lire* of oil a year sells it for more than twenty thousand in New York alone. That is the secret of good fortune. When I observed to him that it seemed to me immoral, he answered:

"It may be true, but we are not the only ones to do it; everyone 'cuts' the arriving olive oil with cottonseed oil, and that's where the profit is. I, when I'm selling it, always speak of oil imported from Lucca, very high quality, and for every 'gallon' I get fifty cents."

But would I be capable of doing this? Could I get used to telling fifty lies to earn fifty dollars? No, I could not, and for this reason I suppose I will always be a gluer of labels at six dollars a week.

But how many unfortunates come to this country! Aristocrats whose wealth melted away in the hands of prostitutes and at the gambling tables; high government officials who attempt to augment their meager salaries by indiscretions that cost them their position; army officers forced by debts to cut short their careers; persons who, rich one day, ruined themselves by satisfying the petty ambitions that grow in the shadow of the town's bell tower, victims of local feuds, harassed by their rivals; young intellectuals who because of their ideas found themselves one day facing the dilemma of either hunger and an occasional prison term, or exile. There are thousands of these unfortunates, and you encounter them everywhere: washing glasses in bars; serving customers in cafés and restaurants, sweating blood ten or fifteen hours a day in bank offices for a starvation salary, moving crates and loading bushels of goods, all of them atoning for a sin carelessly committed.

I knew a young doctor who one day, eager to follow the urgings of his conscience, devoted himself to socialist propaganda, carrying with all the enthusiasm of his twenty-eight years the knowledge and the seed of the new ideas to the houses of the peasants of his town. He was the town doctor, but after a while the job was taken away from him, and when he applied for another the Mayor, on the advice of the authorities of public safety, refused to accept him. Later, for having written an article in which the authorities found the usual incitement to hatred between the classes, the doctor spent six months in prison. Today, when one speaks to him of his country and its institutions, he jumps to say . . . things that only the Consul or the *Cavaliere* would not consider just. How he loves that land where he was born, and how happy he would be to live in his home town, to which he will never return!

And the case of a teacher who often comes to the *pensione* is even sadder.

For twelve years, with a salary of seventy *lire* a month, he taught in the schools of his native town, where he was loved and esteemed, and where he expected to end his days among the blessings of those he had taught and made men, taken care of by his children, to whom he would wish to give a special place in life. How modest was this dream! But fate willed otherwise; and at forty he found himself with five children and the same salary.

"What a struggle!" said the poor teacher, telling me his story. "What torment to dig through my pockets in vain, looking for the money needed to buy shoes and clothes for my family. When my oldest son was ten and, under my teaching, had completed elementary school, I wondered what he should do. Should I send him to study in the city? And how? A few years later my next son would be ten. Send him to study, too? Well: in the best hypothesis one of my sons would have to learn the shoemaker's trade, the second the tailor's, and the third would become a blacksmith or carpenter. The town offered nothing better and I racked my brains to find some way for them to finish their education.

"One night I had a luminous vision: I was alone in a field, where the grain was growing as tall as a man and had ears heavier than any I had ever seen. Here and there in the field were piles of gold that sparkled in the sun and dazzled me, and in the background, against a cloudless blue horizon, were some letters, monumental in size, which I could not distinguish clearly. I sharpened my gaze, making an effort to concentrate on the point, and I read . . . can you guess what I read? 'America!' my resolution was taken: I woke up my wife and told her that I would be leaving immediately, at the cost of whatever sacrifice."

As it happened, the teacher found a distant relative who does whitewashing. Today he gets up at five-thirty and at seven he is already on the job, in a long white smock and with a brush that he sticks in a bucket of lime and he slops, slops it on the walls for ten hours a day.

XVIII

August 2, 189 . . .

Catastrophe! . . .

Coming into the Office I couldn't believe my eyes, and for two hours I was as if stunned, observing that mass of people crowding around my door asking for news of Don Raffaele.

"He's gone," answered my colleague, in a faint voice, while on his face one could read surprise, grief, and rage. "He's gone, leaving me a note on a piece of paper saying I would never see him again."

A farmer who a week earlier had deposited two hundred and seventy dollars in the bank, hearing the news, ran toward the Office, and, making his way through the crowd, asked, with his hair bristling and his eyes bloodshot, for his money.

"I want it, give it to me," cried the poor man, beside himself. "I have to pay my taxes. . . ."

When the only response from Don Raffaele's partner was that he dried his eyes, which were wet with tears, he fell to the floor unconscious, clutching in his hands a long knife, with bloody spittle running out of his mouth.

Another sad scene occurred when a ragpicker asked if the news of Don Raffaele's flight was true. At that moment there were more than sixty people in the bank, many of whom were weeping, while many others were shouting and demanding an account of the money sent ten days ago now, and others were speaking in loud voices. When my colleague confirmed the news to the ragpicker, she let out a cry that silenced all the others, and tearing her hair threw herself at the window, waving her arms desperately, cursing, crying, finally pleading in the name of her two children whom she had to support. The unfortunate woman has been a widow for three years and she had entrusted all she possessed to Don Raffaele: three hundred dollars, which represented the savings of two years of work and humiliation, on the streets of this city.

"Help me," she said to me. "If those little ones get sick, I haven't a cent to buy medicine. . . ."

In her eyes were dark flashes of anger, and at one point I was afraid that she would lash out at me, who knew little or nothing of what had happened. Fortunately, a young man who had lost a hundred *scudi* began haranguing the crowd, saying that the best thing to do was to get a lawyer, and many left with him, including the woman. But still the bank was full of customers who had been robbed, and the worst thing was that I, and my colleague and the boss's partner, could not leave, for fear that one of them, blinded by rage, would attack us, demanding immediate restitution of what we did not have. In the end we telephoned Central Police Headquarters and told them about the mob and the danger we ran, and five minutes later four police officers forced the crowd to disperse. This caused the cries, shouts, and protests to redouble in force. One old man, who every Saturday evening, as soon as he collected his salary, came to the office to deposit four or five dollars, would not resign himself to the loss of that small sum, with which he hoped to buy a little farm where he counted on ending his days. Gripping the window grate with his bony hands, he resisted the efforts of the agents, continuing to look at us as if begging to be protected. Little by little, however, the sparkle in his eyes was extinguished, and the old man went out, unsteadily, murmuring incomprehensible words, gesticulating wildly, examining attentively the faces of the people he encountered. When, in our turn, we went out, accompanied by the policemen, the crowd that was stationed in front of the bank was enormous. Those who had been robbed, men and women, were weeping, the curious struggled to console them, advising them to go to a lawyer, and often joining in the curses directed at Don Raffaele, the single cause of the dreadful catastrophe. As we went off, I saw the old man again, sitting on the step of an abandoned house about forty feet away, gazing at the crowd, continuing to gesticulate, and from time to time emitting inarticulate sounds, which made the passersby turn.

And who can say in how many other places these painful scenes will be repeated—I thought as I got on the tram—how many others, like that old man, have entrusted all their savings to the bank, which has melted away in an instant, like a drop of wax on a lighted coal. Those who have been robbed who live in the city are few, the great majority work scattered throughout the United States, and for many the loss will be like a knife in the heart. How many will die of that pain? How many go mad at the idea that all the savings of one or two years of labor are lost, irredeemably lost?

According to my calculations the stolen sum might be as much as fifty thousand dollars!

※

The loss gave Don Raffaele a motivation for another of his tricks; he remained true to his madcap nature even in the face of the grief that this act of his caused, and which should have sent him directly to jail for the rest of his life. For several hours the safe became the center of all hopes; everyone believed that part of the sums deposited in the bank would be found there; but it was not so.

When the safe was opened, a letter was found in the box where the gold was kept, which said that for two years he had been thinking of the failure as an absolute necessity, since the bank had a deficit of more than twenty thousand dollars!

And so the threats have become reality, you poor peasants who today are overwhelmed by your tears!

XIX

April 28, 189 . . .

Today I don't feel like doing anything anymore, and if I hadn't remembered you, poor diary, I would have gone out to celebrate the third anniversary of my arrival in America. This perhaps will make you think that I have made a fortune and occupy a grand position, but . . . rest assured. Three years ago, when I disembarked, I had in my pocket several hundred *lire*, today instead I have a few hundred cents and some debts, incurred during three months of unemployment after the failure of the bank; as for the grand position . . . let's not discuss it. A Catholic priest forced to spread socialist propaganda; a painter forced to keep account books; a mathematician forced to write verses would not feel more uneasy than I feel in this editorial office, which I came into just by chance, as I might have gone into a salami or macaroni factory.

My professor was right when he told me that this was an extraordinary country, full of resources, where one's situation changes in twenty-four hours, and where it is possible to make a fortune in twenty-four days. Now nothing astonishes me, I have become an itinerant piece of ice, tramping impassively across this unique, incomparable stage that is our immigrant community. And then, why should I be astonished? One morning I picked up the newspaper and read that someone was looking for a young man who knew Italian "discreetly" and would be able to translate rapidly from English. I thought at first that it was a matter of translating commercial contracts that would not be very difficult, and I went. Two other young men had arrived before me, and their appearance made me immediately realize that they must be even more unfortunate than me. A little later I convinced myself that probably English and Italian were not their strong point, and my heart was filled with hope. They will take me, I thought, and at least I will be able to pay my debts. After a two-hour wait, an old man who I later found out was the editor in chief, and for whom today I feel a truly filial affection, had us come into the office and each of us was invited to translate a good half column of a newspaper without using the dictionary.

"If you come across an unfamiliar word," the old man said, "ask me the meaning."

Then he went back to his desk, where there were mountains of newspapers, magazines, and books in all languages, while I, having read the piece that I was to translate, thought it was a joke. It was the telegraphed account of a session of the French parliament, at which the rehearing of the Dreyfus trial was being discussed, and the translation seemed to me extremely easy. My companions—I later learned—had had something similar, but they worked at a snail's pace, and so, even if they had been hired, they would have been a failure. At some point one of them asked me if Gazzetta was written with one or two "zeta"s, the other asked if "been" meant "bean"! I finished a good half hour before them and delivered the translation to the editor in chief, who, after reading it, abruptly asked what I thought of Dreyfus.

"He's a victim," I answered, without hesitation and without thinking that the answer was equivalent to a declaration of political faith and that perhaps it might compromise me in the eyes of the person who was to decide on my suitability for the position of translator. But far from compromising me, that declaration helped me immensely, for we found ourselves in agreement and after a few minutes were talking like two old companions of ideas and battles.

When the others finished they were kindly let go, with the promise that they would be informed by letter if they were to come back or not; I instead stayed, and continued to translate until midday, and was to return definitely the next day.

And that is how I find myself working here as a so-called "immigrant journalist," something as cheerful and sympathetic as the community that supports us. A lot of people envy me this job, but I forgive them because they are ignorant of many things. If I don't look for another job, it is only because here, at least, no one rebukes me for the minutes spent staring into space; because I can read and study; because I have contact with people from whom one can learn things, and above all because . . . because it has allowed me finally to get to know the community. A year ago I believed that it held no more secrets for me; that the past and the present of its inhabitants were thoroughly familiar to me, while today . . . only today do I realize that the more one studies it the more it is necessary to study it; that the more one investigates the wider becomes the field of investigation and observation. How many things pass before my eyes today, how many revelations at every new event where I go to represent the paper, so to speak, and what inexhaustible sources of new sensations are the halls of justice, the law offices, the police stations, the elegant hotels, the fashionable restaurants, the society gatherings, all the places, in short, where my new career calls me! no, then I didn't know the community: the *prominenti* who flatter us to get blurbs and those who offer us drinks to keep us friendly; the illustrious unknowns who notify us of the birth of the seventh heir, and those who announce their next marriage; the misunderstood geniuses who bring us manuscripts to read, and the unrepentant amateur actors who ceaselessly pursue us; the poetry- and prose-writing barbers who poison our lunch, and the inventor shoemakers who want their portraits in the supplement; the hoarse-voiced singers who ask us to announce their next concert and the angry fencers who want us to announce their next tournament; the cavaliers of the Crown of Italy who honor us with their protection, and the supplicants to the cross who confide their hopes to us, unfortunately unfounded; the *prominenti* who come and the *prominenti* who go; the unsettled who arrive and those who leave again. . . . I didn't know any of them, just as those who are not in this place where the slander of the community prevails will never know: where everything, sooner or later, is found out; where cries of joy and grief echo; where the news that a fellow-countryman has been sentenced to death is often confused with the news of a triumph of the Italian name; where we struggle and curse, win and bless.

And I ought to tell you about all this, but, what do you want? I'm tired, it's late, and today I did more than I intended. Tomorrow I will return to you with the passion of an old lover and confide in you all that I have seen and heard in these last months: my hours of joy and sadness, the impressions both beautiful and ugly that my new career has brought me. But no more today, my poor diary! Maria wrote me that tonight she has made ravioli and I'm going to eat some. She is happy, she has a fine boy of eight months, her husband adores her, business at her boarding house is going full sail, and a few days ago her husband told me that if things continue in this way for a couple of years, he will open a hotel on Lake Como, where he hopes to attract a large American clientele. I wish him good luck sincerely, brother to brother.

*Il diario di un emigrato* (New York: Tipografia dell'Araldo Italiano, 1904), 66–70, 167–75.

## A SERIALIZED SOCIALIST NOVEL

Almost nothing is known about the author, but it is noteworthy that a mouthpiece of the Italian American left, *La Parola del Popolo,* sponsored and "produced" its own brand of proletarian novel. Here we have the opportunity to step into the world of blue-collar immigrant workers, caught between the basic needs of survival and the awareness of class divisions and exploitation. The main characters decide to fight for their rights, by going on strike. This becomes an assertion of a new maturity and self-reliance, marking a clear dividing line with the allegiances of the old world. The novel ends with a rosy vision of a Socialist future.

**Toward the Ideal**

SCENES EXPERIENCED BY AN IMMIGRANT ITALIAN IN AMERICA
X

Those six laborers worked like beasts. Although the sweat was pouring off them, they were always running. Around evening, however, they realized that it would be impossible to finish the oven that day, so they slowed down a little. But the following morning they set to work with greater industry, since they were afraid they wouldn't finish the rest of the oven in the five hours that remained. In fact at midday the oven was still not empty although they had worked with all their might. After lunch the seven workers were so exhausted and discouraged that they felt the need to slow down, so they did not see the end of that damn oven until 4 p.m. What a treat! After working like beasts, the seven laborers were giving away three hours of work apiece to the bosses.

In the evening he told about it at home, and learned from Giovanni that those "deals" had been going on for years, and that when they didn't have the unpleasant result mentioned above, some hours were gained that, compared to the double amount of work done, always turned out to the advantage of the bosses.

And he knew also that that fine custom had been in effect ever since the Italians began working there, whereas before, when everyone worked by the day, they worked less and earned more.

The next morning, he asked Bepi to tell the boss that he didn't want to hear anything more about those "deals." Then they began unloading coal from the wagons. Certainly the work was no less exhausting, but at least there was the assurance of being paid for all the hours worked.

All the workers employed in delivering milk to the city had called a strike some weeks earlier, for a small increase in salary, and the various companies, in spite of major efforts, had managed to hire only a few traitors; too few to be able, even superficially, to replace the many strikers, for the daily delivery of milk. The public, tired of not receiving that precious nourishment, demanded an agreement, but the arrogant owners refused to give in to the just demands of the workers, who, certain of victory, maintained an admirable solidarity with their organization.

Nino Perla, who ever since he had disembarked in New York, had been trying in vain to discover where that damn "democracy," so extolled by poor Tonio, lived, hoped that he would finally find it in the great, tumultuous City.

Hence he was anxious to go out into the crowded streets, and to be in contact with all the busy multitudes whom he saw walking on the streets, to learn from them their customs, their habits, their ideas. So after dinner that Sunday, he eagerly accepted Bepi's invitation for a stroll along the nearby avenues. They went down Chouteau Avenue, walking slowly and chatting cheerfully of this and that. Nino Perla, meanwhile, did not let a thing go by without observing, studying the people and their movements: the houses, the trams, the automobiles, the horses, in short the whole cinematographic scene that a main street of a great city offers. Arriving at the intersection of Grand Avenue, the two friends stood in front of the Revely Dairy Co.'s grand building. Their gaze was drawn to a group of twenty-five strikers who were stretched out on a pile of dirt talking peacefully across the street from the dairy. Suddenly a company truck full of men came from the north on Grand Avenue and appeared at the intersection. At that sight the strikers leaped to their feet crying "Long live the strike. Down with traitors!" A fierce discharge of rifles was the response of the scabs. The group of strikers dispersed, fleeing in all directions, but five of them lay on the ground, uttering anguished cries. Meanwhile the truck carrying the attackers turned west and, undisturbed, went in through the main gate of the dairy. Two policemen, who at the moment of the tragedy were in front of the dairy, instead of following the attackers ran toward the strikers, arresting the few courageous ones who had stayed to help the wounded. Nino Perla, who had been present at that swift scene without having time to realize what was happening, stood as if stunned, but when he saw the two policemen raising their sticks against the strikers and dragging them into custody, then he understood the monstrosity of the attack. Enraged, he turned to his friend and asked: "But will those fierce attackers not be punished?" "How can you even ask that? Don't you see they're arresting the strikers?" answered Bepi.

"What about justice, and democracy?" ventured Nino. "Empty words in which only the ingenuous still believe," replied Bepi. And he added: "Justice, democracy, and freedom, my friend, cannot possibly exist in a society that divides the human race into two opposing classes, one of which has the right to live—and prosper—off the sufferings of the other."

Nino Perla was silent. He knew that his friend was right, and he had been foolish to believe blindly that he was truly in a free and democratic country. Meanwhile two automobiles had arrived. Into one the wounded were loaded, into the other the prisoners. Five minutes later the usual tranquillity had returned to the intersection, and of the tragedy of a few minutes earlier nothing remained but a few bloodstains scattered here and there on the mound of earth.

XI

The next day it was learned that three of the wounded had died. At that sad news the strikers' spirits turned bitter, but the leaders counseled calm. They knew that the tragedy of the day before had been arranged by the owners for just that reason, to push the workers to violence so as to be able to let the police loose against them. But their advice was not heeded by all. The next day before dawn a gunshot from an unknown hand made a corpse of one of those Judases, while he was delivering milk in one of the principal neighborhoods of the City. That shot was, in truth, fatal for the strikers. With it, police reprisals began, the leaders of the workers were arrested, the strikers who up to that point had been picketing the dairies were dispersed, and the office of their organization was stripped.

A week later, the strike ended with the utter defeat of those poor men, who had to return to work, under harsher conditions than before. The owners, with the assistance of the democratic authorities, won that strike by means of a crime.

Mister Brain, a good fellow and a tireless worker, having made the last payment on his house, wanted to celebrate the event with a little family party, and he invited all the neighbors. Giovanni accepted the invitation enthusiastically, knowing he would have a chance to get drunk, while Bepi and Nino Perla were reluctant.

But at the good man's insistence they let themselves be won over. He wanted at all costs to make the event memorable. Nino Perla was curious about the reason behind the fellow's impulse to make the party so momentous.

He explained it himself, as soon as all the guests were sitting around the table, on which sat a little barrel of beer. "For twenty years I've been waiting, anxiously, for this day," said the man, "so I have good reason to celebrate."

At a murmur of surprise from the guests, Mister Brain added, "It's true. When I got married, I earned thirty dollars a month. My mother-in-law, who lived with us, suggested that we should save something from my salary in order to buy a house. And so we did. As soon as we had put together the hundred dollars necessary for the down payment, we bought this humble house for twelve hundred dollars, pledging to pay ten dollars a month to the owner, until the complete sum was paid. But after a few months I became sick, and lost my job, and to continue the monthly payments we were forced to mortgage the house. During the first year we endured many days of hunger, but we never failed to make our regular payments. But then the taxes, the interest on debts, and the monthly payments became more than my earnings. In going without a doctor, I lost my father and mother-in-law. By thus reducing our expenses, we were able to continue the payments.

"In ten years, five of our seven children died, probably because of the poor diet that was all we could afford. For fifteen years I wore the same overcoat. Now, however, after so many hardships, at the age of forty-five, we are finally secure in owning our house, and unless there is a cyclone we hope to live long enough to enjoy it."

"How much unknown grief and misery in the land of wealth and gold!" said Bepi.

This Sunday there was to be a big charity fair for the benefit of the Italian Church, which was burdened by an enormous debt contracted when it was built, many years earlier, and which, in spite of all the fairs and contributions, had never been paid off. The gossips whispered that the debt never would be paid off. But the good parishioners continued to attend in large numbers, and to spend their sweaty dollars unstintingly, every time the good "Father" announced a new charity fair. Needless to say, Giovanni's family could not miss the great fair and naturally they invited the two friends, assuring them that they would have a good time, among so many pretty girls.

The fair took place in the spacious courtyard of the church, which was decorated for the occasion with multicolored streamers. When they arrived, it was full of people, of both sexes, thronging the various stalls of the venders who shouted themselves hoarse as they hawked the various items they had for sale. The large noisy crowd gave Nino Perla the feeling of being at the celebration of a national holiday. Only the place that had been chosen did not seem very suitable. Giovanni, who acted as their guide, accompanied them into the basement of the church to have "a drop" to drink. Nino Perla was amazed to see a real bar, with men drinking and . . . swearing, right under the temple of God. But his amazement did not reach its peak until they were in the dance hall, on whose wall hung a crucifix that trembled sadly with the gyrations of the dancers. At that sight Nino Perla recalled Don Giovanni, the priest in his town, who railed against the young people who went to dances, calling them scandalous . . . and he understood the whole plot of that grand comedy.

---

"Verso l'Ideale. Scene vissute dall'emigrante italiano in America," *La Parola del Popolo,* 8 and 15 (July 1922).

## RED SCARE: AN ITALIAN ANARCHIST IS BUSTED

In the winter of 1920, Ludovico Caminita was rounded up along with other anarchists, mostly from Paterson, a historic haven for Italian libertarians, and sent to Ellis Island. His book, *Nell'isola delle lagrime: Ellis Island* [On the Island of Tears: Ellis Island], which chronicles the period he spent in prison, is one of the last expressions of his radicalism; soon after his release, more than three years later, he considerably moderated his views and entered the immigrant mainstream. In both guises, however, he proved a valiant and perceptive writer. Although he was not uncompromising, his tone could be scathing, without giving in to the petty parochialism common in the Italian American press. From a strictly political point of view, his prison memoir may be disappointing; but the verbal and visual energy of its best pages form a poignant, angry introduction to life on the "island of tears."

### On the Island of Tears: Ellis Island

Sunday passed monotonously. We were tired from the long night, and our thoughts were with our families. We spoke from one cell to another, at long intervals and without much interest. Every so often a guard came along, called a name, and gave the prisoner cigars or cigarettes that his relatives had brought.

The wife of the weaver who had lodged and fed Joe Termini, and given him money, thought that he was a prisoner with us, and had had the idea of bringing him some cigarettes. Poor thing! All alone, and far from his comfortable mother, he surely felt, more than the others, the burden of unexpected imprisonment!

"The cigars are for my husband, the cigarettes for Joe Termini."

"Joe Termini? But he's a spy for the federal agents! Who knows where the bum is now!" exclaimed the guard.

You can imagine the amazement of the poor woman!

They brought us breakfast, lunch, and dinner from a nearby restaurant, paid for, of course, by the federal government. I, who with my frequent travels was used to American cooking, considered those meals tasty. The others, who had never left their native dinner tables, received that food like a penance. "Oatmeal" and coffee with milk to a Piedmontese, or a Neapolitan!

Monday came as a relief. We didn't know what they would do with us, but we hadn't slept for two days, and the thought that we would be able to lie down on some mattress or other, at home or in prison or on the island, consoled us a little.

During the wait the minutes seemed like hours. Every time a guard entered we all expected to be called. And it was a great disappointment when instead he called us to deliver a package.

I received underwear and cigarettes.

"Who brought them?" I asked the guard.

"Your wife."

"That's impossible; my wife can't leave the house; she's sick."

"I tell you, she did bring them. The chief recognized her. And she's outside there, in the crowd, waiting for you to come out. They are pitiful, poor women! Since six in the morning they've been out there, and it's six degrees below zero. Such is life!"

He went off shaking his head and repeating: "Yes, such is life!"

I stood there for some minutes gripping the iron bars, then I threw myself on the bedsprings and hid my face in my overcoat so that my cellmate wouldn't see the tears that I couldn't hold back. I wept for the woman who walked heroically at my side, a smile of comfort on her lips, always ready to support me in difficult moments, along the Via Crucis of my fate, lined with thorns. I wept for the wives of the others, frail, innocent creatures, true victims of that judicial error made for the sake of ignoble profit by the new priests of the class struggle, who wore soft hats and fluttering black ties.

Around two o'clock the chief of the local police made a tour of inspection and stopped in front of my cell. He was in plainclothes. He asked me how I was doing, if breakfast and lunch had been good, and urged me not to be discouraged.

"I'm sorry about this mistake. I knew it the night they brought you here, because the federal agents wanted to do everything secretly—they wouldn't trust us. I hope that it will all turn out to be a soap bubble in the end."

"Thank you. I know that our wives have been waiting a long time for us, out in the street, in the cold. Couldn't you let them have shelter?"

"I would do it happily, because the poor creatures really are a pitiful sight; but the federal agents won't allow it. They're already irritated because I allowed you to get cigarettes and clean underwear."

"If I am not mistaken, you are the chief here, not the federal agents."

"Yes, but I would be opposing those people just for a matter of a few minutes. Be patient. Now they'll take you away. I hope that it will all come to nothing, and that you will soon return to your families. Goodbye; rather, see you again. Cheer up!"

A few minutes later the federal agents came to get us. They were agitated. Why? They handcuffed us two by two and lined us up. I was with a young man from the Romagna who had been in the United States only a few months, and who had a pretty little wife and a sweet baby. He knew a few phrases of bad English, and had a confused idea of their meaning. He was an apprentice weaver by day and a typesetter by night. He was small of stature, lively, and talked a lot, too much, but since he had nothing in his mind but an inexhaustible reservoir of jokes, not all decent, he couldn't talk about anything else. He was always laughing. He was so empty-headed that his friends called him a sucker. And he laughed at it. Even that day, he had not lost his stupid good humor, for, knowing that he was innocent of any possible or imaginable crime, he was convinced that within a few hours he would be freed and would be able to recount to one and all his extraordinary adventure in America.

My left wrist was bound to his right by a handcuff, and we were made to leave by a rear door of the building, which opened into a courtyard. There the agents stopped us; they moved my companion in chains a step away, making our arms straighten, and leaving me to face the lens of a camera. An agent ordered me to take off my hat. I refused.

When this function was over, which all great personages must submit to today, we were put on a police bus, with two federal agents and four uniformed local policemen, and the bus departed, bell ringing.

At the sound of that bell, our wives, followed by the crowd, ran to greet us, but they were stopped by a line of police, who were armed with heavy clubs, because they were afraid of a rebellion. I and my companion scrutinized the crowd, but it was so dense and fluctuating that it was impossible to see our wives.

It was only a few blocks from where we were to the train station. All along the way the sidewalks were lined with people, who hailed us waving caps and handkerchiefs. A policeman said to a federal agent, "You see? We told you that public opinion is with them. You wanted to put on this show because you don't know the place."

My companion in misfortune, happy in his ignorance, began waving his left hand in response to the crowd, and cried, "Goodbye! Goodbye!"

One could imagine oneself a truly important person at that moment. One of the federal agents, less restrained than the others, shouted at him: "Shut up!" and he, drunk on his quarter of an hour of sudden popularity, shouted back at him: "Shut up you!"

The agent became furious and quickly landed a punch across his face. Not satisfied with that, he pulled out a blackjack and was about to strike the unfortunate gusher of jokes, not all decent, when a policeman grabbed him by the wrist saying: "You damn fool, you want to get us lynched?"

The agent remembered the crowd, put the blackjack back in his pocket, and giving the prisoner a look like an angry hyena said: "When we get to the island I'll kill you."

The poor man didn't understand, but when I translated the threat into Italian, the color drained from his face, he bent his head, and remained silent.

When we arrived at the train station, the agents wouldn't let us go in because the waiting room was extremely crowded. They backed us up against a wall, under the overhang of the roof, and planted themselves in front of us, so that no one could get near us. Behind us was a window that opened into the waiting room. I looked through the glass and saw that people were thronging to see us. One man had a folded newspaper in his hand, and I could read some bits of the large-type headline: "Arrest . . .Deport . . ." Without a doubt, that newspaper was referring to us. The man understood my wish and unfolded the first page. I read the giant red letters of the headline:

"The king of the anarchists arrested with twenty of his followers— he is to be expelled from the United States."

A subhead in black:

"For eighteen years he has escaped the police searches."

Another, in italic:

"Arms, hand grenades, and dynamite confiscated from his house."

The king of the anarchists, according to the paper, was me!

And prominently displayed was the picture of an ugly mug in a beret, with no collar, who surely had been dug up in the depths of the Bowery, and the paper was passing him off as me.

After about ten minutes the other detainees arrived on foot and were herded under the roof.

I knew that in America reporters took special courses in journalism at the university, where they studied the best means for arousing the morbid curiosity of readers. But I had never imagined that their impudence had no limits. The mob was looking for a human beast surrounded by its terrifying followers and was finding neither the one nor the others. It saw some well-dressed people, with a very civilized appearance, handcuffed.

What a disappointment!

Suddenly there was a scuffle. I saw Grandi's wife, a small woman; Pietro Baldisserotti's wife, tall and robust, with big muscles; and the woman who had brought cigars for her husband and cigarettes for Joe Termini struggling with the federal agents. The three women wanted to break through the police cordon to get to us; they seemed to have lost their senses. They must have suffered mightily to abandon themselves to that open, irresistible rebellion. More than eight hours on the sidewalk in six-degree-below-zero weather! And all they wanted was to be near their husbands for a few moments and say some words of comfort. The crowd expressed its sympathy for those poor women by hurling taunting remarks and cutting insults at the agents. These put up with it, but they did not dare to react with violence.

Finally one of them took out a blackjack.

For those who do not know it, this insidious weapon is a ball of lead tied to the end of a strip of flexible leather. The law strictly prohibits the use of this weapon, even for the police, but there are none who do not carry one openly.

The agent, obviously annoyed, threatened the wife of Baldisserotti, and now the women became furious. But they were three against a group of strong men, armed with every weapon, including the most powerful: the certainty of going unpunished.

The crowd began to shout; one soul, a little bolder than the others, raised his fists at the agents. Then a detective sergeant from Paterson, a certain Billy Hughes, known for his great courage, rushed over to me.

"Mr. Caminita, tell your friends to urge their wives to be patient. What's going to happen if the federal agents get out their automatics?"

"If you let them come through, everything will work out for the best."

"But the agents have explicit orders. I'm afraid there will be a bloodbath."

"You ask them, in our name, to submit for the sake of their husbands."

The sergeant hurried off to communicate our request, and did so in such a way that the women could see us. We made them a sign to calm down, showing them our handcuffed wrists to indicate that we could not give them any help. They understood. Mrs. Grandi called to us, in English, so that the agents could understand: "We wish to go into the station to buy tickets, what right have these brutes to keep us out."

An Italian American detective from Paterson, De Luccia, also helped to soothe them.

The police officers had a lot of trouble trying to pacify some men who were threatening to start a fight.

Finally some calm was restored.

My eyes sought my wife. I saw her. We smiled at each other. And we continued to smile; but suddenly she couldn't keep up the effort to control herself. She hid her face in a handkerchief.

Knowing that she was so ill, I felt that exposing herself to the intense cold was a suicide in disguise.

The Paterson police began to criticize the federal agents, calling them agents provocateurs.

"It's a needless cruelty," said one.

"It's a stupid put-on," the detective sergeant concluded.

Finally the train arrived. We exchanged looks and smiles with our families, and we departed.

During the trip — an hour — my companion, the cheerful young fellow whom his friends called by a name that I cannot transcribe, was cheerful no longer. He glanced sidelong at the agent who had threatened to kill him as soon as we arrived at the island the way a dog looks from under the table at his master who he expects is going to beat him. He didn't dare to speak. Finally he said to me in a low voice, and without turning his head:

"When we get to the island, that big ape is going to get me, right?"

"I don't think so."

"Oh, yes he's going to give me a thrashing. How he's keeping an eye on me! But I didn't mean to offend him. I don't know myself why I told him to shut up himself. Out of the damn habit of always saying 'Shut up yourself' when people tell me to be quiet."

For the entire journey he did nothing but annoy me with his whining.

When we arrived in New York, the agents lined us up and walked us down to South Ferry. People stopped to stare at us, thinking perhaps that we were, at the least, a gang of bandits captured in the wild West.

The pavement was covered with ice, and in order to keep from slipping we had to perform miracles of balance, each tugging on the other's wrist. The handcuffs stuck to our skin like icicles. My hands were frozen. My gloves were of no use. I was afraid that the tips of my ears would freeze, and every so often I rubbed them with my free hand. The agents cursed the cold and took it out on us.

That march of a mile and a quarter was endless. When we boarded the warm ferry boat, it seemed to us we were in paradise.

The boat set off, and during the crossing I watched, heartsick, as New York receded; New York, the great, immense, beautiful metropolis, where I had enjoyed so much and suffered so much; New York, that I loved the way one loves the city of one's birth!

As we approached Ellis Island, I saw through the window the huge, beautiful, proud statue of Liberty that stands near the Island of Tears, and there came to mind the words of Madame Roland, uttered on the gallows, as she looked at the statue of Liberty standing before her.

---

*Nell'isola delle lagrime: Ellis Island* (New York: Stabilimento tipografico Italia, 1924), 29–39.

## A TAKE-OFF ON SOUTHERN LOCALISM: THE CARTOON CHARACTERS OF PASQUALE SENECA

This is a prime example of what the film scholar Giorgio Bertellini has aptly called "Southernist mimicry," that is, the ability displayed by Southern Italian entertainers-intellectuals, especially during live performances onstage, to reflect on their subalternity, in relation to both Italian and American society, while at the same time poking fun at themselves and their audiences, and showing a forthright awareness of the specificity of Southern culture. Seneca's wry extended joke on the divisions that stifled the Little Italys bears a dedication to the king of early Italian American comedy, Eduardo Migliaccio, a.k.a. Farfariello. And the parodic element is omnipresent: in the alternation of roman and italic typefaces, of Italian language and a corrupted version of dialect, in the comic drawings, and most of all in the outrageous narrative, full of double-entendres. As these pages show, ridiculing but also denouncing, there can be no peace among Italian Americans. This is the bitter laugh of early Italian American comedy.

## President Scoppetta

FOUNDATION OF THE SOCIETY

In a corner of our beloved Italy, where the sun, it seems, never sets and the meadows smell sweetly in the gentle breezes of an eternal spring, God willed that, to crown the marvelous picture of rustic beauty, a village should arise, a lovely little spot, certainly deserving of a prettier and more gracious name than poetic fancy could conceive, but to which, instead, whim, or the irony of chance, gave the name of . . . Brigantello.

We say whim or the irony of chance because this bizarre name has nothing to do with the character of its inhabitants, who, if they have ever sinned, have done so through excessive zeal of virtue.

It is a fact now proved by the annals of this village, that in the time of feudalism, when, that is, the nobles got up to all sorts of tricks at the expense of the oppressed peasants, the Brigantellani were the only ones, as far as anyone knows, who sharply opposed that uncivil and barbaric practice that was concealed by the Latin formula *jus primae noctis* and which therefore claimed to be legal. "*Jus primae noctis* my foot!" said the inhabitants of Brigantello, when the meaning of it was explained to them. "We tolerate everything; but don't talk to us about that sort of nonsense because the honor of our women is sacred, and anyone who dares to touch it will lose his hide." And so the nobles of Brigantello had nothing to eat, so to speak.

But the virtue at which the Brigantellani excelled was devotion, and this devotion was fulfilled in the worship of their holy patroness, Our Lady of Peace, which they carried to the point of paroxysm. Everything was imputed to her statue: she rewarded good works and punished bad, and every little phenomenon, however insignificant, was explained in terms of this belief. It was raining? It was Our Lady preparing a good harvest. It wasn't raining? She was punishing the inhabitants for impiety, etc., etc. Some would call this peculiarity ignorance and fanaticism; we prefer, however, to call it robust, indestructible faith, since faith alone conceives true sacrifice.

And so the fine people of Brigantello lived through the years and through the centuries finding peace and comfort in work and devotion. But bad times arrived. Our country emerged from an era of foreign oppression and entered into a period of reconstruction, which meant sacrifices and suffering. But the people who feel the effects and do not question the cause attribute every economic ill to the corruption of those in power; and so, with the curse of "Thieving government" on their lips, the poor workers who were no longer able to find a way to support themselves in their homeland had to leave their poetic villages and look for work across the ocean, the first going to Merica Grande, as they used to call Brazil; the others, the great mass, to Nova Yorka, that is, the United States. This occurred in the last years of the nineteenth century and the dawn of the current one.

What happened in the other cases happened with the Brigantellani: where the first ones went the others followed, in such a way that, gradually, in one of the major cities of the Union, a Little Italy came into being, made up largely of immigrants from Brigantello.

The period of adjustment to the new environment was difficult, but the people prevailed, thanks to the most conspicuous virtue of our immigrant race, the intense love of work; and as a result of this same virtue the community arrived at a level of relative comfort that it could justifiably be proud of. There were shops everywhere, of every sort: banks, offices, and the indispensable Italian newspaper, whose first issue appeared under the enigmatic name of *The Sock of Italy* [*La Calzetta d'Italia*], a name probably inspired by the geographic configuration of the peninsula, which has the shape of a boot! It was founded by a certain Francesco Saverio Scoppetta, who ran a travel agency, what sort of travel we don't precisely know, although there was no shortage of people who claimed that it was a matter of travel from the pockets of others to his own. But these undoubtedly were nasty gossips; who insisted on saying that he was a sinister fellow, that he had a dubious past, and that years before he had had to flee his town and leave his native shores because he was sought by the authorities. In all ways, he was now one of the most prosperous men in the community, and one of the most feared *poletìscene*. Of medium height and rather stout, he had small lively eyes, a prominent red nose, and very thick whiskers, altogether giving him an aspect somewhere between sly and humorous. This was Scoppetta. He did everything and was everywhere. Scoppetta here, Scoppetta there; there was no wedding that he did not know about before the bride and groom themselves, no shooting that he did not know about before . . .those who were shot. Anything but a factotum of Rossinian fame! And his enemies had a big job if they wanted to sully his name! Scoppetta was highly conscious of the great "services" he had rendered to his countrymen and of the credit he had earned with the entire community. "I! I!" Scoppetta used to exclaim. "I have starded Italianism and illiteracy in this nationality!" and in fact, although he had not yet admitted it to anyone, he had for a long time secretly fostered the fond hope that one fine day the government of his country would recognize these vaunted "services" of his and would reward him for his labors. But reward in the form of honor was always delayed in coming, and Scoppetta was getting desperate. Finally he had yet another idea, the foundation of a society of which he would certainly be the president and which, in addition to the prestige he would gain with the consular authorities, would be a great help to him in his travel *besinisso*. To this end he called a meeting of all the leaders of the community, who approved the idea, and Scoppetta himself drew up the act of foundation, which was set forth by him in the following terms:

*"We, the souls who have crossed from the village of Brigantello, are here gathered all together, to found a union of friendship and brotherhood, which it with the help of God must be the best brotherhood of all brotherhoods. The name of this brotherhood, or rather of this reciprocal union, is called brotherhood, or rather "the Our Lady of Peace mutual aid society," which signifies that in this society there has to be peace, or else force will be used.*

*The reason for which this society is called Our Lady of Peace Society must be obvious even to the biggest imbecile, because even he knows very well all the miracles that this statue has performed here in our town, which even a deaf mute could see with his own hands. Now all of our fellow-citizens must recall that when the procession went by and Minguccio, the Blasphemer, refused to raise his hat before the statue, that is the image of the most blessed, the most blessed made him fall face down on the ground. And this was not the first or the last time that the most blessed displayed her power, because when Francisco the Scanzafatica robbed the church behind the archpriest Don Custanzo's garden, not only did Don Custanzo have him put in prison but one evening the most blessed gave him a stomach ache so terrible that everyone believed it was an evil colic. But then the colic was not so evil, because Dulurata, the wife of Francisco the Scanzafatica, who was very devoted to the saint, prayed so devoutly to the most blessed, that then the colic was cured right away. And then, who could ever forget the fear that descended upon everyone when Pascale the Neasante stole the goat belonging to Zi Raffaele, the sacristan of Our Lady. Lightning, thunder, storms . . . we thought it was the end of the world! Then finally the besinisso became clear; and when we caught him, we said, Hey, you rascal, either bring out the goat or we draw blood! And do you believe what he said? You bet! He began to make the sign of the cross and he cursed and swore that he didn't know anything about it. Then finally we heard the bleating of a goat in the bedroom where the big rascal had hidden it. So then we took the goat and we brought both beasts to Zi Raffaele. The storm had already died down. When we arrived at Zi Raffaele's, the goat was content to find herself liberated, and she started licking the hand of her "boss"; and since Zi Raffaele was a man as good as gold and was thought highly of as holy, he forgave the offense that Pascale the Neasante had done him, but before forgiving him he slapped his face so hard that all the teeth fell out of his mouth!*

Signed: Francesco Saverio Scoppetta."

THE SCOPPETTA FAMILY

The *bossa*, that is the wife of Francesco Saverio Scoppetta, was called Addolorata in the village, but now everyone was supposed to call her Dorì, because according to her that was how you said Addolorata in "mericano." Similarly, her oldest daughter had been given the name Maria Grazia, but she was called Cresì and was in love with a Mike Morfi (Murphy), who in spite of his name was not Irish but Italian, having been christened Rocco Trippabella. Scoppetta's oldest son had been baptized with the name Giovannangelo, but now everyone had to call him Sciorì, because, according to Scoppetta and his wife Dorì, that was how you said Giovannangelo in "mericano."

Next to Sciorì and Cresì come Mattì, Serì, and Notti: which names have nothing to do with the "Dance of the Hours" of the "Gioconda" or with the divisions of the day, morning, evening, and night; they are simply the nicknames of Matteo, Sara, and Giovannotta. The same observation must be made with regard to Melì, Perì, Peschì, and Nucì. They have nothing to do with apples, pears, peaches, and nuts; they are nicknames for Carmela, Pierino, Pasquale, and Annuccia. Then came Canì, Gattì, Urzì, and Leonì, and again we beg the reader not to think that we wish to describe a zoo, for here again we have simply nicknames for Arcangelo, Caterina, Orsolina, and Leone. Among these, Canì and Gattì were never to be seen; probably because dogs and cats never do get along. Then, the Scoppetta spouses did not wish to neglect the patriotic side, and so, finally, the youngest, who received all the caresses and all the spoiling, had been given the glorious name of Garibaldi; only now he wasn't called Garibaldi but Gerrì, because according to Mr. Morfi that was how you said Garibaldi in "mericano." Scoppetta's offspring therefore included the following: Sciorì, Cresì, Mattì, Serì, Nottì, Melì, Perì, Peschì, Nucì, Canì, Gattì, Urzì, Leonì, and Gerrì, that is, Garibaldi. The other ten were dead. Sometimes Ursì would hit Canì, Leonì would punch Gattì, and in the blink of an eye what had begun as merely a personal fight degenerated into a frightful free-for-all, from which more than a few emerged with bleeding heads or scratched faces. So that if someone asked Scoppetta how many children he had, he might very well answer, "Twenty: ten dead and ten wounded!" Otherwise peace reigned in the Scoppetta family, for the father commanded with an iron hand: only, no one obeyed him. In effect, they were all in charge there, but the one who was most in charge was Mr. Morfì, Cresì's fiancé.

Sciorì was never at home. Besides, he was very well instructed "in mericano!" Imagine! He knew all the new dances, he knew how to play poker, and he knew how to *sciutticreppo,* that is shoot craps. As for eating, he didn't eat much; but when it came to drinking, it was a known fact that Sciorì almost never drank water. "Uh, never!" said Scoppetta's wife, boasting to her friend Marianna. "My Sciorì drinks *visco* just like Mr. Morfì. Now I give him a bottle and right away he looks for 'nother." And then Sciorì knew how to *faite:* for that reason everyone called him Sciorì the Faitatore, the Fighter. Sometimes even Scoppetta got a punch in the nose, but instead of resenting it he delighted in the great erudition of his son!

## THE ELECTIONS

Great doings, unusual activity in the neighborhood of Brigantello! Let us explain: it is the day, or, to be more precise, the evening, of the election of the officials who will rule the future destiny of the Society of Our Lady of Peace. Many are the candidates for the various posts, but the one who campaigned hardest for the presidency is Francesco Saverio Scoppetta; his adversary, or, as Scoppetta says in his jargon, *my anniversary,* is Angelantonio Squaglianzogna, president of the Brigantello Billone Sucièsceno (Building and Loan Association).

The electoral campaign was fairly peaceful, probably in homage to the patron saint. Scoppetta and Squaglianzogna exchanged some . . . compliments, it's true; but for the most part these were inoffensive words and phrases, like: scoundrel, bastard, thief, murderer, wretch, loser, son of a bitch, pig, dummy, cheat, boot licker, illiterate, scab, monkey face, bloodsucker, swindler, stinker, ass, *cruk, bomma,* etc. On the other hand, nothing happened either to upset or to excite the minds of the electorate. It's true that some supporters of Squaglianzogna stabbed five citizens of the opposite party ten times, but this happened because a week earlier Scoppetta had set off a bomb in front of Squaglianzogna's house. But, all in all, everything is quiet everywhere.

Of the two candidates, the more bellicose, the one who ran a campaign that could be called a campaign, was Scoppetta. What good humor! What friendliness toward all! "Gud mornio, Gimì . . . Auai, Gian . . . Allò, Nick, etc., etc."; and if Scoppetta met some friends in a *storo di grosseria,* he immediately treated everyone: cigars, cigarettes, *situata, aise scrima, cenciarella,* etc., etc. But since he was a big *poletìsceno* and had big thoughts in his head, he always forgot to pay, and the one who usually had to fork out for the *tritto* was almost always one of his friends.

And then there was the bossa, that is, Dorì, who helped her husband in his campaign. Because she was very eager to be the presidentessa. And how! Now all the villagers whom she usually despised because they were too boorish and "dorì," had all become her dear friends. And up to a certain point Mrs. Dorì was forced to adopt this tactic, in order to combat the slanderous campaign that the ladies of the Squaglianzogna party were waging, who said all kinds of things about her: that she was a boor, that in Italy she had carried on with this fellow and that, and even that for a certain period she had left the village and had been away on who knew what business! But Dorì never gave up. In fact on one occasion she came out with this observation, or confession:

*"Hey, these four nasty old gossips had better not talk, because they're not even fit to hang on my dress; and they'd better stop throwing in my face the fact of when I left the village, because I was in those places, yes I was, but I am treated with honor and respect!"*

On the eve of the election, Scoppetta received an anonymous letter written in these terms:

*"Dear dirty rotten imbecile,*
*We know very well that you are never ashamed of anything, but now it is clear as day that you are a great big bum. Now you want to be the president of the society. Oh yeah, oh yeah. And don't worry, it's enough that the members see this monkey face of yours, and they'll all vote for you. Why don't you look in the mirror? See how suitable you are to be the president. Yes, you're right, because even in Italy you were the president when you looked at the sheep and the pigs like you, if I may. And then, everyone knows that you were always honest. Oh yes! Especially the paesane who know you best, and know that in Italy you spent more years in jail than at liberty. Your name was Scuppetta, and don't worry, there's plenty of people who will give you a shot in the heart. Ha! Ha! Ha! How many laughs we'd have.*
*I sign and am,*
*Your affect. enemy, Sombarì."*

Imagine Scoppetta's fury on receiving this missive. Oh how he would have liked to get his hands on the person who had sent it! But . . . go fish for him! Among all the voters he'd have a fine time finding the criminal. So he had to resign himself to venting his anger in threats, curses, and denunciations hurled at Squaglianzogna and his followers, without, however, being able to strike at any of them as he would have liked.

On the eve of the election, there was a party meeting at Scoppetta's house. Still roaring with anger about the above-mentioned missive, Scoppetta gave a formidable speech, of which we report the more salient points:

*"Villagers, friends, and compatriots: a short time ago I received an out-rageous letter, the likes of which I believe no fellow before me ever received. And therefore you must excuse me if I am still trembling with tremors and rage, because the letter was full of insults, to my dishonor and my indignity. Of course whoever did it did so with the intention of discouraging me. But if they expect me to be discouraged, they have added up the bill without consulting the tavernkeeper, as the great doctor Dante Mazzino said. Scoppetta has never been discouraged. In fact, he has always been respected, either with the good or the bad, and as he has done for the future, so he will do for the past.*

*"Now it's up to you to defend the indignity and the insult to our race and our religion. If you are truly unworthy and illiterate persons, that is who understand the reason of the consequence wherein which, vote for me; if you are a bunch of ignorant boors who have never understood the science of illiteracy, then vote for Squaglianzogna, and you can all go to hell.*

*"The matter of the vote is very simple. But in all ways, since there are always persons who have never voted, maybe because of too much ignorance and sensibility, I will explain to you that four and four makes eight.*

*"You have to know that when you go there, they give every voter a ball. Now, you ask me, but what do we do with these balls? Well, I'm going to explain it. That one there, when you go to the urns, as soon as you go in the halla, the election, or voting, room, you see that in the middle there is a table where there are two boxes, one for me, the other for my enemy, that is my anniversary. Every boxa will be pierced on top with a narrow hole. Now, you want to know what these narrow holes are for. Wait, don't go too much in a hurry, because little by little I'm going to explain to you the whole bisinisso. He who goes slowly, goes far and arrives gently, as general Gilormo Capumarola said. You have to put the balls that you have in your hand into the narrow holes, and afterwards, the one who receives more yeses is the winner. And of course if someone is the winner, it means the other one has lost. I don't know if I'm giving you the idea. And this is all. Now it's up to you. If you want me to win, give me your balls; if not, give them to my anniversary Squaglianzogna.*

*"One thing I want to warn you about. You see these the friends of Squa-glianzogna may come here and make trobolo tomorrow night. I say nothing to you. I know they won't frighten you, because God protects innocence and dishonesty, as the ancients said. But it's better if you come armed."*

A deafening crash of applause crowned Scoppetta's powerful speech. The meeting broke up amid cries of jubilee and victory; and given the great number of participants and their feverish enthusiasm, one could be certain of the election of Scoppetta. In fact, when the election took place the following evening, the winners were the following:

President—Francesco Saverio Scoppetta
Vice-President—Arcangelo Pizzafritta
Secretary—Celestino Fasulo
Treasurer—Angelomaria Cetrulo

As soon as the election was over, Scoppetta sent off a telegram to a company to order the uniform of an army general!

---

*Il Presidente Scoppetta ovvero La Società della Madonna della Pace (dalla sua fondazione al suo scioglimento)* (Philadelphia: Artcraft Printing Company, 1927), 7–21.

## THE TALES OF AN N.Y.P.D. COP

Halfway between the genres of the underground urban *misteri* and the new hardboiled novel, between autobiography and spy story, *You Gotta Be Rough*—published in English—is loud, fast, and rambunctious, just the book one might expect from the years of Scarface and Little Caesar. But in fact it is all real, taken down, and embellished, by a professional writer. Michael Fiaschetti revels in his own toughness, intelligence, and kind heart; but over all he enjoys spinning a yarn. There's a directness here that is irresistibly New York, with its braggadocio: a guarantee of a kind of honesty, free of the endless mannerisms of the later "goodfellas." This same story had appeared in Italian, a year earlier, serialized in the columns of the *Corriere d'America*.

### You Gotta Be Rough

CHAPTER V
*WHEN YOUR SWEETIE SQUEALS ON YOU, INCLUDING THE BREAKING DOWN OF THE BIG GIRL AND THE TALE OF THE BLOODY BARBER*

Her brother was wanted. A stiletto party, and he had got in some fancy surgery. I strolled up to her flat in a tenement to inquire for him. You could tell that she spotted me right off for a dick. She was a young Sicilian woman, with gaunt, handsome features and big, burning eyes. Half a dozen children hung around her skirts.

"Good-morning, signora," said I, walking in. "I want to find your brother. Where is he?"

"I don't know."

"Is he in town?"

"I don't know."

"You are married, aren't you, signora?"

"I don't know."

"These children, are they yours?"

"I don't know."

"My God, woman," I began to get mad. "What do you know?"

She raised one hand with a melodramatic gesture worthy of a great actress.

"Listen, Signor Policeman, I know that in the morning the sun rises and in the evening it grows dark. That I know and nothing more."

"*Managia i piscetti!*" I said. "So long." I was satisfied. I knew that all the machinery of the New York Police Department could not get anything out of that lady. And I'm telling about it now to go on record with a summons and complaint of how hard it is to drag a squeal out of a woman.

Yes, I have heard all about how women talk a lot—they tell you everything but what you want to know. The girls ought to be the best of stool pigeons, as sometimes they are—but not often. Men spill everything to women, and crooks open up to their broads as no third degree or dusting off in the back room of a station house can make them. But try to get a cutie to come clean. It can be done sometimes, but it takes a special bag of tricks.

It's only natural. The sweet things know perfectly well that the way to ask a question of a lady is to take off your hat and be polite. The third degree is something less than second where a woman is concerned. And then you can seldom get anything on a moll. She may be in the thick of a crooked mob, but it's only once in a while that you can rake up evidence against her that will make a jury say, "Guilty." If you can't do anything to them, how can you make them talk? Still there are times—and that reminds me of one of the flashiest blondes you ever saw.

She was a presiding genius of swell parties—that was her racket. She had a place up near Broadway in the Forties, something like a restaurant—if it hadn't been before Prohibition it would have been a speakeasy. Anyway, it was slick and full of gold trimmings. The Big Girl knew rich men and beautiful dolls and was the fixer and arranger for clubby little entertainments, where laughter and romance made happy hours. Of course, a bank roll might be missing before the night was over, and a badger game might come off once in a while. She was a stately, golden-haired creature who dressed like a picture in a fashion ad and had the manner of a duchess. And really, in spite of pocket-picking and badger games, she thought herself something of a fine lady and managed now and then to crash into gilt-edged circles.

She knew a lot. I can't say how she was fixed with book learning, but she was wise to a library-ful of what was going on in her own neighbourhood. She was hooked up with a mob that did strong-arm work for her, and her boy friend was a gopher. She may not have been any college professor or literary critic, but she was educated in what was doing.

A gangster was knocked off, and I knew the Big Girl would have the facts right at her finger ends. And that's how pretty soon a big bull happened to murmur into a pink, delicately formed ear:

"Come clean, Big Girl, or I'll have your joint closed up."

She laughed in my face.

"Be yourself, Fiaschetti," she gurgled. And for the present that was all.

I could have had her place closed up, but I wanted a squeal. Something dramatic was needed, a bit of strategy and staging. Nothing like something theatrical, with plenty of black and white, to impress the feminine intuition.

I lined up a friend of mine and got him entrance into the Big Girl's Pale of Shakedown, not a detective, for that might compel me to send the Big Girl away, which I didn't want to do. She had the makings of too good a stool pigeon to be shut in by any prison bars. I gave my confederate seventy-five dollars, and he was to play drunk and flash the roll in such a way that it would be taken, with the Big Girl right in the middle of things.

The plan worked beautifully. Such a sucker that guy seemed. The Big Girl herself grabbed the roll. And that's how it happened that a dreadful dick spoke harshly to a beautiful baby.

"It's six months on the Island for you, Big Girl."

Such a swell dame doing a bit on the low-down Island!

She thought it over and then snapped back like a sportsman who says, "You win, old chap."

"All right, Fiaschetti, what do you want?" I really think she would have stood for being put out of business half a dozen times rather than squeal—but not the Island.

First I took back the seventy-five, and then came around to the murder. She spoke her piece all right, and later on a gangster went to prison.

One good squeal deserves another, and the Big Girl could consider herself signed up as a regular source of information. She turned out to be one of the best stool pigeons I ever had. She tipped me off to various rackets, silk robberies mostly, and the tips were so full and complete that it made detective work a pleasure.

She would tell me who the crooks were and what fence had received the stolen goods. All I had to do was to grab the boys and tell them the fence had squealed, and then grab the fence and tell him the boys had squealed. There were confessions galore.

One case, though, was not so easy. I got two tough mugs. We sweated them properly but could not make them come through. I ducked away just before they were locked up for the night and hid in a cell next to their two cells. They thought the cell where I lay was empty.

I waited there for eight hours. They talked from one cell to another, but warily kept to subjects that didn't mean anything, family matters and such. Finally, though, one couldn't help calling out to the other: "Listen, all we have to do is keep our mouths shut. We did that job right, and everything's covered. Don't let that big wop scare you."

"No," responded the other. "We made a clean getaway, and the wop hasn't got a thing on us."

That was all, but it was enough.

"Haven't got a thing on you?" I roared suddenly.

In a minute I was asking them a few questions again. They were so startled they weakened and came through.

The Big Girl is still going strong—in the bootlegging racket now. She is more splendidly gowned and carries herself with a more stately dignity than ever. The Island for her? No wonder she emitted various and sundry squeals in her well-modulated voice.

But, on the other hand, give me the old Green-eyed Monster. That's the animal, insect, or fish that draws the information from the fair. Hell hath no fury—well, it hasn't the fury, nor does it turn stool pigeon so enthusiastically, as a woman scorned.

I can still see the jealous rage in those black eyes. She was slender and young, not more than nineteen. She walked into the office of the Italian Squad at Police Headquarters, timid and hesitant. Timidity and hesitancy gave place to anger and a flood of words the moment she got going on her story.

"I did everything for him," she raged across my desk, "and now he has left me for that other creature."

Her name was Carmela Pino, and she lived in Brooklyn. She fell in love with a handsome barber and soon afterward discovered that he was a Black Hander of purest ray serene, member of a savage Camorrist gang. He was, in fact, Bartolo Fontana, who later on was to be blazoned in the newspapers as "The Bloody Barber of Kenmare Street." Carmela was startled to learn this, but, if love is capable of making the world go around, it can make a woman forgive her lover for being an assassin. Carmela clung all the more loyally to her Black Handing barber. Now, though, he had given her the air for another dame. And love will have to make a number of worlds go round before it will persuade a woman to forgive that.

"I want to get even with him," the girl screamed, clutching the edge of my desk with her finger nails. "I want to see him punished for what he has done."

I always liked to oblige a lady, especially in circumstances like that. I inquired what the worthy beard scraper had done.

"You know of Camillo Caiozzo who was found in the river in New Jersey?" she said in a low voice. "It was Bartolo who killed him."

The murder she mentioned was fresh indeed in my mind. A man's body was fished out of the Shrewsbury River near Red Bank, New Jersey. The back was riddled with the charge of a shotgun. We were able to identify the dead man after a lot of trouble as Camillo Caiozzo, an obscure labourer. That was as far as we got. There was no clue to the murderer. It was a baffling and disappointing case. And now the entrance of the mortally jealous Carmela on the scene was an unexpected stroke of luck—the break.

"It is strange." She continued her story in a tone of terror and mystery: "I don't know why he did it. They were good friends, like brothers. They had been friends since they were boys in Sicily. And Bartolo killed him."

"Perhaps they had a quarrel," I suggested.

"I don't think so," she mused with a puzzled expression, and could afford no further enlightenment.

I sent her back to hang out with the gang as much as she could and report to me what she could learn.

That's how the tip came through. All that remained was to build up a case. Put it this way: You get a bit of information, and then you grab the suspect and break him down. That is how detective work is done—a general formula. It's liable to a lot of variations. You ring many a change on it. Sometimes there's a chance to pull a Sherlock Holmes, with clues, deductions, and the cigar ashes.

Bartolo Fontana, member of a gang of Black Handers, had murdered his best friend. I could make a stab at the explanation. It is common in criminal gangs for a member to be nominated to do a killing, and it has been heard of more than once that a man has been compelled to knock off a friend against whom he had nothing and whom he cherished affectionately. That's a situation for you. It's likely to be charged with emotional explosive.

It happened that I knew the barber and his Brooklyn shop—it was on Kenmare Street. As the head of the Italian Squad, I was acquainted with most Italians engaged in business around New York. I didn't dream of getting rough with Bartolo. He was a swarthy, grim fellow, the kind you can't bulldoze into talking. I had another line of attack. You've got to use psychology in this detective business. Psychology will catch more crooks than a mile of rubber hose. Rubber hose, you know, has at times raised welts and unlocked jaws.

Bartolo was just getting ready to close up. I sauntered in. We exchanged greetings—he with a rather startled "Hello, Mike"—and I sat down and lighted a cigar. No, I didn't want a shave, I said. I was afraid he might lose his poise and cut my throat. I started to talk, asked how business was and about the health of his family, and whether he had heard from Italy lately, and so on. He gave these pleasant inquiries pleasant answers. A crook is usually as polite as a policeman will let him be. But I could see that Bartolo was puzzled. I was not a comfortable kind of guest. What did I want? What was it all about?

"Eh, Bartolo," I exclaimed, after I had given him time to grow thoroughly perplexed, "I am tired— been working hard. I need a little relaxation. Come on and let's have dinner together."

He glanced at me, more puzzled than ever, and quickly made an excuse. I wouldn't take it, and said, friendly like, "Aw, come on, Bartolo." He didn't want me within miles of him, but it is hard for a crook to refuse a policeman.

I treated him to an excellent dinner, with good wine—not too much wine, because I didn't want him to suspect that I was trying to get him drunk and make him talk, which I wasn't. Afterward I proposed that we take in a show. He didn't want to go, but again dared not refuse—I was such a persistent pal.

After the theatre I said it was late and the trip home a nuisance and took him to the hotel for the night.

The next day I kept him with me, and the day after that. It was the same racket, everything very chummy and a hot time—big eats, a card game now and then, and theatres, and at night we stayed at the hotel. In bed I lay with my gun in my hand, keeping a half-open eye on the barber, and didn't sleep a wink. I was afraid he might kill me. Never once did I make a break about any such unpleasant thing as Black Hand, best friend, Shrewsbury River, or murder. From the way I acted we were just a couple of Boy Scouts out for a little fun.

It got Bartolo almost nutty. He couldn't understand. He wondered and tried to figure it out. His perplexity tortured him. This game I was playing with him was like some ghastly enigma. It was a thing to break any man's nerve, and Bartolo was the brooding kind. His hands kept moving uneasily, his eyes grew haggard, and he couldn't sleep at night. Sooner or later there was going to be an emotional upheaval— that was what I wanted and had planned for. It came at the breaking of dawn on the third night, and in a stranger, moodier way than I could have dreamed.

He tossed in bed from one side to the other, then got up and wandered around the room. He went to the window and stood looking out, silhouetted against the gray light. After a while his arms went up in a gesture of utter despair.

"My God, my God!" I heard him exclaim in his native dialect. "He was my friend, a brother, and I killed him. But you know, my good God, I didn't want to do it. I had to do it. They made me kill him."

He went prowling around the room again, like a caged animal.

"I've got your number, boy," I said to myself. I stirred, as if awakening, asked Bartolo why he was up so early, received a muttered reply, switched on the light, and walked over to him.

"I've been taking you around for three days, Bartolo," I started in on him. "Do you want me to tell you why?"

That was what he wanted to know above all things. He stood there in his underclothes, glaring at me, as I went on with a dose of hot shot.

"You know what has been going on, and they know all about it at headquarters. They know all about how you killed Camillo Caiozzo and threw his body in the river."

I gave him a long drink of that particular medicine. Carmela, whose jealousy was holding out nobly, had sent me messages during the past three days, nothing important, but the kind of detail that makes a convincing narrative. I shot everything at Bartolo to deepen his impression that all was known and all was lost.

That line of argument is always good, although it is not likely to work with a staunch Black Hander, whose tradition it is to die without squealing. And I had a still better line with Bartolo, nerve-racked, half crazy, and tortured with brooding over what he had done.

"I should have arrested you, Bartolo," I said, "but I didn't want to. I don't want to see you go to the chair when you are not to blame. You didn't want to kill Camillo Caiozzo. He was your best friend. They made you do it, and it was a dirty thing for them to do. You were always white with them, and they handed you a rotten deal like that. They are to blame, and I want to get them. I want to get them for having made you kill your friend."

Bartolo muttered and cursed, and I kept whipping up his rage against the gang. Of course, I didn't neglect the soothing little argument that he would go to the chair if he shielded them, while if he came clean he was in no danger of burning for what was really their crime—no promise, just a hint. And by the time the sun had fairly risen he had spilled everything and was lined up as a witness for the prosecution.

The gang, it turned out, was one of the worst Camorrist organizations on record. It had ramifications throughout the United States and was responsible for a score of murders. The killing of Camillo Caiozzo had been one of its characteristic acts, a barbarous episode fit for another and utterly barbarous era.

A meeting of evil-faced men in a smoky room, and Bartolo Fontana is there.

"Eh, Bartolo, you know Camillo Caiozzo, don't you?"

"Know him? We were boys together in Italy. Our fathers were friends. He is like a brother."

"Very good, you must kill him."

"Why?"

"Back in Italy his uncle killed the brother of one of our members. We execute the law of the vendetta for our members. You are his friend—it will be easiest for you to kill him."

Bartolo is half crazy over what he has to do—but he has to do it.

We rounded up the whole mob, and the case of "The Bloody Barber of Kenmare Street" was a sensation of the day. It really marked one of the important stages in the breaking up of the Black Hand in New York. The electric chair had its bit to do with several victims. Bartolo Fontana got a heavy prison sentence. And as for Carmela, she disappeared from sight shortly afterward. I happen to know that she married a decent fellow, a workingman, and they cleared out to distant parts to get far away from the criminal scene in which she had been thrown.

That case got me a good deal of credit, and you couldn't blame me for giving the Green-eyed Monster three cheers. It certainly took an awful bite out of the Black Hand. It wasn't the first time and won't be the last a jealous woman turns stool pigeon. But sometimes you have to woo the Monster, coax it along. Sometimes you can tip a moll off to the fact that her man loves another. Or you can tell her that, even if her man is as faithful as a husband locked in a cage. You can play on her feelings like a malicious neighbourhood gossip, and it helps to uphold the majesty of the law. And that's one way the detective gets his man that you won't find in any of the yarns about Sherlock Holmes and the other Great Detectives.

Like Frankie and Johnny, they were lovers. And a handsome couple they made. Bill was tall and athletic and as slick a dresser as you will find on Broadway, and Marjory was an image of brunette pertness and fire. They billed and cooed the way you see in the movies. The star of love was superbly in the ascendant in their lives. It is true that he beat her once in a while, but it was all jake with her. I suppose the thing to have done was a "bless you, my children" act, but then the cops were never sentimental. And Bill was a stick-up man.

I was out to get him and his mob, and pretty soon I was giving advice to the lovelorn. Up to Marjory's place, and a few questions, which she didn't answer. I hadn't expected her to.

"You're a simp moll," I said. "You're getting yourself into trouble by protecting him and he's double-crossing you. He'll be giving you the air pretty soon. He's got another jane, and he's nuts about her."

"You're a liar," she came back at me, ready to claw my eyes out. "Him play me crooked? It ain't so."

It is, it ain't, it is, it ain't—that's the way it went more or less for a couple of minutes. She didn't weaken.

"Bill's true blue, and I'll trust him to the limit." She said this with that utter and unswerving trust which you find only in a woman. It was sour music in my ears—still, the more fervently they believe the sorer they get when they are shown.

"You're a sucker and a dumb-bell," I told her. "What would you say if I showed you the dame, and him with her, and all lovey-dovey?"

"All right, you show me," she replied scornfully.

I told her to wait and say nothing for a couple of days and I'd show her.

For all I knew, her man Bill was true love and faithful devotion itself, but, after all, he was only human, and there wasn't any harm trying.

I knew a girl about as pretty as they come. She was keeping out of the way of a rough and exceedingly angry husband. She had left him and was living with the other chap. Anybody situated like that seeks to oblige, especially if you hint you might possibly say something to the husband. I told her what I wanted, and she said, "All right."

"There's a guy," I said; "he hangs out at a speakeasy. You go there and give him the glad eye and get him to shine up to you. All you have to do is to talk him into taking you to dinner or the theatre and tip me off to it. You won't have to see him again." She was rather pleased,

I think, with the conniving assignment, went about it enthusiastically, and made a good job of it. If she had failed I would have gone right on and lined up other beauties. One finally was bound to succeed in catching the fish. After all, he was only human.

Taxicab waiting in front of a doggy cabaret. In it the agitated Marjory and I. She became almost jubilant as time went by and they did not appear. Then they did appear. The girl had the man by the hand. She raised her lips, and he kissed her. I had told her to put on a love scene as they came out, and she rose to the occasion.

"Go ahead, driver," I called to the chauffeur. I didn't want a scene, didn't want Bill to have any suspicions of what was going on. The girl beside me was raging with hysterical sobs.

An axiom—get them to squeal before they go back home, else they'll have a row with the guy and make up. I got everything Marjory knew, riding her in the taxi while she exhausted her jealous fury. Then I sent her back to Bill to find out some more. Once they've squealed they're caught, definitely committed, and will go through with the job.

Arrests followed in the regular course of things, and when the boys were safely in jail I think Marjory was relieved. A moll sometimes is when circumstances drag her from her criminal associations. I never told her of the game for which she had fallen.

*You Gotta Be Rough: The Adventures of Detective Fiaschetti of the Italian Squad as told to Prosper Buranelli by Michael Fiaschetti* (Garden City, N.Y.: Doubleday, Doran & Company, 1930), 65–80.

## NON-ADJUSTMENT:
## THE "FARAWAY PEOPLE" OF CORRADO ALTAVILLA

The "faraway people" of Corrado Altavilla are a fitting image of the demise of Italian-speaking Little Italy. As this grim, well-crafted novel unfolds, each and every instance of contact with the various aspects of American life drags the four main characters, parents and children, closer to tragic self-knowledge. Father and son in particular are caught between, on the one hand, the glitter and the fascination of a completely different way of life and, on the other, an anxious drive to deny their past and their former selves. This is clearly an underlying element even in the otherwise stereotypical experience in the Chinese opium den downtown. For once, the oversimplistic representation of racial differences appears instrumental to a better understanding of the character: chronically undecided, drifting, tormented, and, with a little help, growing detached and "faraway."

**Faraway People**

John was so intensely absorbed by this vision he didn't realize that the
Chinese man sliding slowly along the bench had come close enough
to graze his elbow.

Turning abruptly, he met the oblique gaze of those slanted eyes.
The Chinese smiled at him and asked for a match. How old he was it
was difficult to say, perhaps thirty, perhaps sixty. What he did was easy
to imagine, since all the refuse of the city flows to the Bowery. And in
fact a moment later he leaned over and said in a low voice: "I've never
seen you around here." Then he added: "Would you like to have an
hour of bliss?"

He turned to examine the effect of that proposal on John's face
and completed the sentence: "An hour when you can forget all your
troubles, here, in Chinatown, just a few steps away, with a pipeful of
opium."

John was struck by the words: "An hour when you can forget all
your troubles." He needed repose for both heart and mind.

He asked: "Is it far?"

The other got up, inviting him to follow, murmuring: "Here, just a
few steps."

Chinatown was in fact very close. The Chinese man went ahead.
John followed, a few steps behind him. They went along two or three
narrow, dirty streets with small shops on both sides, on whose windows incomprehensible hieroglyphics were painted. Two expensive
cars were sitting in front of an entranceway, the chauffeurs asleep at
their wheels. On the second floor people were dancing. A thin, cot-
tony music reached the street. John was tempted to enter that "chop
suey" joint, leaving his guide in the lurch. But just at that moment the
Chinese looked back, to make sure the client was still following. They
walked for a few more minutes, then the guide turned into a little
doorway and stopped. John entered after him. In single file they
climbed a wooden staircase that creaked under their weight. On the
second floor, at a prearranged rapping of knuckles on the door, a
woman appeared, with almond-shaped eyes and painted cheeks, and
wearing a blue dressing gown thickly embroidered in gold and tur-
quoise. They went into a tiny parlor, on whose walls hung worn, faded
carpets. The man who had brought John left right away, to go in
search of other clients, while the woman, dressed in the fashion of
her country, pointed to a low couch and sat down beside him crossing
her legs in the modern fashion. He noticed that she was wearing little
clogs on her bare feet, cut out at the front to reveal her red-painted
big toenail.

"Is this the first time you've come up here?" the woman asked, giving him a close look.

"It's the first time."

"Have you ever smoked opium?"

"Never," John answered, almost ashamed of having to admit it.

"Will you stay all night?"

"Two hours, no more than two hours."

She smiled and, standing up, led him through a long narrow hallway with a low ceiling, like a maze at an amusement park. Then they went into a vast room illuminated by a single lamp covered with a red and black shawl, whose long fringe grazed the floor. A sharp sweet smell struck him as he crossed the threshold. He remained standing there and after a few moments began to distinguish the outlines of things. There was no furniture along the walls; the floor was covered with carpets and piles of cushions. Three men crouched on the floor, holding in their mouths rubber straws that converged in a large vessel where tobacco and opium were burning. A white woman was lying in a corner. She was asleep and beside her on the floor was the pipe that had fallen out of her mouth.

The woman took him by the hand and drew him to a corner, inviting him to make himself comfortable on some cushions. Then she squatted down beside him and asked in a very low voice what time he wanted to be called.

"At midnight," John answered.

The woman got up and a few seconds later returned holding in the palm of her hands a small porcelain vase with a single straw attached to it. She set it on the floor and went off, with tiny, dancing steps, like a sparrow. The three men were silent. The white woman from time to time let out a weak sigh followed by a heavy breath.

John clenched the straw between his teeth and drew in a mouthful of smoke that tasted sweet. He took another puff, and each time a little cloud of smoke rose above the little vase, transparent as a veil. He stretched out with his head and his back on the cushions, and suddenly he saw Kitsy as he had never seen her before: she had pale skin and hair the color of beaten eggs. Then, slowly, her eyes changed their shape and became more and more slanted, like those of the woman who had led him to the room. He touched a hand to his face, moved it in front of his eyes and wiggled the fingers to convince himself that he was still awake and not dreaming. He couldn't understand how that woman could so quickly change color: with the hair, oh! with the hair it was easy, but how had she managed with the skin? She came closer, he felt her beside him, and even heard her voice. She pronounced strange words that he couldn't make out, she spoke in a sibilant language, all *sss* and *zzs*, that at times seemed a whistling, at times a buzzing resembling the language of quinine that fills the ears and pierces the eardrums.

Suddenly he had a sensation of lightness and he touched the cushions to be sure that he was not floating in the air like a balloon. The cushions were still under him but he seemed to have the insubstantial lightness of a feather, as if his body had dissolved. He felt suspended in a void and then fell with a jolt, making his heart race. Kitsy was again beside him. She was dressed in veils, veils so thin that she seemed to be wearing nothing. She turned slowly around him and he felt the coolness of the air stirred by her movement. Then he saw men running, running, and as they got close to him they grew bigger and bigger. They seemed an army of monstrous giants. Suddenly the first one fell to the ground, and the others fell on top of him, forming a heap, and then a black mountain of legs and arms waving in the air, a huge mountain whose weight he could feel pressing on his chest. He couldn't breathe; laboriously, he turned over. The straw fell out of his mouth.

When the woman woke him he felt as if he had slept for a hundred hours. His head was like a weight and he couldn't get his bearings. He rubbed his eyes, but still the room appeared completely strange. The woman helped him get up. He looked around. The three men were asleep. A couple of newcomers were squatting on the cushions. They were young, a man and a woman. She had taken off her dress and was wearing only a silk slip. He was without jacket or collar. Neither had shoes on. They held each other in an embrace as they smoked, without saying a word, as if they were waiting in anxious fear for the poison to take effect.

Groping his way along, and supporting himself against the walls of the narrow hallway, John followed the woman into the first room and gave her without a word the three dollars she asked for. Then he went slowly down the stairs trying to remember how he had gotten there, and when he was out in the deserted street he looked around to orient himself. It seemed to him that the vise in which his head was stuck was getting tighter and tighter. In his hand he was still holding the newspaper he had bought near the pool hall, and it was the newspaper that led him to remember in part what had happened that day.

---

*Gente lontana* (Milano: Medici Domus, 1938), 136–40.

# 2

## Stowaway on Board: Ezio Taddei

> Don Abbondio wonders: what merits did Carlo Tresca have?
> And he answers: none. And he concludes: therefore it is a
> question not of tragedy but of comedy, and the Carneadi have no
> merits.
>
> —Antonio Gramsci

By common consent, the war years mark a watershed in the history of the immigrant community. In spite of hesitations among the masses and the sometimes devious or simply opportunistic tactics of the political and union leaders of the community, the Americanization of the Italian Americans was consolidated. The stigma of "enemy alien" had to be concealed, one's loyalty to America proved; frequently, and sometimes of necessity, people took new names. In the newspapers and the theatrical farces of the period after the war (the latter less often performed in public and more and more widely broadcast by the local radio stations) there is no sense of the bustling activity of the years just passed but, rather, an almost sudden sensation of a survival, of a weird provincialism, of at times a petty disdain. This change of climate is clearly the result of a great historical upheaval that involves and overwhelms the communities, and, at the same time, acquires meaning and solidarity from individuals, from a multitude of individual revolutions in which personal identities are overturned.

This happens in literature as well, as the meteoric passage of the "difficult" and isolated militant and writer Ezio Taddei (Livorno 1895–Rome 1956) confirms. His life was singular and atypical, and yet it can be situated within that crisis, or confusion, that makes a rough line of demarcation in the social and cultural history of Little Italy.

### The Life and Works of an Unorthodox Individual

In attempting to understand Taddei's life and work, we are prompted to begin, not by chance, on Manhattan's lively, imposing Fifth Avenue. Here the Public Library preserves many of his publications: in

152

fact, it probably has altogether the largest archive of his works in existence. First of all, Taddei appears in the heterogeneous "Collection" deposited by the Italian American anarchists of *L'Adunata dei Refrattari*.[1] Second, his works are included in the United States history section, as documents on America in the forties and fifties. Finally, on the New York shelves there are some true rarities: volumes printed in Italian, by the Società Editrice Americana (S.E.A.) and by Edizioni in Esilio of New York, between 1941 and 1944, as well as English translations, which testify to a brief but significant success in East Coast publishing and liberal intellectual circles. Moreover, this material fragmentation of the works echoes the mobile, elusive features of the man: Taddei is a writer to unearth in the special collections rather than in general institutional catalogues.[2] Similar difficulties in uncovering the man are the result of the almost complete oblivion into which his name has fallen: there was a bare mention of the tenth anniversary of his death in 1967, in the old Chicago socialist journal, *La Parola del Popolo;* and, some years ago, there was a precious but fleeting mention by the great Italian historian of emigration, Emilio Franzina.[3] Imprisonment and exile seem to have been elevated from facts of his real life to emblematic figures of his (understandably meager) posthumous fortune.

But that location on Fifth Avenue, far from being simply a bibliographic reference point, also marks a bloody break that provokes what is perhaps the most decisive turn in Taddei's path: on the pavement of that very street, in fact, at the intersection with Fifteenth Street, Carlo Tresca was assassinated, on 11 January 1943. Tresca had been for forty years the charismatic spokesman of the radical left, the fluent and polemical editor of *Il Martello*, in whose editorial offices Taddei had been welcomed. Apart from the suspicions involving the editor himself, and the charges and counter-charges within the diverse and, to put it mildly, dynamic Italian American political, business, and gangster worlds,[4] what is important to note here is the leap that Taddei then made, with disconcerting rapidity, which led him to contribute just a few months later to *L'Unità del Popolo*, a New York paper tied to the Italian Communists. It was the prelude, following the liberation, to a long, stable relationship with *L'Unità*, in Rome, and then a definitive return to Italy a free man.

Fifth Avenue and the assassination of Tresca can, in short, function as a geographic, historical, and political marker, providing a chronology of the brief but intense success of Taddei as an independent writer and highlighting a trauma that we must keep in mind in order to explain the writer's progressively realist perspective. Taddei's life and work are closely intertwined, illuminating each other without being superimposed. This is an important reason for the discordant fascination he exercises and, at the same time, for his more ingenuous and ephemeral features. The autobiographical, memoirist formula emphasized in his books helps delineate the features of a writer-character, and we should keep in mind that it is in fact Taddei's writings that constitute the primary source of our knowledge of his life.[5]

But let us look briefly at the story. The first stop involves the sentence imposed on Taddei in February 1922, along with thirty-two other anarchists, by the Court of Assizes in Genoa "for having gathered together for the purpose of destroying buildings, private and public structures, by means of bombs and other explosive materials" (Bartolini). The facts (as well as preventive detention) went back to March of the preceding year, when, in the big cities of the north, a wave of disturbances had accompanied the hunger strike of Errico Malatesta in San Vittore, Milan. Ezio Bartolini, a member of the defense team, recalled Taddei as an "angelic bomb thrower": an irregular who, because of his shy demeanor and lack of support, ended up—between delays and imprisonments, between brief periods of release and commutation of the sentence to internment—living until 1938 under a regimen of limited, closely guarded freedom. But the young anarchist was already acquainted with the jails (military prison, to be exact) of his homeland: as a young veteran of the trenches in Friuli (with a bronze medal), with years of service on the front line, he had done a clumsy job of counterfeiting a leave. Before that, enlistment had put an end to a mixed-up, delinquent adolescence and youth. He fled Rome and his bourgeois family home at the age of thirteen, becoming a vagrant, acquainted with the world of *la leggera* (the Italian popular underworld), living by odd jobs and his wits, spending his first nights in jail, and briefly frequenting the proletariat and subproletariat milieus of central and northern Italy, from Terni to Milan and Livorno. The experience of war solidified his anti-hierarchical spirit and fostered a more urgent desire for justice, reinforced by his reading, which included, most significantly, the realist novels of the nineteenth century, particularly Russian. Anarchism, populism, and literature merged chaotically in the formation of the young Taddei; Bakunin, Malatesta, and Tolstoy are the names that recur as models for the fictional alter egos under cover of which Taddei evokes those years. It should be noted, however, that it is with the liberal government that he expresses dissatisfaction, and that it was the bourgeois government, not the regime of Mussolini, which punished his subversive activities; not until later, in prison, did he join the school of anti-Fascism, as through newly arriving fellow-prisoners he was able to observe the progressive closing off of every revolutionary prospect, along with the bitter and even violent divisions in the camp of the opposition.

More and more, meanwhile, prison (or prisons, rather, given the prisoner's many transfers) takes on the features of a parallel world, with its rituals and characters, its stories handed down from prisoner to prisoner, even its folklore. In prison, the young anarchist writes the words to a *Hymn for the Barricades*, which immediately becomes part of the clandestine tradition of anti-bourgeois and anti-Fascist protest. Jail is not, for Taddei, a passage, a punishment to be endured; rather, it coincides substantially with an entire historical period of nearly twenty years—that of the dictatorship, outside the walls, and of his own coming of age, in the cells and places of confinement. His first stories were written at Bernalda, in Basilicata, and they have a bland, school-like flavor.

In 1938, he made an adventurous flight into Switzerland, then France (where *Gli umiliati* [The Humble], a story that he took up again later, came out in the first issue of the Parisian anarchist journal *Il Pensiero*), and finally the United States, where he disembarked clandestinely in the port of New York, on the infamous docks near the bohemian neighborhood of Greenwich Village: fitting coordinates for the wandering and worn spirit of the exile (who would later get to know the mean neighborhoods of Harlem, Astoria, and the Lower East Side). His anarchist and anti-Fascist companions on the other side of the ocean had already, during the year 1938, been able to read his political pieces and stories in *L'Adunata dei Refrattari*. In the United States, Taddei immediately came out with an autobiography of the interminable years of imprisonment (*L'uomo che cammina* [The Man Who Walks]) and wrote his most convincing fiction, *Alberi e casolari* [Trees and Barns] and *Il pino e la rufola* [The Pine Tree and the Mole]. In confirmation of a period of happiness, the collection of stories *Parole collettive* (brought out in English as *Hard as Stone*, in a delightfully designed edition) and, almost simultaneously, valuable English translations appeared. But his time in New York was darkened, as noted above, by the shadow of Tresca's murder; and, while he attended to literature, he abruptly ended his more than twenty-year militancy as an isolated anarchist to join the Communist ranks (which, in his prison autobiography, he had been sharply critical of).

When he returned to Italy (September 1945), his inspiration continued. First, within a brief period in 1945 and 1946, a series of volumes that had been written or even published in the United States came out: *Le porte dell'inferno* [The Gates of Hell]; and the Italian editions of *Il pino e la rufola* and *Rotaia* [The Sowing of the Seed]. In the following years, from 1950–55, in spite of the gap in chronology, his output was constant, although the results appear in general to be repetitious and sometimes trite: the memoir *La fabbrica parla* [The Factory Speaks]; and harsh testimony on the criminality of capitalism in the United States, *Ho rinunciato alla libertà*[6] [I Renounced Freedom], and on its moral decadence, *C'è posta per voi, Mr. Brown!* [You've Got Mail, Mr. Brown!]. Taddei also worked on behalf of the party, composing articles and pamphlets that were often marked by a falsely ingenuous sectarianism; it was a new role for him, that of the simple-minded propagandist who puts his years of forced exile to use in the divisions of the Cold War. In the meantime, he made an attempt, worthy in its intentions, at least, at what we might call a national-popular eclecticism, with works that range from an apocrypha of the left (*Il quinto Vangelo* [The Fifth Gospel]) to a story of the Resistance (*"Potente"* ["Powerful"]) and a very short contemporary historical serial novel (*Michele Esposito*). This last constitutes the main event of a notable literary initiative that Taddei undertook, bringing out, from April to December of 1955, eight monthly issues (the last a double) of a journal of stories, *raccontanovelle*, which had a clear realist and didactic purpose but is nevertheless admirable for the gravity of the choices.[7] It was an operation that in terms of literary history would be called retrograde; for the writer, however, it represents the most important attempt—perhaps not very successful but undoubtedly generous—to give a non-partisan meaning to his own militancy. It was an attempt, that is, to confer a broad sweep and an authentic inspiration (both with the serial novel and with the various "pieces" from the anthology) on the populist realism that he had practiced for years. With his monthly, though it lasted only a couple of seasons, Taddei tried to assume a greater public role than had previously been possible, after agreeing to spread—at times with disconcerting partiality—the watchwords of the party. The following year (1956), he died, leaving various unpublished writings.[8]

## CONSTANT NARRATIVES

After his death, in the leaden climate of the Cold War (which the writer and journalist had in his way contributed to), Taddei was made, on the part of opposed alliances, a banner for humanity. The "case of Taddei" was that of a writer who is "with" the people even before he "speaks to" or "writes for" the people; yet one gathers in the praise of contemporaries a certain reserve, as if ultimately his art did not equal in dramatic engagement and intensity the quality of his character and the singularity of his destiny; one notices, that is, regret for a failed promise, in the words both of his editor Davide Lajolo and of his sympathetic biographer Domenico Javarone (whose book has an intelligent preface by Giancarlo Vigorelli), and in those of a group of admirers united around Longanesi (among them his friend Guglielmo Peirce, who commemorated him in *Il Borghese,* and the great Giancarlo Fusco, who made a vivid portrait of him). This sensation is, over the years, only reinforced, in fact intensified, yet does not keep one from wishing to understand in more detail the meaning, the values, and the contradictions of the work.

I will begin by singling out—among repetitions, actual superimpositions, variations on the theme—some large narrative blocks connected to little noted biographical matter. What is evident from the first volume (*L'uomo che cammina*)—disorganized and uneven, and yet with an almost raw power—is a strong desire to recount the sufferings of an unimportant man, led on and overwhelmed not so much by restlessness as by a simple wish for freedom and basic justice: an inner impulse that is enough to turn his youth upside down, sending him on the path of the vagrant. This story is, with greater speed and less effectiveness, taken up again ten years later, in *La fabbrica parla;* while the period that immediately followed, that of the Great War and the traumas linked to the return to civilian life, is amplified in *Rotaia,* a novel with more plots and more protagonists. In the unpredictable, corrupt climate of the postwar years, which *Rotaia* represents in an almost grotesque manner, the first-person narrator of the two autobiographical novels predictably follows the route taken by their real author: assassination attempts organized by the anarchists, arrest, the tomblike caesura of prison. A similar but more ambitious arc, with a portrait of an entire society (the Livorno of those years, in its various social strata, from marginalization to conformity), emerges in *Il pino e la rufola.* Rather than explain, Taddei—consistent with his personal history—foresees, anticipates, signals the approach of Fascism as the response that cuts off the freedom of both the individual (with a pitiless, repressive turn of the screw) and society as a whole. But it is to prison life—and justifiably—that Taddei devotes the most lucid, most meaningful pages of his oeuvre. And there are also sketches and glimpses of life in confinement.

A second large narrative block originates, just as clearly, in the desire to bear witness, from a critically informed point of view, to the fundamental errors and abuses of the American system. It is a critique of the deceptions and illusions whose main victims are immigrants and people of color; in control are judges, politicians, and gangsters, their activities so closely intertwined as to make invisible to the average man the network of collusion that is euphemistically baptized democracy. In the end, the leaders of the workers were themselves caught in that web, as were the more prominent representatives of the émigré communities; the system inevitably marginalizes or eliminates the just and the pure of heart: Tresca, or Daniel— the figure of the old Wobbly (the revolutionary union member)— who appears here and there. This painstaking, one-sided critique of the American system—not immune to the excesses of stereotypical anti-American rhetoric—is delivered in the pages of *Le porte dell'inferno, Ho rinunciato alla libertà, C'è posta per voi, Mr. Brown!*, in addition to some chapters of *La fabbrica parla* and pamphlets of the early fifties (catalyzed by the Rosenberg case).

As we can see, upon returning to Italy, Taddei, although he maintained his characteristically humble profile as an independent voice, became an intellectual who lived on the revenue from his writing, both journalistic and literary. The adventurer Taddei of those years, shabby, generous, watched by the American military authorities who had expelled him, survives in the pages of others, such as his biographer, Javarone, and the reporters Fusco and Peirce; in his own pages, on the other hand, integration into the republican postwar climate is recounted with less urgency. A crafty literature and the short works brimming with good feelings prevailed (*Il quinto Vangelo, "Potente," Michele Esposito*); the daily, anecdotal version of this fervor—repaid not with irony but with a certain amount of incredulous good-fellowship—consisted in the propaganda missions carried out for *l'Unità*, in the course of which, traveling from one end to the other of the peninsula, he had the chance to meet Communist leaders such as Ingrao, Amendola, and Togliatti (he recounts this in the vast container that is *La fabbrica parla*).

Evidently, the close connection between life and work cannot explain Taddei completely (as we will see, more freely inspired works are equally important); in fact, as his integration into the activities of the party guarantees stability and security, that connection loses its cogency.

## BETWEEN EXPRESSIVENESS AND CONFORMITY

In any case, the interest that an author like Taddei arouses does not lie only in the testimonial character of his writing: especially in the early books, along with the need to communicate, there is evidence of a search for a personal means of expression, for narrative formulations and stylistic innovations. In fact, the differences between the books published in New York during the war are so striking that it is tempting to call Taddei an experimental writer.

Autobiography and "engagement" are ultimately irrelevant in attempting to explain two novels like *Alberi e casolari* and *Il pino e la rufola,* happily saturated in their Tuscan locale—in their language, and in a sort of dark, popular ambience where fate takes the form of a mute violence. (The evocation of Pratesi and Tozzi is inevitable, even if difficult to support at the intertextual level.) In the first book, a silent drama of love, rivalry, and jealousy unfolds slowly in a small country town, where three men are competing for the beautiful Norma: the story is told with immediacy and starkness, and without explicit intrusions on the part of the narrator, who remains outside and almost impersonal, confining himself—and it is not a small thing—to observing, in short sections of hallucinatory intensity, the gestures of the characters and the signs of natural life. The environment is evoked not through descriptions but in instantaneous images that have a strong sensuous charge: the tension of the human plot spills over into the animal and vegetable world. Similarly, in the passages where, because of the characters' reticence, there is no direct discourse (although it is present elsewhere), some fragments of free indirect discourse lead the reader to a better understanding as the concluding catastrophe approaches (with the death of Norma and an innocent friend). With its tragic intensity, this short novel of exile represents one of the most successful, original results of Taddei's art. -

*Il pino e la rufola* also presents an interesting narrative solution, which is only in part a later version of *Alberi e casolari.* There is not, as in the earlier book, strong unity of action: the novel takes form gradually, following the intertwining of various plots. Each level presents a different milieu, with a correspondingly distinct style and point of view: in the foreground is the world of the petit bourgeois professionals of Livorno (in particular lawyers, from rivalries at work to adulterous relationships) and an infamous underworld, without any romantic attraction. More in the background are high society— which to satisfy its vices has recourse to the corrupt criminal element—and the healthy, pure, and idealistic sector of the people, embodied by the anarchists and, secondarily, the socialists (it is the turbulent period after the Great War). From time to time, short third-person paragraphs keep us informed on the political situation, following the slow kindling of Fascism, which takes in the barely motivated energies of both individuals and groups as they are introduced. Thus the novel follows, if not explicitly, a moralistic, teleological scheme, although it is a negative teleology, for it marks the progressive, violent affirmation of Fascism, against which personal reform and the rediscovery—outside corrupt Livorno, in the countryside of Lucania—of the solid old values of honesty, justice, and moderation count for little in the end. It is a social novel with a moral, disjointed, uncentered, and for that reason vague even in its ideological point of view. What is interesting is the broad sweep of Taddei's portrait, depicting, if in a fragmentary way, a community in a period of crisis and confusion, both moral and material. As a result, the language ranges from the crude vernacular of the lower classes, often indicated by quotation marks, to the more refined realist bourgeois style in which the story of the lawyer Michele Pellizzari is told, and the almost neutral and impersonal pages that function as historical connections. This diagrammatic character, at once historical and individual, decided the consensus on the book, both in the United States and in Italy: the novel won high appreciation among contemporaries. *Il pino e la rufola* is valuable in that, even though it is disorganized and somewhat mechanistic, it manages to present at once both the individual and the community during the crisis after the First World War, whereas in the autobiographical works the two remained divided, with the first clearly predominant, and could be put together only in the mind of a willing and eager reader.

It is a pattern analogous to that which Taddei traces from *L'uomo che cammina* to *La fabbrica parla,* passing through *Rotaia:* his own story as an emblem of change, of defeat, and of the end of an epoch, reflected—above all in the middle book—in the stories of so many other young war veterans, of every origin and orientation. This path can also be seen in the style and narrative method: the first volume displays tremendous spontaneity, characterized by a parataxis that is not only syntactical but almost axiological, and corresponds to memory that is fluid and linear, rather than hierarchical; in *Rotaia,* there is a complex juxtaposition of individual stories, and unrelated narrative sequences, which, continually interrupted and then taken up again, make one think of an ambitious but failed historical novel; in *La fabbrica parla,* a simpler division into short sections and a focus on the first-person narrator clarifies the individual segments but risks sinking the whole under the weight of an excessive consistency and self-referentiality. Later, in fact, this becomes a feature of Taddei's writing: the autobiographical formula gets progressively more rigid, a situation made worse by the insistence on being exemplary.

When it comes to (anti-) American subjects, however, whether in the form of testimony or of invention, Taddei displays little interest in stylistic methods. Anonymous evocations or revelations of a journalistic type alternate with "black" sketches on the ordinary horrors of American society. But the absence of a literary project is palpable beyond the polemic intention (which, moreover, is openly partisan).[9] The last phase of Taddei's activity is more interesting, making up for such dullness by proposing a realist poetics: without neglecting the importance of the "message," Taddei succeeds in producing apologias and narratives complete in themselves (*Il quinto Vangelo, "Potente," Michele Esposito*). It is a literature of "service," far from engagement and from the broad sweep evidenced in the past, but not, as had also been the case, pure propaganda.

## PRISON, POVERTY, AND CRITIQUE OF THE UNITED STATES

It is much more important to recognize the phases of Taddei's writing and their characteristics than to distinguish the few consistent themes. These, in fact, run in subtle fashion through the whole of the author's oeuvre, and could, if analyzed in isolation, so to speak, overload it with responsibility. Given that premise, the primary importance of the theme and topos of prison must be reaffirmed. Taddei does not fail to offer an interpretation of that reality, however allusive and never insisted on (the two central works, in this sense, are yet again *L'uomo che cammina* and *La fabbrica parla*): prison as the emblematic place of suffering, of isolation, of society's abuse of the individual; historically a microcosm in which Fascism performs without pretense its freedom-destroying work. Yet what might be called the ethnographic and topographic approach to the penal system is more emphatic and more deeply felt. The "bath," the big house, the pen (the use of synonyms is understandable) are concrete realities, depositories of stories that verge on a macabre folklore (in *L'uomo che cammina* the story of the assassination of Gaetano Bresci, the anarchist responsible, in 1900, for the murder of King Umberto I), places with specific rules and attributes that are learned through slow and agitated messages whispered from cell to cell, and where, above all, the prisoner, if he wants to survive, must recognize the inmates' differences, characteristics, needs. Every house of detention, every cell has its Lares, its physical and architectural features whose influence on the prisoner is definitive (there are memorable pages in *Fabbrica* devoted to the small gloomy windows at Marassi, in Genoa; to the sacred images at Ucciardone, in Palermo; and to the hard cells at Santo Stefano and Sassari). Whether the prisoner is in prison or in detention, vicarious versions of life filter through the interstices of segregation, keeping him watchful, a witness of camorra-like vendettas, of senseless divisions among political prisoners, of petty episodes of corruption, of small abuses and cruel summary executions (the so-called Sant'Antonio, the beating, often fatal, ordered at night by the warden). It is the mass of details, set forth naturally and meticulously, that makes this portrait convincing, and remarkable for its breadth, its spirit of observation, its equanimity.

A theme with a more uneven outline, open to multiple expressions, underlines Taddei's consistent attention to politics and society. It is the theme of poverty and equality, which in his characters—who are always just a step ahead of indigence—becomes an incentive to "understand the masses" (*Rotaia*, 158), to recognize the end of the "era of the artisan" and the start of the age of the factory (*La fabbrica parla*, 88). In even more explicit terms, this need to be "for" the people explains both his youthful anarchism (providing a justification for direct action, sabotage, violent demonstrations, in the name of adherence to the supposed vitality of the "masses") and his passage from individualism to the organized politics of the party (claiming that in the age of the factory "every worker, even the riveter, feels pride not in his own work but in the work performed collectively." [*La fabbrica parla*, 312]).

From the first book to the last, Taddei's attention to the concrete manifestations of poverty is unwavering; if it often has painfully personal causes (the breakup of the family, flight, abandonment, failure), it also always finds social expression, in vagrancy, in various forms of criminality, in the harsh life of the urban tenements, in the dark misery of the countryside. Given these premises, one understands how populism and pauperism are two temptations that run through all Taddei's work. This example, taken from the chapter *L'ultima cena* [The Last Supper], in *Il quinto Vangelo*, is typical:

> Now the apostles were silent, and Jesus spoke sadly:
> "The hours are counted out. The Priests, the Scribes, and the Pharisees have gathered to pronounce my sentence. So I will give you my last words. But in truth I have time enough to tell you that I leave to you the poor. And you, do not separate yourselves from them, for he who separates himself does so not only with his body. . . ."
> And Jesus fell silent, then he began again:
> "And do not separate yourselves from me, for the poor will not leave me by myself, and will go on, and will again find apostles." (*Il quinto Vangelo*, 77)

Therefore, to remain on the side of the disinherited not only is the spontaneous gesture of a writer without home or legitimacy but takes on the significance of a privilege, of moral salvation, and of complete historical and social consciousness. It is by identifying with them that the various narrators—transparent spokesmen for the author—can observe from a critical and unconventional point of view the great traumas of war and the Fascist dictatorship. Ultimately, without this closeness to the world and consciousness of the people the supporting structure of Taddei's art would fail, both in its narrative incidents and in its attitudes of thought. It is a peculiar form of "arte povera" because of its own radicality, rather than because of a convenient adherence to a poetics of realist reflection.

Not that Taddei was immune from a more purely instrumental use of his favorite themes. Consider his longstanding, pervasive focus on American society, explicated by means of a remarkable variety of stories, situations, particular events. If it is true that, on any random page, the hostility of the isolated, marginalized intellectual of the left appears, it is equally clear that Taddei lacks a firm set of values, an alternative frame of reference, since that insistent, multifarious condemnation cannot be transformed into a comprehensive critique of the system. In truth, he lacks an overall understanding of United States culture; it is replaced by a gallery of anecdotes, all or almost all in the category of power being concentrated in the hands of criminals (confirmation is paradoxically provided by the final pages of *Ho rinunciato alla libertà,* in which there is a brief, condensed history of the United States, centering on racism and the creeping, hidden influence of the Ku Klux Klan). One does not mean, obviously, to take issue with the individual charges (which are more than justified: recall at least the anti-Truman, anti-atomic campaign); rather, it is to signal the artistic limits and the ideological weakness of a content that is an end in itself, able to repeat and reproduce as if by parthenogenesis. The encounter and clash with American reality is resolved in an accumulation of more or less sincere and effective stories and sketches (a portrait of Italian American Fascist sympathizers, the funeral business, to mention just a couple), but the American theme remains a disjointed one; it is not expanded into a view of the whole, nor is there any narrative development. As testimony that is authoritative in its own way, it has a certain value within the varied but limited account undertaken in those years by the journalists of *l'Unità* in constructing a "countermyth" to the stars and stripes.[10]

A rereading of Taddei cannot ignore an evaluation of the individual works—especially since, if the author's name has been forgotten, some titles have by now fallen into the unenviable condition of collector's items. In spite of the family resemblance that unites the texts and the "cyclical" temptation, or, more simply, the pure repetitions, we should recognize the expressive personality of the more successful ones: the urgency and unmitigated power of *L'uomo che cammina*, with its autobiographical energy made more touching by the insertion of unexpected, almost gnomic reflections; the masterly climax, at once tragic and sentimental, of *Alberi e casolari*, a little gem of "provincial" literature; the dissonant harmony of *Il pino e la rufola*, which, with a mobile and pitiless gaze, follows, in each social class, the drift toward the suffocating resolution of the Fascist order. On a lower level are novels on a broader scale, ambitious in terms of overall design but not very convincing from a narrative point of view: the book on the outcome of the Great War, *Rotaia*, and the other long autobiographical tract, *La fabbrica parla*. Off to one side is the apocryphal exercise of *Il quinto Vangelo*, stylistically eccentric but fully in keeping with the deep roots of Taddei's "popular" diversity.

Each of these works brings a special note to the engaged realist context of the literature of the forties and fifties, which can be summarized, perhaps, as a sense of raw spontaneity. Taddei is not a "programmatic" writer whose stories come from on high. His populist realism can be supported, if necessary, by extemporaneous declarations of intention (rather than a real poetics) and does not retreat before the sirens of Manichaean didacticism, but it does not insist on constructing typical, formalized characters and situations, and so it reserves for itself a margin, an anti-dogmatic side. The confused, unresolved, or inconclusive scheme of the more extensive works indicates a structural limit, a narrative weakness, but also communicates a certain ingenuous belief in the relative and changeable value of "engagement." What is fragmentary, elliptical, and casual in his plots may remind us of the contemporaneous use of real-life stories on the part of the neorealist directors: employing figures viewed in the midst of other, minor ones, and not characterized with great psychological care, Taddei presents a slice of contemporary Italian history.

In part, as I have tried to emphasize, reading Taddei invites us to explain the origin of his choices, in a long past of isolation and a present as exile and outsider: the human experience is not simply one of the many facts of his literature but constitutes its very source. Further, it is possible to indicate a stylistic course, a formal search (certainly not of long duration and perhaps not completely clear to the author himself) that indicates, however, a willingness to experiment and a need to adapt language to the various objectives of expression. An analogous dynamic, which oscillates between originality and repetitiousness, can be seen in the use Taddei makes of his chosen themes.

Placed under a single spotlight, and put back into the context of the whole, the works of Taddei—successful or not—reemerge, with greater clarity, as the product of a recognizable personality, with its naïveté and its limitations but also with its direct, sometimes touching, truths.

※ ※

*Anthology*

## SCENES FROM THE INFERNO: EZIO TADDEI

To the anarchist exile Ezio Taddei, America is not a destination like any other. Fleeing from Fascism, and eighteen years of prison, he still views the big city of entry into the new world as a gateway to Hell. Indifference, rusting steel and decay, an unbearable din, and anonymity are only a few of the physical and spiritual wounds that scar his feverish alertness. A fellow traveller in the immigrants' world, he will soon add to the picture dire poverty and exploitation: briefly, a total lack of freedom. His writing, while obviously based on autobiographical experiences, is intended as a form of agit-prop addressed mainly to an audience in Italy. But there's something that risks going unnoticed: it is in this hell that Taddei starts his new life as a writer.

### The Gates of Hell

> *To the Italian immigrant in the land of America who,*
> *enduring danger and derision, built a nation*
> *that never became a homeland.*

*In Astoria there is a bridge that crosses the East River. It is built like a cage, with massive sheets of steel, and the trains pass through, and at night, at the top of the span, a small red light is lit.*

*People say that these are the gates of Hell.*

*Beyond the bridge is the city, with streets like grates, and an endless sky above.*

*The swallows do not come to nest on the roofs, and down below, in the two great Rivers, the water is full of dark streams that ripple, and lengthen, without ever breaking.*

NEW YORK

The *Normandie* was sailing at its regular speed and you could feel the slight trembling of the motion along the sides of the ship.

I was huddled in my hiding place, and when a crack of light came from the hole below, I saw the eyes of the three Jews who had escaped from Austria and were at the bottom, one beside the other, as if they were about to sink.

Under us was the first-class dining room, and we could hear the radio when it broadcast to the passengers the distance traveled and other shipboard news.

One day the radio broadcast the sound of bells, and my traveling companion said to me:

"Those are the bells of St. Patrick's."

"Are we close?"

"We arrive tomorrow."

Then the *Normandie* stopped, the people disembarked, went about their business, and no one knew any more about them, and when everything seemed to be forgotten it was our turn. The sailor came to get us one at a time.

"O.K., pay attention."

"We're there?"

"Yes. As soon as you're out turn to the left. . . . Walk naturally. No one will say a word to you. Go . . ."

The sailor stood there watching me.

As soon as I got to the end of the dock I found myself on one of those streets down there, and I would have liked to turn back to hear the sailor's voice again, but when I turned he had vanished.

The first day was like this, I remember it very well: I walked with my companion, who was my guide, and I asked him:

"Where are the skyscrapers?"

"You'll see them later."

At a certain point we went down to the underground train, which is called the subway, and right in the midst of all those people standing there, crushed together, I imagined I would be able to talk to someone. I touched the arm of one man and he seemed not to have felt it.

When the train stopped there were more waves of people ready to push their way on, because it was the time when work was over and they were all in a big hurry.

In front of me was a tall young woman who stared at me as if I weren't even there, and I couldn't decide if I should smile or not.

When we got to Union Square I saw the young woman get off. I, too, was getting off.

She walked away among all the other people. I saw her blond head go up the stairs. Everyone went up.

So finally I found myself in the open air.

What was my first impression?

What shall I tell you, maybe it was because evening had just begun, but on the spot I saw nothing but legs walking in light-brown stockings, and it seemed impossible that they wouldn't stumble.

They went into stores and vanished immediately.

All along the streets were office buildings with lighted windows, one beside the other. And farther up, you could see at the end of 16th and 17th Streets all those silent houses that looked like big asylums, with no hope.

Down, down the stairs that lead underground to the subway, people crowded in.

*Le porte dell'inferno* (Roma: Alcide Mengarelli, [1945]), 7–10.

## I Gave Up Freedom

Dear Sir,

Perhaps you no longer remember me, but I have always thought that I owed you an explanation of my behavior when I was called into the office of the New York immigration police.

Many years have passed, and I will try to remind you of my case, and also of myself, one of so many who passed through the glass door of your office, and sat down on the opposite side of that big desk, to answer the strange questions of your interrogation.

It was 1940, a June evening, and the person who arrested me was Agent Fink of the F.B.I.

From that moment I began to climb stairs, traverse corridors. I went before a judge who said to me:

"Did you know that you entered the United States illegally?"

The lawyer had told me to say no. To me it seemed strange, because there I was, but the lawyer convinced me, telling me that it was always done that way, and if I answered differently I would immediately be sentenced. So I answered:

"No, I didn't."

And I went out on bail of 500 dollars.

Then came other questioners, papers, bills, citations, and every so often I had to come to your office.

I was a poor fellow then, as I am now, and you, when I appeared before you, told me that I was expelled from the United States, and that I had to go within that day.

I said to you that there was a war, and that it was impossible. It went on like this, for quite a while, and we saw each other about every six months.

Something happened unexpectedly that, it seemed to me, had

nothing to do with your police department. Dial Press published my novel, translated by Putnam. It was mentioned in the papers with a certain persistence, the book was successful, and you called me into your office again.

I will not hide from you the fact that it was a big nuisance. In any case, I came to see you.

The woman who was there that day was pretty, your secretary. She was very pretty, and she looked at me. You, too, were very nice, as were the other people who were standing around.

My lawyer, however, had his usual preoccupied and worried look.

I will summarize here our conversation. You said to me that I was a writer and this gave you great pleasure.

"We're glad when people like you stay in the United States."

"But . . ." I wanted to answer.

"They will give you a preliminary visa. You will go to Canada. In a week you will be back legally, and after a year you will be able to be a naturalized American citizen."

The secretary smiled as if to congratulate me. I answered, in annoyance:

"But the war is over. I can return to Italy."

"No, perhaps you haven't understood."

And you started to explain again to me.

My lawyer was silent, as if drawn into his shell.

I insisted that I wanted to return to Italy, and I even told you the reasons.

"All right, you can go back to Italy."

"Thank you."

"But I can't understand your decision. It seems incredible! Think about it . . . You are giving up America! Giving up freedom . . . Millions of people would like to come to the United States . . ."

Finally you decided to make one last try: the test.

At that moment you seemed reassured. You said to me affably:

"Listen to me: in Italy, who was in charge before? Who was the boss, Mussolini or the people?"

"Mussolini," I said.

"Good."

There was a sigh, you looked satisfied, and the young woman smiled.

"Now, listen carefully. Here in America who is in charge: the government or the people?"

"The government."

"No! think about it . . ."

"But, I don't know. The government."

And for this reason I was declared anti-democratic and my expulsion was confirmed.

## AT THE NIGHT NURSERY

Meanwhile I had decided not to learn English. Then without realizing it I became more violent, and argumentative, so that my landlady—I have to say that I had found a place in one of those furnished rooms downtown—as I was saying, my landlady had to kick me out, and, not content with having made me a long speech, she began to complain on the stairs and I heard her say:

"Ghini."

"Ghini?" I repeated.

I threw at her all the dirty laundry that was piled in the corner of my room. Piece by piece I threw it at her, she was going down the stairs, and I kept going as long as I could, then I left.

Ah, how free I was that day!

I went in search of a friend of mine, an old Irish revolutionary. His name was Daniel.

I said to him:

"Daniel, I have no place to sleep."

He began to laugh.

"Where do you sleep?" I asked him.

"On the Bowery."

"Will you take me there?"

He laughed again.

"It's the night nursery."

"Fine. Tonight you come and get me."

"Where?"

"At the Life."

When it got to be late Daniel looked in at the windows of the cafeteria, I saw him and went out, and we walked along in silence. From time to time we'd see a woman on the street who was drunk.

One stopped us, and spoke some words that she struggled to pronounce, and then in irritation she went off, continuing to mutter her incomprehensible speech.

The Bowery has the deep darkness of mean streets. Only the bars were open, with their names illuminated in red over the doors, and through the windows you could see the usual customers around the bar, as if they had been locked up there. High up, the bottles stood against the mirrors; and then, after that sparkle of light, the street was deserted for a while, and the elevated train went by at regular intervals, making the only sound.

The drunks stood peeing next to the sidewalk.

Daniel said to me:

"We're here. Be careful that your shoes don't get stolen."

He looked at them.

"They're falling apart," I said.

"They'll take them anyway . . . Be careful while you sleep."

He went up a stairway. On the second floor a door. Daniel pushed it open.

Inside was a big room that must once have been a factory. Near the entrance a high desk, behind it an old man with a big book, writing down a name.

"Your name."

"John Smith."

The man continued to write as if it were habit.

"Your name?" he asked me.

Daniel answered for me:

"John Smith."

After he wrote the name he gestured to me with his free hand.

"Over there."

In the room was an old lamp whose illumination barely reached the back corners. There were seven or eight tables, on which men were sleeping. Others were lying on the floor, this way, that way, every which way. Some had brought newspapers and spread them out.

You could hear snores, and a few words, but everyone there was breathing painfully hard.

Daniel kept on: he walked over bodies, moved legs.

"Goddam!" someone said and went back to sleep.

Daniel said to me:

"You go there, I'm here."

Just then the door opened, another man came in, and I heard the name repeated:

"John Smith."

Afterward, everything seemed to be quiet again.

There was a smell of alcohol mixed with breath and every so often someone coughed.

At one point I saw a man get up, maybe he had to go to the toilet. He started walking around, stepping over others. Now he stood still, staring as if he had changed his mind. He was standing with one foot on one side, one on the other, and in the middle was a fellow sleeping on his stomach.

The man kept staring at the one who was sleeping, then suddenly he leaned over and began to pull down the fellow's pants. He pulled very slowly, you saw the shirt, a piece of his skin. Meanwhile with the other hand he was unbuttoning, took out . . .

The one who was sleeping woke up unexpectedly, and the other bent over farther.

The one underneath tried to turn.

"St!" he said.

"What do you want?"

The one who had been standing lay down on top. I saw them rolling over. The sound of a fist in the face.

The people nearby woke up, began to laugh, and pulled down the pants of the man underneath.

Then someone turned out the light, and you could hear a tussle that went on for a long time.

In the morning the man who had taken the names gave us each a towel. I really hadn't expected this: the towel, although it was dirty, had been ironed in such a way that it seemed stuck together

I turned it over in my hands, unfolded it.

"What's this?"

I looked carefully. In the middle were three fleas. I touched them with my fingernail. They had been ironed, too.

I had never seen fleas in that condition: they looked starched.

BLACK MISERY

And yet those fourteen million unemployed had to live.

The government had filled the stomachs of a good number of them with cabbage and apples, but there were others. All day the poor went looking for relief, and late at night:

"Where are you going to sleep?" said one.

"I'm not going to the nursery."

"Let's go to the people's hotel."

"And the fifty cents?"

"How much do you have?"

"Thirty."

"For twenty cents . . . I have mine."

"Let's try asking for it."

"You take the other sidewalk . . ."

". . . Sir, please! Five cents, for a bed."

The man went by.

". . . Ma'am, all I need is twenty cents, please can you spare me five . . ."

The woman didn't respond.

After an hour.
"Nothing!"
"Me neither."
"It's late. I'm tired . . . if I don't sleep I won't make it tomor-
row . . ."
"Look, there's a guy."
"He won't give us anything!"
"You'll see . . ."
The man approached, the two waited.
"Hands up . . . Look in his pocket . . ."
The friend stuck his hands in, took out: a few dollars.
"O.K."
Soon afterward, the police whistles can be heard in the nearby
streets, and the white cars arrive.

## LINEUP

I started to get to know the city well; the Avenues go up and down, the
Streets across.

On 10th Avenue are the Irish drunks. On 8th Avenue the employment agencies for waiters and dishwashers, who line up outside. On
1st Avenue the carts of the Italian vegetable sellers. In the middle is
5th Avenue, with its skyscrapers, Park Avenue, Madison Avenue,
where the millionaires live.

But the Avenues are so long that at the ends they change, and on
Park Avenue around 110th Street the neighborhood's full of blacks.
The black prostitutes say to you:
"Honey!"
"How much?"
"A dollar . . . Come on."
She walks into the darkness, goes up a stairway. There are eyes
looking out from behind the wall.
Then she says:
"Give me a dollar."
That's Harlem.
They say that after midnight it's hard to pass through there.
Here's how I went to live there. I took the elevated train, I got off at
106th Street, I went into a filthy house.
In America the cockroaches have red skin like mahogany, they're
small and you find them everywhere. They run along the walls, on the
floor, in the water. There they call them *cacarocci*. In Harlem I watched
them moving around my pillow in every direction.
At night I went out and wandered around. I walked along the
sidewalks and every so often at the door of a bar I saw the shining eyes

of the Negroes who were waiting. Then all at once you heard a shout from somewhere that ended suddenly, and you didn't see anything anymore.

"They've pulled him inside."

I went to various bars, but the one where I spent my time most nights was known as the gangsters' Bar.

In that strange place things happened silently. Even the bartender didn't say much, and the clientele was sparse and always the same. Generally, the clients arrived two at a time, and they spoke an abbreviated language that was often reduced to movements of the head.

I was considered friendly, I talked with everyone a little, and especially with a young gunman who often came and sat at my table.

"How's it going?" I asked him.

I don't know why this young man had such trust in me, but the fact is that he confided many things to me that he would certainly not have said to others.

For that reason I cannot mention the name of the young gangster. On the other hand he was aware of my interest in those things and he willingly explained them to me.

"Mind you," he said to me one day. "It's only the children of the poor who do this for a living."

"But at the movies you sometimes see . . ."

He interrupted me.

"Ballshiettes," he said bitterly.

He was silent, then I began again:

"Do you think you'll stop someday?"

"When they shoot me dead."

Once I saw this young man get into a car with another gangster. He saw me, but he didn't say anything.

That evening when I ran into him he was excited and happy, he was drinking and bought me a drink. Suddenly he said to me:

"Don't think about it."

Another time I was at the Bar and suddenly, not far away, a shot rang out. Then more. The gangsters were attentive, as if they were counting.

"They've shot a Negro."

"Why?" I asked. "How can you tell?"

"The police are in the habit of discharging their guns into a Negro even after he's dead."

My friend had promised me long ago that he would tell me about the white female slave trade and I awaited the moment eagerly, without knowing why he kept putting it off. In any case I had decided not to insist.

One night a man came into the Bar and said in a whisper:

"There's a lineup at 325 110th Street."

My friend nodded to me, I went out with him.

"What's a lineup?" I asked him.

"It's a girl on the roof . . . Now you'll see her. You want to go up?"

While we walked I got a better idea of what a lineup was.

A man meets a girl, at a dance, in a bar, somewhere. He gets friendly with her, buys her drinks, then leaves with her. This always takes place in Harlem.

Arriving at a predetermined street, the man makes the girl go through a doorway, and up the stairs. On the top landing there's a door to the roof that can be opened from the inside. The man pushes it open, and so the two of them are on the roof of the building.

There he grabs the woman, lies her down, gets on top of her, and meanwhile others are arriving through the door to the roof, in silence, they sit down to wait, one beside the other.

They keep coming through the door, they sit there ready, the hand that unbuttons the pants in front.

She says nothing . . .

Down in the street someone goes into the nearest bar and spreads the word.

"There's a lineup at 110th Street."

The men go out in silence.

My friend had me go in another door; when we got up there, you could see in profile the men waiting for their turn.

"How long does it last?" I asked.

"Keep your voice down . . .Until day."

"And then?"

"Then if she's pretty they take her to another roof and she does it for another night."

"And then?"

"Depends. Sometimes she does two or three nights."

"And when she goes home!" I said, worried.

"She doesn't go home."

"What?"

"He comes to get her . . . You saw the guy in the gray coat down in the bar?"

"Yes."

"He's the one who gets her. He lets her sleep. When she's rested, he buys her a dress because the one she was wearing, well, by now you can imagine what it's like . . . then he tells her it's pointless to go home and sends her off."

"Where?"

"Depends. Where there are requests. Chicago, Boston, Mexico, Chile."

"And she?"

"It's over."

"Why doesn't she protest?"

"To whom?"

"To the police."

"What police?" the gunman said to me.

### THE COAL IMMIGRANTS

The bus was ready. By now all the passengers had got on. The man closed the door from the outside and the driver settled himself so that he was comfortable, before starting to maneuver out of the bus station.

Next to me was a man who seemed preoccupied, on the other side was the window, and so I could look out at the street: first the streets of the city, then the tunnel that went under the Hudson, with all the other cars trying to get out. The curves, the chimneys of the factories, the plants with their rows of windows, and the warehouses out in the open, along the edge of the grass.

After Scranton, the towns seemed darker.

There were wooden cabins, huddled together as if they were cold.

The bus stopped, I looked around.

Down in the street was a group of workers whose faces were barely visible. They called me by name, then all of a sudden I felt happy.

"How are you?"

Each one tried to get near me.

The bus drove off, and we headed toward a cabin at the edge of town where I was to hold my first meeting.

On the table was a lantern with a low flame and in front of me benches filled with the anthracite miners who had come to hear me.

When I finished, the men came up to me, silently, someone put a hand on my shoulder.

"Come to my house?"

"I have to leave."

"You need to rest," they insisted.

"I'll sleep on the bus."

"At least come and have a bite to eat."

The house where we went quickly became crowded, and I listened to all the voices.

"In Pittsburgh you have the miners of soft coal. They earn less there."

"Say hello to Di Cecco. Tell him to come see us."

When we left it was very late. We walked a little way together.

At the railroad crossing we stopped to let the train go by, with its single bright headlight.

One miner tapped the rail with his foot.

"We laid these here. You remember Pierino?"

The old man nodded his head yes.

"How many miles?"

"What do you think now!" said the old man.

"Get him to tell you what we did."

The bus heading west was ready.

Before arriving in Pittsburgh I had begun to see occasionally along the road groups of houses whose windows appeared to be boarded up.

This time a local worker was sitting next to me.

"What's that?" I asked him.

"Nothing. It was a mining camp, and now they've closed the mine. When the mine closes they send everyone away."

"Why?"

"Because they don't need them anymore. The houses in the camp belong to the mine owners."

"Who are the mine owners?"

"The bank," said the worker.

"Which one?"

"Eh! Who knows anything about that?"

"Where do the people who live there go?"

"They emigrate."

"Where?"

"To another mine! . . . My friend," the worker gazed at me, "have you seen the anthracite miners?"

"Yes."

"They worked at this mine, too . . . In the mines everywhere in the United States . . . They all know each other, they marry here, then the family breaks up . . . Here's another one . . ."

He, too, looked out: it was like a beehive that had been emptied by smoke.

"Who can say how many children were born there, how many have made love! . . ."

"Tell me," I asked suddenly, "if someone were to go and live there?"

The worker shrugged his shoulders.

"They'd arrest him."

"Why?"

"Because it's the property of the mine! If it didn't work that way, then the miners wouldn't emigrate anymore and the cost of labor wouldn't keep falling."

In the mine in Avella there are only Spanish and Italian workers.
At night they come from work in their hard shiny hats with the
lamps at the front.

When I saw them it seemed to me that they were so exhausted they
couldn't even hold their soup bowls. Their arms hung down.

"Oh, you've come?" they said to me.

They went to wash their faces, their chests, their backs, and their
eyes, which were ringed with black as if the white were just temporary.

I stayed for a few days in one house.

At night Mirra was drunk, and he lay on the bed vomiting and said:
"The mine . . . the mine . . ."

Fioretta patiently cleaned him up.

The others were talking of a miner who had died and were saying
that the funeral would be the next day, and Mirra wanted to say that
he understood.

"Then when they send us away from the camp, he'll stay . . .
Where's your father? . . . If you had known the mine . . ."

After Pennsylvania I went to Michigan, and arrived in Detroit.

*Ho rinunciato alla libertà* (Milano: Le edizioni sociali, 1950), 5–7, 37–41, 58–64.

# 3

# The New World of the Second Generation: Pietro di Donato and John Fante

*"You too are here for the World's Fair!"* he smiles happily as the
elevator stops, and the door opens wide.
—Pier Antonio Quarantotti Gambini

THE RISE OF THE SECOND GENERATION, WHICH OFFERS A VERY DIF-
ferent expressive world, is well represented by two notable "neo-
Americans," Pietro di Donato and John Fante. By the end of the
thirties, as I've said, narrative in Italian was clearly on a downswing.
Bearing witness to this is the scarcity of production, the dark and
problematical plots, and above all the quantity and the quality of
books written in English, which are no more, as in a long and glorious past going back to the eighteenth century, the isolated fruit of
strong personalities but the expression—individual and traumatic, if
you like—of a collective adjustment within the adopted society. For
this very reason it is important to pick out the points of contact
between the two generations, to observe, so to speak, the young
writers as they leave the house of their parents.

When *The World of Tomorrow* appeared, in English, in the yearbook
*Leonardo* at the beginning of 1939, Pietro di Donato (1911–92) had
not yet published *Christ in Concrete,* the proletarian novel that immediately roused a "wave of emotion" (Rimanelli), impressing the name
of the self-taught writer on the attention of America. The novel came
out a little later, in April. A few months afterward, with enviable
timing, it was mentioned in Italy by Elio Vittorini (at the peak of his
work for *Americana*) in the weekly *Oggi* (28 October 1939), on a page
that, after seventy years, seems to express the high quality of the
Italian literature of that period. Landolfi denigrates Panzini, Gian-
siro Ferrata reviews Gadda's *Le meraviglie d'Italia,* and, finally, Vittorini
presents *Christ in Concrete* with harsh disdain:

> For long stretches, the book is loaded with tedious old-fashioned psychol-
> ogy; with characters drowning in details of pure contingency . . .; and

178

with scenes developed according to a taste for an almost provincial realism that recalls the Italian realism that originated with Verga. . . . This
useless firing of big guns is due perhaps more to bad habit and sluggish-
ness of taste than to an ineluctable personal inclination.

It should be noted, however, that, despite these criticisms, di Donato's novel was soon offered to the Italian public.[1]

But we are still at the start of di Donato's career, a step back with
respect to his masterpiece. With painful irony, the "world of tomorrow" that is mentioned in the story in English refers to the promo-
tional title of the massive construction project of the World's Fair
(completed in 1940), conceived and directed by the demiurge of
urban architectural modernism in New York, Robert Moses; and it is
at a construction site at the fair that the narrator temporarily finds
employment.[2]

The physical exhaustion and daily hard labor of the autobiographical protagonist are in stark contrast to the unrestrained speculative,
innovating energy symbolized by the citadel of commerce. The
description of waking up and traveling from home to the job in a
cold, windy dawn immerses us immediately in the dim, dark atmosphere of the commute. Rapid, almost inessential, the names of the
"stations" of this ordinary collective calvary rush by: the Sound (the
arm of the sea that separates Long Island from the mainland: the di
Donatos had just moved from West Hoboken, New Jersey, to North-
port, on Long Island), the railroad hub of Jamaica, the crowded
neighborhood of Flushing, in Queens, and finally the arrival at the
Fair site. Similarly, signs of a corrupt, already threadbare modern life
creep into the narrator's not-quite-awake senses: from the ring of the
alarm clock to the rumbling of the cold engine, from the metallic
rhythm of the train to the disturbing appearance of advertising
posters. And even meetings with a young blonde and two Irish cops
are little more than flashes, instantaneous, which allude impres-
sionistically to a stimulus of the senses and a curiosity about the small
details of the day (it is not hard to pick up, if fleetingly, a certain
imaginary Italian American, caught between ethnic rivalry and the
wish for assimilation).

Even before setting foot on the site, therefore, the writer-worker,
along with a crowd of similar types, has had to endure the weight of
the most trite mass rituals. Meanwhile, the "tomorrow" announced
hopefully in the title and in the final passages as the horizon of
freedom for future generations must pass "through the darkness,"
traverse a today of a completely different nature. And yet even the
harshest and most ungrateful reality is contained within a profoundly

religious vision of the world, which despite rejections and gestures of rebellion allows one to accept even tragedy in the light of redemption, of a positivity that is also social. It is, understandably, the same ideological diagram that is behind the mesh of desperation and solidarity, of rage and pity, in *Christ in Concrete*. One should pay attention, here, to two indications of different value, evident in the final lines: the "internationalist," engaged reference to the Spanish and Chinese civil wars, on the one hand; on the other, the insistent recourse to the semantic sphere of light and shadow, from an "all-shining Sun" that sanctifies the work of man, to a "darkness" and "sightlessness" that plunge him back into the gloom.

If we keep in mind di Donato's obsessive faithfulness to his themes and his figures, we can understand how difficult it is to speak of a plan or a preparatory sketch of the novel. Certainly one can find in it the homology between work and tragic labor implicit in the use of the term "Job," which is always capitalized and never preceded by the article: Job-work as the personification of the biblical Job, with the obvious implications of that. One can read, as in the opening of the novel, passages that are stylistically "modernist," with the display of verb forms made into adjectives, onomatopoeia, simulations of speech, noun phrases, typographical effects. Above all, di Donato manages to insert here his "primal scene," that is to say the topos of the death at the construction site. It should be noted that a foreshadowing of the death appeared fleetingly in the anecdote recounted by the Irish policeman on the morning bus: a macabre-grotesque premonition.

Thus the text has its more specifically individual characters as well as those which connect it more generally to the work of the author. In both cases, *The World of Tomorrow* displays a commitment, a seriousness that is hardly in line with the pietistic and nationalistic stereotypes of a proletarian literature that is in some ways contiguous. Through a revealing irony of fate, the circumstances of publication of *The World of Tomorrow*, if they allow us to emphasize the fact of the author's belonging to the world of Little Italy, in a certain sense have hidden its existence for decades. The story, in fact, came out, after *An Appreciation of Pietro di Donato*, by the editor Lambert Davis, and an advance excerpt from the novel (the solemn passage on the funeral of the father, Geremio), as one of the rare inserts in English in the annual review *Leonardo* (1939, edited by Onorio Ruotolo). This elegant magazine was the yearbook of the Leonardo da Vinci Art School, at the corner of East Tenth Street and Avenue A, on the Lower East Side of Manhattan, which was founded in 1923 by a group of artists and intellectuals in the Italian American community and headed by the sculptor and activist Ruotolo.[3] From 1924, the prestige of the school, introduced in ardent nationalistic tones by Ruotolo in the monthly *Il Carroccio*—the arena of intellectuals closest to the new regime in Rome—is reflected annually in the issues of the journal, in which some significant names appear: D'Annunzio and Papini, Marinetti and Prezzolini, Barzini Sr., and the American Dreiser, as well as those of the futurist and militarist old guard such as Auro d'Alba, Paolo Buzzi, and Armando Mazza, and of the writers of the immigrant community, from the essayist Italo Stanco and the poet Antonio Calitri to Ernesto Valentini. In other words, just as, in the twenties in *Il Carroccio*, new voices of Italian American literature in English, such as those of Pascal D'Angelo and Louis Forgione, were encouraged as an emblem of Italianness, so at the end of the thirties the Italian-speaking establishment of the immigrant community became the promoter of a second-generation youth, di Donato. It was an isolated incident, to such an extent that *The World of Tomorrow* was preserved in the pages of *Leonardo* as if in mothballs for seventy years;[4] but it is also the sign of a certain vitality in the more traditional Italian American literary scene, which in the period after the Second World War ended definitively within its narrow confines, in a slow sunset punctuated by self-celebrations. Only then did its distance from the new Italian American literature and experience, in English, appear truly unbridgeable.

## FANTE AND FANTOLOGY

Today, authorized by the imprimatur of two other cult writers, Charles Bukowski and Pier Vittorio Tondelli, and happily amazed by a small but passionate editorial and expository industry, we are at risk of considering John Fante (1909–83) one of those writers who are neglected in life and appreciated only later. The retrieval, from the depths of the Prezzolini Archive, of this short letter allows us instead to return briefly to that period of the thirties and forties when the name of Fante figures in high relief as an expression of the "new legend" of America. The quotation is taken from the concluding pages of *Americana;* Vittorini ends the historic 1941 anthology with his own translation of the final pages of the first chapter of *Wait until Spring, Bandini*. And 1941 is also the year when Vittorini publishes, in Volume 125 of Mondadori's *Medusa, Il cammino nella polvere* [Ask the Dust]. But it appears on closer examination that the anthologized excerpt (*Una famiglia neo-americana*) had been preceded by other Fantian offerings to the Italian public: beginning with *Il conto del droghiere*[5] (subtitled, here as in the two publications mentioned below, "A Story by Giovanni Fante"), which is to say the entire fourth chapter of *Wait until Spring*, although freely cut. In the pages that follow, a succinct column by "Caliban" introduces the writer in a few lines, encouraging the hypothesis that this is his first Italian appearance. The role played by Longanesi's illustrated magazine *Omnibus* in the work of modernizing journalism in those years, at all levels, was definitive: in its pages literature became a stimulus for letting in the new energies from abroad (including the American myth); the editors were open to the contributions of all the best young people around, and the novelty of the graphic style had a strong impact.[6] The experiment of Longanesi's weekly came to an abrupt end, and the following year Fante appears in a journal with double ties to *Omnibus*: *Oggi* (second series), edited by Mario Pannunzio and Arrigo Benedetti. Here we read *Un muratore nella neve*,[7] evidently taken from its original place of publication, *The American Mercury* of January 1936; *Bricklayer in the Snow* was included in the collection *Dago Red* (1940) and reemerged, in Italian translation, almost seventy years later.[8] Shortly afterward, another excerpt from the first chapter of *Wait until Spring* appeared: *La moglie troppo saggia* [The Wife Who Was Too Wise].[9] *Oggi* also published, with almost constant regularity, excerpts from American literature (witness Vittorini's canon: Steinbeck, Caldwell, Saroyan, Cain, etc.), reports on American events, customs, and culture sent by Prezzolini, not to mention contributions from other writers active in reporting news from across the ocean (Tito A. Spagnol, Roberto Campagnoli), and pages by other Italian Americans (Edoardo Corsi translated by Prezzolini, Angelo Bertocci in Maria Martone's version). It is interesting to note that the first part of *Wait until Spring* stops exactly at the point where Vittorini's excerpt in *Americana* begins, which might furnish a valuable hint as to the paternity of the three translations.[10] But we should keep in mind that a systematic survey of the periodicals of those years might lead to further discoveries.

All in all, however, the names of Vittorini and Prezzolini emerge as scouts and promoters of Fante, among others; the engagement of the latter is more obscure and difficult to reconstruct, as the brief epistolary relationship documented here confirms. Prezzolini was examining the nature and significance of the Italian spoken in the communities in the United States around the same time,[11] and so it makes sense that he would turn to Fante (given Fante's literary baptism by a figure whom Prezzolini esteemed highly, H. L. Mencken),[12] impelled not only by curiosity as a reader but by his interests as a scholar and privileged observer.

As for Fante's response, it is not going too far to suppose that it might confirm the addressee in his apocalyptic interpretation of the Italian American "linguistic tragedy," about to manifest itself in the second generation as "*schizophrenia,* or rather the splitting of the soul of the immigrant into an Italian and an American, oftentimes represented by two different generations."[13] Certainly some pages of *Dago Red* would authorize one to speak of a dilemma, if not of true tragedy, and a source of frustration ready to become a creative burst. Fante's admission of a lack of familiarity with Italian has, however, left in his letter confirmation marked by a serene, even amused, tone of confidentiality.[14]

## A STEP BACK

In her autobiography, Mary "Mother" Jones, the legendary union organizer, recounts that after the 1914 massacre in the workers' camp in Ludlow, Colorado, set in motion by the militia in the pay of Rockefeller's Colorado Fuel and Iron Company, a delegation went to Washington to meet President Wilson. One of the most outspoken among the delegates was a Mrs. Petrucci, whose three children had been burned alive in that inferno. Mother Jones does not specify what her words were, or the language in which they must have been spoken.[15] But that Italian was common among the miners in Colorado is confirmed by, in addition to contemporary testimony,[16] the novels of Fante and Jo Pagano (especially *Golden Wedding,* 1943) and by the activity of the local press. A brief reconnaissance allows us to note such journals as *Il Risveglio,* in Denver (1906–55), and, in Pueblo, *L'Unione* (1897–1947) and *La Voce del Popolo* (1925–49: the voice of a community from Trento with polemically conformist positions). The "common ground" of the sensibility displayed in these papers is not very different from that of the other Italian American journals in Italian, with a generous selection, throughout the forties, of the more or less well-known serial novelists, from Invernizio to Richebourg (the novelist Bernardino Ciambelli appears as an editorialist). These are certainly peripheral voices, but of necessity aggressive yet careful in the face of the news from Italy and changes taking place in their audience. It is sufficient to recall, in the case of *L'Unione,* the circumstances of publication in 1934 of Silone's *Fontamara* as a serial novel, and the gradual replacement in the middle and late thirties of Italian by English, even in the literary pages.[17]

Behind the words of Fante to Prezzolini, behind the touching gift to his father of a copy of *Ask the Dust* found by an English soldier in

Venice, the outlines of a broader story can be made out, as in a palimpsest: the story of emigration as the story of looking for a job. And labor represents the alpha and omega, the text and pretext, of the best Italian American literature.

※ ※

*Anthology*

## PIETRO DI DONATO, *THE WORLD OF TOMORROW*

A new generation of Italian American writers comes of age in the thirties, if not eschewing, then refashioning, the overly autobiographical modes of the first books by Italian immigrants, which had appeared during the previous decades (often linked to strong personalities like Carnevali, Panunzio, D'Angelo, Forgione, Villa, and others). Garibaldi Lapolla, Pietro di Donato, and John Fante (and soon many others) wrote primarily novels and short stories, preferring narratives to memoir. Nevertheless, their pages display everywhere the cultural origin of the authors. Italian American and Italian literati, on both sides of the Atlantic, were well aware that something was happening—that the "old" world of the first generation was slowly fading away, making room for new characters, new plots, and a new language. In the robust literature of Lapolla, the fabric of life itself, the scene, is still distinctly Italian; it is less so in di Donato and Fante. But it is highly significant that a resounding title such as *The World of Tomorrow* was published in an obscure art magazine, *Leonardo,* circulating only within the Italian cultured élite of New York; and that John Fante, from Los Angeles, could spark the interest of Giuseppe Prezzolini, the most influential intellectual and mediator between Italy and the United States, then director of Columbia's Casa Italiana, and a fervent admirer of H. L. Mencken, Fante's mentor. That new generation was using its own language to express the social, psychological, and political plight of a different kind of Italian, in a crucial moment of the relations between the two countries.

### The World of Tomorrow

"You contacted me just in time," he said. "We're all set for the bricklayers. Show up first thing in the morning, and tell the foreman I sent you."

"Thanks, Sam, you don't know what this means to me. Thanks." I meant it. At night I had the sad and quelled feeling which always preceded my communion with the walls. After preparing my tools and work clothes I set the clock and went to bed. Before I actually went off, the rent, gas and electric, food, laundry, and other facts loomed such impregnable things, and I nervously saw myself very very small.

The belling in my head told me it was five o' clock, but the darkness made it seem as though it were still the dead middle of the sleeping night world. I jumped from bed. The kid brother Joe got up also and began to dress.

"What are you getting up for?"

"Oh, I don't care to sleep."

He put the light on in the kitchen and made some coffee and eggs while I shaved and washed. When I put on my heavy work shirt and trousers I felt fortified and in the chill kitchen breakfast was warm and nourishing.

"Have you enough clothes on?"

"Yes," I said.

"The thermometer must be below freezing."

I nodded. It looked gloomy outside the window.

"Take your time," he said. "Have another cup of coffee while I go out and warm up the chariot.—Don't forget your rubbers when you come out."

While we talked we looked at each other and then away. I had the extra cup of coffee. The wind was blowing up from the Sound. I heard the old Chrysler's starter churning. And as I left the house I wondered how it would be to stay home—just stay home, and listen first to the Sunrise symphony and then the Master-work hour. The wind met me like a ghostly veil of ice. I said it was good for me. And the Sound below our hill was a tormented metal sea. It was wild and I had to leave it. Joe backed the Chrysler up to me. I put the tools in the rumble seat. While I was driving Joe asked:

"What kind of job is it? Is it high over the ground?—You know, if it's dangerous—".

"Hell," I said. "Job's a job. Nothing to worry about."

We drove on to the next station and did not say anything more. The train chugged in. I got my tools from the rumble seat.

"O.K.," I said. "Watch your driving."

He looked at me with his big eyes.

"Chief, *you* watch yourself."

When the train left the station I could not help thinking how deep, how manly his voice had become.

The train rumbled and chattered through the potato fields and woods, as morning quietly sent up over the countryside sweeps of scarlet lume. Opposite me was a sleepy blonde girl. Her clothes were poor and much worn. She had a jaunty hat set over a pleasant face. She did not look out the train window to see what Nature was doing. I wondered what kind of work she did, whether she were single or married and happy, and how things were at home. Someday she would be white-ishly fat. She was tired. There was submission in her face.

At every station more workers came on; laborers, railroad men, telephone operators, small tradesmen, and factory girls. The short thickset girls carried brown paper lunchbags oily spotted, popular love magazines, and their rough fingers showed red-blazoned nails. Coming into the train was important. They liked to be seen and heard. And no one would ever say to them tenderly, fervently: "Darling, you are beautiful . . . Sweet, how I love you . . .!!" But they laughed loudly at every little thing.

Many of the men had their heads tipped back and soundly caressed in sleep. They were heavily dressed in cheap dusty clothes. Above one lean old sleeping laborer were car posters that featured Esquire for entertainment, the Sherry-Netherland for the ultimate in fine living, and further along was the Life-saver ad that said "It is not a Life-saver if it hasn't a hole." Looking at the gnarled faces of the laborers I wondered if they had had anything to say about the making of their faces, and I tried to picture them as when they were young, what they thought about, and what they had dreamed of someday being.

A few stations before Jamaica a girl got on and sat next to me. I could tell she was a salesgirl. She wore an inexpensive polo coat and a pert little saucer of a hat. Her face was sensitively attractive with the shadow of conscious inferiority that kept her from looking up and about. She knew I was observing her and could feel her hunger for romance. It was unfair of me to pay close attention to her—to let her think that I another worker had found "the" girl—and God knows, perhaps for her, I would have conveniently answered her dreams . . . At Jamaica she also got off. She met a girl friend. They hurried away along the platform arm in arm, and I saw how pitifully thin her legs were.

The Flushing bus was crowded. I had to stand near the driver. He sent the huge vehicle hurtling along the highway, manipulating levers and pedals. The passengers admiring him. Our safety was in his hands. His employers depended upon him. He was earning his bread. And he was proud.

Two young Irish-American policemen came aboard at one of the stops. The bus roared on to Flushing as day was lighting gray. A drab girl looked up from her novel and asked her companion what "Franz-wah" was; to which he said conspicuously: "Oh, Franz-wah, don't you know? Franz-wah is French in French. Sure, Franz-wah." The two policemen were talking of their work, one telling of his dislike of a "snotty bastard lootenant who'll get a dose of my rod one of these fine days." His buddy symphatized boyishly with him and related of a suicide he handled the previous day.

"Yeah, this bloat was hard up and took the easy way out. When I got there the inspector and internes were standin' round. I says: 'Looks like he did a good job.' Nobody said nothin'. And believe me I felt like a dope. Anyway, we hadda take the stiff down in the freight lift. Couldn't lay him out—hadda prop him up in a corner. Nobody said nothing on the way down. The stiff fell against me. So I says: 'Bo, if you're tired lean on my shoulder—I can take it.' "

"Was he rigor mortis?"

"What's rigor mortis?"

The bus turned onto another highway and the World's Fair city came into view. Among far spread buildings bescaffolded Trylon and Perisphere stood sharply up. With straight and circled line their amazing simplicity suddenly seemed to geometricize in lucid answer the rhythm of being, posed there as first man and woman . . . And I wanted to raise my heart and sing through the skies Life, oh Life!

The bus stopped and we assorted humanity quietly, respectfully, unloaded. Through the gate and into the Fair grounds. An hysteria of buildings—Wooden-scaffolded, steel-pipe-scaffolded structures meeting vision's perimeter—battle-field of toil with dug-up earth in piles and building's big toy-pieces awaiting—buildings' walls severely straighting-curving-angling-rolling-rising-fuguing in liberated phantasia from the living minds of men—and in rough streets we laborers pour as shabby army to siege.

"Are you mister Kilo? I'm the bricklayer Sam told you about."

"Yeah. Go with this guy in the Hall of Nations and lay up the fireproofin' walls."

"Yes, sir."

Two hodcarriers, another bricklayer and I went into the vast Hall of Nations. The hodcarriers quickly shoveled sand lime and cement into the mortar box, turned the water hose into the box and hoed the mortar. The wall was a sixty foot partition of twelve by twelve inch celled tile block: to rise to the roof a hundred feet above. I got into my overalls. A chorus of thin whistles shrilled. Before their vibrations had carried off Job went into action. I dug my trowel into the mortar. Sixteen years of trowel and mortar's feel surged along the conduits of my physical intelligence. From the thrust and weave of my substance a corner of block masonry raised. Automatically I noticed the other bricklayer keep pace. We had not yet spoken. But we measured each other. When we had put up our leads he came over to me.

"Got a line, kid?"

We stretched the line between our leads and began piling in the blocks. I know. On the wall we have no personalities. No distinctions. The most important thing in life is to get endless blocks mortared and bonded up and up and they don't care if a black man or a white man or a tall man or a short man or a good man or a bad man or if the Devil or if God layed them they have to go up! The army of carpenters crucified beam on beam and hammers' heads on spikes piercing fibrous timber echoed lively through the morning—Trucks snorted and snarled—hit steel belled in metal voice—and the many buzz-saws cried their irritated poignant Maahh-ahorrrr-RRR-yeh! Over and over and over . . . but don't you see I can't live if I don't lay blocks! don't you see I was born and let to live to lay blocks! don't you see that all living other than laying blocks is not real but make believe!

Did I not somewhere dream of love? Was she not tall light Goddess? Or red-lipped blackeyed velvety brunette whose beauty strengthened and melted? And did I not see myself singing, running naked over sand by water and loved of sun? But no, that must be in another world, and how shall I find that world? Who will tell me? Please! please! Crash my senses oh furious reality of Job! Louder, Discord! Stretch farther beyond oh sweated fighting flesh and shout to myself the complete beauty of life's gift is the pushing up the walls for my father did it and his father and his father's father's father and their fathers since the beginning was a straight and rounded line and I have been raising the earth above me since and what God will glorify this melody?

"Look out below!"

"Watch out BEE-LOWW!!!"

I swiftly flattened against the wall. A huge wooden beam shot down from the rooftop. A man stopped in the center of the floor. They had shouted above. He instinctively bent his head. He had heard. Eyes were electrically fastened upon him. The beam chopped insanely through his head. I wanted to vomit on this world. I wanted to run. The man went into quivering sleep, cuddled by the beam, went into another world. He was an ironworker. His rugged hands, his athletic body were divorced from things. He was quickly taken away. The machine of Job had not stopped, and no one single man had cried: "Men! Men let us gather and talk about our lives!! Let us know each other! Let us help each other!"

At noon I made friends with the two laborers and the other brick-layer. I had never seen them before. But I knew them. They were workers. And what more can I say of them than that they were workers?

With afternoon the sixty pound blocks were heavier, my back ached, and my hands were bruised. It wasn't the first time. And when work-day quieted Job I left my fire and fluid on Job and departed a purposeless worn thing. The ride home, though blurry, was a reward. I was in the tired stream of labor. Yes, I remember seeing some of the faces that rode with me in the early morning, and there were other beings; well-dressed lovely girls and tailored men chatting from tooth-pasted mouths about school, maids, weekends, brokers, sport, prices, who didn't know they could not live without laying blocks and seeing the ironworker quiver! So I was nothing; just a whipped face, a trickling body, and clothes powdered of mortar. In the train we had all paid the same fare, only some of us died for the money, and others—And I knew there was a right side and a wrong side, and all I wanted to do was cry tears for my side, to wet down the pain.

Joe picked me up at the station. The wheel of day had brought cold dark glowing evening, and it seemed a long time since I had last seen the kid.

"How do you feel," he asked. "How did it go?"

"Not too bad," was all I could say.

At home the kid brothers and sisters had supper ready for me and my special place at the table. Their quietness meant they were sorry, and appreciated. They know that when I was a kid I was smart and a great dreamer who liked to make acting about people until papa was carried home from the walls. They know I want them to do the studying I had to forget about so that the world will have to suffer up its buildings without any more Di Donatos.

After supper we sat at the fireside. I told them about Man at the World's Fair, of his painful genius, that above the commercialism, and cowardice, beyond the bazar of color and goods, beyond the slashing whirling blind blows struck against each other's precious lives there was a major music rising as invincible as the all-shining Sun.

In bed day's struggle dilated and flashed through the tubes of my being. They were *my* aches and *my* pains and they told of days pay. I thought of the ironworker's family. Yes, *their* elegy had begun. I thought of the men with whom I silently wrestled, whose souls I could not reach. I saw them but in their darkness they could not see me. I thought of how they were being sent in their darkness to kill each other in Spain and China, and I was frightened to think that some day—somewhere they would kill me also in their sightlessness. And before I wandered away to nothing I followed the faces of my kid brothers and sisters, the faces I helped free from the old world and all its poison, the faces whose light will radiate through the darkness to illumine the world of tomorrow.

"The World of Tomorrow," *Leonardo,* Yearbook 1938–39, edited by Onorio Ruotolo, 37–39.

### A Letter from John Fante to Giuseppe Prezzolini

February 18, 1940
Dear Mr. Prezzolini,

When I come to New York—but God knows the time—I shall be very pleased to visit you people at the Casa Italiana.

Thank you very much for the interest you express in my writings. Doubtless you shuddered at the spelling of those Italian words in my Wait Until Spring, Bandini. If you have had any experience with printers, you know how I must have felt. That was over two years ago, but I still clinch my fists and spit on the floor when I think about it.

The truth is, I can't write Italian, except phonetically, but I had my proofsheets carefully checked and double-checked by an expert. It made no difference to that damned printer. When I found out about it the book was already for sale. I offer this explanation because Prof. Altrocci at California U. commented about it, and I assume you too were surprised.

Sincerely yours,
John Fante

904 Manhattan Ave.,
Manhattan Beach, Calif.

Courtesy of Archivio Prezzolini, Lugano.

# 4

## Poetry of the Italian Americans

Perhaps never more will I return here to you where I struggled
  and gained
The ample treasure of affection,
But never will I forget you, oh beautiful Golden Gates.
               —Pietro Gori, *Farewell to San Francisco*

### POETRY IN THE IMMIGRANT COMMUNITIES

ONE OF THE LARGEST AND MOST INTERESTING MANIFESTATIONS OF "immigrant" literature was poetry, which accompanied the immigrants from the start, one could say, even before the historic exodus bridging the nineteenth and twentieth centuries. The poetry of the Little Italies is a constant, as attested by its long history in the immigrant press and publishing, which consistently promoted poetic voices, whether of recognized authors or simply of ordinary readers. The chronology might begin with the activity of the first important Italian American newspaper, *L'Eco d'Italia,* founded in New York in 1849, and end with a polemic that, in 1959–60 (and, later, in a decade of private correspondence), on the occasion of an announced visit to New York by Ungaretti, presented two diametrically opposed figures of Italians in America: Giuseppe Prezzolini and one of the last, obscure representatives of immigrant poetry, Giuseppe Incalicchio, a contributor to *Il Progresso Italo-Americano,* the major paper of the post-Second World War period.

Even if the Italian American papers of the second half of the nineteenth century preferred literature in the form of serial novels or the various types of prose addressing the aftermath of the Risorgimento, their pages, and often the first page, always featured attempts at an indigenous poetry, so to speak, alternating mainly between comments on current events in Italy or the United States and conventional sentiment, either romantic or nostalgic. More than a century later, in the 1960s, this type of poetry survived, although with obvious and predictable differences. But, while one can pick out a small group of writers who contributed to the more important journals (*Divagando,* in New York; and *Il Compasso,* the supplement to *La Parola*

191

*del Popolo,* in Chicago), it is equally clear that that industry, although prolific, was already anachronistic, because of the foundering of the Italian language in the post–Second World War period. However, even if the Italian poetry produced in America was correctly called "the fruit . . . of a double alienation" (Durante), that does not mean that it has no relation to the substrate of the Italian tradition.

We must keep in mind, at the start, a series of "external" features of poetic production; for one thing, the sheer quantity makes it clear that the first task of the literary and historical critic is to search for the work and prepare biobibliographical documentation. This poetry, by its very mass and vitality, played a recognized and important role in the history of the Italian American immigrants, offering significant testimony about their taste, their linguistic usages, their cultural baggage. Proof lies in the fact that not only outside observers like Prezzolini but also some of the more informed activists and intellectuals of that world noted the phenomenon, although their evaluations and emphases were different (names of some resonance can be mentioned, such as those of the anarchist Luigi Galleani and the public official Edoardo Corsi, or of forgotten journalists and poets such as Rosario Ingargiola and Giuseppe Zappulla). My intention is not, let it quickly be said, to legitimatize aesthetically works that, for the most part, exhibit in dramatic fashion provincial and retrograde attitudes but to understand them in a broader context. This particular area of immigrant culture, despite its obvious backwardness and contradictions, represented in the twentieth century one of the most relevant ethnic components of United States culture; and in recent years there has been a rigorous rereading of American history through the numerous texts of the non-English-speaking communities.

In spite of the fact that in many ways this work is just beginning, there exist, to facilitate the task, some collections of a general nature that are well known to specialists, as well as some brief studies, both historical and more strictly literary; in short, a vision of the whole is available, even if it requires expansion, correction, modification. The dimensions of the poetic culture and a comprehensive sense of it can be closely approximated; what is lacking is a direct examination, a close reading of the authors and their important works. It is time, that is, to recognize some of the major voices and try to gain a better acquaintance.

## THE MULTIFORM PRESENCE OF RICCARDO CORDIFERRO

Riccardo Cordiferro was the favorite pseudonym of the many-faceted Alessandro Sisca (1875–1940), born in San Pietro in Guarano (in the province of Cosenza). His father, Francesco Sisca, had, in his old age, written an expressive and ironic poem, in octaves of eight cantos, in Calabrese: *Lu ciucciu* [The Donkey] (1913). The son, influenced very early by the Neapolitan bohemia of the end of the century (as the poem *Ad Alarico* demonstrates), arrived in the United States in 1892; the following year, together with his father and his brother Marziale, he founded the satiric-literary weekly *La Follia di New York,* which remained for decades his preferred place of publication. Incidentally, a history, with an anthology, of *La Follia* (which is still alive today, the long-lived dynasty of the Siscas having only recently ended), would in itself offer, in the variety of its genres and language and its lively, militant style, a representative slice of Italian American literary culture. In addition to poetry in Italian, Cordiferro composed fluently in Calabrese and Sicilian dialects and, under the pseudonym Sandro, in Neapolitan. Some of his Neapolitan songs, set successfully to music, have entered the Neapolitan repertoire (in particular, *Core 'ngrato* [Ungrateful Heart]). He was also a contributor, if less well known than others, to the dramatic theater scenes that were then popular in the halls of the urban "ghettoes," alternating with Yiddish theater pieces. Here, too, the texts, often presenting a critical vision of society, were composed both in Italian and in Neapolitan (two shows noted by the major Cordiferro scholar, Emelise Aleandri, are *Mbruoglie 'e femmene* [The Trickery of Women], 1894, and *L'onore perduto* [Lost Honor], 1901); in addition, Cordiferro contributed to the notable immigrant success of farces and sketches (some poems, too, center on the figure of Pulcinella). He was an eloquent speaker, tending toward socialism, but not unpopular with the anarchist press (later, among other typical fluctuations, *La Follia* established itself as one of the most interesting platforms for a certain type of popularizing, "spontaneous" anti-Fascism); and he also wrote brief narrative pieces. The mere versatility and abundance of his writing, and the success documented in the chronicles of the time, make him in every sense one of the champions of the literature of Little Italy.

Cordiferro's popularity brings up an immediate comparison between his work and the attraction of his picturesque, impetuous personality in the life of the immigrant community, especially in the urban areas of the East. In fact, as a poet he was anything but a naif. Even at the time, his Neapolitan poems would in all likelihood have been read as a late-nineteenth-century variant of a vigorous lyric tradition, which it seems hasty and reductive to call "local," since a great part of the southern intelligentsia converged on Naples and was active there. As for the poetry in Italian, its deliberate refinement is striking: the literary nature of its elements was such that Prezzolini branded them excesses of artifice, "literary blisters," which were "always false

and rhetorical, the offspring . . . of memory and rhyming dictionar-
ies."[1] Keep in mind, however, that for Cordiferro his dignity as a man
of letters was based on the call of tradition. In part through uncritical
acceptance by a network of scholars, in part as a "nationalistic" reaction to the detachment caused by emigration, a poet like Cordiferro
could still compose as if the ideology and practice of the *imitatio* were
fully alive and valid. Entering into his poetic workshop, which preserves its expressive, historical texture, allows us, among other things,
to grasp the profound, I would say genetic, reasons for the floodlike
production, contemporary and later, of poetry in Italian that is, to
quote Prezzolini, irremediably "embalmed." Precisely because imita-
tion confers a seal of literariness, homages to other authors are abundant, the sources are clearly displayed, and the ability of the poet lies
in the restatement of themes, situations, styles, and meters of others.

Sticking to this tradition, Cordiferro emerges as a voice belonging
to a composite but well defined area of nineteenth-century poetry.
One need only skim the epigraphs attached to passages in *Singhiozzi e
sogghigni* [Sighs and Smiles], of 1910: the names of Carducci and
D'Annunzio (a good eleven mentions) appear, alongside those of
Giuseppe Aurelio Costanzo, Ada Negri, Giusti, Praga, Tarchetti, Stecchetti, and Rapisardi; and we might add, looking at the catalogue
with which his father, Francesco Sisca, closes his Calabrese poem, the
politically and geographically notable names of Cavallotti, Aleardi,
Parzanese, and Imbriani. It's true that, as early as 1911, *La Follia*
hailed Marinetti as a courageous innovator; but the weekly and its
guiding spirit remained solidly in the sphere of a nineteenth-century
classicism, weighted toward the last decades of the century, between
evocation of the three great poets (although Pascoli appears of more
problematic usefulness) and openness to social themes and the satirical, unruly accents of protest of the "poets of revolt" (presented in
1978 by Pier Carlo Masini in a useful anthology). At the lexical and
metrical level, Cordiferro's talent for assimilation expresses itself
with such facility and abundance as to become tedious: his sincere
adherence to a historically and rhetorically determined poetic "feeling" is beyond doubt. In results that are not, perhaps, more beautiful
but more convincing and consistent, in spite of awkward rhythms and
embarrassing apotheoses of a rebel and exiled "I," Cordiferro does
not seem unworthy of standing beside some of the names that he
himself invokes. It goes without saying that such exaggerated literariness would quickly be seen as inadequate to a public that was strained
not only socially but culturally, by a different, traumatic process of
assimilation, symbolized by the melting pot. The Italianness of this
poetry, even at its liveliest and most accessible, ultimately signals a

close: Cordiferro's *trobar clus,* although significant and even at times fascinating, displays only a partial understanding of immigrant culture.

Many elements bear witness to this, indicating the poet's long critical isolation; he was overtaken by a generous devotion to political and union battles (*Primo maggio* [May Day]), and the insistent parallel with the figure of a blond, combative Christ is strident, if comprehensible within a certain radicalizing tradition (*Resurrexit* and *Gesù sul Calvario* [Jesus on Calvary]). From New York, Cordiferro followed events in Italy, and among his verses we find the obligatory names, places, and dates of Umbertine Italy, from Dogali to Crispi and the twentieth of September. Before the establishment of Columbus Day, in the twentieth century, 20 September was the most important holiday in the various Little Italies; it was an occasion for parades, which were ridiculed with biting satire by the poet (*La festa del 20 Settembre a New York* [The September 20th Parade in New York]). The hexameters of *Publio Ovidio* [Publius Ovid] also refer back to the situation of the immigrant, reworking the topos of unjust, forced abandonment and painful distance (a theme on which, some years later, Cordiferro constructed a long *Ode alla Calabria* in octaves). The poem to the Latin poet is a precious archeological allegory (affirmed by the choice of meter) whose programmatic limitations and incongruousness leap out, but which, in its shameless arrogance, confirms the insistent search for dignity and the sublime on the part of this forgotten poet-seer of the immigrant community. Perhaps the vein most congenial to him can be found in extemporaneous pieces, some of which have been collected—ordered according to the person addressed and the occasion—in the good-humored, satirical anthology *Brindisi ed Auguri per ogni occasione* [Toasts and Good Wishes for Every Occasion] of 1917.

## GIOVANNITTI, THE BARD

With its highs and lows, its periods of intense activity and, in fact, celebrity, and of constant but little-noticed low-profile work, the biography of Arturo Giovannitti, a native of Molise (Ripabottoni, Campobasso, 1884–New York, 1959), is, until the outbreak of the Second World War, a typical story of a leader and intellectual of the American left—and, as such, deeply rooted in the ethnic community. In fact, the main stages of his life are contained within the broader history of Italian American socialism and unionism, as the best work on the subject, published in 1991 by Elisabetta Vezzosi, tells us. Arriving in the United States in 1904 (after three years, including university, in Canada), Giovannitti served as a Protestant minister in the mining towns of Pennsylvania. He quickly abandoned this to move, with an impulse no less prophetic and propagandistic, to union organizing, which, following the founding in 1905 of the Industrial Workers of the World, was then at the height of its most dynamic, aggressive period. Giovannitti was one of the prominent Italian spokesmen for the movement: he worked closely with Carlo Tresca and wrote for militant papers such as *La Plebe* and *Il Proletario* (of which he was briefly the editor, in 1911–12). He was among the leaders of major strikes, such as the strike of the textile workers in Lawrence, Massachusetts (1912), which led to his imprisonment and trial—and acquittal—on charges of assassination (his eloquent self-defense, in English, before the court of Salem should be noted), and a brief moment of international glory;[2] the strike in Paterson, New Jersey (1913); that of garment workers in Manhattan in 1916 (beside his contemporary Fiorello LaGuardia). His rhetorical passion made him a fixture at workers' meetings in those decades. At the same time he cultivated a more literary vein, editing or contributing to the more original and innovative periodicals of the Little Italies (*Il Fuoco, Vita, Il Veltro*), as well as to *The Masses,* which brought together the liveliest exponents of American radicalism in the second decade of the century.

After the First World War, and with the progressive exhaustion of the IWW experience, Giovannitti continued to work in the organizations that represented workers of Italian descent, binding himself forever to the new political exiles expelled by Fascism. (In 1923 he was the secretary general of the Anti-Fascist Alliance; from 1928 to 1930 he was the editor of *Il Nuovo Mondo;* later he joined the Mazzini Society.) Two English translations, notable in themselves for their mastery of expression, synthesize these two periods of Giovannitti's career: in 1913, in a revolutionary climate, he translated a famous pamphlet by Emile Pouget, *Sabotage,* which was published in Chicago by the anti-establishment house of Charles H. Kerr (with an introduction by the translator); in 1934, he made a translation of a long, novelistic biography explicitly entitled *Mussolini: Storia di un cadavere* [Mussolini: Story of a Corpse], by the former socialist deputy Vincenzo Vacirca, who, consistently rejected by American publishers, ended up printing it much later at his own expense in the original Italian. These translations represent, in the first case, the political and intellectual fame and direct action of years of union leadership, and, in the second, the indifference, if not actual hostility, with which, twenty years later, Little Italy and official America viewed a strongly critical portrait of Il Duce. The old, forgotten Giovannitti of the final period reemerges, decades later, as a character in the affecting autobiography of Joseph Tusiani, one of his principal exegetes.[3]

Giovannitti's poetry can be easily found, in two volumes of collected works that appeared a little before and a little after his death— *Quando canta il gallo* [When the Cock Crows] of 1957, and *The Collected Poems of Arturo Giovannitti* of 1962—brought out by another socialist publisher in Chicago, the Trieste native Egidio Clemente, of *La Parola del Popolo*. It should be pointed out, however, that many other lyrics, as well as a notable number of prose writings (characterized for the most part by heatedly and obscurely oracular opinions), must be retraced to the publications they originally appeared in, and that Giovannitti also contributed to the Italian American theater.

His *Come era nel principio* (*Tenebre rosse*) [As it Was in the Beginning (Red Darkness)], an anti-militarist drama in three acts, published in 1918, was performed in New York in both Italian (in 1916 at the People's Theater, on the Bowery, with Mimí Aguglia) and, the following year, in English, at the Gayety Theater.

In his practical politics, in his journalism, and in his creative writing, Giovannitti displayed an ornate and fluent bilingualism, more significant, of course, in the case of texts composed in both Italian and English. The frequent uncertainty of the dates of composition and, especially, the remarkable freedom with which he moves from one version to another suggest that the two expressive spheres were relatively independent, and this is confirmed on a case-by-case basis by his use of rhetorical strategies strongly representative of the respective national literatures: Whitman and his free verse, and Markham and the socially engaged poetry of the early twentieth century (Tusiani mentions, among other poets, Carl Sandburg and Vachel Lindsay); Carducci and D'Annunzio in their more heroic veins, and the ostentatious nonconformism of Stecchetti paired with the pomposity of Rapisardi, adapted as necessary to the rhythms of the Dantesque terzina (*Parole e sangue* [Words and Blood], is the pointedly suggestive title of another important collection). Aside from the variety of the particular works and the greater or lesser felicity of expression, aside from the lexical and metrical display, what is significant is that this juxtaposition of Italian and English in the end gives life to two contiguous, ideologically homogeneous, yet distinct poetic experiences. Giovannitti sees himself and presents himself as the bard of the Italian American working people; but the failure to fuse the two traditions seems to reflect, with characteristic "sublime" accents, the travails of assimilation experienced by his public.

Linguistic and sociological considerations apart, the encounter with the texts, if it is useful in becoming familiar with a style that is not exactly personal but certainly recognizable, at the same time reveals the general failure of the oeuvre as a whole. There exist (survive?), of course, pieces packed with energy, with a strong and unmistakable imaginative and verbal charge; there are hymns, ballads, and prose narratives that at times demonstrate a certain vibrant density, an expressive flame. But the very possibility, offered by the two anthologies, of a broad reading of this work demonstrates immediately the rhetorical excess, the unbearable vagueness, the monotony, the overblown, myopic revolutionary emphasis. We shouldn't forget that Giovannitti did not stop writing poetry after the IWW stage, but had a long "second period," unfortunately distinguished, at the expressive level, by a triumphalist, hagiographic vision of the Soviet revolution. This enthusiasm was later transformed into unsought adulation, creating an effect that Tusiani, kindly, calls "comical political propaganda."

The (relative) ease of finding the collections allowed the development of a small critical discourse, whose primary function was to choose, with largesse, the works and passages less likely to be censured by the taste of later generations. The worst Giovannitti is perhaps less misleading and more "typical"; but the less uncertain fate of other works guarantees continued attention on the part of alert readers equipped with an erudite historical and literary point of view. It is his most obvious contradiction: the desire to be the singer of the proletariat stifled by a diligent adherence to an inhibiting rhetorical and thematic arsenal; it is the sore spot of a long rhetorical tradition within the socialist workers' movement, and of a rich outlying area of nineteenth-century literature, but in Giovannitti it informs with "comic" and, at times, perverse ineffectualness an entire creative output.

Thus the choices for a possible course of reading are obvious: starting with *The Walker,* which appeared in 1912 in the prestigious *Atlantic Monthly,* and in 1914, in the author's first and most valuable plaquette, *Arrows in the Gale.* (Various versions in Italian circulated in Italy; *Colui che cammina,* by the sculptor and poet Onorio Ruotolo, evidently approved by Giovannitti, had the honor of its own small volume in 1950.) *The Walker* is a prison ballad in which the autobiographical occasion becomes an obsession and a "supplication" (Tusiani), sustained by a slow, dark rhythm. Giovannitti is more effective when he manages to stay with an object or a figure, avoiding at least temporarily his preachiness: here, the steps of the "walker" and the jingling of keys; in the hymn *O Labor of America: Heartbeat of*

*Mankind,* the list of cities invoked, through vivid, picturesque description between the Dantesque and the expressionistic; in *The Day of War—Un comizio a Madison Square,* the young orator and his band of spectators. Elsewhere, other styles and attitudes can prevail: the Nordic romanticism of the ballad *The Nuptials of Death—Le nozze della Morte;* popular tunes, as in *Nenia Sannita—Samnite Cradle Song* (several models can be adduced, from Parzanese to Carducci and Trilussa; in the development of the theme the difference between the English and Italian texts is noticeable); or, again, a mannerist invocation to an avenging, justice-bearing violence, as in *Il canto della scure* [The Song of the Axe]. Reread today, at a distance of only a few decades, these poems appear accessible only in the perspective of a historiographic evaluation; yet we should remember that, even after the blaze of the early century had been extinguished, a certain type of Italian American culture continued to celebrate itself in the name of Giovannitti—even with a prize—well into the seventies, which is, in a way, just before yesterday.

## THE SONNETEER RIGHI

Less encumbered, and therefore more easily appreciated, is the poetry of Simplicio Righi. An esteemed doctor, Righi was able to preserve through the years the respect of even the most far-flung groups of the community; and in this a certain role was no doubt played by the modest fame he had won as a "nice" and lovably dilettantish poet who composed well-crafted sentimental love songs and verses in praise of working people.[4] He signed himself, especially in his youth, with the pseudonym Rosina Vieni ("Come, Rosina"); the course of his ideology is interesting, and not completely atypical, moving from a deep involvement with the socialists (he was the editor of *Il Proletario* in 1901–2) to collaboration with the nationalist-Fascist front, from the columns of *Il Carroccio.* The essential New York topography of his five *Sonetti di Manhattan* of 1924,[5] characterized by an academic literariness, precedes by only a little the complex, varied "historical" Americanism of Cecchi, Soldati, Borgese and so on. But in Righi, not unnaturally, the critique, if one can call it that, is still pre-modern; it originates in familiarity with the daily sweat of the people rather than as an adventurous exercise in comparison between the "civilization" of the Old World and the barbaric energy of the New. In another sonnet, the exemplary and touching *Vennero i bricchellieri . . .* ([The Bricklayers Came] signed with the pseudonym),[6] the liberal use of the hybrid Anglo-Italian lexicon is not a linguistic game (besides,

Righi was neither the only nor the first to take up the "speech" of the immigrants)[7] but a rigorous, emotional adherence to the real world of the construction workers; in fact, it is precisely the close texture of neologisms that suggests how, through the travails of work, a new identity was painfully coming into being as well, that of the Italian American.

## THE "CIVIL" AND TRADITIONALIST POEMS OF THE RED BARTOLETTI

Within the trio of the most outstanding Italian American proletarian poets in the twentieth century—Giovannitti, the Sicilian dialect poet Antonino Crivello, and Efrem Bartoletti—the last is distinguished by a more active, intimate faithfulness to valuable models from Italian literature, as well as by careful attention to the events of contemporary Italy's tragic political history. In contradiction to the titles of some of his collections (the first and the last: *Nostalgie proletarie* [Proletarian Nostalgias], 1919, and *Evocazioni e ricordi* [Evocations and Reminiscences], 1959), Bartoletti, aside from the plaintive, formulaic tone of the exile, displays in his most interesting work a vigorous and, in its way, notable engagement. The work that is signed with the pseudonym Etrusco is from the thirties and forties, during the decline, that is, both of the union-revolutionary activism of the IWW, of which Bartoletti had been one of the first advocates, and, more generally, of Italian American literature in Italian itself.

The Umbrian Bartoletti (Costacciaro, Perugia, 1889–Scranton, Pennsylvania, 1961), came to the United States in 1909. He was self-taught, and was a miner, with only a few interruptions, for his entire life (iron and coal, with a short stint in Luxembourg, at the age of eighteen). He was a prolific contributor to the organ of the Italian Wobblies, *Il Proletario,* from 1916 until it closed thirty years later, and in both his poems and his so-called "battle" prose he used various pseudonyms (Porsenna, for example). From the early teens he had been among the contributors to local papers such as *L'Operaio Italiano* in Altoona, Pennsylvania, *Il Messaggero* in Ohio, and Carlo Tresca's combative *L'Avvenire.* He made a name for himself in *Il Proletario* in 1916, as an organizer and a correspondent, from Hibbing, Minnesota, covering the iron miners' strike there, which became a symbol of the American workers' movement; in 1917, in the heat of the moment, he wrote a draft of a hymn to *Russia ribelle* [Rebellious Russia], for *L'Avvenire.* From 1919 to 1930 he was back in Costacciaro, where in 1920–21 he was the mayor, heading a socialist administration that was soon overthrown by Fascist violence. Bartoletti's political and union activity, at least until the March on Rome, also included speeches, for the most part marred by an insistent recourse to the most trite commonplaces of patriotism: "After the advent of Fascism he kept in the background, giving the apparent impression of not being concerned with politics."[8]

Two years after the centenary of the death of Leopardi, celebrated with fanfare by the Fascist regime, there appeared in *Il Proletario*, in Brooklyn in 1939, *Il carme a Giacomo Leopardi* [Ode to Giacomo Leopardi], framed by a clearly anti-Fascist dedication to Randolfo Pacciardi (then among the leaders of the Mazzini Society) and an equally symbolic date, 1 May, representing the "international solidarity of the proletariat and social revolution" (Vecoli)—and chosen deliberately in place of the usual national or nationalist holidays, both American and Italian (4 July, 20 September, 12 October).[9]

Leopardi is invoked and, at times, appropriated in a tour de force of quotation and updating that offers itself as the solitary product, a "distant echo," of a generous and undoubtedly sincere "proletarian classicism." The poem affirms (anticipates?) a progressive reading of Leopardi, impelled by the calamity of the prewar present. The two principal textual reference points are the *Canzone all'Italia* and the *Palinodia al Marchese Gino Capponi:* two poles, which are also chronological, of Leopardi's civil engagement, heroic and satiric. Thus it indicates, on the part of the poet-miner, a struggle and a critical view consistent over time (and at the particular moment an irreproachable credential of anti-Fascism), and a variety of ideological and linguistic attitudes, from the sublime to the comic (in fact the latter are almost completely stifled by the former).

In the foreground, therefore, we find, as in Leopardi's civil odes, the Italian martyrs (here Matteotti and the Rosellis) and the glories of poetry (Pascoli: not only and not necessarily the Pascoli of the "great Proletariat," the father figure of the immigrant people, who had been mourned in an elegy of 1912). But behind the eulogy, as in the model, is a biting contempt for decadence, both political and literary: the dictatorship of Il Duce, a "traitor," "piglike and bald," who brandishes "a savage club" (the vocabulary and iconography are socialist, almost in the Scalarini style); and the "ignoble servility" of Marinetti, who pollutes the Muses (in the post–Second World War poems the anti-modernist polemic became even more pronounced and predictable). The whole poem is interwoven with such opposites, which are certainly too vehement and programmatic to produce a rhetorically worked out irony; but the insistence of the parallels still reflects a kind of nobility. The marvelous achievements of technology are similarly distorted: radio used for the purposes of propaganda (one of the subjects of Etrusco, as another interesting poem confirms: . . .*ascoltando la Radio* [. . . Listening to the Radio], in *Il Proletario*, 10 February 1940); electricity as the instrument of death; the "dream" of Icarus which has produced "bombers/flying monsters." Not without reason, his colleague Pucelli, in a rare critical piece, suggests a debt to the civil poetry of Monti.[10]

This constant distortion of ends appears to the "Leopardian" Bartoletti the truly triumphant internationalism: from Italy the vision spreads to Germany (where the same involuted process is replayed: from Kant, Wagner, and Schopenhauer to the "foul painter's smock") and to war-torn Spain. But this decline falls not only on the West, as verses on China and Japan and a mention of Ethiopia suggest. And interestingly the poem, with a skepticism not, it appears, entirely shared by other comrades, including Giovannitti, mutes the early post-revolutionary enthusiasm, and does not present a hagiographic, redemptive vision of the Soviet Union: accomplices of this vision are the bitter internal party and union divisions of the left, stigmatized by one who nevertheless can produce the expressive hendiadys *Capitalismo e delinquenza* [Capitalism and Criminality]. Criticism of the "fatal" complicity of the European democracies is fleeting but unequivocal; on the other hand, among so many verbal assaults the silence, perhaps purposeful, that surrounds the land of exile is striking, though it is easy to imagine it covered by a "democratic fleece, dripping / tears and blood of the betrayed and oppressed."

The poem begins with old-fashioned eloquence, crudely mixing biography and Leopardian poetic fiction, to end with a facile and incongruous exhortation; but in between, thanks to the image-filled, digressive unfolding, it acquires its recognizable pace, sustained and fluent. We find ourselves before one of the last "organic" fruits of Italian American culture in Italian, and one of the most "prodigious," a hymn at once artificial and spontaneous that is both Italian and international. Although Bartoletti also loved short poetic forms (epigrams, sonnets), he was better suited to the broad measures of the ode, to "triumphal hymns," even to the clearly immigrant genre of the "satire of the immigrant communities."[11] Within a rich oeuvre, the ode to Leopardi manages to stand out not in spite of but by virtue of the linguistic and figurative emphasis. Unlike in the great majority of his other texts, here his highfalutin tone seems to coincide with the patriotic and anti-Fascist rhetoric: this could be called oxymoron poetry, the result of mixing a high culture, laboriously acquired, and the political myth of "direct action" of the people.

Another, shorter and more explicit "May Day" is the work of Giuseppe Bertelli (1869–1943), a native of Empoli, in Tuscany. A sort of lament for laborers, it displays a similar repertoire of almost slogan-like, and therefore contrived, words and images that exhibit, for the same reason, signs of strain. Bertelli, who settled in the United States in 1906, was a central figure in the history of Italian American socialist and workers' organizations, and notably of their press (he was one of the founders of *La Parola dei Socialisti* in 1908, and of *La Parola del Popolo* in 1919); in 1940, at the end of a life as a proselytizer and prolific writer of pamphlets for the left, he published a short volume, *Rime d'esilio—Il bacio* [Rhymes of Exile—The Kiss], in which nostalgia, senile reflections, domestic scenes, and a kindly, paternalistic tone are prevalent. The private, humble face of the tough organizer, whose poetic militant outbursts are rare, as if muted by a palpable sense of defeat. An observation of Croce's, in *Letteratura della nuova Italia*, still holds true for this minor and occasional author: "Deep within these fierce socialists, there was always the good 'bourgeois' and the good Italian patriot."

## DIALECT POETS: MENNELLA AND BORGIANINI

From the point of view of a history of taste, *Rapsodia napoletana* [Neapolitan Rhapsody] and *Napule d'aiere* [Naples of Yesterday], both published in 1944, by the Neapolitan Federico Mennella (1894–1954; in the United States from 1913) are easily defined by the realist, storytelling spirit that informs the poetry of an inspirational writer like Ferdinando Russo, who was fond of broad historical frescoes presented in series of sonnets (the resemblances between Mennella's *Rapsodia* and Russo's *'O Cantastorie* [The Storyteller], are notable, but Russo's poem is only one among many possible examples). And a preface to *Rapsodia*, signed by Agostino De Biasi (the founder of *Il Carroccio* and its man of all work from 1915 to 1935), helps to place the author in the circle of the middle-high Italian American bourgeoisie. This is confirmed by his voluntary enlistment and return to Italy during the Great War (he took the occasion to publish, with Morano in 1918, his first collection, *Sempre e ovunque* [Always and Everywhere]); by his contributions to Cordiferro's *Follia di New York* (where he appeared on the dialect page) and to the more conformist *Progresso Italo-Americano;* and, finally, by his career as an official employed in trade relations between the two countries.

There is not much to add to this profile of Mennella, an amateur poet (in spite of a handful of other publications, in Naples and New York) and a public figure in the immigrant community. In fact, his work in Italian, both as a poet—with the overelaborate, pretentious *Canzoni de l'ora* [Poems of the Present], of 1945—and as a short-story writer, seems completely negligible. His interest lies almost solely in the *Rapsodia*, an epic of Neapolitan history, in 105 sonnets (from the founding of the Greek colony to the entrance of the Allies), and has quite a lot to do with the timeliness of the inspiration and the execution: there is, in the *Rapsodia*, a freshness unusual in the panorama of Italian American letters, which can be explained by, among other things, a faithfulness to the emotions evoked by events. One of the better elements of *Napule d'aiere*, entitled *Guagliune'e Napule* [Kids of Naples], begins as a sentimental comment on a clipping from the *New York Times* of 7 October 1943, dedicated to the heroic days of the anti-Nazi revolt. The determining choice of dialect was not in itself a guarantee of authenticity, since it could also have meant falling into another type of convention. Instead, the weight given to the setting, with a popular storyteller, Don Pasquale Forte, "'o presidente 'e tutt' 'e guardaporte," [the president of all doormen] presiding on a fateful winter evening in Naples in 1944, successfully and realistically anchors an ancient story in the travails of the present, and, in addition, inspires reflection on unexpected aspects of southern emigration.

Thus the themes of war and the return to the South of the sons of the first immigrants are expressed with obvious immediacy and cathartic freedom: "'Nu bellu marenaro americano / capille nire e uocchie a fa' ncantà, / se chiamma Pasqualino Califano, / 'a nonna sta' de casa 'a Sanità" [A handsome American sailor / jet-black hair and enchanting eyes, / his name is Pasqualino Califano, / his grandma lives in the neighborhood of Sanità]. Within the setting, the broad historical design unfolds in a tone somewhere between folklore and legend, with a popular point of view that de-heroicizes the figures and events of a great past without, however, denying their importance. The epic is diminished, made more "true"—in both moments of glory and moments of tragedy—by a comic vein that runs under the surface. When it comes to the revolution of 1799, for example, it recounts up to a certain point the clear, almost Manichaean opposition between the "glory" of the Republic and the perverted, traitorous spirit of its enemies; to Mennella–Don Pasquale it is particularly important to construct a micro-narrative, to draw, with quick brushstrokes, some of the characters, following a secular vox populi. And here the pawns of that dramatic game reappear, from Admiral Caracciolo to Re Nasone, from the treacherous Ruffo and Emma Lyons to the traitor Nelson. The attitude toward the Risorgimento and Garibaldi is similar. Moving therefore in its own way between detachment and intimacy, between irony and didactic intent, the voice of the narrator gradually gains credibility: the *Rapsodia* is an isolated, unique work within the Italian American dialect tradition, and deserves to be placed in the group that includes the *Galleria*, by J. H. Burns, Malaparte's *La pelle*, and *Naples '44*, by Norman Lewis, in addition to the masterpieces of Eduardo. The two names of Mennella and De Filippo appear deliberately in succession in Pasolini's great study of dialect poetry (1952); both are examples of the move from "the catchy digiacomismo" (that is, the lyrical mode fashioned after Salvatore Di Giacomo) to "more recent, twentieth-century literary experiences."[12]

Closer to the surrounding reality, at least in the better works, is another noteworthy dialect poet, Alfredo Borgianini (he was an automobile designer in Trenton, New Jersey; he seems to have arrived in the United States in 1907, at the age of twenty-five). The volume of his collected works, *Sonetti e poesie romanesche* [Roman Sonnets and Poems] (1948), certainly has documentary value, with representations of immigrant life including banquets, picnics, and appearances by prominent figures (including first and last names). The usual tone is a "reassuring good humor" (Durante), with frequent sighs of nostalgia for "Rome my beauty" or, on another level, ironic nods to American modernity. There are cycles of sonnets (*Sonetti reclame* [Advertising Sonnets]) and narrative sestinas (*Flapperismo; Le delizie der matrimonio* [The Joys of Marriage]), which acquire a more consistent pace, although they are marred by embarrassing displays of misogyny. Borgianini's trump card, so to speak, is his words—not the language but, rather, strictly a lexicon that gives generous room to American English loan words (some examples: *Brodestreto*, "Broadway [street]"; *muvimpiccio*, "moving picture"; *cotti*, "coats"; *arrioppa*, "hurry up"). This brilliant and in a sense informal expressiveness constitutes the principal interest of poetry that is on the whole anecdotal, as much in its style as in its content.

## THE "HARMONIES AND DISSONANCES" OF RUOTOLO

The less obviously formless or lachrymose texts of Onorio Ruotolo, a native of Irpinia (Cervinara 1888–New York 1966; emigrated in 1907), can be seen as the end point of a certain type of poetry that goes back to, as a common historical denominator, the epochal break represented by the great migration. Ruotolo was an extravagant promoter of New York's Little Italy, as Pietro di Donato affirms. He was a champion of the "average" member of the Italian American population, as faithfully reflected in a public life that may at first glance seem disconcerting because of its openness to so many disparate views and mental habits. Yet Ruotolo's conformist permeability to the prevailing moods corresponds precisely to the vacillations (including electoral ones) of his audience. Thus, in the teens and the early twenties, he fought beside Giovannitti (for whom he translated *The Walker* in 1950), founded or edited journals such as *Il Fuoco* and *Minosse,* and supported the United States Socialist Party. Soon afterward, however, we find him as an "artistic contributor" to *Il Carroccio* and the other major conservative immigrant journals; he took intensely chauvinistic positions, praising D'Annunzio's invasion of Fiume and placing himself squarely among the nationalists; and in the following decade he joined Fiorello LaGuardia and Edward Corsi, that is, the Republican establishment of his city. After the war, he appeared among the animating spirits of *Divagando,* the last large-circulation Italophone weekly, an advocate of the *pax americana*—but at the same time he published in the ever more moderate socialist journal *Parola del Popolo,* and assumed cultural positions in the union world. Finally, as the late collection *Accordi e dissonanze* [Harmonies and Dissonances] of 1958 demonstrates, he embraced a vague but accommodating religiosity. During these forty years Ruotolo was active as political commentator, prose writer, and playwright. But his name is associated above all with his work as a sculptor and as the founder, in 1923, and director of the Leonardo da Vinci Art School in Manhattan, which was for twenty years the crossroads of the Italian American art world (and not only Italian American: Isamu Noguchi and Louise Bourgeois also passed through it) and, in addition, an arena for cultural exchange between the two countries (notable in this regard are the institute's annual yearbooks).[13]

The poetry, produced more assiduously in his last years, seldom rises above the personal occasion; the verse of this hardworking activist is forgettable, lacking, as it does, a recognizable purpose. Nor can one speak of models, except for a slight influence of Ungaretti. But precisely this lack of interest in the tradition signals the impoverishment of poetry transplanted from nineteenth- and twentieth-century lyricism. Ruotolo's more sincere verses, with their relative freedom and modernity, unfold in a strictly personal key, corresponding to the vivacity of the man, guileless even in his commentaries on art and politics. At times, in the scenes of daily life in New York, gracefully nostalgic or lighthearted, we seem to have an unusual example of "ingenuous" Italian American poetry (*Nel parco della Union Square* [In Union Square Park]; *La mia vacanza estiva* [My Summer Vacation]; *Notturno di rimembranze* [Nocturne of Memories]; *Il passato non muore* [The Past Does Not Die]). But one might rather acknowledge there the final stop of poetry that has been stripped of ornamentation and is on the point of extinction, at least as an expression of a community. The simplicity of Ruotolo's poetry, which is so readable, especially in comparison with the literary rhetoric that precedes it, is in fact an indication of weakness, of not belonging, and, as its author clearly saw, of "dissonance." The paradox is only apparent, for a closer look demonstrates that neither naïve spontaneity nor the traditions of the twentieth century ever represented true points of reference for the neglected work of this "historic" Italian American poetry. (This may also explain the longtime reluctance to study it and the often contemptuous tone of the rare critical works.)

The panorama, of course, does not end here. In addition to the writers presented above, others should be mentioned who are of interest, for reasons either external (historiographical, publishing, and polemical), or internal (thematic, linguistic, and, in a loose sense, aesthetic value or lack of it). One could enter, in short, what Francesco Durante has proposed calling the "undergrowth" of Italian American poetry in Italian: a territory as broad as it is feverish with enterprise, but in essence distinguished by a strict, loving traditionalism, and for this very reason by a more and more pronounced isolation.[14]

❊ ❊

*Anthology*

## CORDIFERRO-IRONHEART: VERSATILE VERSIFIER

The language, rhythms, images, and themes of Riccardo Cordiferro's poems reveal a breadth that could only be called eccentric, and, with their fluency and lack of restraint, they appear to best advantage in a brief selection. Apart from the occasional portrait of a character or event in the immigrant community, the work remains closely tied to the vast field of nineteenth-century Italian "minor" poetry. This is its strength but also its limitation. It might not be too far-fetched to praise Cordiferro now mainly as the soul of the weekly *La Follia di New York*.

## May Day

*To my friend Luigi Bizzarri*

There's a crowd that rumbles and shouts,
that beats the streets of every town.
Riotous, furious, it defies today
the parasites of society.

Red waves the flag, a beacon
for those who ask for work and freedom,
for those who trust in the triumph of the oppressed,
in a peace now unknown to the people.

Oh! perhaps the day when the red
flag of rebellion becomes a banner,
the fated day of liberation,
anxiously anticipated, has already come?

No: but it is near. From an unknown depth
the Messiah is rising who will lead us.
The phalanx of men is swelling
that will sweep away every injustice.

## To Alarico

So do you remember, my cheerful friend,
the happy days we spent in Naples?
Not even I, rambling Alarico,
not even I have forgotten them.

Our youth was like a spring
smile, and Naples, then, a charm.
Why did we leave that sweet Paradise?
Why did we come to this graveyard?

Here, where the best of our lives fades away,
is a land of headless people and snakes.
It is not worth wasting paper and ink
if the public misinterprets or does not see.

Heart and soul, lock, stock, and barrel,
you devoted yourself to the art of cartoons.

I, I am but a rattlesnake
kidding myself that I inspire fear.

And like an automaton I write, and Judas'
sneer is chasing me like a cat.
Better, then, to stay in my Trivigno
and, among the peasants, turn into a hick!

Here boredom kills you little by little,
here all is hypocrisy, all is deception!
Gone is the fire of our youthful days,
of ourselves and the others we're ashamed.

He who swears friendship is a traitor,
he whom we think an apostle is a cheat.
We know what Sorrow means,
and what illusion means!

Yet we were so happy in Naples,
and so carefree, O *Viafòra!*
I remember all our friends,
how I still remember those joyous days!

You made love with the seamstresses
of via Roma, and I, an impromptu poet,
was scribbling verses to the Nanninas,
the Olgas, the Marias of the neighborhood.

Then, inside the Gran Caffè all day and night
with Mignone and Labriola and Sarno and Alfano,
with Bruno, Trevison, Cocchia, and Guarino,
we made such an awful din.

Caffè De Angelis was the meeting place
of the radicals and outcasts.
Some evenings it was packed to the rafters.
Still we were all "desperadoes."

We were all broke, and yet
our youth was like a smile.
Why did we come to this graveyard?
Why did we leave our Paradise?

Do you remember, then, the joyous days
of that sweet time, my young Alarico?
Not even I will ever be able to forget them,
my sweet, my courteous friend!

## The 20th of September Parade in New York

Oh! the houses are all decked with flags today,
the streets much livelier . . . What in the world is it?

Proud and smiling, they promenade here and there,
the illustrious *prominenti* of our colony.

They're dressed in uniform. Take a look . . . it's natural!
For those who still don't know it, this is Carnival.

There he is on a prancing horse, conceited and smug,
in front of everybody, sitting tall, motionless, the grand marshal.

Lined up behind him according to hierarchical rank
are all the people of the community . . . (And they look like
     brigands from the Sila.)

You find colonels, and generals,
and soldiers and officers galore.

See that fellow who . . . looks like a captain,
they all know him . . . the famous scoundrel.

And that one, who holds his sabre like a stick,
he has the easy job of the pimp.

The other one, dead drunk, who's come out of the ranks,
he mumbles prayers from morning to night: he's a hypocrite.

That thing so long and lank, almost like a baldachin,
he's a professor, but really he's just an imbecile.

That pigmy who shouts as loud as he can,
he's a doctor who should still be in school.

And that eccentric, that cheeky fellow,
he's the editor of the *Bug*, an illiterate notary.

You have Don Mamozio here, the ignorant banker,
who in his home village herded the sheep . . .

You have Father Sausage, Father Eat-the-Immigrants,
Lawyer Strip Him, Esq., the king of cheats.

And the one they all call cavalier Carlino,
together with the famous writer Don Agostino.

You'll find Papà Luigi, Zucca, Vito, Cambria,
Mr. Ambassador, the consul, Mr. Turncoat & Co.

It's a holiday today! The 20th of September! The parade
is passing by. Hear how the music is out of tune!

Hark! Hark . . . They're playing Garibaldi's hymn.
O! damned race! Liars and lowlifes!

Could this be the Italy you dreamed of,
you Lion of Caprera, fearless figure?

Is this the Italy for which you, strong and brave,
fought a hundred times, crying: Either Rome or death?

Here, Italy is passing by . . . You see how happy
the *prominenti* are, greeting the crowd.

See how they clutch their swords,
while one is lecturing and barks like a dog.

See how attentively they listen to the speaker
who with his elbow wipes away the sweat.

Oh, how many, how many veterans of our nation's jails
are talking about honor, and country, and virtue! What a pleasure!

And how many who in Italy were sentenced
to life are now cheered and praised!

Italy is passing by . . . Take off your hat . . .
Would you want to see a nicer and more exciting show?

Without paying a penny, you will see
things which in other times may seem incredible!

The Society of San Rocco takes the lead . . . then
here's the Bruno. What, are you laughing?

No, no need to laugh . . . The one that's walking by now
is the Club named after the *Progresso.*

It is followed by another, the Bandiera,
and right in front you'll find the Prayer.

O! What a rich banner! See: it's all made of silk.
And embroidered above: "Holy Virgin Mary from Meta."

But the other is richer still. It belongs to the patrons
of the society of Mother of the Seven Chains.

Here's Italy passing by . . . And you laugh! It's true:
these are things to make the whole world laugh!

If at the echoing sound of the raucous trumpets
the martyrs who made Italy could

for a little time rise from their tombs,
what would they say? . . . Who can say?

They'd cry out repenting: But this is a bacchanal!
Who knows! Maybe we were resurrected at Carnival!

**Publius Ovid**

Dark and horrid Tomos, covered by gloomy clouds,
is sleeping. No star clears the thick darkness
of the Getic horizon that on the desolate city
like a lead cloak falls. The bare, squalid countryside
never seemed so grim to the eyes of the thoughtful poet
who, while everything is silent, like a living ghost wanders
along the dark deserted roads known to him alone,
the empty roads that he has already bathed in his tears.
The wild sea moans, the angry sea that never
calms down. As the sea is storming, so is
the poet's anguished soul, remembering time past,
and it shivers with outrage, regretting the joyous beautiful days
    gone by.
The Pontus Euxinus murmurs. What strange news does the river

tell in its language? What does it ask the poet? What is it looking
  for?
It may listen to the exile's long lament, to Ovid's
despairing cries the river may listen, and echoes
the pain of him neglected, banished by the wrath of Augustus
to fierce Scythia, among the barbarians forever.
"O how monotonous in this icy necropolis,
seething with people who pass by like ghosts!
O how monotonous this town, wrapped in
a shroud of thick fog, always, even when the sun
shines in the heavens looking like a huge veiled disk—
a huge disk of fire cast into the deep void!"
Thus, weeping, the sad poet laments, he who sang
of the splendor of ancient Rome, the glories of imperial Rome.
And while in the depths of night all the people of Tomos sleep
in Morpheus' arms, in tranquil slumber: he alone,
he alone confides his grief to the land and the sea,
and he talks to the breezes, and his slow lament reaches the sky.
Yet the sky, the sea, the land, the wind, all he sees,
all that surrounds him, all that he touches and hears,
takes pity on him, pities his boundless grief;
even the Gods are moved, and mourn his fate.
Augustus is deaf to every prayer, he alone remains distant; he's not
listening to Ovid's laments; he alone, impassive, is waiting
for Death with her fateful stamp to seal the mouth
of the man from Sulmona. Sad and silent, Publius wanders in the
  woods,
he weeps and begs, thinking of Rome, now old,
and of his rich house, splendid with luxury and good taste;
he thinks of knights and ladies, of poets and artists, of the
  hospitable
gathering gladdened by sweet Fabia's smile.
Only Augustus' heart is never moved, only
his incestuous heart does not ache at Publius' faraway lament,
feeble and thoughtful, concealed forever from glory
and from Perilla's kisses! (O sweet daughter, o graceful
girl, the favorite of Art and the Muses, nevermore will you
be able to kiss your father's pallid face!)
He is writing to you and in those epistles is all his heart,
a father's, a poet's, his sad and wounded heart.
He writes to you, and before sending his torn heart,
he covers the trembling letter with tender kisses.
But while all mourn Publius' cruel fate

and ancient Rome eagerly awaits his return, only Augustus,
ruthless Augustus, does not give in to the poet's entreaties and
   prayers.
He alone does not want him to return. Everywhere,
since the world began, kings have always been cowards,
always harsh and depraved, always, everywhere tyrants!

❖

"O this murky sky, forever hooded with clouds,
this heavy humid air that stifles and suffocates," moans
the exile. "O, nevermore will I see you again, O beautiful sky,
O beautiful, smiling sky of Italy! As each day passes,
my wretched life like a flower sheds its petals, and my hair
turns white, and all, all crumbles around me!
Will this anguish that freezes my soul be eternal,
rending these poor fibres, compressing my
brain, like a sinister instrument of death?
Oh, will this atrocious torment be eternal, never
giving me peace, will there be no relief from the weight that for so
   long
has oppressed my yearning soul, filled with doubt, shattered
and shaken by enormous, overwhelming sorrow?!
Have pity at last, Augustus, on your old friend!
The mild sky of Rome, oh, let me see it again! Let me
kneel one more time in front of the benevolent gods!
My rosy hopes are all vanishing! Each day
I see them fade, and now they have left me, and I feel
alone . . . (O my aching heart, be resigned to your cruel fate!)
Beloved motherland, I'll never see you again! The endless
agony that consumes me has made me an automaton, a tree!
Roving, roaming, prey to a cruel fate,
I'll end my days here, cursing my unlucky lot,
which condemns me to live far away from my beloved mountains!
But at least let my sad heart cease, cease to beat!
let death come! For so long now I've wished for death and waited!
There is no sweetness, I think, that will ever
equal death. It alone can soothe every human pain.
And in the unknown grave (let the Scythian arrow die!)
I will feel at peace, much happier than amid this
deep incessant desolation of humans and things,
which like a fog clouds my dark life, and takes my breath
away. O, come, come death, which I've wished and waited for
from the day when I was snatched forever from my beloved
   motherland!"

Thus the abandoned poet moans, who was dear to the gods, and
   whose brow
was wreathed with flowers, once, with sweet-scented flowers.
Thus moans the grieving poet who in vain awaits Augustus'
pardon, in vain prides himself that he can appease Caesar's
   disdain.
Icy the air that touches his face, and as he looks at that dark
sky that never smiles, tears roll down his gaunt
and faded cheeks. Could he at least sleep
the last, eternal sleep beside comely Falisca,
the dear and good and sweet creature who first loving him
let him taste the supreme pleasures of the senses!
She now lies cold in the silent sepulcher, but
he'd rather have that pit than this den of living men!
Why is he sighing in that savage cave, amid unshaved barbarians,
he who one day chose Rome the unconquered as his adopted
   motherland?
What brought him there? Augustus would have been more
   humane
had he signed an edict of death instead of foully
damning Publius to perpetual exile! Everywhere
since the world began, kings have always been kings,
longing for revenge, thirsty for blood, cowards,
always cruel and contemptible, always, everywhere, tyrants!

O Publius, O Publius, stop begging forgiveness from the unjust!
Stop crying, alas! Augustus rejects your prayers.
Augustus crowned you with laurel on the Capitoline
and weaves for you now a blood-red crown of sharp thorns.
Die a brave man, at least! Do not cry! . . . Kings are everywhere
beasts clothed in gold and worshipped by the people. Be strong!
He whose soul is proud does not fear, does not weep, does not
   pray:
no, do not kneel at the feet of Caesar who despises you!
Giulia, Giulia alone, charming Corinna, who appears
in your uneasy dreams, she alone might soothe
your pain, which bitterly racks and gnaws at you;
but she, too, is in exile, banished by Augustus,
and weeps on a foreign shore, she whose heart you asked for in
   your songs,
and she gave it to you, indeed, conquered by your immortal songs.
O Publius, O Publius, stop begging forgiveness from the vile
monarch acclaimed by the mob of cowardly subjects.

You, incautious, unveiled Maximus' secret. Cursing
ambitious Livia, your faithful friend killed
himself, and you shed tears for him. O Publius, the olive branch
you await from Augustus will never reach you in exile!
Horace is interceding for you. Humbly he prays, and swears
that at last the king will retreat from his cruel purpose. But in
    vain!
Tibullus weeps for you in feeble couplets, while in suave
pentameters Virgil greets his onetime friend,
remembering "Medea," the beloved "Medea," which first
brought you fame, and in vain he implores harsh Augustus.
Augustus sends everyone away. O Publius, do not entreat him
    anymore!
Even by Tiberius, even by cunning Tiberius, you, anxious,
will wait in vain to be pardoned. He, too, sneering, indifferent
will read your poems, and scorn
your boundless pain . . . And Fate, pale Fate, O poet,
to your cold exile will finally come and seize you!
Who will scatter flowers on your desolate tomb?
Who, O Publius, will say the elegy over your sad bier? At last,
O Publius, you will close your weary eyes on the beloved
volumes, your companions in painful exile.
And as you bow your white head over the white pages,
your last word will be for the motherland: *Ave Roma!*
*Ave, Ave, Roma,* praised be the sword of Brutus
the avenger! Blessed be the sword of Brutus!
For then the world will be cleansed of all infamies,
when broken forever the thrones will crumble and the false
idols will be thrown down. He who is about to die lays his head
on the sweaty pages, and the echo replies: *Ave, Roma!*

*New York, November 26, 1903*

---

*Singhiozzi e sogghigni* (New York: L'Araldo Italiano, 1910), 41, 109–110, 135–137, 202–206; translated by Martino Marazzi and Ann Goldstein.

## The Bard Arturo Giovannitti

Giovannitti, like Cordiferro, can only benefit from an anthological
selection. His voice loves expansiveness, bombast, imperative moods,
and rhetorical calls to arms and justice. He almost always writes as if
he were standing on a stage and preaching to a transfixed audience,
employing Whitmanesque prose poems, or the incantatory repeti-

tions of an oral, folkloric tradition. His assertiveness, although far from current tastes, underscores the honesty of his inspiration; and for many decades he was considered the name to remember in Italian American letters, thanks in part to his brave bilingualism. Such fame may appear to be historically deserved, but a close reading of the texts reveals, among other things, a heavy debt to the late romanticism of the Scapigliatura and to the decadentism of the turn of the century.

## "O Labor of America: Heartbeat of Mankind"

Come, then, come now, sweat, sooty red-eyed,
Flame-scorched vestals of the eternal fire of
steel and coal and steam and wood, and stone
and tools that make bread and surcease from want and woe.

Human machines actioned by hope and ambition
and oiled with blood, miners, stokers, hammersmiths,
builders, converters, puddlers, engineers of chasms,
escalators and defiers of the Babylon heights—
O Labor of America, O heartbeat of Mankind,
Come before and beyond all authorities, rules, edicts
ukases, injunctions and excommunications and
foregather and proclaim yourselves in the great
deed of Liberty.
For you have lightened the night of your dream
even to the humbling of sunrise.

Welcome, dark, fierce cities, daughters of volcanoes,
hearths and matrices of the new world—
Duquesne, Homestead, Calumet, Buffalo, sleepless and
tortured and flint-faced.
And you, Braddock, fevered with an endless
contemplation of the Satanic glow,
And you, Pueblo, titan-limbed, monster biceps
bursting in the almighty effort of gestation and
agony of the implacable fecundity of our
ferocious industry.
And you, McKeesport, mountain-ribbed, and you
Akron and Youngstown, rubber-thewed, washing
your stolid blank faces in your rusty creeks,
And you, astraddle the Styx and the Acheron,
Pittsburgh, wrathful resting grave of

spent meteors, gateway of Hell,
All ye, unhallowed grails of the last eucharist of sweat,
Welcome to the home of Labor, the last stricken
Archangel,
For your resurrection has come.
Detroit has its hand on the lever,
Gary maneuvers the brakes
and Chicago, feeder of the world,
Rules the switches of the two-fisted earth.

If this is not the fullness of your glory,
O American Labor, there is your New York
Cosmopolis of Mankind,
Whose towers you raised to mock the hurricanes
and to shame and debase the clouds,
Whose harbor swallows the nations, whose
people, myriad-tongued,
absorb and reshape and amalgam
all creeds, all races in one humanity.

Stand up, then, and take the earth unto your bosom,
Gather the oceans in your mighty cupped hands,
Cleanse the heavens of the scourges of the black demons
Of war, hate, fear and death and destruction,
Remold and reshape the soul of mankind
Into brave exploits of compassion and the dazzling
splendor of reason and brotherhood.

Take most of our bread to the starving,
Whoever they be, wherever they be
Fill your countless argosies with milk and honey
For the livid parched lips of the children
Of your erstwhile enemies and your detractors,
Uprise the fallen heroes, sustain the weak,
Comfort the widows the orphans and the bereft
Tear down the gateways to freedom to the imprisoned,
Turn the flood gates of light upon the entombed in darkness
Dry up the tears of shame and remorse
From the eyes of the harlot and the thief,
Smoothe the scowl of hate and revenge from the brow
of the earth
And make of all her children the new, eternal united
Israel of mankind.

And now we as Italian-Americans bow in
both humility and pride as we ask you
to stand by and acclaim
your brothers from the land that
gave a new hidden world to the world.

From that venerable mother of
America, from the land of
ecstasies and sorrows, of
Ancient glories and unbearable
humiliations,
From the garden of the earth, from the
only land of many tender and mystic names:
Etruria, Augusta, Enotria, Esperia,
Saturnia, Vulcania, forever Italia,
we call upon you to stop her weeping over
earthquakes, eruptions and floods,
and the desolation of ancient and new battlefields,
to mingle with you in an everlasting embrace
in amity and liberty and love.
Let our two nations, the Mother and her
last Child march on together indissolubly until
we weave forever
A shroud to all oppression
A bridal gown for the young earth,
Till we build together,
The city of the Sun,
The new Jerusalem,
The Peaceful House of Man.

## The Day of War

A hawk-faced youth with rapacious eyes, standing on a shaky
    chair,
Speaks hotly in the roar of the crossways, under the tower that
    challenges the skies, terrible like a brandished sword.
A thin crowd, idle, yawning, many-hungered, beggarly-rich
With the heavy booty of the hours of dreaming and scheming,
Imperial ruins of the mob,
Listens to him wondering why he speaks and why they listen.
The fierce incandescence of noon quivers and drones with the
    echoes
Of distant clamors, grumbling of voices, blaring of speed-mad
    fanfares,

Of suddenly drowned outcries.
But as the roar reaches the group, it turns and recoils and
    deviates,
And runs around it as a stream runs round a great rock.
Stirred by the blue fans of the skies his black hair is caught
    and entangled in a little cloud between the tall roofs
And only his voice is heard in the little island of silence.
His arms go up as he speaks; his white teeth fight savagely with his
    black eyes,
His red tie flies tempestuously in the wind, the unfurled
    banner of his heart amidst the musketry of his young
    words.
He has been speaking since dawn; he has emerged from the
    night, and the night alone shall submerge him.
They listen to him and wonder, and grope blindly in the maze
    of his words;
They fear his youth and they pity it;
But the sunshine is strong on his head,
And his shadow is heavy upon their faces.
Suddenly, like a flash of yellow flame,
The blast of a trumpet shoots by, smiting the white tower like
    a hail of gold coins.
The soldiers march . . . Tramp, tramp, tramp . . . The soldiers
    march up the avenue.
And lo! the crowd breaks, scatters, runs away,
And only six listeners remain:
A girl, a newsboy, a drunken man, a Greek who sells rugs, an
    old man and the stranger I know.
But he speaks on, louder, with the certainty of the thunder
    that only speaks after the bolt.
"Workers of America, we alone shall acquit this generation
    before history. We must and shall stop this war."
Tramp, tramp, tramp—the soldiers are marching . . .
The Greek vendor moves on; wearily the old man turns to-
    wards a seat, far away in the rustling park.
But he speaks on.
"The great voice of labor shall rise fearlessly today, and the
    world shall listen, and eternity shall record his words."
Tramp, tramp, tramp—the soldiers march near by.
The drunken man grumbles, stares at his open hands and
    lurches away towards an approaching car.
But he speaks on.

"Our protest and our anger will be like a cloudburst, and the
masters will tremble. Brothers, don't you see it? The
revolution is at the threshold."
The newsboy swings his bag over his shoulders, and dashes
away through the park.
But he speaks on.
"As sure as this sun shall set, so will tyranny go down. Men
and women of America, I know that the great day is
come!"
Tramp, tramp, tramp—the soldiers sing as they march!
The stranger I know shrinks in the hollow places of himself;
he fades and vanishes, molten in the heat of that young
faith.
But the girl stands still and immovable, her upturned face
glowing before the brazier of his soul,
As from the tower drop one by one at his feet the twelve tolls
of the clock that marks time, the time that flows and
flows on until his day comes . . .
And the girl and the tower and he
Are the only three things that stand straight and rigid and
inexpugnable
Amidst the red omens of war,
In the fullness of the day,
In the whiteness of the moonlight,
In the city of dread and uproar.

**Words Without Song**

O distances, rival sisters of the altitudes!
I who have given up floating on the mists towards the stars
That I might follow the tracks of trains and the hoofs of
horsemen,
Shall I forever stay here in the Bronx?
Shall I never see the red linen sails gliding through the
amaranth of the Bosphorus?
Shall I never plant a young sapling by an Indian pagoda
Or beat with my sweaty hands the silences of the Sahara
waiting for a human echo?
Shall I never curry a colt at dawn in the plains of the Pampas
Or turn my back on the minarets of Moscow and follow the
wind and say:
This sun is going back to whence I came?

Shall I be forever immobile in the Bronx saying to the tailors
  and the dressmakers
The glory of man is on the picket line downtown?
And the end of life is two hundred dollars a week?

## The Walker

I hear footsteps over my head all night.
They come and they go. Again they come and they go all night.
They come one eternity in four paces and they go one eternity in four
  paces, and between the coming and the going there is Silence and
  the Night and the Infinite.
For infinite are the nine feet of a prison cell, and endless is the march
  of him who walks between the yellow brick wall and the red iron
  gate, thinking things that cannot be chained and cannot be
  locked, but that wander far away in the sunlit world, each in a wild
  pilgrimage after a destined goal.

Throughout the restless night I hear the footsteps over my head.
Who walks? I know not. It is the phantom of the jail, the sleepless
  brain, a man, the man, the Walker.
One-two-three-four: four paces and the wall.
One-two-three-four: four paces and the iron gate.
He has measured his space, he has measured it accurately, scrupulously, minutely, as the hangman measures the rope and the
  gravedigger the coffin—so many feet, so many inches, so many
  fractions of an inch for each of the four paces.
One-two-three-four. Each step sounds heavy and hollow over my
  head, and the echo of each step sounds hollow within my head as I
  count them in suspense and in dread that once, perhaps, in the
  endless walk, there may be five steps instead of four between the
  yellow brick wall and the red iron gate.
But he has measured the space so accurately, so scrupulously, so
  minutely that nothing breaks the grave rhythm of the slow, fantastic march.

When all are asleep (and who knows but I when all sleep?) three
  things are still awake in the night: the Walker, my heart and the
  old clock which has the soul of a fiend—for never, since a coarse
  hand with red hair on its fingers swung for the first time the
  pendulum in the jail, has the old clock tick-tocked a full hour of
  joy.

Yet the old clock which marks everything, and records everything, and to everything tolls the death knell, the wise old clock that knows everything, does not know the number of the footsteps of the Walker, nor the throbs of my heart.

For not for the Walker, nor for my heart is there a second, a minute, an hour or anything that is in the old clock—there is nothing but the night, the sleepless night, the watchful, wistful night, and footsteps that go, and foot-steps that come and the wild, tumultuous beatings that trail after them forever.

All the sounds of the living beings and inanimate things, and all the voices and all the noises of the night I have heard in my wistful vigil.

I have heard the moans of him who bewails a thing that is dead and the sighs of him who tries to smother a thing that will not die;

I have heard the stifled sobs of the one who weeps with his head under the coarse blankets, and the whisperings of the one who prays with his forehead on the hard, cold stone of the floor;

I have heard him who laughs the shrill, sinister laugh of folly at the horror rampant on the yellow wall and at the red eyes of the nightmare glaring through the iron bars;

I have heard in the sudden icy silence him who coughs a dry, ringing cough, and wished madly that his throat would not rattle so and that he would not spit on the floor, for no sound was more atrocious than that of his sputum upon the floor;

I have heard him who swears fearsome oaths which I listen to in reverence and awe, for they are holier than the virgin's prayer;

And I have heard, most terrible of all, the silence of two hundred brains all possessed by one single, relentless, unforgiving, desperate thought.

All this have I heard in the watchful night, And the murmur of the wind beyond the walls, And the tolls of a distant bell, And the woeful dirge of the rain,

And the remotest echoes of the sorrowful city

And the terrible beatings, wild beatings, mad beatings of the One Heart which is nearest to my heart.

All this have I heard in the still night;

But nothing is louder, harder, drearier, mightier, more awful than the footsteps I hear over my head all night.

Yet fearsome and terrible are all the footsteps of men upon the earth, for they either descend or climb.

They descend from little mounds and high peaks and lofty altitudes, through wide roads and narrow paths, down noble marble stairs and creaky stairs of wood—and some go down to the cellar, and some to the grave, and some down to the pits of shame and infamy, and still some to the glory of an unfathomable abyss where there is nothing but the staring white, stony eyeballs of Destiny.

And again other footsteps climb. They climb to life and to love, to fame, to power, to vanity, to truth, to glory and to the scaffold—to everything but Freedom and the Ideal.

And they all climb the same roads and the same stairs others go down; for never, since man began to think how to overcome and overpass man, have other roads and other stairs been found.

They descend and they climb, the fearful footsteps of men, and some limp, some drag, some speed, some trot, some run—they are quiet, slow, noisy, brisk, quick, feverish, mad, and most awful is their cadence to the ears of the one who stands still.

But of all the footsteps of men that either descend or climb, no footsteps are so fearsome and terrible as those that go straight on the dead level of a prison floor, from a yellow stone wall to a red iron gate.

All through the night he walks and he thinks. Is it more frightful because he walks and his footsteps sound hollow over my head, or because he thinks and speaks not his thoughts?

But does he think? Why should he think? Do I think? I only hear the footsteps and count them. Four steps and the wall. Four steps and the gate. But beyond? Beyond? Where goes he beyond the gate and the wall?

He goes not beyond. His thought breaks there on the iron gate. Perhaps it breaks like a wave of rage, perhaps like a sudden flow of hope, but it always returns to beat the wall like a billow of helplessness and despair.

He walks to and fro within the narrow whirlpit of this ever storming and furious thought. Only one thought—constant, fixed, immovable, sinister, without power and without voice.

A thought of madness, frenzy, agony and despair, a hell-brewed thought, for it is a natural thought. All things natural are things impossible while there are jails in the world—bread, work, happiness, peace, love.

But he thinks not of this. As he walks he thinks of the most superhuman, the most unattainable, the most impossible thing in the world:

He thinks of a small brass key that turns just half around and throws open the red iron gate.

That is all the Walker thinks, as he walks throughout the night.

And that is what two hundred minds drowned in the darkness and the silence of the night think, and that is also what I think.

Wonderful is the supreme wisdom of the jail that makes all think the same thought. Marvelous is the providence of the law that equalizes all, even in mind and sentiment. Fallen is the last barrier of privilege, the aristocracy of the intellect. The democracy of reason has leveled all the two hundred minds to the common surface of the same thought.

I, who have never killed, think like the murderer;

I, who have never stolen, reason like the thief;

I think, reason, wish, hope, doubt, wait like the hired assassin, the embezzler, the forger, the counterfeiter, the incestuous, the raper, the drunkard, the prostitute, the pimp, I, I who used to think of love and life and flowers and song and beauty and the ideal.

A little key, a little key as little as my little finger, a little key of shining brass.

All my ideas, my thoughts, my dreams are congealed in a little key of shiny brass.

All my brain, all my soul, all the suddenly surging latent powers of my deepest life are in the pocket of a white-haired man dressed in blue.

He is great, powerful, formidable, the man with the white hair, for he has in his pocket the mighty talisman which makes one man cry, and one man pray, and one laugh, and one cough, and one walk, and all keep awake and listen and think the same maddening thought.

Greater than all men is the man with the white hair and the small brass key, for no other man in the world could compel two hundred men to think for so long the same thought. Surely when the light breaks I will write a hymn unto him which shall hail him greater than Mohammed and Arbues and Torquemada and Mesmer, and all the other masters of other men's thoughts. I shall call him Almighty, for he holds everything of all and of me in a little brass key in his pocket.

Everything of me he holds but the branding iron of contempt and the claymore of hatred for the monstrous cabala that can make the apostle and the murderer, the poet and the procurer, think of the

same gate, the same key and the same exit on the different sunlit
highways of life.

My brother, do not walk any more. It is wrong to walk on a grave. It is a
     sacrilege to walk four steps from the headstone to the foot and
     four steps from the foot to the headstone.
If you stop walking, my brother, no longer will this be a grave, for you
     will give me back my mind that is chained to your feet and the right
     to think my own thoughts.
I implore you, my brother, for I am weary of the long vigil, weary of
     counting your steps, and heavy with sleep.
Stop, rest, sleep, my brother, for the dawn is well nigh and it is not the
     key alone that can throw open the gate.

**Samnite Cradle Song**

Lullaby, baby, mamma's own child!
Who sang the evil dirge about thee?
Thou camest in March time, wee as the tart
Berries of hedge thorns, pale, as the wild
Roses that have a wasp in their heart.
Who has to thee the witchy words spoken?
Who read to thee the malevolent star?
Who cast on thee the spell of the dead?
A hunchbacked wizard thy cradle has broken,
A lame old fairy embittered my teat,
And the blind priest with unblessed water wet
At the font thy poor, innocent head.
Thou art so sleepy, but numb are my arms;
Thou art so cold, but chilled is my breath;
Thou art so hungry, but dry is my breast.
Lullaby, hush-a-by, baby mine, rest,
Sleep for thy mother, who is tired unto death.

Lullaby, baby! The corn was so full,
The vines were so heavy, the season so pleasant,
And happy, so happy, the heart of the peasant,
Who was preparing and sweeping the bin
For the new wheat that was bristling so fine,
While his nude youngster was laughing within
The casks he was scrubbing to fill with new wine,
But God dislikes them whose heart is content,

God loves only them who starve and bewail;
And so he sent us the wind and the hail.
All has been carried away by landslides;
All has been buried beneath the brown mire;
All has been ruined by storms and by tides,
Nor vineyards nor orchards the water did leave.
The mice now dance in the empty meal keeve;
The ashes are cold of the last cauldron fire;
The dams and the flood traps the torrent has torn;
And poor we! the mill that once ground our corn
Now grinds away the last hope of the land.
Lullaby, baby, the morning is nigh.
Hush-a-by, baby, thou must understand,
The tale of my woe is as long as thy cry.

Lullaby, baby, thy grandfather plowed
And thy father mowed the grain,
And thy mother winnowed the chaff,
And at evening many a spool
Spinned with spindle and distaff,
Threads of hemp and threads of wool.
But granddaddy was broken and bowed,
The land was hard, the winters were cold;
But thy father was twenty years old,
So they took him away and sent him to war.
One was old and one was young,
One was weak and one was strong,
One was too tired to till the sod,
One was fresh in the heart of spring.
So thy grandpa was killed by God,
And thy daddy by the king.

Lullaby, hush-a-by, baby mine, sleep, Lullaby, softer than thine is
   their bed!
Mother will sing thee, mother'll not weep, Mother'll not mourn
   for the dead.

Lullaby, baby, grow strong and brave!
They are no longer hungry now;
Only us two the bad luck smote.
The gravedigger took away the goat,
For digging an eight-foot grave;

The curate has taken the sow,
For saying mass by the biers;
And the Government for its toll
Has taken the earrings from mine ears,
Lullaby, baby; they took our all,
The walnut chest, the iron bed,
The silver brooch, the marriage ring,
The black fichu in which I was wed;
I have not even a scarf to mourn
And honor my young love forlorn
And the faith I swore to him.
I have only the sack of straw,
The bident with the broken horn,
And the medal which the law
Has sent to thee, an iron thing,
Which in his honor bears the trace
Of his young blood upon one face,
And on the other side the grace
Of God about our gracious king.

Lullaby, hush-a-by, baby mine, sleep,
    Lullaby, softer than thine is their bed!
Mother will sing thee, mother'll not weep,
    Mother'll not mourn for the dead.

Lullaby, baby, the winter is near,
The mountains put on their clean hood of snow.
What shall I do? Where shall I go?
In the sieve there is no more flour;
In the bin there is no more coal;
In the jug there is no more oil.
What shall I do, my desperate soul?
Am I to die of hunger and cold,
Or beg for bread from door to door,
Or be a wanton about the inns?
Ah, what do I care what I shall be,
What do I care, so you do not die?
My grief shall stop where your joy begins
And our good day shall surely come by.
And when it comes, and I am in my grave
Or past the age of thy pride or blame,
If I keep true to all that aid me,

Give back a hundred for one they gave,
But if I rear thee with sweets and with shame,
Lullaby, hush-a-by, harken, my life,
For every dollar of silver they paid me,
Give back a stab with your father's keen knife.

Lullaby, hush-a-by, baby mine, sleep,
   Lullaby, softer than thine is their bed!
Mother will sing thee, mother'll not weep,
   Mother'll not mourn for the dead.

Lullaby, baby, the rope is so frayed
That down the well soon the bucket will dart;
The whip is broken, the yoke torn in twain;
But see, how sharp is the hatchet's blade!
The ass has broken away from the cart,
The hound has shaken and slipped from the chain
And I am singing away my fierce heart
Just for the rage of the song, not the pain.
Behold, the dawn fingers the shadows dispel,
Soon will the sun peep at thee from the hill;
The cocks are crowing, the starlings grow shrill.
Wait, and my song with the matin's glad bell
Shall fill the morning with omens of glee.
For now no longer I sing unto thee,
Mamma's own wolflet, the tale of my woe,
But now that the sun is near, my man-boy,
The night is gone, and my sorrow will go;
List to my prophecy, vengeance and joy.

Lullaby, baby, look! Our great king
With all his princes and barons and sons,
Goes to the church to pray to the Lord.
Ring all the bells! Fire all the guns!
For all the chapter is wearing the cope,
And the bishop himself will sing the high mass.
How came this vision to me, my wild hope?
How came this wonderful fortune to pass?
Behold, the bishop lifts up the grail;
The king is kneeling upon the gray stone;
The trumpets hush, the organ heaves deep:
"*Te Deum laudamus* . . . We praise thee, O Lord . . .

For all thy mercies, Lord, hail! All hail!"
Hush-a-by, lullaby, listen! Don't sleep!
Lullaby, hush-a-by, mark well my word!
Thou shalt grow big. Don't tremble! Don't fail!
The holy wafer is but kneaded dough;
The king is but flesh like the man with the hoe;
The axe is of iron, the same as the sword;
This I do tell thee and this I do sing.
And if thou livest with sweat and with woe,
Grow like a man, not a saint, nor a knave;
Do not be good, but be strong and be brave,
With the fangs of a wolf and the faith of a dog.
Die not the death of a soldier or slave,
Like thy grandfather who died in a bog,
Like thy poor father who rots in the rain.
But for this womb that has borne thee in pain,
For these dry breasts thou hast tortured so long,
For the despair of my life, my lost hope,
And for this song of the dawn that I sing
Die like a man by the ax or the rope,
Spit on their God and stab our good king.

Sleep no more, sleep no more! Show me you know,
Show me you listen, answer my sob!
Drink my blood, drain my heart! Just one sign . . . so
Bite my breast, bite it harder, mother's tiger cub!

---

*The Collected Poems of Arturo Giovannitti* (Chicago: E. Clemente & Sons, 1962), 2–4, 31–33, 116, 147–152, 200–205. Reprinted from *The Collected Poems of Arturo Giovannitti* by courtesy of E. Clemente & Sons, Publishers.

## A SONNET ON CONSTRUCTION WORKERS

A keen linguistic inquiry together with a dignified pathos gives a near-perfect balance to this sonnet by Rosina Vieni (Simplicio Righi), which, with its elegance sustained by outrage, echoes the wrenching representations of labor left by other, greater Italian Americans of the period, from Pascal D'Angelo (*Son of Italy*) to Pietro di Donato (*Christ in Concrete*). Unfortunately, the list of Righi's poems is far from complete, and a thorough assessment of his oeuvre, which shows strong ties with the popular, Socialist, grass-roots oral tradition of the Italian working class is problematic. *Vennero i bricchellieri* [The Bricklayers Came] was soon recognized by no less an authority than H. L. Mencken, who culled the sonnet from a 1926 issue of *Zarathustra,* an art magazine, written in Italian, that was sympathetic to the struggle of the anarchist and labor leader Carlo Tresca.

**The Bricklayers Came**

The *bricchellieri* came in the hundreds
a whole *ghenga* with callused hands
to build a house four stories high
not counting the *ruffo* and the *basamento.*

Now it seems to challenge the firmament
to the honor and glory of the Americans;
but who thinks of the *grinoni,* the peasants
dying suddenly, without the sacrament?

What does it matter, if bad luck or *mistecca,*
you're smashed to pieces at the bottom of the *floro—*
poor *ghinni,* unfortunate *dego?*

In front of the half *ponte* of beefsteak
the *bosso* sneers and displays his gold teeth:
who's dead is dead . . . I'm alive and I don't give a damn.

---

"Vennero i bricchellieri," in H. L. Mencken, *The American Language: An Inquiry into the Development of English in the United States* (New York: Knopf, 1947), 642.

## Efrem Bartoletti, the Miner-Poet

Most early Italian American poetry could hardly be called spontaneous, burdened as it is by the weight of the Italian formal poetical tradition; yet much of its stiffness and excesses can be attributed to the fact that its makers were for the most part self-taught. Among them, Bartoletti probably best exemplifies this craving for a higher culture, which might allow him to express with a heady thrust his class-consciousness. Most of the time, he ends up with a sort of self-induced hauteur, in which he mixes the two sources of his inspiration, homesickness for his rural Umbria and a robust solidarity with his fellow proletarians. At his best, he brings a harsh reality to the foreground, infusing new life into a language that echoes, sometimes to a disturbing degree, passages, rhythms, and structures of the classical Italian masters. The consistent political tone is not necessarily a way of taking a position; rather, it is a sign of his awareness and understanding of the surrounding world, from the mines underground to the airborne waves of radio wartime propaganda.

## Proletarian Nostalgias
### I.

Verses of anguish, rhymes of sorrow,
of pious remembrance, of outrage and ire
flowed sadly from my heart,
from my poor heart sighing in vain,

go, go messengers of love,
there where squalid Hunger is roaming;
where there's a languishing wretch, and a dying one, too;
on the gallows of the martyr, exhaling.

And if ever some merry fat critic
tries to bite you,
tell him: We were born with the lights out,

we're the cry of the buried people,
of those who sweat and labor underground for you
and, unavenged pariahs, often die.

## The Mine

Like an infernal smoky black mouth
filled with Death and disgrace,
fatal the mine opens up, dire and dark
in the huge bosom of the earth.

Like pale shadows, the ranks
of the oppressed pariahs, uncertain and never sure
they'll ever see the Sun again, labor and endure
from morning to night in its deep horrors:

and in the pale glow of waning lamps,
amid fumes and gas and deathly cave-ins,
they defy the Unknown and sometimes die;

while in the shining Sun, huge idol, the Trust
is partying with its armed cohort
denying, the misers, bread to the wretched.

Hibbing, Minn., April 2, 1912.

## The Miner's Morning

When in the morning the screaming choir of horns
makes a horrible harmony in the ear;
and waking the humble pariahs
awakens the anxiety of the feverish work,

I, weary, leave my hard bed and wonder
if I'll ever be able to lie down again:
I dress and eat, and along the dead road
that leads to the narrow smoky hole,

sepulchre of the living, I walk
in pain and in sadness. My wounded soul
laments its ruthless, tragic destiny.

And I say: Here's the sad uncertain life
of the miner, who goes down in the morning
not knowing if he will come out at night!

## The IWW

To be, or not to be
among the beings who are alive;
to live, or not to live;
it's the audacious program!

Free acts and thoughts,
in line with the existence
of all humankind
and of all human science.

Reclaim the trampled
rights of the poor,
and break the chains
of so many outcasts.

Cleanse the shame of the centuries
suffered by the oppressed;

level the high and the low,
and free yourself.

Equal work for men,
and equal pay;
children of the free world
wherever you tread.

And eternal war on tyrants,
on the Crœsuses, on Capital;
on the hypocrisy of religion,
on sword and crosier.

Death to Bellona: rise
from nothing to unity;
call for Peace among peoples,
for Equality and Freedom.

The untamed iconoclast,
ready to destroy;
the Big Union, the Nemesis,
that's the IWW!

*Nostalgie proletarie. Raccolta di canti poetici e di inni rivoluzionari di Efrem Bartoletti* (Brooklyn, N.Y.: Libreria editrice dei Lavoratori industriali del mondo—Italian IWW Publishing Bureau, 1919), 3, 75, 110, 117–118; translation by Martino Marazzi and Ann Goldstein. Special thanks to Robert Kulesz.

## NEAPOLITAN RHAPSODY

All roads lead to Rome, but Naples was the first big city that the Allied forces entered. And to many immigrants that seemed the fitting closing of a circle that had opened decades before, when the steamships left from the piers facing the town, and even more so with the U.S. Army that included Italian soldiers. Charles Poletti (and Vito Genovese) had not been chosen by accident. In any case, the well-oiled machinery of dialect poetry produced within Italian America was able to reflect the Italian American Zeitgeist, so to speak, and bring it all back home. Federico Mennella, by all accounts a minor and amateurish writer, stood up to the task with a hundred and five sonnets on the history of Naples, to the edification of two Italian American boys newly engaged to the daughters of the fictitious storyteller.

## Neapolitan Rhapsody

*A rainy, cold evening in February 1944. Don Pasquale Forte, the doorman of a building in via dei Ventaglieri, in Naples, recounts the historical vicissitudes of his city.*

I

— All right then . . . since you really care
I'll tell you the story of my town,
because Naples, in case you didn't know,
is the best thing God ever put on earth.

Look at the sky, and around, wherever you want,
every morning when the sun shines,
or when, at dusk, the moon rises above the sea
silvery, like a queen . . .

With these words, don Pascale Forte,
a respected man, a good soul,
the president of all the doormen,

smooths his mustache with two fingers,
swallows a quick and tempered cough,
and darts off, like a *cicerone.*

VI

War, bombs, hunger and fright,
entire nights in the cellar
beneath the building, to save their skin,
don Pascale, family and tenants.

He's sixty, and then . . . a *carabiniere,*
mind you, nobody's afraid
but it's not a pleasure, you see,
to cheer those who are not brave.

Thinking like that he held himself,
poor man, uplifted,
*the war's got to end,* he said

and when a shoot-out quieted down
the world was back to normal as before,
and thank God, whatever happened had happened.

XIII

— The story goes, I read it myself,
that some foreign sailors
came to these shores for glory, more
than for pleasure.

Because, you know, back in those days
the art of running around the world,
call it tourism if you wish,
did not quite exist, not at all.

I can't remember well what was the reason
that brought them here,
it's clear they had something in mind,

something really made up in their minds,
otherwise, not for a million
would they have faced this well of trouble.

LVIII

— Naples' best blood has been spilled
and written into the history of this town,
words made of burning fire known
wherever civilization exists.

Ferdinando came back with the queen,
and so did Emma Lyons behind them,
an endless bloody party is thrown
to celebrate a victory without honor.

The kingdom's been saved, yes, but who cares
if the crown stinks of rot and sorrow,
is by chance Re Nasone feeling any shame

or the queen, thick as thieves
with the mistress of sluts,
Emma Lyons, viper and disgrace?

LIX

— This hellish woman, the most beautiful one,
married to the English ambassador,

wrapped around her little finger
the minds of men, the sea and the earth.

But, more than others, Horatio Nelson
like a dead weight fell for this witch,
he who was a great man fighting
at Trafalgar, who defended the might of his flag.

The life and glory of this sailor,
on account of this disgraceful woman,
have a stain, and a bitter taste,

and a stain, alas, that's here to stay.
The murder of another sailor
is the worst deed of cruel jealousy.

## LXVIII

— Young girls and daughters of mine,
now you see how battered has been
this Naples, the land of joy,
made for love, for songs and serenades.

We wanted to live like flowers
in the fine air, all merry and gay,
this was what the Lord had in mind
for this little garden of Paradise.

But men are evil-minded,
they could have left us in peace,
these shameless and arrogant ones.

But here they came with the fixed idea
of enslaving us, for no reason,
just like a donkey from Pantelleria.

## XCII

— This evening I told you in earnest
the most important facts of this town,
and if you think them over,
think that they are all true.

This town suffered many wounds,
it bled and was hungry,
and now once again is waiting for some good,
for that bread you can eat without fear.

And when you go back home,
with these roses as your wives,
may you be happy that all is over, and all is past,

but don't ever forget this night
and the story that was told to you sincerely
by Pascale, the doorman of the Vintagliere.

### CII

—Tell it far and wide when you return,
the story of this sweet Naples,
not only songs and serenades
but the fever of freedom that cries and seethes.

Italy brought light into the dark,
like a noble lady in decay,
I assure you, hold out a hand to her
and the light that disappeared will come back.

It was an Italian who discovered America,
and do you think it is a little thing
to let the whole world open wide?

You go and tell them the time has come
to repay that life with a hand,
tell them that this is a debt of honor.

### CIV

Then Don Pascale pulls himself together,
smooths his mustache with his fingers,
wipes the handkerchief across his eyebrow,
stands up, stretches, settles down.

From inside his wallet, slowly,
amid the pictures, the papers and the scraps,
the Saints and the ticket for the breadline,
he takes out a little flyer.

*The Nazis are worse than the Bourbons,*
*We're coming to free you,* he reads aloud.
He believes in this, just like *Communion.*

All the rest is nothing, it doesn't matter,
a piece of bread, watching a door,
and the sky, the sky, his until he dies.

---

*Rapsodia napoletana* (New York: Cocce Press, 1944), 17, 22, 29, 75–76, 85, 109, 119, 121; translation by Martino Marazzi and Ann Goldstein. Special thanks to Domenico Scarpa.

## ROMAN DIALECT

Alfredo Borgianini offers further examples of the close and simple metrics common among the "popular" poetry of Little Italy. The central issue of labor is deftly given a twofold meaning here: as a parable of the socially and psychologically devastating fight between workers and bosses, Labor and Capital, and as the emergence of a mechanical modern age, whose vocabulary demands a great number of newly coined words. As in Righi-Rosina Vieni, these instances of so-called Italglish are a means of being precise, and are not intended to amuse the reader, although it may seem that way, just a few decades later.

### The Dream

I

After fourteen hours of work,
dead tired, panting, exhausted,
after working so many hours
under the burning rays of that golden sun,

With the sickle over his shoulder, shirtless,
baked by the sun, black as a Moor,
to have some rest and some relief,
he went into a house in the middle of the field.

He was hungry, pitiful to look at,
and while the boss was throwing money away,
spending a hundred bucks for dinner,

This martyr, who was giving his life
to make that rascal rich, ate
a plate of savorless polenta . . .

## II

Then he fell asleep and dreamed; he dreamed of a dawn
with a brighter and more beautiful sun,
two swans that pulled a cart
beneath that rising sun above.

He dreamed of a train at a hundred miles an hour,
and at a hundred miles a beautiful ship, too,
and saw a slave tearing down a gate
and another who screamed: "Onward still!"

He dreamed of thousands of people
crossing meadows of violets
running all together in the same direction.

They arrived in the foreordained spot
and they all knelt down to the sun
that beautiful sun so often dreamed of . . .

## III

Then the dream changed, and on a road
he saw his boss approaching
and as if he were a friend of his
he shook his hand, and the boss did the same.

Labor and Capital kissed
under the burning rays of the summer sun,
and the proletarian was satisfied
to see at last his ideal fulfilled.

Equality ruled everywhere
and waving alone in the middle of the field
was the big flag of brotherhood.

That vision seemed to him true,
and it seemed to him that fulfillment had come
to those sacred words: "Onward and Hope" . . .

## IV

That dream lasted for hours and hours,
until the church bell

sounding the dawn louder and louder
woke the gentle dreamer.

He woke from the deceiving dream
and felt a rage never known before,
now it was time to go to his work,
he was still another man's slave.

He rose in pain greater than the night before,
in a cold sweat, wiped his forehead,
picked up the sickle lying on the ground.

He went out, and as he walked
the sun was rising behind the mountain,
but it wasn't the sun he had been dreaming of . . .

**Advertising Sonnets**

When you need a little gasoline,
a tire, a pipe, a jack, an oilcan,
a sparkplug of a fine brand,
or a good carburetor,

When you need a headlight
or oil to lubricate your motor,
come to Fritz, come, and right in the window
you'll find everything you're looking for.

If your car has taken sick
and stops after starting
I can charge your battery.

For charging, I got a trick
and after I recharge it
your car will flee faster than the wind . . .

II

My gasoline, excuse me,
is the best of all, is right on top;
just touch the accelerator
and the car will jump like a cricket.

Uphills will be a joke
with such a powerful motor,
and as for trouble with the carburetor,
don't worry, don't even talk about it.

If sometime you have to travel far
buy my gas, try it, and you'll see
that not even a plane will go that far . . .

If you do as I tell you,
you will be convinced like many others
that among the gases, mine's the best . . .

*Sonetti e poesie romanesche* (Trenton, N.J.: White Eagle Printing Co., 1948), 70–73, 146–47; translation by Martino Marazzi and Ann Goldstein. Special thanks to Francesco Durante and Giuseppe Antonelli.

## THE EASY POEMS OF ONORIO RUOTOLO

Ruotolo, who had been active since the teens as a militant intellectual, sculptor, and educator, waited until the end of his life to collect his verses (to which should be added his rendition in Italian of Arturo Giovannitti's classic *The Walker*). The collection, rather than recapitulating a lifetime of achievement or the decades of a homegrown, Italian American poetic tradition, expresses a sort of "writing degree zero," of free-wheeling perceptiveness tainted with nostalgia and senile humor. It is an odd close to the highly rhetorical tones of early Italian American poetry and a very personal one; but its simplicity does capture, at last, a feeling of togetherness and a sense of familiarity which otherwise might have gone unnoticed.

**My Summer Vacation: A Scherzo**
    (for Dr. Nicola Brunori)

I, even I, had
to take
a long
summer vacation.
My learned medical
friend
made me.

"Go to the beach, go swimming,"
he said.
"Play, you need to play,
or else you'll be sick."

I wanted, this time,
to obey him
and so I took—
in my own way—
the . . . prescribed vacation.

I sent away
my family,
with the angora cat
and the yellow canaries,
to a distant beach.
Then I wrote to my wife,
and to my faithful friends—
who are many—
"I'm setting off
on a long crusade.
See you in September."

Then I had the importunate
telephone turned off.
Then I cut the wires
of the squealing
doorbell.
Then, so as not to see bills
or accounts,
at the post office
I stopped my mail.

Then, so as not to accumulate
toxic piles of paper,
at the newsstand I stopped
subscriptions
to journals and reviews.
And then, with sufficient,
fairly frugal, yes,
but well-chosen provisions,
I locked myself in the house

alone . . . alone . . .
And then? . . . And then? . . .

In revenge I unplugged
the radio,
damned hussy,
who howls, shouts, mutters,
laughs and cries,
plays, sings, and brays,
and lies, always lies,
in all the tongues of Babel,
to induce you to buy
all sorts of stupid things:
who day and night,
whether you like it or not,
breaks your eardrums,
because the bully
always has in the family
powerful allies,
among your dear children,
or in your beloved wife,
who protect her,
who defend her . . .
Always! . . . Always!
And then? . . . And then? . . .

I burned the calendar,
the ever-living—everlasting,
inexorable, voracious
paper gauge
of this tiny
terraqueous globe,
ceaselessly spinning
around the immense
glowing sun . . .
I burned it, the implacable
curtailer
of this already
too short
too stormy life of ours:
the gendarme
of the landlord

in our houses,
the cynical mute autocrat
who with his edicts,
daily, weekly,
and monthly,
implacably intrudes on
domestic peace:
Everywhere! Everywhere!

And then? . . . And then? . . .

I stopped
all my clocks:
the metallic, infinite, and most murderous
children of this calendar cop:
devices
with an honest, innocuous,
and gracious look,
considered most useful,
indispensable, and indeed
by many, by many possessed . . .
and by all loved,
and by all desired,
especially if encased
in a precious dome
of gold or platinum,
and studded with jewels:
devices
with delicate hands,
that turning and turning,
mark on the fine face
the hours, the quarters, and the half hours;
the first minutes and the seconds;
and so turning silently,
so they extinguish,
little by little,
softly, softly,
without uranium
and without fireworks,
human existence;
more than the swift,
and less diabolical,

frightening atomic bomb;
at the gentle, hidden, unsuspected:
tick tock, tick tock . . .

And then? . . . And then? . . .

I closed the blinds
and all the windows,
to immerse myself
in the shadows,
so I wouldn't hear
the street noise,
of the ball players:
dear boys . . . dear boys!

And then? . . . And then? . . .
I emptied
of useless furnishings
the cool neglected
little room
of the apartment,
and there, as if in an oasis,
I installed myself . . .
Bliss! . . . Bliss! . . .

And then? . . . And then? . . .

Now by day I sleep;
I am never tired of sleeping
my longest, nicest
sleeps,
refreshed and soothed
by a heavenly peace
never before
enjoyed during the day . . .
Nor hoped for! . . . Nor hoped for!

And then? . . . And then? . . .

Now at night I wake
in the weak light,
in the solemn silent
solitude of my house,

and I pray and I contemplate,
smoke, write or read
when I feel like it,
without being disturbed
and without disturbing;
and in perfect joy
I work on my now manageable papers—
alas, so disliked by my family—
without hearing the irate voice
of my beloved wife
who calls me to bed . . .
yes, now, as never ever before,
I'm happy! . . . I'm happy!

And then? . . . And then? . . .

I've told you:
thus happily I spend
my summer vacation,
my only
responsibility, a pleasant one,
to water, every evening,
on the kitchen windowsill,
the basil and the mint,
in whose country fragrance
my sense of smell revives! . . . revives!

This is how I live, outside society;
in eternity,
ignoring the nonexistent
existence
of that abstract illogicality
that—who knows why—
ever since it was invented,
was called Time . . .

I live in the company
of silent learned men
who never annoy me
with their voices,
or their vanity;
who never
ask anything,

and know only how to give
those highest and rarest things
that can't be bought
not even with all the gold
in the world . . .

I live with the books
that I love,
in the sweet illusion
that September
will never return . . . never return . . .

And then? . . . And then? . . .

Alas! . . . Alas! . . .
I don't want to think about it!

## In Union Square Park

Those who never saw you,
or don't know you well,
are almost frightened of you,
remarkable little park
of Union Square;
where the sage rebuilders of the New Deal
made a haven at last for the statues
of Washington, Lincoln, and Lafayette.

They have described you and painted you
as a den of raving reds,
fomenters of strikes and treasons,
and yet you are no more
than a lovely oasis of coolness,
for the disappointed, the lost, the rebellious;
for the vanquished, the survivors, the destitute,
and for all the tired walkers
in the immense desert
of burning human sand
that is Manhattan,
the Babel-like Imperial city:
O maligned, O calumniated,
green and leafy island
of Union Square.

A hundred languages and accents
alternate, meet,
and dissolve freely
into the most variable arguments
among the strangest ethnic groups,
shouting every day,
assembled in the shade
of the fine Stars and Stripes
that, reaching to heaven, flutters in the breeze,
over that narrow but free space
of Union Square.

Beside the white paths—
that outline the grassy central space,
in the shape of a cross—
sitting or lying
on the wood and concrete benches,
are the drunks and the homeless,
snoring openmouthed,
emaciated, languid and dull,
mingled with pairs of lovers
disparate in color, age, and dress;
who in each other's arms are kissing,
whispering words of love,
in the traditional manner
of Union Square.

Here, a thin pale poet,
staring wildly, yes, but surely infatuated
by a chimera, or a beautiful woman,
entrusts to the frail pages
his fanciful thoughts:
he writes, erases, and writes again;
he stops; looks for a moment at
the bright clouds dispersing
behind the tall Edison Tower;
he smiles to himself, happy;
pats a friendly gray dog,
and then, indifferent to the din,
goes back to writing, again for hours,
under the clear blue sky
of Union Square.

There, shabby and taciturn, sits
a plump old bearded fellow
with a socratic-looking head and face.
His eyes and lips are half closed;
he seems to be absorbed . . .
He is a philosopher-misanthrope, a madman;
who is he?—A noted model he,
sought by painters and sculptors,
and very well known to the habitués
of Union Square.

Farther on, a group of the curious
are wide-eyed with amazement
at the pleasant entertainment of a long-haired artist
who draws rapid likenesses
in pretty or grotesque profile,
for the price of twenty-five cents.
He is the most admired
and, after the pigeons, the best . . . fed
in Union Square.

Scattered everywhere;
crouching on the steps,
or leaning on the railings;
standing still,
or sauntering slowly,
are people smoking pipes, or reading,
eating fruit or chewing gum,
or slaking their thirst
at the cool gush of the little fountain;
and then there are some who love and care for
only the small winged creatures and the dogs
of Union Square.

Around the three circular terraces
of red granite at the base
of the bronze "Emigrant Pioneers"
and the neglected
"Tablet of Independence"
of the golden monument to the Flag,
children and babies, ugly and cute,
white girls and black rascals,

fling their arms at each other, roll around,
run, shout,
in genuine fraternity,
intoxicated with innocent gaiety . . .

Only the paternal eye
of the Martyr, liberator of slaves,
humble, cloaked,
and sadly smiling,
motionless, watches them, protects them
from the height of the pyramidal base
of his unadorned pedestal
in Union Square.

Under the heroic equestrian statue
of the noble Father of his country—
First Soldier and First President—
rather, under the rump of his horse
with the arched and flowing tail,
crowd the most ardent rebels.
That seems to be the site
most favored every day
by the Tribunes of pure American blood,
because there only English is spoken
to the miscellaneous listeners:
too often protesting,
and at rare moments applauding.

There the most loquacious, the most learned,
the most fearless, the most red,
the most persuasive,
the most prepared to overcome,
lecture and harangue
on the most abstruse international problems,
of war and peace,
of politics, economy, religion,
of new heresies and old utopias.

There the cleverest ask
and the sharpest answer,
wave their arms and shout,
thundering and threatening.

But in truth, in truth,
those harmless verbal explosions
frighten no one;
not even the well-fed pigeons,
nesting and drowsing
in the hospitable trees
of Union Square.

And no one can overpower
the voices of the other haranguers;
neither that of the ice-cream vendor
who, from morning to sunset,
sells thousands of Good Humors
to the comrades and drifters
of Union Square.

Why has it never, ever happened,
nor perhaps ever will—
despite the absence of a cop—
the simplest scuffle,
the briefest fistfight,
the commonest crime,
and not even the hint of a robbery,
in Union Square?

Perhaps because that oasis, an island
ill known and ill famed,
lost and forgotten
in the heart of the boundless city
swarming with greedy and grasping beings,
is a true, integral democracy:
so that the wandering pilgrims
of all ages and all races,
of all faiths and all ideals,
like its hundred varicolored doves,
find a place of refuge, outlet, and peace
in Union Square.

Ah, if they knew you better,
little park, with no other laws
than free and brotherly tolerance
and mutual respect
for the civil liberties of all! . . .

They might then discover,
your ignorant detractors,
that the shining America augured
by Jefferson, Mazzei, Washington,
Franklin, Lincoln, and Whitman,
is honored daily only in you,
small green and leafy space
in Union Square, in Union Square!

---

*Accordi e dissonanze* (Milan: Convivio Letterario, 1958), 73–80, 221–29; translation by Ann Goldstein.

# 5

## Prose of Testimony: the Color Line

Shining shoes at the side of the street
      —Giovanni Pascoli, *La grande Proletaria si è mossa*

Ah got some boss shit, man. Ah mean its dy no mite, right from
the *eye*talians.
                              Hubert Selby, Jr., *Requiem for a Dream*


A FEW YEARS AGO, MARIO MAFFI, INTRODUCING THE FIRST IMPOR-
tant anthology of stories and essays by Latinos in the United States to
appear in Italy, deliberately spoke of "writings" rather than writers.[1]
Despite the obvious differences, many writings of a critical and creative nature by Italian Americans, too, could only remotely be
categorized as "literature." Many of these contributions would not fit
into even the most flexible subdivisions of genre, and yet they express
a high degree of intelligence and sociopolitical engagement. Furthermore, these are testimonials that within the immigrant world
were readily considered to be part of a discourse with many voices on
the principal themes of the American experience. One such theme,
constant and inescapable, covers encounters with and reflections on
racial diversity in the United States.

The history of the relationship between Italians and blacks in the
United States during the decades of the Great Migration is a story
that the written sources recount almost incidentally. It's a story that
for the most part has been overlooked, in part because of the formal
diversity of the sources, but that to a contemporary reader appears to
have a strong coherence and unexpected duration. One finds, in
fact, a substantial discourse on race articulated according to impressions of the moment, current ideologies, and common sense, and
punctuated by significant repetitions over the decades. It is, all in all,
an organic vision, even though it has often been based on incidental
observations.

The main documents that I intend to focus on date from 1888 and
1906, the golden years of the migration: but there is a series of
writings on the subject from the 1860s up to the First World War

(with a remarkable coda after the Second World War, as we will see). These were decisive decades for both America and Italy, especially in terms of confrontations, both internal and external, with the "other," whether the slave of the American South (the Civil War), the "subaltern subject" from the center or south of Italy, impelled or forced to emigrate, or the black victim of Italian colonial aggression in Africa at the end of the nineteenth century (the campaign's main events were eagerly followed by the thriving press of the Little Italies).[2] These historical processes leave an explicit mark on the works of Italian writers and officials in the United States, particularly in passages in which an attempt is made to account for the presence of blacks and understand their relation to the masses of new workers from southern Europe.

The documents I am going to look at demonstrate actual instances of interracial contact, but, apart from their value as documents, they contain elements of judgment and, to be more precise, racism, or at least extreme uneasiness. We find an inarticulate or "vague" kind of thinking that on the one hand produces highly figurative language and on the other does not hesitate to take well-defined social or political positions. It is a tantalizing domain, where stereotypes mingle with sincerely motivated attempts at reform directed toward narrow, local realities, especially in the southern states and the Mississippi Delta. What in effect emerges is a conceptualization of race expressed in figurative terms.

## COLORS AND NAMES OF THE FREEDMEN

In 1849, when the first Italian newspaper of record in the United States, *L'Eco d'Italia*, was established in New York by Giovanni F. Secchi De Casali (a political exile then of Mazzinian leanings, and soon in the pay of the Washington representative of Piedmont), Italy was still a word, an aspiration, a political idea, but not a reality. The Italians documented in the United States (in 1850, between 3,600 and 3,700, according to the sources)[3] were for the most part from a cultivated, politically conscious élite, exiled members of the Risorgimento, under various guises, and often with republican tendencies.[4] The weekly *L'Eco* provided its readership mainly with news of the homeland; its first real commitment to the news of American policy and society came a decade later, with the outbreak of the Civil War. This is not surprising if one keeps in mind that the readers of *L'Eco* were in essence representatives abroad of that Italian public which in previous years had shown a keen interest in the question of slavery, giving, for instance, a swift, warm, and soon solid success to *Uncle Tom's Cabin*, which was praised by Jesuits and liberals, monarchists and republicans alike.[5]

With the war, American news took over the headlines, even though it was tangential to the interests of Italians. *L'Eco*—which, as far as we know, was a one-man undertaking, written by the owner and sole editor, Secchi De Casali—gave on the whole a meticulous account of facts, showing a strong interest in the military and political aspects of the war. Emphasis on the anti-slavery struggle was accompanied by dispassionate, matter-of-fact observation of the divisions in the United States, both north and south of the Mason-Dixon line. *Ammutinamento di bianchi e neri* [Mutiny of Whites and Blacks][6] recounts the violent reprisal of white workers (mainly Irish) in Brooklyn against the employment in a tobacco factory of blacks (including women and "youths"), who worked for less pay. "Ever since the question of the abolition of slavery was raised," the anonymous author of the article observes, "blacks have lost more than they have gained in the great cities of the North." What was previously a mere matter of racial difference has now grown into a major cause of disputes in the workplace, where blacks are "exposed to the jealousy and hatred of a whole class of white workers."

Following Lincoln's assassination, *L'Eco,* while considering counterproductive any rekindling of the divisions created by the slave question, denounced the unrest that was shaking the nation, commenting: "We're living in an epoch when it is better to be black than white, but the future will decide which of the two races will prevail in the United States."[7] And a few days later it devoted two brief but telling articles to the topic, informing readers about a huge religious gathering of blacks in Brooklyn and about violent clashes between freedmen and white soldiers in the South.[8] In typically ambiguous fashion (ambiguous, that is, from a contemporary point of view), the first piece mixes racist remarks with a condescending admiration: the people belonging to that "African race of impure origin" behaved well, in a dignified manner, "and unlike the Irish knew how to enjoy themselves with order and decency." The article that follows has very different implications: the white farmers of the South (specifically in Louisiana and North Carolina), who are in trouble because of the racial disorders that broke out at the end of the war, are trying to replace the black work force with new "labor," which "although more costly may be more useful." This expresses a prophecy that will be widely fulfilled in the coming decades: "The Southern states offer to industrious European immigrants a broad field of action on which to better their conditions." Here the articles end: no more, when all is said and done, than brief news accounts. But we cannot grasp their full significance without taking into account their liveliness of expression and relative linguistic richness. The breadth of reference to skin color, for example, is astonishing: the former slaves are designated as "neri" (blacks) and "Negri" (Negroes) in the titles, but in the body of the articles as workers "di colore" (of color), frequently as "liberti" (freedmen), or as "africani," "discendenti di Cam" (descendants of Cam). Finally, in the description of the mass gathering along Myrtle Avenue in Brooklyn, the palette becomes in its own way virtuosic: "fantini neri nerissimi" (the blackest of black jockeys,) and a complexion "chiaro-scura, nera, giallastra" (light-dark, black, yellowish), as well as "qualche tinta di cioccolata" (some chocolate tints). This meticulousness of expression underlines the diversity, at the same time reinforcing an implicitly judgmental evaluation of race.

## "KNEELING AT THE FEET OF A NEGRO"

The historically definitive expression "color line" (aptly translated as *la linea del colore*) appears near the conclusion of one of the first reports in Italian journalism on the American school system—a report that does not conceal the system's strictly segregated nature. The year is 1884, and the context is one of the most thorough and interesting volumes devoted to American habits and customs by nineteenth-century Italian intellectuals: *New-York*, by Dario Papa and Ferdinando Fontana.[9] The authors are representative of the highest level among Italian immigrants. Although they stayed for only two years, Papa and Fontana were able to spend their time in the New World working at the newborn *Il Progresso Italo-Americano*, as, respectively, editor-in-chief and editor, and on their return to Italy they introduced themselves as experts in things American.

The mention that Fontana makes of the "color line" comes at the end of his report, but it is not at all casual or unexpected; in fact, it is preceded by a *Lettera aperta ad un amico*, an "open letter to a friend," dated New York, 23 January 1882, in which he expresses a deep personal disillusionment with America. At its origin is the shock he felt in witnessing a "scena . . . disgustosa": the "appalling sight" of an Italian shoeshine "kneeling at the feet of a Negro" to perform his job.[10] It is an eight-page letter that has to be read in its entirety if one is to grasp the rhetorical framework (which hinges above all on repeated images), and the slow unfolding of a sort of specious reasoning by means of which the different identities of the two men are made to acquire the more grandiose status of racial and pseudo-historical entities. It's a real outburst of racism, suffused with both nationalist pride and a personal sense of shame and embarrassment, which is all the more revelatory because it comes from a "democratic" writer clearly trying to leave a perceptive and unprejudiced account of his experience of immigration.

Fontana's "Negro" is introduced almost as a cartoon character: in his yellow-gloved hand he holds "a gold-handled cane of precious wood," as, "with his broad chest puffed out, his person in an exaggerated pose of hauteur, and dressed 'in fashion,' like a mountebank, with his mouth hanging open in a big smile," he boastfully smokes "a big Havana cigar," as if to take vengeance on the "irrefutable right of supremacy" that whites have exercised over his people. He is the descendant, after all, "of cannibals"; he is "related by blood to the Zulus"; his "race" has won political freedom, but from a civil and moral point of view it still "cannot be called redeemed"; it hasn't managed to "work for its own rehabilitation," continuing to demonstrate its "childlike and cruel" nature, with the result that "now it is almost pleased with the contempt of which it has become the symbol."

To produce its effect, this demology (and demonology) relies on a dark litany, playing on the repetition of the image of the Italian man "kneeling at the feet" of his black client. The image of the shoeshine presents the unprecedented Christlike "passion" inflicted on a son of "humanity's greatest race,"[11] whose ancestors include the clichéd but significant names of Italian heritage, from Julius Caesar to Marco Polo, from Dante to Raphael and Michelangelo, from Giordano Bruno (an obvious nod to freethinking and anticlericalism) to Garibaldi and Cavour (symbols of the Risorgimento, understood as a genuine movement of freedom and independence, unlike the Emancipation). Fontana's sensibilities are bruised in particular by the suspicion that the black client seems to be making fun of this pedigree.

A few months later, in 1885, another encounter with the color line was published—a nearly identical situation but recounted in terms far less dramatic—by an Italian professor of French and Italian active in New England, Luigi Donato Ventura, in *Peppino,* a rare text that is considered one of the first examples of Italian American literature.[12] What attracts our attention is a passing observation by the narrator: I "strolled downtown and came upon Peppino at the corner of Prince Street, where he was busily brushing the boots of a colored man." At first glance, a simple memory fragment, but on closer examination it seems to indicate a "defensive/aggressive"[13] attitude and perhaps anticipates something larger and more significant. We should keep in mind that, especially during the years of the Great Migration, the literary activity of the immigrants developed by virtue of a constant, intense, and complex relationship with Italy, or, rather, a relationship between certain artistic and intellectual circles in Italy and the narrow, polemical world of the literary élite of the Little Italies. This emerges, above all, in the individual biographical facts and in the circumstances of publication, but in a more coherent form in the strong correspondence between the conceptual and ideological attitudes of the early Italian American intellectuals and those of their counterparts in the homeland. In the case of Ventura, this bond is exemplified by his contributions as a correspondent for the Italian press (a circumstance that has up to now been almost ignored).[14]

A long article on *I negri d'America* [Negroes of America] (dated "Boston U.S.A., September 1888") came out the following February in *Cuore e Critica*, a moderate forerunner of the glorious *Critica Sociale*, the socialist journal edited by Filippo Turati. It is a correspondence (described in an editorial note as "bizarre but frank") that is essential in order to understand Ventura's position. During the four years of its existence (1887–90), *Cuore e Critica* published many articles on the United States, concentrating on the economy, the racial question, and the phenomenon of immigration.[15] Ventura's piece stands out as less rigorous and more open to personal observation; the result is a hodgepodge of professorial condescension, paternalistic analysis, and expressions of a racism that is at once offhand, evolutionary, and colonialist. It is all too easy to extract typical sentences, but it is difficult to try to unravel the tangled skein of his thinking. Ventura claims that a philanthropic and humanitarian approach to the racial question is harmful: insisting on the practice of a "modern and intrusive" realism, he says that a personage like Frederick Douglass should be considered "an exception, a wonder," like a trained horse in a circus. According to Ventura, blacks have been used by Republicans for electoral gimmicks, with the result that they have lost their former state of innocence and "the supreme blessing of ignorance." Yet this is not simply a matter of ideology; Ventura notes from the start that he can observe the interaction between blacks and whites every day. A black shoeshine, instead of being grateful for his work, literally at Ventura's feet, still has the impudence to ask for his money; a black doorman earns more than an Italian officer who risks his life in Eritrea, and so on. The behavior of blacks is characterized by an instinct for "aping all the vices" of whites, which isn't surprising, since they are an "inferior race," "akin to apes," who should be "caressed like pedigreed dogs when they're good and put on bread and water when they're not." The Italians, now embarked on a dubious African colonial venture, receive a warning from their fellow citizens on the other side of the ocean: "We have wasted money and lives of civilized people to bring civilization to Massaua," gaining no advantage from it, in fact running great risks and paying for them personally. If science provides irrefutable proof of the physical inferiority of blacks, firsthand observation condemns the licentiousness of their habits. That is why southern white Catholics are wrong when they try to promote the education of former slaves: blacks are the same everywhere, in Africa and the United States, and white philanthropists— American abolitionists or the radical socialist readers of the Italian journal—should learn "not to stop at mere images of freedom."

Although Ventura's article lacks a coherent structure and is in many ways derivative,[16] it does have a shameless originality, which consists in giving voice to sentiments of white supremacy and therefore being useful outside the American context as well, in any interaction between Italians and blacks. This explains, among other things, the polite but firm stand taken by *Cuore e Critica*: "We prefer the epithet *despised* . . . to that of *inferior* races."[17]

## LABOR CONDITIONS AND PLANS IN THE SOUTHERN STATES

Within a few years, the huge wave of immigrants had changed the nature of the discourse. What had been perceived as an individual insult and, at worst, a threat to nationalist expansion was replaced by the problem of regulating and rationalizing the flow of labor. Granted, beneath the surface the substance had not much changed; but the surface difference was significant. By the beginning of the twentieth century, there seemed to be less need for a popularization of evolutionary racism, for something new was happening: in 1901, an Italian journalist who also founded agricultural settlements in Alabama wrote that in Louisiana and Mississippi Italians (mostly Sicilians) "are rapidly dislodging the Negroes from the sugar-cane plantations."[18] At the same time, the planters were seeking new workers to replace the descendants of the slaves, and Italian officials began working on an unprecedented and ambitious idea of sending Italian immigrants to the rural South. One such advocate, for example, was E. Mayor des Planches, the Italian ambassador to Washington, a Piedmontese aristocrat who in *Attraverso gli Stati Uniti: Per l'emigrazione italiana* [Crossing the United States: For Italian Emigration] (1913)[19] extols the virtues of agricultural work, without neglecting the "problems" of racial divisions between whites and blacks (but also Chinese and Chicanos).

Other voices reveal a much closer relationship with the immigrant communities. Many issues of the *Bollettino dell'Emigrazione*, published by the Italian Ministry of Foreign Affairs, contain evidence of this. In 1904, Guido Rossati—an agricultural expert who two years later became the first head of the new Labor Information Office, opened in New York by the Italian authorities—was sent out to scour the country with Adolfo Rossi, a former editor of *Il Progresso Italo-Americano* and a dean of Italian American journalism. Rossati drafted a report on the "colonization" of Mississippi, Louisiana, and Alabama, where, he observes, with scientific detachment, the arrival of a white work force: "preferable in any case . . . especially for its higher intelligence, steadiness and morality, is preferred also on political and social grounds, to hold in check the threatened preponderance of negroes."[20] Considered as individuals, blacks can be "good . . . less good . . . and evil," but in any case Italian immigrants are wise not to place "too much confidence" in them, since the presence of this "inferior race" has to be considered a serious obstacle to any plan of future settlement. The words of his fellow traveler, Rossi, while open to a more narrative style, take a similar tack. In a passage whose setting recalls an analogous situation described in the influential *The Souls of Black Folk*, by W. E. B. Du Bois (1903),[21] issued just a few months earlier, Rossi reports on a conversation with a black cart driver in which the interviewee ascribes the differences between the poverty of the blacks and the thrift of the Italians to the fact that the former disdain hard work and are fond of gambling, liquor, and women. Rossi thus manages to put in the mouth of a black man (treated, typically, as an honest, uncouth fellow who marks his words "with a noisy laugh") the admission of the moral disparity between those who lead a licentious life, end up supporting as many as "four women," and would rather "have fun," and those who, like the honest Italian, are an example of moderation.

For a variation on the theme, we can turn to the work of one of the most interesting members of the Italian American élite, Camillo Cianfarra. When Cianfarra published his memoir *Il diario di un emigrato* [The Diary of an Immigrant] in 1904—one of the most remarkable narratives written from "within" the exodus—he was already a prominent figure,[22] above all as editor-in-chief of the socialist journal *Il Proletario.* Yet he was hardly partisan; a few years later he was writing in the columns of the more mainstream papers. The *Diario* overtly indicts the so-called padrone system and the ruthlessness of the bosses, who signed up workers newly arrived in America and then took advantage of them; but at the same time it holds out the hopeful vision of a not too distant future when "a strong and healthy race"[23] like the Italian will assimilate within the broader whole of America. As things stand at the moment, however, Italians can consider themselves lucky not to be treated "like the Negroes,"[24] for Mulberry Street—whose doors are opened to the protagonist by a "Professor" who has fallen on hard times—presents a demeaning spectacle of immorality, lack of hygiene, and illiteracy. Later in the narrative, when the narrator stops to watch the Italians who are working on the railway tracks, the arrival of some priests and some black prostitutes triggers a moment of dismay as he thinks of the "likelihood of a union between a black woman and a white man—even if he is a starving Southern Italian peasant."[25]

Shortly after the publication of the *Diario*, Cianfarra was enlisted by the Italian government to work as an inspector in the Labor Information Office, in New York. He made five tours of inspection, which his superior, Rossati, praised publicly for their "worthy zeal,"[26] dwelling in particular on the last, which took him to the South, from Virginia to Tennessee and Florida. Cianfarra had anticipated the results of this mission in a report published in the monthly *Gli Italiani e l'America* in November 1906.[27] His conclusions, interestingly, are similar to those of another expert sent to the South during the same period by the United States Bureau of Labor, Emily Fogg Meade, who, in full agreement with Cianfarra, ends her report: "All things considered, the Italians have been found to be good citizens, and their presence has proved an obstacle to the increase of negro labor."[28] In other words, Meade views favorably the noticeable movement of labor from Italy (and especially Sicily) to the agricultural areas of the South.

In Cianfarra's view (as in that of Ventura, another intellectual whose debts to socialist culture need to be more closely examined) the "superiority, as a citizen and as a worker," of the Italian with respect to the Negro is incontestable. Although relying mainly on the opinions of the whites he interviewed, Cianfarra also calls on Darwin, Lombroso, and the authority of other scientists and experts to corroborate the hypothesis of an "anatomical, physiological, and psychological" inferiority. Now familiar observations and comments are repeated: blacks are lazy, indifferent, sexually intemperate, and inclined to alcoholism and absenteeism. Without regret, he points to the definitive collapse of plantation life, supported by an old aristocracy, which has now been supplanted by the *economia a salario*, or "wage economy," of the "capitalists and merchants of the North." From an "evolutionary" point of view, however, it has had some unpredictably negative repercussions, since it used to be that "the master oversaw the physical development of the race, promoting marriage between the strongest and most physically perfect of the two sexes, and the mistress educated by example and by the rod the children born of these unions."[29] That is the past; and yet the rejection of violence by the bosses of today leaves open the problem of the relationship with the "Negro work force" that is, one hopes, to be replaced.

In Florida, the inspector dutifully documented the employment of Italians as longshoremen in the port of Jacksonville and as laborers in the sawmills in Mountbrook. Company towns like Tyler were eager to attract European immigrants to what turned out to be a trap, a place made unlivable by the climate, the activity of "aguzzini bianchi" (white torturers), and the nighttime surveillance of "molossi" (watch-dogs). It is therefore understandable that Cianfarra's diligent in-vestigation warmly counseled Italians to avoid this hellish destiny, leaving it for blacks. But it is equally obvious that humanitarian obser-vations should not be misunderstood as a wish to question the color line. Thus, a policy of protecting the national labor force (Italian, but here already clearly seen as an ethnic component of the American melting pot) confirmed, however passively, the practice and ideology of segregation.[30]

We have little information on Cianfarra's later work.[31] The Labor Information Office for Italians, though it continued its efforts on behalf of Italian immigrants for some years, changed its official policy favoring rural settlement and a larger presence in the South, noting that such projects were to be opposed as long as "our fellow citizens are treated on the same level as blacks."[32]

## CODA

A century after the outbreak of the Civil War and the publication of the articles in L'Eco d'Italia, one of the most authoritative voices in the history of relations between Italy and the United States, Giuseppe Prezzolini, discusses, in I trapiantati [The Transplanted] (1963), the aforementioned writers. And he does so in detail.

I have tried elsewhere to outline Prezzolini's role, which to me seems ambiguous yet fruitful, and certainly undeniable, in shaping current Italian images of and prejudices about America.[33] In I tra-piantati, devoted to Italian American subjects, he dwells on Ambas-sador Mayor des Planches's journey, insisting on its success while recognizing as a mistake the plan of settlement in the South; com-mendably, he unearths the figure of Adolfo Rossi (a predecessor of his, so to speak, in the narrow field of Italian American studies) and suggests a rereading of the great work by Papa and Fontana. He also discusses, of course, the Italian shoeshine kneeling in front of his conceited black client, commenting, "Luckily, Fontana wrote these racial pages at least fifty years before fascism gave way to nazism."[34]

Anyone who has the patience to take up that nineteenth-century text will, I think, be able to decide easily about its racist or racial nature. What is insidious is the implied historical judgment. That a racist policy, within and outside the boundaries of Italy, was adopted without pretenses by Mussolini's regime, and broadly applied, is one of those facts that cannot be argued. But here the distinction is more subtle: bringing in the chronology, or rather proposing one that suits his purposes, Prezzolini reinforces and highlights the myth of the "good" Italian compelled to act ruthlessly by the "bad" German. And yet in the early sixties it was known that explicitly racist laws and provisions had been put into effect in Libya, Somalia, Eritrea, and Ethiopia long *before* the infamous anti-Semitic laws of 1938, which were indeed *fascistissime,* and indebted to Nazi ideology, even if they were not promulgated as an automatic response to Nazi pressures. The omissions and the lack of clarity on these points suggest that we should consider Prezzolini's point guilty of a conscious falsification, as if he had undergone a trauma, similar to the one freely admitted by Ferdinando Fontana. That is, decades after Fontana, a whole series of historical and psychological reactions seems to be put in motion when a member of the Italian intellectual élite happens to observe (in this case, through the mediation of reading) the simple but humiliating action of an Italian shining the shoes of a colored man: not least, the wounded pride of colonizers and immigrants, in Africa as in the southern states. It was 1963: we might add that the last Italian troops had left Somalia only a few years before, in 1960.

Furthermore, expressions of this racial unease were not confined to comments on texts: with an immediacy that today might seem embarrassing and dismaying, Prezzolini a little later clarified his own position in an "analysis" of the relations between whites and "Negroes" published in 1967 in both countries, in the daily *Il Tempo* in Rome and the following month in Boston in the *Post-Gazette.* Yet again, the declaration of racial inferiority takes an unmistakable tone: "One cannot speak exactly of the fault of the Negroes, as one cannot say it is the fault of the child of an alcoholic or a syphilitic." According to Prezzolini, the historical phenomenon of slavery has up to now kept Negroes from being fully incorporated into modern life, "from adapting to the conditions of an ever more specialized workplace which requires a certain mental habit of order, tenacity, and organization which is unknown to the majority of Negroes." But a comparison between the idleness in terms of work and the dubious sexual and family morality of blacks, on the one hand, and on the other the success of "Italian, German, Jewish, Japanese, and Chinese" immigrants allows Prezzolini to slyly place beside the historical reasons an old pop-psychology theory of innate inferiority. The fact that this aspect of the essay was taken up and emphasized in an introduction by Giacomo Grillo—an old acquaintance of immigrant journalism—says it all on the persistence of separatist (and in the mid-sixties anachronistic) positions. Furthermore, this constitutes an example (a "fine example" one might say) of the direct responsibility on the part of intellectuals in the secular work of constructing an Italian American identity even from the point of view of racial diversity underlined by racist arguments and remarks.

❊ ❊

*Anthology*

A BLACK AND WHITE VIEW FROM THE SIXTIES

When Prezzolini wrote this article, he had left the United States and his tenure at Columbia, where he had spent more than three decades, and had already collected most of his Italian American articles and essays in *I trapiantati*. The crystal-clear quality of his prose does not demand much interpretive effort; what is significant is the reprinting in America of this tirade, specifically for an Italian American audience. Prezzolini's usual assertiveness of tone is accompanied by the additional authority of the renowned professor, and the end result, rather than a journalistic bout of racial prejudice, seems to dangerously approach a sort of microtreaty, turning personal and highly debatable observations into double-edged truisms.

***Whites and Blacks: An Analysis by Prof. Prezzolini***

In mid-September (1967), a New York periodical will publish an article by the journalist Prof. Giuseppe Prezzolini, of Perugia, which appeared in *Il Borghese* under the title "The Civil War, in America, is some two hundred years old [*sic*]." The author has allowed me to publish this penetrating analysis, in which, with admirable clarity, he presents what seem to me to be new ideas regarding a problem of topical interest that is shaking America and sowing seeds of hatred, now that the fierce struggle has been revived, as a result, in particular, of the Negroes who have immigrated to the North, torn from their natural agricultural society in the South. In the article in the *Post-Gazette* this week, sent to me by the illustrious writer, after it appeared in *Il Tempo* (13 August 1967), Prof. Prezzolini presents some other aspects of the problem that Italians are not aware of, since in Italy the only cohesive ethnic minority that has caused trouble is that of Alto Adige. But if there were twenty-three million blacks among the Italians in Italy, or even whites of a different race, then it would be less difficult to understand what is happening in the United States, where the Italians of the past generations have, through thrift and cleverness, through organization, overcome the barriers of the ghettoes. They have flourished economically, gone into the schools, and become recognized as an element of American politics. In other words, the Italians were able to use the benefits of American life and, as Prezzolini says, "if the Negroes had their skin color as a disadvantage, the Italians had against them ignorance of the language and, later, their coarse accents and religious prejudice. But they had men of talent in the banks, in business, in construction companies, and skillful men in local politics. This did not happen for the blacks." Here follows Prezzolini's article.

—Giacomo Grillo

When two races are brought by the events of history into the same nation there are three ways of resolving the conflicts that arise: the stronger destroys the other, as the Anglo-Saxons did to the Indians, or it absorbs them, as happened to the Mexicans with the Spanish, or they live together, but with separate institutions, as in South Africa and Rhodesia and, soon, in Alto Adige. A system that gives the two political equality but does not take account of their differences creates friction and, in extreme cases, conflict. This is the case of the Negroes in the large American cities, where they are isolated from whites by their customs but are equal under the law.

### SLAVERY

Only when the percentage of a race is minimal or small, so that it is unable to form a corpus of habits and opinions and gain a racial consciousness, can the members of the two races live together peacefully. The Italians, who until they acquired Alto Adige had never faced a cohesive ethnic minority, are not aware of the problems that arise when two races live together in one nation; if they had among them ten million of the yellow-skinned races, blacks, or simply whites of a different race, they would understand what is happening in the United States. It would suffice to look in the classified advertisements and listen to private conversations in Italy to see how much weight the difference between a southerner and an inhabitant of central or northern Italy is given in society; and yet between a Sicilian and the central or northern Italian there is nothing like the difference that exists between a Negro of the American South and an inhabitant of Massachusetts.

Generally in Italy whites are charged with being racists, but today racism is becoming the doctrine of Negroes in the United States, including a remarkable number who call for the formation within the United States of a nation made up only of Negroes. For many years this was the program advocated by the Communist Party in the United States and Negro groups found it unacceptable. The ideal of the leaders of the movements for the improvement of conditions in the United States was a peaceful cohabitation, and as, gradually, equality under the law was achieved for the two races, the conviction developed among them that political equality would not be enough but, indeed, separation was required. As a result we are now faced with the curious spectacle of the more advanced American Negroes advocating a program that is the same as the Apartheid of South Africa and Rhodesia. Naturally the cases of cohabitation have their differences and the specifics of each must be studied; yet certain ironies of history cannot be ignored.

In America the upheaval caused by cohabitation and, finally, the open conflict between the two races had as its basis a particular historical condition of one of them. This historical condition is slavery. Between the Flemish and the Walloons in Belgium, the Finns and the Swedes in Finland, between Ukrainians and Russians or Georgians and Russians in Russia, between Croats and Serbs in Yugoslavia, between the English and the French in Canada, between Chinese and Indonesians in Indonesia, between Hindus and Muslims in India friction arose from differences in language, culture, race; but none of these peoples were slaves of the other. In America there are many different races, and some are notably concentrated in certain regions, so that Wisconsin can be considered in a certain sense German, as Rhode Island is Italian, Louisiana French, and New Mexico Spanish or Mexican—but between one race and the other there was not the moral difference that one of them had been enslaved and had accepted slavery. It had not done so by legal means, but of course the consensus of society manifests itself in other ways besides the vote. Blacks accepted slavery in the regions of the South, because they didn't rebel, or rather because their partial revolts did not have sufficient strength; and their liberation from slavery occurred through the efforts of whites who fought and died to maintain the unity of the United States. The freedom of the Negroes was not the product of sacrifices on their part but of the sacrifices of the whites. The reasons for it were more complex, but the moral fact that emerged was this.

Slavery always leaves deep traces that are not easily erased. The law that freed the slaves did not consider that free citizens cannot be created with a flourish of the pen even if it is preceded by military victories.

Among the more or less silent reproofs that whites give to the

Negroes in the United States there is, for example, the deplorable family morality of many of them. This does not apply to all blacks, of course; but the consequences of the sexual behavior of many of them have repercussions throughout the colored population. Certainly the Negroes under slavery could not have ordinary families. Not always, but often, the masters of the slaves did not hesitate to sell their children, to separate husband and wife, and they considered it their right to take as a mistress the most beautiful among the young slaves. This left among the Negroes a notable percentage of mulattos; in fact one might say that the examples of pure Negritude are fewer than those of mixed race. But the effects of this can be seen in the lack of family stability among Negroes. The number of illegitimate children is much higher than among whites.

In the schools of Washington where the Negroes have made great progress in number in recent decades, the number of unmarried mothers of fourteen and thirteen years increased in a surprising manner. When I did some research in a neighborhood in Harlem and spoke with various Negro pastors, they all told me that the most serious problem was the instability of the Negro family. The crime of rape occurs more frequently among Negroes. The real reason that whites do not want to send their children to the public schools is the lax sexual habits of the Negroes.

THE UNEMPLOYED

Another legacy of slavery is a character flaw generally attributed to the Negro, and that is his tendency to laziness, his carefree manner, his going about singing and dancing, good-natured but ineffectual— an image that is part of the folklore. Along with this is his inability to save money and his inclination to drunkenness (during the recent riots it was not the bakeries that were ransacked but the liquor stores).

Now these few features (to which one might add the inability of the Negroes to establish and manage a business) explain, at least in part, why in a society that is more and more industrialized, such as that of the United States, Negroes have a more difficult time finding work, and hence around 70 per cent of the unemployed are Negroes. I don't mean that in certain cases the antipathy of a white management is not the cause of Negroes' being fired or their failure to be promoted; but I mean that much more often unemployment is caused by the inability of the Negro to adapt to the conditions of work that has become more and more specialized and which requires orderly, tenacious, and organized mental habits that are unknown to the majority of Negroes. And they are unknown because the condition of slavery did not allow for the experience of them, and the seed was absent in the original African civilization.

Naturally, one cannot speak, exactly, of the Negroes' fault, as one cannot say it is the fault of the child of an alcoholic or a syphilitic. That does not remove the fact that any industrialized society, even a Communist one, has to recognize the reality and not entrust to a disabled child tasks that require a precise mind and a steady hand. In the Bible one reads that the guilts of the fathers are visited on the sons, and among all peoples it is a rule of common sense to judge the sons and fiancés by the family in which they were brought up and the country where they were born. That creates some personal injustices, but the system whereby anyone is accepted only on the basis of his accomplishments has the serious flaw of often producing commercial failures and bad marriages.

Refuting the complaints of the Negroes that they are victims of discrimination is the success in America of the Italian, German, Jewish, Japanese, and Chinese immigrants, who endured oppression similar to that of the freed blacks, with the aggravation of ignorance of the language. Italians who have relatives in North America ask them for explanations about what is happening: nine out of ten will explain how even they do not place much confidence in the Negro worker and are not too happy to learn that their women cannot go out at night on the streets of the city without an escort.

In response to the Negroes' demands to have in positions of authority a percentage equal to their percentage in the population (that is, I believe, eleven per cent), one should keep in mind those Negroes who have excelled in the abilities common to their type, that is the arts of dance, singing, sport. No one hesitates to recognize the Negro champions in singing, dancing, and boxing and to reward them with success and money, as is characteristic of American or European civilization.

Jobs will be found in a proportional number for Negroes who wish to become policemen or guards; but not among professors of physics.

No government or congressional commission will ever find a cure for the scars of slavery. One does not remedy the damage made by centuries with decrees and laws only a few years old. It will have to wait a long time. Negroes, enslaved by their African brothers, sold to the English slave traders, and transported to America to work in an agricultural society, today have against them the industrial mentality and automation.

---

"Bianchi e negri: un'analisi del prof. Prezzolini," *Post-Gazette* (Boston) 1 September 1967.

# 6

## At Ellis Island

"Liberty? It's a statue."

—F.

THE ESSENTIAL COLLECTIVE, SHARED EXPERIENCE, THAT NEARLY IN-evitable passage through the halls of Ellis Island, was closely observed by Edward, or Edoardo, Corsi, in a classic text, *In the Shadow of Liberty*. Corsi was a son of the exodus who rose to become commissioner of immigration, a ferryman of souls, so to speak. His autobiographical account of the history of "the island of tears" was, in rapid succession, translated, analyzed, and then brought "home" to Italy, through the efforts of one of the most authoritative intellectuals active in the United States, Giuseppe Prezzolini. Unlike the preceding discussion of racial interaction, in its way choral and attentive to the "great" geography of the republic, this testimony emphasizes the strong personalities of the two writers and mediators against the background of the preeminent urban context: New York.

Today, Ellis Island, in the upper part of New York Bay—the imposing tip of Manhattan in front, the Verrazzano Bridge and the Atlantic behind—is the site of a museum and, like the Statue of Liberty, is a destination for tourists. One can retrace there the thread of memory, now belonging to distant immigrants, to try to imagine at least vaguely a collective drama of great historical and human significance: thus, this cluster of buildings, the crossroads of peoples and in many aspects the matrix of a substantial part of the body and soul of the United States, continues to inspire narratives, visions, and journeys of acquaintance. And if the historical bibliography on Ellis Island is by now remarkably extensive, in the last decades there has been a notable renaissance, in a heterogeneous, intensely literary group of texts of "this isle of quarantine / fading in a cloud of memory."[1]

Very different, however, are the impressions transmitted to us by these "invaders" and "immigrants," retrieved from an Ellis Island of more than sixty years ago. It's hard not to feel the tragic, burning

270

present of these ancient passages, now that the points of landing are so much closer to the Italian "motherland," and bear names that are much more familiar to an Italian ear. But it is not, I believe, a matter of a mere recurrence, of a chance nemesis of history. Behind the representative evidence of these pages, which capture today as they did yesterday the attention of readers, one perceives the direct involvement of the author, who explicitly puts himself and his own experience in play to create a work of testimony. It is therefore worthwhile to stop briefly on the figure of Edoardo Corsi, which among other things will allow us to better put in perspective his partial translation into Italian.

Edoardo, or Edward, Corsi (Capestrano, province of Aquila, 1896–Kingston, New York, 1965) came through Ellis Island as a child in 1907, arriving in the United States with his mother and her husband (his father, Filippo, the Republican representative to the Chamber of Deputies for the district of Massa Carrara, had been dead for several years); the family quickly settled in the crowded Italian neighborhood of East Harlem, one of the most run-down but dynamic areas in the city. After a difficult childhood, marked by the depression of his mother (who finally returned to the Abruzzi and died there soon afterward), Edoardo participated eagerly in the local life; soon after receiving a law degree, he began working as an administrator and official in social services, in which he had a long career, and was at the same time active as a journalist and writer. From 1926 to 1931 he was the director of Haarlem House, a historic point of reference of sociocultural activism in the neighborhood;[2] his work with the immigrants of New York's Lower East Side earned him the attention of the Republican political machine (within which Corsi held, from 1925 on, important posts), which was in search of a "clean" figure to head Ellis Island, after a scandal had compromised the credibility of the administrators. From 1931–33, he was commissioner of immigration at Ellis Island, under President Hoover: "From my position, similar to that of St. Peter, I consider that I have learned a certain degree of humility and patience."[3] In 1932 in Rome he met Mussolini, "to discuss, among other things, the possibility of starting another Fascist-friendly newspaper in the United States."[4] In 1934, while Fiorello LaGuardia was mayor of New York, he entered the economic crisis as director of the Emergency Home Relief Bureau, a job he held until 1935.

At this point, Corsi already had behind him distinct journalistic experience: he was the correspondent for *Outlook* and, in 1928, for the *New York World* in Rome, where he tried unsuccessfully to interview Mussolini; in addition, he appeared often in the pages of *Il Carroccio*, to which he contributed excerpts from his speeches and previews of the volume on which he was working. He also edited a local Italian tabloid, the *Harlemite*. In 1935 *In the Shadow of Liberty: The Chronicle of Ellis Island* was published (in New York, by Macmillan)— the broad history and chronicle of emigration from which the pages presented to the Italian public were taken—and Corsi founded *La Settimana*, an elegant and cultivated bilingual weekly to which some of the most well-known names in Italian journalism and culture in New York contributed, from Amerigo Ruggiero to Beniamino De Ritis, from Alfonso Arbib-Costa to Angelo Patri.[5] On the literary plane the choices of the weekly were consistent with the belletristic taste of the major organs of the immigrant press: a lot of "romantic" sentimentality, exoticisms, a more mannered range of mysteries (from Luciano Zuccoli to Gaston Leroux). And ideologically it displayed—in accord here, too, with the mood of the majority of Italian American voters and their leaders (the so-called *prominenti*)— a benevolent attitude not only toward Mussolini but also toward Hitler.[6]

In 1937, Corsi was a delegate to the convention to revise the constitution of the State of New York, where he concentrated on unemployment and health in relation to insurance issues. This partly opportunistic mixture of active humanitarianism and a politics of "law and order" did not, however, win him election when he ran for the Senate in 1938 (later, in 1950, he ran unsuccessfully for mayor of the city). In this period he was also, literally, an important voice for Little Italy; on the radio, for much of 1941, he broadcast a series of high-level talks on American and Italian history and culture, which were published regularly in *La Follia di New York* (to which he had been contributing since 1924, serving for a brief period as editor).[7] From 1943 to 1954, under Governor Thomas Dewey, he was the head of the State Industrial Board, and as such he represented the State of New York in labor politics and controversies. In 1954–55, he did a brief and much discussed stint in the Eisenhower administration, as special assistant for immigration,[8] a delicate task, which Secretary of State John Foster Dulles made impractical for him within a few weeks, because of the severe divergence of views between the government's "protectionism" on the subject of open borders and Corsi's "immigrationist" attitude. A lucid reflection in an autobiographical key on that political battle appeared some months later in *The Reporter,* the weekly edited by Max Ascoli. Ascoli was another figure of Italian immigration in the United States,[9] but a very different one from those mentioned above. Even after he lost his government position, Corsi occupied various other high-profile posts (in particular, that of director of the New York World's Fair in 1964–65), but his symbolic weight as a public figure was severely reduced. That is the outline of his career; but his work as an Italian American intellectual, official, and politician in the most humanly and historically complete sense of the term awaits more detailed research and analysis.[10]

Meanwhile, we can follow the singular Italian success of *In the Shadow of Liberty*, which was entirely dependent on Prezzolini's careful work in publicizing it. In fact, the promotion of Corsi's text, aided by the smooth translation of the two excerpts (it does not seem to me farfetched to see Giuseppe's hand in the lucid style of the article signed "Giuliano"),[11] constitutes one of Prezzolini's most well-concealed, but not for that reason less relevant, activities as a path builder between the two cultures, and, more specifically, as a participant in and observer of the Italian American world. *I trapiantati* (issued by Longanesi in 1963, and dedicated by Prezzolini to the "tragedy" of immigration) is only, in short, a selection of the author's work on the subject; much of the earlier as well as the later material is found in other publications.[12] We should also keep in mind Prezzolini's influence as director of and professor at the Casa Italiana at Columbia University: several years before, figures important in that world, such as Leonard Covello and Garibaldi Lapolla,[13] had come through Columbia, and in the thirties the Casa Italiana had the opportunity to collaborate with Corsi's Haarlem House and, around the corner, with the Aguilar Branch of the New York Public Library, which, with a rich collection of Italian books, was an attraction for the more engaged Italian Americans of East Harlem.[14]

For Corsi, almost uniquely, Prezzolini manifested over the years a constant admiration,[15] even reprinting in *I trapiantati* a brief, positive profile written in 1955 after his abrupt dismissal (*L'affare Corsi*). Already, in those few pages, there is much of Prezzolini: the rigorous documentation, relieved by the conversational flow of the prose; the rapid succession, almost intermingling, of information and opinion; the caustic tone, the sudden flareups, the equivocal changes of direction. An eloquent sample:

> I have often said that Corsi is one of the best products of the American influence on an Italian character.
> When an Italian immigrant has not become a delinquent, has not ended up in a mental ward, and has not swelled up into a "notable," he is truly a fine fellow.[16]

But what seems to me noteworthy above all is the (relative) "investiture" implicit in the work of translation. It is this dimension of Prezzolini as a "cultural worker" (an expression that probably would have horrified him) which today stands out with particular effectiveness, because one feels less of that often ungenerous spirit that kept him from a more historically justified understanding of Italian American culture. Consider the utter timeliness of this and other reports, relative to authors whom we have learned to read and evaluate only at a distance of decades, accepting tardily his invitation: in addition to Corsi, he mentions Eduardo Migliaccio, John Fante, Jo Pagano, and also, disparagingly, Cordiferro and the great daily of the immigrant community, *Il Progresso Italo-Americano*. In fact, simply by naming names Prezzolini was performing an elementary but indispensable critical gesture, guided by a taste with which later generations showed themselves in the final analysis in agreement.

To better understand the meaning of this "militance," it may be helpful to mention the external circumstances of the two publications. *Gli invasori* [A Picture of 1907] came out in 1938, on the front page of Longanesi's *Omnibus*, below a large, six-column photograph from the Spanish Civil War: "Rebels surrendering to a government unit." The story of immigration is thus placed beside prewar polemical articles and commentary that is disdainful of French fears and the indecisiveness of the Chamberlain cabinet regarding the Sudeten question, and with a poison dart of anti-Americanism in the second-page photograph, showing injured demonstrators, after an anti-Nazi protest in New York ("Demonstrators, after the attack on Nazi headquarters, waiting for a doctor") as if smugly to suggest that in Manhattan veteran members of Fascist action squads had disembarked along with the immigrants.

*L'isola degli emigranti* [Racketeers and Human Contraband] appeared in 1939 in *Oggi*, which was in many ways, in its early days, the heir of *Omnibus* (a mere glance at the bylines, the subjects, and the graphics is sufficient). *Oggi*, like *Omnibus*, devoted considerable space in every issue to United States news and culture, and was generous in its attention to Italian Americans. The same names ricochet from one publication to the other: Steinbeck, Caldwell, Saroyan, "Giovanni" Fante; it is the cradle of *Americana*, and in fact Vittorini, its editor, is alongside Prezzolini in the discovery of transatlantic literature. But they are not alone: one reads articles, essays, and reportage by Giaime Pintor, Tito Spagnol, Roberto Campagnoli, and others. This is the literary parterre, even though *Oggi* regularly gave more space to the present. Thus the "American" Prezzolini, commenting in the first issue, on the front page, on Dewey as the Republican candidate for the presidency, found himself in the company of a piece—not so incongruous at the time—by the *fascistissimo* Manlio Lupinacci which expounded with obvious enthusiasm and conformity on the return of the Fascist troops from Spain. At the top left, as if to bless the launch of the new weekly, is the profile, in high relief, of a radiant Mussolini: "Il Duce welcomes the victorious legions." A few months later, in an advertising section, Corsi's memoir was preceded by a note on the magnum opus of thirties anti-Americanism: *America amara* [Bitter America], by Emilio Cecchi.

The assiduous and valuable work of disseminating Corsi's pages must, in brief, be evaluated not only diachronically, within the broad, multifaceted militancy of the "American" Prezzolini but also synchronically: placed, on the one hand, beside the more passionate documents of an influential pro-American "myth," and, on the other, beside a series of clearly propagandistic, not necessarily literary signs. "It is a pity," Prezzolini wrote in 1955, "that a book like this has never been published in Italy."[17] In a certain sense, sincere regret kept the existence of those two long-ago offerings hidden. Outflanking the forgetfulness or excessive modesty of their editor, they reemerge today, still strong, in a time of new immigration.

*Anthology*

EDWARD CORSI, *IN THE SHADOW OF LIBERTY*

One evening in 1931, on the triangular walls of the old *New York Times* building, where in blazing characters the most important news of the day appears, one could see the following announcement circulate: "President Hoover today named Edoardo Corsi commissioner of immigration at Ellis Island."

In this way the people of New York learned that an immigrant, who thirty years earlier had been introduced as a child to the narrow gate through which 35 per cent of the inhabitants of the United States had entered, had been named its guardian.

Edoardo Corsi is one of the children of Italians who have distinguished themselves in America without denying their country of origin, but bringing to their compatriots the support of a disinterested heart, a clear mind, an uncommon political ability. He emerged through social work performed at his Haarlem House: a charitable institution founded in the center of the poorest Italian neighborhood in New York.

At Ellis Island, where he was called by Hoover, he introduced fundamental reforms dictated by his spirit of humanity and his experience as an immigrant and friend of immigrants. Among the other things that he did, and that were important to the social life of

America, he had the good idea of digging in the archives of the institution intended to watch over the entrance of immigrants in the United States, of questioning old inspectors, interpreters, and doctors of the great establishment and of writing an anecdotal book, rich in human documentation, on the cases that presented themselves in almost fifty years in the offices, corridors, and halls of Ellis Island.

Asians and Europeans, anarchists and South American dictators, celebrated singers, famous divorcées, actors, the lowest scum and great failures of Europe, international swindlers and cheats pass through his pages; and their memories, their struggles to enter the United States are narrated by Corsi in a wonderful book, in English, entitled *In the Shadow of Liberty.*

Corsi also had the advantage of going to Italy in 1923 and writing for the *World,* a newspaper opposed to Fascism, a series of reports that interpreted, with a spirit of truth and sympathy, the renewing movement of Italy. Today Corsi occupies an important post in the city government of New York, and represents the Republican Party at the Albany Convention, where the constitution of the state of New York is being revised.

—From the original introductory note to the 1938 Italian translation

## A Picture of 1907

I am sure that most Americans will be astonished to learn that during a single year of the depression eighteen thousand men and women from foreign shores, debarred from our gates by immigration quota restrictions or for other reasons, sought surreptitious entry and were arrested and turned back.

The figure eighteen thousand is a measure of quantity only. Without an examination of specific cases there could be no conception of the intensity, the burning hopes of success, and the countless personal considerations which impelled these eighteen thousand who failed to reach our hearthstone. From each specific case some of us might gain a truer appreciation of our citizenship.

Approximately five thousand of these "gate crashers" stowed away upon ships, living in many instances for days and nights upon bread and water, voyaging to our ports in bales, crates and boxes, in water tanks, and a strange variety of hidden compartments. Sometimes the international racketeers in charge of the smuggling venture foresaw possible apprehension and capture, and then they threw the alien's living body to the sharks. . . .

Those who did not stow away on ships, that most hazardous of all methods of entry, tried to enter in bales of Canadian hay or crates of Mexican freight. They came concealed in wagons, automobiles, railroad cars, or the airplanes of international racketeers. Some, it is true, merely posed as former citizens at points of entry, and walked across the border amid holiday crowds returning from Cuba, Mexico, or Canada. Others affected the disguise of priests or nuns. Then there were those who swished through the night in high-powered launches or speed boats, to seek out lone stretches of coast line or isolated lagoons and inlets.

Guns flashed in the darkness along these wild strips of shore. Sometimes it was the alien who was killed; not infrequently it was the immigration inspector or a member of the Coast Guard.

One case came up during my administration which showed me the depths of misery which men will suffer in the hope of sharing what we accept as a matter of course. This is the story of Nicholas Prazza and his comrades. Their tragedy has such a dramatic quality that it is easy to piece together the events into a logical and poignant whole. It began on the night of July 10, 1933.

The setting is the tropical port of Balboa, in the Isthmus of Panama, amid a great bustle and hurry. The *California* is taking on cargo preparatory to her departure for New York. Scores of singing, sweating, swearing stevedores are rushing up and down the gangplank in rhythmic confusion, while the huge piles of freight upon the dark wharves dwindle as night wears on.

Finally all the wharves are nearly emptied. Midnight is drawing near and the eerie noises are subsiding. Now the empty-handed stevedores shuffle down the gangplank more slowly, mopping their grimy faces with grimier handkerchiefs, their bare backs glistening in the moonlight. They plod wearily toward the few remaining crates and boxes and bulging gunnysacks which fringe the docks, and take them up with an apathy that belies their great physical strength.

Lights appear intermittently upon the great ship. Then her engines throb with a low drone, getting up their first heat for the long voyage ahead. Their sound mingles with the clang of signal bells, and the stevedores arouse themselves to a renewed and final burst of energy.

Removed from this age-old scene of the sea, but by no means apart from it, stand three silent, motionless figures deep in the shadows at the rear of the wharves. They await the word from the seaman who has agreed to smuggle them into the United States.

They wonder whether he will ever come, whether or not they have been betrayed, while the interminable minutes drag slowly by, each contributing to the intensity of their suspense. If he does come, will

they succeed in boarding the ship? Otherwise, what will be the consequences? They murmur to each other in tense, excited whispers.

For three years they have awaited the opportunity for this supreme
adventure. Each has suffered extreme self-denial, each has stinted to
save actual pennies in order to get together the money demanded by
the smugglers.

No wonder that Satero Zattos whispers, "If he does not take us, it
will be too bad if he ever comes back to Balboa!"

"We can do nothing but trust him," Peter Spiro whispers back.

Nicholas Prazza smiles gravely, but says nothing, for he is a quiet,
rather melancholy man. And finally Satero Zattos and Peter Spiro
stop whispering.

Satero Zattos thinks of his eight-year-old son, of his wife Elene,
both far away in his native Grecian village of Tsemanta. For their sake
he has been a peanut vendor in Balboa for three years. He hopes that
in America it will be different, that soon he will make enough money
to be able to send for them. Elene's brother, Michael, who lives in
Massachusetts, will help him, and all will be well. What does it matter
that he is risking his life when the reward is success and happiness for
all?

Peter Spiro is thinking too. He has two sons, one six, the other
nine, and they are with his beloved Anthoula in distant Albania.
Staring into the darkness, he pictures the happiness he will feel upon
reaching his cousin in New Haven. Perhaps there he will not have to
drudge for hours over hot stoves and wash greasy, smelly pans. Perhaps he and his cousin will be able to have a restaurant of their own,
with someone else to do the cooking. But anything will do for a while,
if later he can bring Anthoula and the little sons to share his success.
This is a desperate chance he is taking, but getting to America, just
getting any kind of chance in America, is, in his opinion, worth the
sacrifice.

As for Nicholas Prazza, he never talks and no one ever knows what
he is thinking about. No one even knows if he ever had a wife, or if he
has any relatives anywhere.

Now the last of the stevedores comes down the *California's* gangplank, and the shouts of the crew reverberate across her dim-lit
decks.

Suddenly the three men who wait in the darkness stiffen and stare
ahead. Two shadowy figures are coming cautiously towards them.
There is a low whistle, and the trio advances to meet them. It is the
Spanish sailor, Sebastian Rivera, with a companion, Peter Heule.

"Keep quiet," warns Rivera. "Follow us, and hurry!"

The seamen smugglers lead the way up the gangplank, then down narrow iron steps into the curious abyss which is the hold. Through lanes flanked by piles of freight they file in the dim light, until they reach a darker chamber which is oppressively hot and stifling. Sebastian Rivera stops.

"Aquí!" he mutters in Spanish, motioning toward the smokestack casing above the boilers.

He has indicated a small trapdoor in an extremely inaccessible place. It leads to the shafting, and a bolt and nut have been removed in order that it may be opened. Below, and with nothing but scorching iron rods between, are the ship's boilers.

"We will die!" exclaims Satero Zattos.

"Don't be fools," snaps Rivera. "Soon you will get used to it." Before he finishes speaking there is a gentle sway of the ship and acceleration of her engines. She has weighed anchor, and the three stowaways look up in bewilderment. They stare at each other in frightened silence. It is Nicholas Prazza who shrugs his shoulders in futile abandonment and crawls head first through the trap door. A moment later he is followed by Satero Zattos, then Peter Spiro.

Within the miniature inferno they hear the door bang shut behind them. They hear Rivera and Heule reaffix the bolt and nut.

Their three years of waiting are over. They are on their way to America.

It was agreed at the beginning of their negotiations, and at the time they paid him their money, that Sebastian Rivera was to furnish food and drink for the duration of the voyage. Will he comply with his part of the bargain? They can only wait and see. After several hours he brings the suffocating trio a hunk of hard bread and a can of water.

Courageously they suffer the torture of their cramped quarters: through the long night and through the next day when Rivera returns with more bread and water. For the most part they have been silent, conserving the strength which they can feel ebbing out of their bodies.

One—two—three—the days pass like so many eternities. On the morning of the fourth day, just as Nicholas Prazza is expressing the fear that all is lost, Rivera comes with the bread and water again. With a mighty effort Nicholas Prazza lifts himself on one elbow and attempts to drink, but he slumps backward before he can take the can from the hand of Satero Zattos.

"Drink, comrade," Satero Zattos urges, helping him up and forcing the can to his lips. "It is too late to give up now."

"I try, but it is no use," says Nicholas Prazza, after gulping a swallow of the tepid water.

"It is noontime," remarks Peter Spiro. "Those are the whistles we hear."

"I hope we shall hear them in New York," replies Satero Zattos.

"Maybe in hell," Nicholas Prazza whispers hoarsely.

All three are silent again. More long hours pass. They are hours of indescribable misery. The quarters of the three have commenced to smell foul and sickening. Nicholas Prazza is breathing heavily, as though in deep sleep.

Through the rest of the fourth night Peter Spiro and Satero Zattos pray. For both it is a nightmare during which they battle to retain consciousness, and literally cling to life. Already Nicholas Prazza is delirious. The heat from the boilers rises in terrific waves; their water has long since been exhausted, and Sebastian Rivera has not come for almost twenty-four hours.

Suddenly there is a whistling sound, a rattle in the throat of Nicholas Prazza, Satero Zattos bends over him, extending one hand in the dark. He feels Prazza's swollen tongue protruding from his lips.

"Comrade!" he shouts. "Comrade!" But the rattle has ended, and Nicholas Prazza cannot reply. With his death have passed the dreams he had of life in America.

Peter Spiro and Satero Zattos utter hysterical prayers. High above them the noon whistles are blowing. They have but one alternative now, and that is to surrender. Sebastian Rivera has not returned, and it occurs to them that perhaps he does not intend to come back. Who will climb up the funnel shafting, the only outlet from their hole of imprisonment? Peter Spiro volunteers.

This is the official report of the outcome:

From H. Manning
Chief Officer, S.S. *California*
To: Captain T.H. Lyon
Marine Superintendent,
New York, N.Y.

Subject: Finding of Peter Spiro and Satero Zattos, stowaways, and body of Nicholas Prazza, deceased stowaway.

Sir:
Facts pertaining to the above are as follows:
At about 1:00 p.m., on July 16, Mr. J. English, 6th Assistant Engineer, while pacing on the fiddley deck, found a stowaway climbing up the funnel shafting (inside). Mr. English notified Mr. Bishop, Jr., 3rd officer and myself.

Investigation revealed another stowaway and body in the shafting around the bottom of the funnel casing over the boilers. Cross examination of the stowaways revealed that they had contracted with Sebastian Rivera and Peter Huele, firemen on this vessel to stow them away to New York. Peter Spiro claimed to have paid S. Rivera the sum of $60 in cash prior to boarding the said ship at Balboa. Satero Zattos promised to pay a similar amount to the two firemen on arrival in New York . . . . . . . . . .
. . . . . . . . . . . . . . . . . . . . . . . . . . . . . . . . . . . . . . . . . . . . . . . . . .

The time of Nicholas Prazza's death was established by Spiro as he heard the noon whistles.

The doctor examined the body of Prazza, found him to have expired from heat, exhaustion and suffocation, no doubt due to the intense heat from the boilers.

The belongings of Nicholas Prazza were very few. A small pocket book contained $1.65, several small pictures, and a small note book. I mentioned this as there appears some doubt as to the correctness of his name. No written or printed evidence has so far appeared. I have written out the name merely from the hearsay of all his companions, who did not seem to know him prior to the meeting for the purpose of stowing away.

The body of Nicholas Prazza was committed to the deep on July 16, 1933, 0:10 a.m. in Lat. 32–36 N., Long. 77–19 N., with due ceremony in the presence of Commander, Officers, Doctor and other members of the crew.

Rivera #145 and Heule #147, Porto Rican and Hawaiian, respectively, placed in confinement in ship's brig until arrival in N.Y.

The denouement of this tragedy, which grew out of the desire of three poor Greeks to live in America, occurred a few days later at Ellis Island. Peter Spiro and Satero Zattos were held as alien stowaways and arraigned before a Board of Special Inquiry.

At the official prelude to their deportation both begged imploringly for a chance to live in the United States. But the deportation statutes, rigid and inexorable, permitted of no discretion in either of their cases. They were held, however, by their own consent, until trial of the smugglers was completed and both Rivera and Heule had been sentenced to terms of imprisonment.

---

*In the Shadow of Liberty: The Chronicle of Ellis Island* (New York: Macmillan Company, 1935), 71–89.

## Racketeers and Human Contraband

Edoardo Corsi (who was named head of the United States Immigration and Naturalization Service by President Hoover) is an Italian immigrant. His memoir of being an official at Ellis Island, the island

that has seen millions of European immigrants come through and has seen, similarly, millions of other Europeans rejected who in the golden age of immigration tried to be admitted to the States, is a lively and moving human document that is not without literary effect.
      —From the original introductory note to the 1939 Italian
translation

   Many friends and officials of the Immigration Service called at my office during the first few days after my arrival to take up my duties at Ellis Island.
   One day, when the flood of visitors had subsided somewhat, and I was discussing various phases of the work with Assistant Commissioner Byron H. Uhl, the conversation happened to turn to the year 1907.
   "Who was here," I asked him, "when I came through the Island?"
   "Well, I for one," he replied, laughing. "I'm nearly as old a fixture as the first buildings. I've been in the Service about forty years, you know."
   "But an Italian immigrant boy coming through in 1907," I said, "surely wouldn't have seen *you*."
   Again he smiled. "We couldn't see the individuals for the crowds we had in those days," he said. "But wait—Martocci! Why didn't I think of him before! He probably admitted your family."
   Seeing my eager interest, he explained: "He's the same Italian interpreter we had when you came through the Island. Wouldn't you like to talk with him?"
   A few days passed before I had the opportunity to see Frank Martocci. He came into my office and congratulated me in Italian, having already read in the papers of my appointment and my immigrant background. When I asked if he had escorted me personally into this country, he paused reflectively, going over in swift review his many years at Ellis Island. His merry dark eyes twinkling, he ran a stubby hand through his shock of iron-gray hair, which, despite the years, had not thinned. Finally he said:
   "Of course I can't remember whether I inspected your family, but I can tell you that the millions of other Italians who came through Ellis Island and now live in America are glad to see you here."
   I thanked him and we chatted for some time. Finally I said, "Tell me, what do you remember of the days when I came in? What were the conditions in those days?"
   Eyes twinkling, he rubbed his hands together and leaned forward.
   "We went to work, of course, from the Barge Office at the Battery. From there the ferryboat took most of the employees to Ellis Island at

nine in the morning. Hundreds of other people were always eagerly waiting and clamoring to get on the same boat. These were the friends and relatives of immigrants expected during the day, or already being detained at the Island. . . .

"Fortunately or unfortunately—however you look at it—I was a native Italian, knew the language, and had already been in the service a long time. This combination made me a sort of godsend to many of these people, who, recognizing my nationality, would seize me by the coat, by the arm, and even by the neck, and insist on following me everywhere I went, babbling out their problems and pleading for aid. I did my best to keep clear of them in a kindly way, but sometimes I couldn't help but lose my patience. Waiting for friends, brothers, mothers, fathers, or sisters, they looked at me so hopefully, so anxiously, that my sympathy for them was quite a strain on my nerves.

"Once at the Island, we employees had to plunge immediately into our work, for in those terrifically busy days whole boat loads of immigrants were waiting to be inspected every morning. They came from everywhere: from England, Germany, Russia, Italy, France, Greece and other countries.

"At quarantine, inspectors had already boarded the boats to examine the first- and second-class passengers. Those found eligible were landed at the pier. Many less fortunate, who were considered ineligible, were brought to Ellis Island, where they had to undergo the experience of being judged by the immigration authorities on the following day."

"How different the inspection routine must have been in those days," I mused.

"It certainly was," he answered, "I can well remember, for at that time I was in the registry department, assigned to decide the eligibility of aliens to land. To make things run fairly smoothly in that mixed crowd of poor, bewildered immigrants, we would tag them with numbers corresponding to numbers on their manifest, after they had been landed from the barges and taken into the building.

"Here, in the main building, they were lined up—a motley crowd in colorful costumes, all ill at ease and wondering what was to happen to them. Doctors then put them through their medical inspection, and whenever a case aroused suspicion, the alien was set aside in a cage apart from the rest, for all the world like a segregated animal, and his coat lapel or shirt marked with colored chalk, the color indicating why he had been isolated. These methods, crude as they seem, had to be used, because of the great numbers and the language difficulties.

"All the other aliens were passed down a long line and grouped according to their manifest numbers, and the inspection continued. There were twenty-two lines of inspection, as well as a number of side sections where the aliens were grouped according to letters.

"Every manifest held thirty names, but one inspector never got all thirty. Some were detained by the doctors at the medical inspection, and others were held back for other reasons. Those aliens who were passed were told by the principal inspector to follow the line to a point where another inspector sat with his manifest before him."

"And there, no doubt, occurred the essence of the work," I interposed. "You had to question the aliens to find out if they were eligible to enter the country."

"Yes, and that's where most of our headaches began. If, for example, a woman with three children came before the inspector, she was asked her name. Then she had to produce her vaccination card, which the inspector would compare with her name on the manifest and the line number of the manifest. Her age was asked, and again the manifest was consulted. These manifests, of course, had been prepared by the purser or some other official of the ship, so that they were all ready when the alien came before the inspector.

"Before a barrage of questions such as: Sex? Married status? Occupation? Where born? Where last resided? Where going? By whom was the passage paid? Is that person in the United States or not? If so, how long? To whom is the alien going?—the alien would do his best, wondering what it was all about and when and how it would end. These crowds, this pushing, this hurrying to get things done, this red tape, those cards containing he knew not what damning information against him—it was not at all like his peaceful life back in his native country. Would he get along in this new and strange land? Maybe he should never have come. These thoughts must have been in the minds of most of them. . . .

"With those who were being detained matters were still worse, for it was almost impossible to provide strict sanitation. . . . One Sunday morning, I remember, there were seventeen hundred of these women and children kept in one room with a normal capacity of six hundred. How they were packed in! It had to be seen to be appreciated. They just couldn't move about, and whenever we wanted to get one out it was almost a major operation.

"For example, I was one of the four employees whose duty it was to distribute their detention cards. That day it took us all of four solid hours to distribute the cards to the seventeen hundred people, because, added to the general noise in several different languages, we were simply unable to work our way through the massed crowd. . . .

"With so many people packed together under such conditions, it was naturally impossible for them to keep clean, for the clean ones were pressed against aliens infected with vermin, and it was not long before we were all contaminated."

※

"As for sleeping quarters, please don't imagine they were anything like what we have now. Not only were they inadequate, but what we had were not of the best. There were iron bedsteads, which folded like a pocketbook, and these were in three tiers. The aliens who were unfortunate enough to be without beds had to sleep on benches, chairs, the floor, or wherever we could put them. Today there are usually about two hundred detained every night, but in those days we averaged about two thousand. In the detention room there were never less than nine hundred. It was an endless affair, like filling a trough at one end and emptying it at the other.

"And the feeding of the immigrants! It was a sight, back in those days, and I hate to think of it. One employee brought out a big pail filled with prunes, and another some huge loaves of sliced rye bread. A helper would take a dipper full of prunes and slop it down on a big slice of bread, saying: 'Here! Now go and eat!'"

※

"There were quite a number going back, too."

"Plenty. And in the case of aged people it was particularly pitiful," he acknowledged. "You see, in nine cases out of ten, an old person was detained until called for by some relative or friend. At the Island, these poor unfortunates would wander about, bewilderment and incomprehension in their eyes, not even knowing where they were, or why they were being kept. It was touching to see how, whenever they saw anyone who spoke their language, they would ask hopefully: 'Have you seen my son? Have you seen my daughter? Do you know him, my Giuseppe? When is he coming for me?'

"There were times, of course, when all our efforts to locate the immediate relative failed. Sometimes a married woman had come to join her husband or a young woman to marry her fiancé; and the man could not be located. Perhaps he had died, or moved, or the correspondence hadn't reached him — who knows? In any event, the results were tragic indeed, as I well know from personal experience. There was no way of soothing these heartbroken women, who had traveled thousands and thousands of miles, endured suffering and humiliation, and who had uprooted their lives only to find their hopes shattered at the end of the long voyage. These, I think, are the saddest of all immigration cases.

"Sometimes these women were placed in the care of a social agency which agreed to be responsible to the Commissioner, caring for them or placing them in some appropriate occupation. But if everything possible had been done, and the missing husband or fiancé still could not be traced, the poor alien, despite all her tears, had to be returned to her native country.

"Occasionally cases of this kind did not have the element of tragedy, but were queer and hard to handle. There was, for instance, the second-class passenger from Vera Cruz booked under the name of Alejandra Veles. Boyish in appearance, with black hair and an attractive face, she proved to be, upon examination, despite her earlier insistence to the contrary, a young woman. Vehemently she insisted that her identity had not been questioned before. When Dr. Senner asked her why she wore men's clothes, she answered that she would rather kill herself than wear women's clothes. Perhaps some psychoanalyst can explain it, but she said she had always wanted to be a man and it was no fault of hers that she had not been born one!

Finally she broke down and pleaded with us not to expose her. Then, being threatened with arrest for her defiance of rules, she sent for a very prominent lawyer of the city, who, it turned out, had received a fund for her support. He identified her immediately, and after having exacted a pledge that the girl's identity would not be revealed, he told her amazing story.

" 'Alejandra Veles' was the daughter of a cultured Englishman who had married a wealthy Spanish woman, and then had been sent to represent his government in the Orient. The girl had been born in the Far East and, when a little child, for some reason or other unhappy at being a girl, she had insisted on dressing as a boy. Although her parents did all they could to discipline her, she would tear her dresses to shreds. She defied all control and finally was allowed to grow up as a boy.

"At the age of fifteen she deserted her parents and started drifting. She came to this country and for two years worked as a hostler in a New York stable, after which she went to the West Indies and bossed men around, nobody ever suspecting she was a girl. Her father, frantic and at his wit's end, had provided this lawyer with a liberal sum for the girl's support. Was there anything else she wanted, she was asked. 'Yes—give me two plugs of tobacco and a pipe.'

"These were given to her, and she was allowed to leave the Barge Office on her promise to leave the country at once. This she did, sailing for England to visit her parents."

"Did she," I wondered aloud, "sail for England in a man's outfit, or dressed as a woman? But I suppose, having seen thousands of cases, she was just another case to you, and no doubt you are already thinking of someone else."

"Right you are," was his response. "I'm thinking of another strange human specimen we once had detained on the Island—José Maria, who baffled all our officials. Until then I had thought that among all of us interpreters we could find someone speaking the language of most every alien. But José Maria was more than our match. He understood none of the many languages we tried on him. Even the Chancellor of the Japanese Consulate who had a reputation for speaking and understanding almost every dialect of the Orient, and whom we called on for assistance, could make nothing out of José Maria, who looked like a mixture of Japanese, Chinese and Malay. All he ever said to anyone was, 'Me no sabe.'

"There was nothing about his person by which he could be identified. The newspapers got hold of the story and played up its human interest. They even went so far as to offer us suggestions. One paper guessed offhand that the man was Burmese, and he may have been for all we knew, but he was the only one who could tell, and he couldn't or wouldn't.

"In his satchel he had two envelopes, one addressed to 'José Antonio Chins, Rua de Mancel, Rio de Janeiro, Brazil,' and the other covered with Chinese characters which told a lot about a restaurant somewhere, but nothing about himself. He had $1.50 in German money, and he was heading for Brazil. We never found out anything definite and my memory is a little vague now as to what became of him, but I do remember that Dr. Senner decided that, in sailing from Bremen, José Maria had taken the wrong steamer, and had landed in New York, when in fact he had meant to take the boat for Rio de Janeiro." . . .

"Tell me," I said, "do you remember particularly any case of a man being deported to a country that refused to take him back? A man without a country is a tragic person."

"There were many such cases, but none more strange or more tragic than that of Nathan Cohen, who came to us again in 1916. He was insane, and try as we might we could not establish his nationality. As a result, he was shipped back and forth, again and again, between South America and the United States.

"Although we had but few facts to go by in this case, we did manage to find out that he had been born thirty-five years before in Baush, a little village in the province of Kurland in Russia. As a boy, he had left home and gone to Brazil. Three years previous he had landed in America, married, and gone into business in Baltimore with several thousand dollars. All seemed to be going well with him. Then his business failed, followed closely, as happens all too often in life, by other catastrophes. His wife ran away with another man, and Cohen lost his memory and his power of speech, and had to be taken to an insane asylum in Baltimore.

"Now he was a public charge within three years of the time he had first landed in the United States and, under the alien law, had to be sent back to the country from which he had come, by the line which had brought him originally. The Lamport Holt Line was therefore instructed to return him to Brazil.

"The Brazilian authorities, however, would not accept Cohen, and the Argentine, where he was next sent, also refused him entrance. Back he was sent to the United States, which promptly shipped him back to Brazil. Since the steamship company could produce no evidence of his Russian birth, he could not be returned to Russia. Such a situation might be funny in fiction, but in real life it was too tragic for humor.

"At last the Knights of Pythias found that he had joined their order in Jacksonville, Florida. With the help of former Justice Leon Sanders, the immigration authorities were induced to let Cohen land, on condition that he be deported to Russia after the war if he proved to be a Russian citizen.

"So Cohen finally was sent to the sanitarium at Green Farms, Connecticut, as a charge of the Hebrew Shelter and Immigrant Aid Society and the Knights of Pythias. It was there he died.

"Of course it wasn't all tragedy in those days. Now and then bits of humor and comedy drifted in at the Barge Office and on the Island. For instance, there was something about the Italians, especially the women, that would not let them leave their pillows behind. No matter what else they relinquished, they usually brought along bulky pillows and mattresses. And very often this was just about everything they did bring!

"But whether they were Italian or Russian, Swedish or Spanish, German or Greek, many of the immigrants came in their native peasant costumes—a strange and colorful procession of fashions in dress from all parts of the world. One would think we were holding a fancy dress party, judging by the variety and oddness of the styles. And the gypsies!—I mustn't forget the gypsies!

"The Cunard liner, *Carpathia,* brought them in September of 1904, two hundred and eighty of them, in all the picturesque gorgeousness of their various tribal costumes. But what wasn't so picturesque was the fact that forty-eight gypsy children had measles and had to be sent by the immigration doctors to the Kingston Avenue Hospital in Brooklyn.

"This taking of the children was what started things; and what fanned the fire was the fact that several members of distinctive families were taken from the detention room and placed before the Board of Special Inquiry.

"More and more gypsy forces arrived—gypsies from Long Island, New Jersey, and other adjacent points flocked into the Island to meet those detained. Then some gypsy spread the rumor that all the children taken by the doctors had been drowned, and you can imagine what happened!

"At eleven o'clock that night a doctor, who tried to feel a gypsy child's pulse, was attacked by the gypsies as a murderer. This started a riot which could not be checked or stilled, and which raged all night. Every time the gypsies saw anyone wearing an immigration uniform or cap they opened fire, using as weapons anything on which they could lay their hands.

"But at last a way of explaining things was worked out. The next gypsy child who developed measles was sent to the hospital like the others, but the parents were allowed to go along and see how the other gypsy children were being cared for. They brought the news back to the other gypsies, and this was successful in appeasing them. But as long as I live I shall never forget the picture of those gypsy women pulling off their heavy-soled slippers, and sailing into us inspectors and the doctors with fire in their eyes! . . .

"One of the most disgusted men we ever had on the Island was a young Hungarian who, in 1905, had, as he complained, to marry his own wife!

"They were two young Hungarians, and I remember them well, though it was back in 1905 that they got to Ellis Island. They had come from London separately, on tickets bearing different names, and at that time they had said they were cousins.

"Once they arrived at the Island, however, they explained that they were really man and wife, adding that they had bought return tickets for other people, and so had been forced to represent themselves as the people whose names were on the tickets.

"The immigration authorities brought the case to the attention of the superintendent of the Home for Jewish Immigrant Girls, requesting her to become responsible for the girl. She agreed and took the girl to the Home. Later the man appeared with several of his countrymen and demanded his wife. A conference followed, in which they were asked for evidence of their married status. Their explanations, given convincingly, were that they had been too poor to get a wedding ring and that the wedding certificate had been in a trunk which was lost.

"Finally the superintendent said: 'Well, if you're married already, it won't do you any harm to be married all over again. If you will marry here and now, you can go away as you like, but if not I will have to keep the girl, for in spite of what you say, you have no real proof that you are her husband.'

"The man looked dazed. 'What kind of country is this,' he asked hoarsely, 'that makes me remarry my own wife?'

"He agreed, however, to the proposition, and after a rabbi had been called in they were married again, to the bewilderment of the bridegroom and the amusement of his naturalized friends. The couple went away happy, however, with clear sailing ahead."

"It's good to hear that with all the squalor and bewildered crowds and misfortunes," I said, "a little occasional humor or romance lightened the day's work. Perhaps it would have been unbearable without that."

"Oh, we had plenty of that! It seems to me now as I look back that in those days there were crying and laughing and singing all the time at Ellis Island," he recalled. "Very often brides came over to marry here, and of course we had to act as witnesses. I have no count, but I'm sure I must have helped at hundreds and hundreds of weddings of all nationalities and all types. The weddings were numberless, until they dropped the policy of marrying them at the Island and brought them to City Hall in New York.

"Incidentally, as you may have heard, there is a post at Ellis Island which through long usage has come to earn the name of 'The Kissing Post.' It is probably the spot of greatest interest on the Island; and if the immigrants recall it afterward it is always, I am sure, with fondness. For myself, I found it a real joy to watch some of the tender scenes that took place there.

"There was a line of desks where the inspectors stood with their backs towards the windows and facing the wall. Further back, behind a partition, the witnesses waited outside for the detained aliens. As the aliens were brought out, the witnesses were brought in to be examined as to their rights of claim. If the inspector found no hitch, they were allowed to join each other. This, because of the arrangement of the partitions, usually took place at 'The Kissing Post,' where friends, sweethearts, husbands and wives, parents, and children would embrace and kiss and shed tears for pure joy.

"I have shown how the routine was held up and how complications arose when an alien was unable to give the information required of him. When an alien refused to give this information, the complications that resulted were still more serious. Take, for example, the case of Joaquin Nabuco, the Brazilian Ambassador at Washington, who arrived in November 1906 on the White Star Line steamer, *Baltic*, from Liverpool.

"Senhor Nabuco refused to answer the following questions which were put to him by immigration authorities purely as a matter of routine: 'By whom was your passage paid? Have you fifty dollars in your possession? Have you ever been in prison or in an almshouse or in an institution for the care and treatment of the insane or supported by charity? If so, which? Are you a polygamist? Have you come here under the promise, offer, or solicitation to labor in the United States?'

"Although it was explained to Senhor Nabuco that these were certain set questions, the answers to which were required by the immigration laws, he persisted in his refusal to answer, drawing himself up to his full height and saying:

" 'I have answered every question which I believed would add to the necessary statistical governmental information; but these other questions are different. I am not a visitor to this country in the implied sense of the word. I am here as the representative of another power, and as such I am to a certain extent the guest of this nation. This is the ground I take, and for this reason alone I refuse to answer certain questions. There is no friction over the affair, and I should like nothing said about it.'

"Lord Curzon, the English statesman, was also a passenger on the *Baltic* at that time, and he had answered the same questions, although this did not establish a precedent, for Lord Curzon was not an official representative of a foreign power.

"At any rate, the purser of the *Baltic* reported the matter and the desired information was asked of E. L. Chermont, secretary of the Brazilian Embassy, but Mr. Chermont could not provide it. Again the information was requested of Senhor Nabuco, and again he refused to supply it.

"It was then that Secretary of State Root, upon being unofficially notified of the situation, got in touch with the Department of Commerce and Labor and requested that the courtesies of the port be extended to Senhor Nabuco and his secretary.

"There was talk for some time of an apology being made, and for all I know it may have been; but under customs regulations, a country sending a diplomatic representative to this country is required to notify the Secretary of State in advance, and the State Department then informs the Secretary of the Treasury, who orders that the customs laws be suspended in the instance of the incoming individual. Brazil had not given such notice, and we, as a result, had received no word to suspend such questions in the case of the Ambassador."

*In the Shadow of Liberty: The Chronicle of Ellis Island* (New York: Macmillan Company, 1935), 130–36.

# 7

# Italian Americans and Italian Writers

And then I don't even want to speak to you about
Italian Americans, they're all raving mad.
—Giose Rimanelli, *Peccato originale* and *Biglietto di terza*

## VINDICATION OF IGNORANCE

Broadway, the writer Luigi Donato Ventura recalled at the end of the nineteenth century, also existed in Viggiano, in Lucania. And after more than half a century Carlo Levi confirmed it: Christ stopped at Eboli, but not the green dollar bill, the photographs of President Franklin D. Roosevelt, the dream and the memory of emigration for the "Americans" who returned. In terms of the texts, within this history, how much and what of Little Italy ended up in the pages of writers at home?

In fact, the lack of attention given to the experience of emigration and its developments in the emigrants' country of arrival by spokesmen for Italian culture has often been pointed out. Now, this apparent failure lends itself to diverse interpretations. The long-standing unease of the Italian intellectual toward another Italy plays a part: an Italy so subordinate as to be far away, unknown at home, and not easily defined using the tools of an abstract ideology, an Italy, therefore, that is not compatible with the ritual apologias and curses uttered in relation to the New World.

In her recent *Italy's Many Diasporas*, the historian Donna Gabaccia argues that the history of that cultural territory which we call Italy has been intrinsically shaped, molded and transformed by the myriad individual and collective emigrations from the peninsula beginning at least at the end of the eighteenth century. Although I am convinced by Gabaccia's argument, and by her rewriting of Italian history, I do think it is also a provocative claim, insofar as this knowledge is still shared only by a tiny minority of scholars. In fact, it is not even denied or contested, it is simply ignored, as has been the case all along. There are exceptions, of course, and one could pull together the threads of a "subterranean" scholarship aware of the phenomenon. Yet although this would benefit the scholars' self-esteem, it would not change the fact that a deliberate act of ignorance has become itself, over time, an element to be accounted for.[1]

Has Italian literature been an accomplice in this strategy of silence? Overall, it is easy to answer yes. And, given the role and influence that literature has always played in Italian culture, this is no small indictment. It is telling that even the presence of Italian Americans in the U.S. is largely tangential to a history of Italians' perception of America. In fact, it was precisely this discovery which sparked my interest, after years of research on the journals, books, and novels dedicated by Italian writers to the New World. Once again, one does find exceptions, but also daily confirmations: September 11 has produced a mass of written reactions and comments in Italy, only very few of which even mention the reality of an Italian America.[2]

Yes, *The Sopranos*, DeLillo's *Underworld*, and David Foster Wallace's *Infinite Jest* (which carefully avoids dwelling on the Italian American origins of the Incandenza brothers—an omission that I find acute and bewildering) have brought renewed attention, in Italy, too, to the immigrant experience. And so have diverse works such as Shell and Sollors's *Multilingual Anthology of American Literature*, the insightful comments of Alessandro Portelli, and the widely read, contested, and acclaimed libel by Oriana Fallaci. Reading these, one can catch more than a glimpse not only of the exodus of Italians across the Atlantic but also of their contribution to the history and literature of America and of Italy. However, what I have tried to present in the previous pages is different. It is not necessarily the history of those Italian heroes who, during the Risorgimento or threatened by Fascism, found hospitality under the beacon of American liberty. Rather, it documents quite another story, with many beginnings and not a few codas, a story that has not ended yet, and might even produce in the future some belated effects, reawakening the Italian collective conscience to a part of the past that has made Italy what it is. Note, though, that my critique should now be verified and maybe reassessed after the success of *Vita* (published by Rizzoli in 2003), a hefty historical novel on Italian immigration in the U.S. by Melania G. Mazzucco.

Then again, has Italian literature reacted to this forgotten, popular wealth of writings? Clearly not, because it did not know them, did not have any interest in them, and because, after all, *non c'è miglior sordo di chi non vuol sentire* [there's no better deaf mute than the one who doesn't want to hear]. Tolstoy famously asked a young Rachmaninoff if he thought that his music could be of any interest to Russian audiences—and history has given an answer. "Dagoes Read," argues

294     VOICES OF ITALIAN AMERICA

a leading specialist in the field, Fred Gardaphé. It is crucial at this point to know that they also wrote. We—Italians, Americans, Italian Americans, and a more general public—have the right to read what they produced. But let's turn back, for the time being, to a more thorough examination of what Italian writers have had to say on Italian Americans in the twentieth century.

If it is undeniable that in works written in Italy about the United States Italian Americans occupy for the most part a marginal, accessory position, and that very often only an impressionistic use is made of their habitats, the simplistic formula of silence and absence that our literature is guilty of is, at least in part, being reexamined: a number of contributions demonstrate that one can and must account for that relative reticence. In the notes that follow, however, the pairing literature and emigration is in a certain sense taken for granted, considered a necessary antecedent, since the prevailing interest is to verify the existence and meaning of a literature that confronts (at times even in spite of itself) the phenomenon, however varied, of the actual immigrant communities. Given that expressions like "Italian America" and "Italian Diaspora" designate a by now established cultural dimension, it is a matter of seeing if and in what terms the literature of the country of origin has been able to approach this particular world, beyond the individual traumas and dramas of the first generations.

I will not, therefore, dwell "on the Ocean" or in the lands of return, which means excluding some important works. First, there are the remarkable novels that center entirely on the problem of emigration, as a product of the historical, social, and anthropological conditions of the south: *Peccato originale* [Original Sin], by Giose Rimanelli (1954)—one of the books I am about to mention that I am particularly fond of—and *I quattro camminanti* [The Four Wayfarers], by Rodolfo Di Biasio (1991). Then there is a series of narratives, of varying value and importance, that have as their focus powerful figures of "Americans" struggling with their native Italy, or in search of an identity that is uncertain and difficult to decipher after the years spent in America: *Una posizione sociale* [A Social Position], also by Rimanelli (1959; republished under a new title, *La Stanza Grande*, [The Big Room], in 1996), *Ninna nanna del lupo* [Lullaby of the Wolf], by Silvana Grasso (1995), *Silvinia*, by Giuseppe Bonaviri (1997), and *Dall'altra parte degli occhi* [From the Other Side of the Eyes], by Dario Buzzolan (1999). Finally, there are autobiographical writings, works published either during an author's lifetime or posthumously, and those which are still deposited in public or private archives.[3]

## An Interpretative Perusal

An initial consideration, influenced perhaps in part by more recent works, has to do with the greater openness toward the Italian American experience demonstrated by narrative, despite the presence of an overwhelming number of travel books, journalistic investigations, and various types of essays, which at first glance would seem more suited to looking at particular communities, yet which instead often tend to avoid them, in pursuit of individual stories. In other words, to generalize, Italian Americans have been re-created in imaginative prose and as novelistic characters (with intensity and sincere faithfulness) rather than described and analyzed by qualified observers. We touch here superficially on a sore point in the relations between Italian culture and that of the United States: those who venture to read the writings of journalists and intellectuals on the States will quickly realize, to speak with the Lévi-Strauss of *Tristes Tropiques,* that many of our "emissaries" were unready for or uninterested in perceiving the wealth and meaning of American diversity. For this reason, it's not surprising that a lack of preparation, in addition to the unease mentioned earlier, would suggest that one refrain from touching such a delicate place in the relations between the two countries. And at times one has the impression that this attitude is still valid.

But to go into detail, with an attempt to balance the requirements of a picture that is historically organized and at the same time follows, at least broadly, type, I would distinguish—from Fascism to the present—three principal areas of investigation. The first corresponds to *tradition* and, as such, can in a sense be seen as a foundation with respect to the others, continuing to show its vitality today; the second corresponds to a particular stage of *crisis* and some cases of real *silence,* largely coincident with the first three decades of the Republic, from reconstruction to the economic boom and the birth and spread of mass culture; the third is that of the *present,* with all the cautions that contemporaneity imposes, since, beyond the texts and viewpoints contingent on current reality, I think there has been a turning point, an expansion, in the perception of Italian American identity.

## Tradition

It is not difficult to identify a topos for the encounter between Italian writers and Italian Americans, an approach that appears detached but is ready to unfold in directions anything but neutral. It's a matter, so to speak, of the zero degree of relationship between the intellectual away from home and his distant Italian American cousin, and the achieving of this relationship by means of the *visit* or some form of *hospitality*. In Mario Soldati's famous *America primo amore* [America, First Love], of 1935, the rapidity of contact allows with an embarrassing clarity the expression of the most bitingly candid preconceptions. The acute observer, who notes, for example, the complex relationship that unites and divides under the same roof the immigrant parents from the second-generation Italian American children, or the bond of the immigrants with the now vanished Umbertine Italietta, becomes one with the paternalistic commentator and the severe, indeed pitiless, critic, in the name of a banal appeal to the primacy of the old country. Recalling a Sunday spent in the Bronx at the home of the Costantino family, Soldati incorporates, in passing and almost politely, some terrible comments:

> Furthermore, their welcome was as human and affectionate as it could be, poor things. And unfortunately it's not cordiality that Italian Americans lack. An arm around your neck, a slap on the back, and calling you by your first name almost as soon as you're introduced.[4]

Most of the time, naturally, the visit to this strange type of compatriot, precisely because of the train of negative reflections that accompanies it, is a single, unrepeatable and unrepeated experience; in addition, it suggests a conclusion about the immigrants' "betrayal" of the mother country by setting up comparisons, with a clear anti-modernist bias, between the soundness of domestic customs and what Michela Nacci has justly defined as the "barbarity of comfort":

> Come back next Sunday! And in spite of letters, notes, phone calls, and even some visits they made to me without finding me in, I never went back. In compensation I knew other Italian Americans, many others, and I knew and visited them. More or less wealthy, more or less educated, the scene was always the same: with a few sympathetic and bizarre exceptions.
> And of course, sadness, spiritual blindness are characteristics they have in common with all the immigrant peoples in the States. But it is much more agonizing in them, who descend from one of the oldest civilizations and from a sense of dignity that even in the most miserable eras and the most wretched regions has never failed our people.
> The poorest peasant in the poorest town in central and southern Italy preserves always, both in hardships and in disasters, a gravity, a humanity of behavior. But they, in their affluence, with the Ford, with the Sunday paper, and the electric icebox, have lost everything: equalizing, dark, obtuse, the immigrants of whatever nation.[5]

A similar pattern, although distinguished by a fellow countryman's greater superficial sympathy, can be seen in an encounter with a couple of old upstate New York Waldensians, or with a so-called Duke of Solimena, in a modest trattoria in Chicago. The Italian American met in his family environment is rebuked both for an anachronistic attachment to the traditions of a postcard Italy and for the too casual adoption of the exterior signs of the American lifestyle; what follows in both cases is a sort of sin of lèse-nationality. Half a century later, in *Addio diletta Amelia* [Farewell, Beloved Amelia], of 1979, Soldati is pacified and on the whole more benevolent. But the modalities of the encounters with Italian Americans on both coasts, which here, too, are frequent, are not that different. Visits are sometimes affectionate, but they are always quick and in essence politely touristic; and there is still the tendency to offer bold interpretations, trusting in a sort of divining virtue:

> One would say that [the Italian Americans] are trying, thus, and certainly without realizing it, to forget something, to deafen themselves by stifling the echo of an intimate and unconscious remorse that continuously bothers them. One could say that there remained in them the visceral doubt, unconfessed, unconfessable, as to whether they had indeed made the better choice.[6]

In the same period of *America primo amore*, a more tolerant and well-documented essayist, Giuseppe Antonio Borgese, has the same view, practically anywhere in his interesting *Atlante americano* [American Atlas] of 1936. The tone is less aggressive and more relaxed, but the basic concept recalls Soldati. Here is the beginning of a visit to Italians stationed in California: "The house is like all the others: a cabin of clean and whitewashed wood, full of mechanical comforts. The habitations of men are barely dug into this soil, they have no roots."[7] A little later, another young writer on a journey, Quarantotti Gambini, makes use of Italian American companions. The central themes of his diary, which was revised, and so, in a sense, still approved, decades later but published only recently, reveal, perhaps in the extemporaneousness of the notes, a shrewder and more realistic view, not only of the Chicago underworld and the asphyxiating parochialism of the immigrant press but also of the reasons for nationalism shading into Fascism, the uncertainties of the Italian Americans in the face of the anti-Semitism of the Wasp majority, and the different stages of assimilation, as embodied in three distinct characters, who are presented in physiognomic closeups. And yet the strongest image is of the immigrant community as a "herd," a formless group of uncivilized people:

This instinct to stay crowded together, close and confused at the same time, which unites men with certain animals and is a survival of the lowest human condition, does not abandon the immigrants when they disembark or afterward. . . .

Leaving the immigrants to themselves was one of Italy's great mistakes. To be convinced of this it is enough to know some of them. It is they themselves (notwithstanding their attachment to their native land) who have spread across the Atlantic the idea of an Italy that cannot align itself with civilized peoples. . . . They, who were the most disinherited sons of the peninsula, ended up believing (and those who listen to them believe it along with them) that all Italy is like the village they left, and that all America, on the other hand, is like New York. It was in good faith, since they continued to love the Italy of their poor memories, and often returned there; but many of them didn't know, and probably don't know today, that in Italian cities there is running water, that we, too, have bathrooms and gas and electric light (what worse propaganda across the Atlantic?); and they admired the Statue of Liberty ignorant of Michelangelo.[8]

Evident are the pride of comfort, so to speak, together with symptoms of a superiority complex; a short circuit between modernism and the eternal primacy of the two-thousand-year-old civilization; and, barely concealed, a strong distinction between North and South (between the lines devoted to the "herd" and the "tribes" of the immigrants the memory of "an Italian village, I don't remember if in Calabria or Sicily" stands out). And, beyond the conceptual outline, the method and the assertive tone of the discourse should be noted.

The approach that I propose to call traditional thus assumes the conceptual but also narrative centrality of a writer-visitor who expresses with absolute clarity his point of view, highlighting the difference and the distance between the two worlds: that of the immigrant, filled with work and domesticity, and that of the intellectual, who in a sense provides homeopathic doses of America to his public at home. A grid of reading of this type can help us understand, for example, the lucid observations as well as the ambiguities of the most important study of those years, the direct source of the horrific fresco presented in Emilio Cecchi's *America amara* [Bitter America], of 1939: *Italiani in America,* by Amerigo Ruggiero (1937). It is a model that lends itself to revival, and is not necessarily confined to the thirties or to the multiple metamorphoses of anti-Americanism. With streaks of nostalgia and profound empathy we find it in action again in a tender aside in the sentimental journey of Mario Maffi through the Lower East Side. Here we relive, among many other things, a chance visit to a group of Italian Americans, which takes on the flavor of the final salute to the common heroes of a great history: on the one hand the peripatetic writer-essayist, on the other a "little half-deserted butcher shop on 'Elisabetta Stretta,' in mid-afternoon," with Moe and Mary Albanese and their friend Sal, recalling the Little Italy of a bygone time.[9] Or, again, think of *I segreti di New York* [The Secrets of New York], the best-seller by Corrado Augias, which dwells on some "classic" figures of Italian immigration—old and contemporary, famous and less well known.

Another frequent approach is the *cronaca,* or feature article, a short piece that combines journalism and narrative: the special province of those who know America with a particular continuity and closeness, and who as a result can tell the ordinary stories of daily life. In this case, too, both the quality of the observation and the individual evaluations can be spectacularly diverse, and the constraints imposed by the fixed time and space of publication ends, often, by leading the writers on flight paths that are completely divergent and yet homologous. I think of the curious mixture of novelty and cliché, of genuine curiosity about lesser known aspects of the lives of Italian Americans paired with almost official portraits of Mafia criminality or local associations. The names I have in mind above all are those of our two most influential and constant mediators of things American: Giuseppe Prezzolini, the anti-democratic muckraker, who for more than thirty years has continued undaunted to whisper his great refusal, and Furio Colombo, the exact opposite, democratic, earnest, a friend of America and Americans, conscious of the complexity of their world, including both misery and splendor. Of the first I would mention the ample, well-crafted fourth chapter—*Gl'italoamericani: Leggenda e realtà*—contained in his first important collection, *America in pantofole* [America at Home] (1950); and, for an enjoyable and paradoxical acceptance of clichés, the biographies of gangsters, in particular *Vita di Luciano il fortunato e storia della sua partecipazione alla "liberazione d'Italia"* [The Life of Lucky Luciano and the Story of His Contribution to the Liberation of Italy].[10] But the mixture of hostility and proximity in Prezzolini's articles shines forth especially in the ponderous, wide-ranging *I trapiantati* (1963), a volume for the broader public and at the same time an irreplaceable source of information on the culture of Little Italy and testament to the profound gap between the Italian intellectuals (who are, by implication, "true Italians") and the immigrant communities.[11]

In Colombo, the shrewd analyst coexists with the editorialist and observer who over the years maintains the special correspondent's taste for discovery, and almost anywhere in an article or, later, a book, I would say, a critical observation appears beside a description or a portrait. The Italian intellectual at home in the United States is led to declare that the two societies, [the] two historical traditions, [the] two countries . . . have nothing in common. . . . Thus originates that sort of painful and endless lack of comprehension that leads, in a continuous spiral, to love too much or hate too much this nightmare country, this dream country, America the powerful and America the utopia, whose symbols are by now planted at the center of contemporary culture and imagination.

But the Italian Americans of Greenwich Village are quick to make a flesh-and-blood appearance:

Under their evening clothes it is difficult to distinguish who has succeeded through a fury of hard work, who has accumulated and taken advantage of the work and fear of others. The same gray faces, dark under white hair, the same suspicious eyes, identical, masterful and good-natured gestures of hands adorned with rings.[12]

There is another approach to the American experience, and it is that of those who go home, recover, and recount that experience to the Italian public. From the thirties until today we have had a series of *testimonials from within*, perhaps not as many as one might expect, but almost all, in different ways, of great interest, because of the profound engagement of the writer who speaks not as an isolated intellectual, thinker, or traveler but as one who has shared with others the vicissitudes of life in a place never entirely familiar. Among these are the works, lying halfway between memoir and autobiographical fiction, of Fausto Maria Martini, Luigi Barzini Jr., Marcella Olschki, Paolo Milano, Giose Rimanelli, and Aldo Rosselli. What distinguishes and characterizes them, with respect to the other approaches, is the broad choice of subjects treated, a greater capacity to read the differences and peculiarities of the various American and Italian American milieus, an emphasis on the meaning of work as a means of survival and social ascent, and, as a result, a more complex and reliable picture of relations with the rest of American society. The problem of assimilation, of loss of identity—feared by some, hoped for by others—seeps out, not unintentionally, and sometimes becomes a theme. The American dream and the American nightmare emerge in strong relief. Sometimes such testimonials do not contain images or scenes of the Little Italies, for the simple reason that everything is said and filtered through the voice of an immigrant—however privileged. The intensely individual point of view brings to life stories and characters that are anomalous and at times marginal but, for this very reason, more convincing.

Let's go south of Houston Street, in Manhattan, to Martini's bitter comments, as he speaks for a small group of Roman boys:

Hunger . . . what is it but the specter of hunger that nails us all three before this sign hanging in front of the door of a barber shop at the corner of Mulberry Street with a section of the great road? On the card is written: Shoeshines wanted, and the formula "wanted"—common to all signs in shops and offices where work is offered and of which we all three immediately grasped the significance—attracted us, none of us rebelled at the thought of the kind of work that here was offered to us.[13]

An encounter with the boisterous audience in an immigrant theater in Brooklyn, almost at the start of a memoir by the war bride Marcella Olschki, a novice writer and journalist, makes a strong impact because of its spontaneous freshness. Probably by virtue of her uncertain, destitute personal situation, she observes with amusement the gap that separates her from the crowd without, however, slipping into a supercilious condescension. As for the theme of consciousness of one's own identity, entrusted to a first-person narrator who reflects on his childhood years, between school and family (and what a family!), we have the lucid reflections of Aldo Rosselli:

All in all, however, instead of hating my companions I envied them, wishing in my more or less prohibited dreams to become like them, in fact to be embodied in one of my little enemies, until my hateful identity, permeated by the mysterious will to be the victim, was destroyed.

And my rough American, coin of exchange with my schoolmates, helped me turn my back on that world of old people where everyone was murmuring in a tired, obscure Italian and choose the present, the brightly illuminated stage where every gesture had a precise meaning and everyone was allowed to have a role.[14]

An exhaustive if eccentric example of a travelogue is *Biglietto di terza* [Third-Class Ticket], in which Rimanelli physically and symbolically traverses many of the scenes of immigration and the literature devoted to it, from the family dinner to the hunt for a "giobba," from observation of the intellectual and creative aspects (journalism, Italian American speech, jazz orchestra) to anthropologically stimulating encounters with the opposite sex, from a coast-to-coast journey to an autumn farewell that today, keeping in mind the author's own story, we can almost interpret as yet another literary convention, with a decisive difference: that the house, the work, the car, and many of the people he meets belong to *his* family, which embodies, in its generational divisions, the courses and recourses of a secular story of exile, from pre-union Molise to New Orleans before the Civil War, and bilingual Canada after the Second World War, in a protracted dream of "doing America."

Rich in allusions—first of all, again, to the tortured relationship with the Italian language and, more broadly, to the literary tradition expressed by it—is *Lettere a Manhattan* [Letters to Manhattan], by Manlio Cancogni, a novel that, appearing in the wake of these testimonials, demonstrates, as perhaps only Paolo Milano before him did, a notable achievement in the portrayal of the characters and their relationship with the authorial voice, in this case a narrator in the Mulberry Street community whom at times we are tempted to call the voice of the chorus, the old sages of the neighborhood. What's central is the account, both nostalgic and ironic, of a botched attempt to resurrect the Italian American theatrical scene—an apt metaphor for the intricate and at times ambiguous nature of any "ethnic revival."

A flight from Lucania in the late seventies to the thousand lights of New York, from the family offices on Wall Street to the mansions of the Mafiosi in Brooklyn, is the easy climax of the picaresque *Parenti lontani* [Distant Relatives], an expansive, dramatic novel by Gaetano Cappelli, who, sticking to the narrator's point of view, unfortunately fails to truly develop the portrait of the immigrant scenes, although they are largely present on the page. As one can see, the area that I have called "tradition" lends itself to continuous expansion and enrichment.

## CRISIS AND SILENCE

In the period stretching from the end of the Second World War to the middle of the seventies, it is possible to distinguish an extensive area, if not of shadow, of uncertainty and dissatisfaction regarding the more well-established modes of the relationship between Italy and the United States. It is not accidental that during these years the interchange between the two countries and their interdependence undergoes a dramatic acceleration at every level. In this respect, one can speak of a decline in the myth and its replacement by an American model, a much more concrete, exportable, and reusable term of reference.[15] From the prosperity of Eisenhower America through the counterculture and the civil rights battles of the sixties, touching on the crisis of the seventies and predicting the domination, from one side of the Atlantic to the other, of a postmodern and postindustrial culture of images, Italian intellectuals attracted by the United States offered broad analyses of the American world. And I am speaking of some of the most completely representative authors of the post–Second World War period: Piovene, Calvino, Arbasino, Parise, Eco. A detail relevant to the end of this discussion informs their work—that is to say, the nearly total absence from it of Italian Americans. The fact is that the United States was more than ever seen as the land of modernity, of the future, from technology to the economy, from architecture to artistic production and civil engagement: an example for the wavering, newborn Italian democracy. In this context Italian Americans were perceived as a trace of the United States' past, not of its expansive present—not, certainly, as an anachronistic and damaging presence, as a Prezzolini would have it—but in any case as a factor irrelevant to the purposes of the critical and cultural militancy of intellectuals at the peak of their most aggressive, experimental years.

A narrative, novelistic use of the Italian American experience works as an antithesis to this silence. The stories of Mario Rigoni Stern and the novels of Gianluigi Melega, Angela Bianchini, Guido Morselli, and Ennio Flaiano (here, too, the names stand out) dramatize, almost always in the first person, an experience of immigration, with variants that deserve brief consideration. Only two feature "classic" Italian American figures: Rigoni Stern's miner and tireless construction worker, with his fame as a pioneer of the Midwest, and Walter Ferranini, Morselli's hero, a worker in Chicago in the late thirties, a prominent opponent of the American system and yet the husband of one of its model daughters. The others are an enthusiastic and euphoric Milanese student (Melega), a young wife who is a victim of suburban comfort (Bianchini), and an intellectual in a creative and erotic crisis (Flaiano). One way or another, these characters encounter defeat, sometimes confirmed by a tragic journey and homecoming, or, owing to the shock produced by the American experience, they endure a prolonged period of instability (one might mention here the attraction of an archetypal figure such as that of Anguilla in Pavese's *Luna e i falò* [The Moon and the Bonfires]). In any case, the cliché of the United States as the land of opportunity, as an enormous and alien space to be confronted in groups, in neighborhoods subdivided according to the regions of origin, is broken. The United States is on the way to becoming, for our literature, a setting for coming-of-age stories. In this phase the social and historical dimension of immigration moves to the background, while the main task becomes that of defining an individual story. It seems to me equally symptomatic that most of these books have had an extremely difficult publishing history, as if the Italian public were still unprepared to penetrate the veins of America.

## A LOOK AT THE PRESENT

Under this completely provisional heading I would place a group of texts (novels, memoirs, stories, essays) that reflect vividly and often with remarkable intelligence phenomena representing not so much the daily condition of the "old" Italian Americans—whose traces are found in the discussion I have called traditional—as new faces, I would say almost the new clothing and new habits of first-generation Italian Americans who come to the United States pushed not by hunger but by a more or less clear desire to give a decisive turn to their own destinies. It should be noted parenthetically that in the last twenty years the field of studies—both historical and ethnological— devoted to the classic decades of immigration and its protagonists has seen formidable growth, in a certain sense freeing the writers from the weight of the past. And while in the area of American studies in Italy there has been some expansion of a fascinating middle ground, highly creative and essayistic (not to repeat names already mentioned, I would here add those of the timeless Fernanda Pivano, of Guido Fink, and of Marco d'Eramo), in the case of concentration on Italian Americans the divide between the scientific sphere and the personal creation appears clearer. Even the autobiographical pages of a master like the sociologist Franco Ferrarotti immediately and directly proclaim an acute partiality, which is useful in explaining, from the inside, the increasingly widespread phenomenon of academic and intellectual immigration.

The family disappears almost completely, along with the scenario of the Little Italies, the cliché of goodfellas and godfathers (now a formulaic genre with a refined style on the big screen);[16] the narrators and characters of Andrea De Carlo, Pia Fontana, Luigi Settembrini, Sergio Campailla, Rossana Campo, Gina Lagorio, Lidia Ravera, Gianni Celati, and Daniele Brolli are precarious and restless monads, who are "different," and who live not without a narcissistic self-satisfaction in having succeeded in breaking the thousand ties with the old world.[17] A distracted reader might take them for travelers or tourists. To be sure, we find them, too, usually as mediators, vis-à-vis other Italians, who, in new ways and at the limits of good sense, "have done it": exponents of a sometimes ambiguous, socially anarchistic nomadism, which, originating in the ashes of the crisis and restlessness produced by prosperity and the counterculture, comes to occupy, within the anthropological supermarket of the United States, particular, recognizable niches.

Paolo Valesio has spoken with full knowledge of the facts of a "passage . . . from the rhetoric of immigration, of abandonment . . .

to the rhetoric of mediation, that is to the discovery that one can live on two continents."[18] There are characters whom one would be tempted to call post-youth: perennial students without degrees who survive on the art of getting along; young academics in enforced self-exile, at once fragile and determined, isolated and proudly "situated"; true or false nouveaux riches caught in the whirlpool of Manhattan, in sex, drugs, and hanging out with celebrities; gays who wander from one occupation to another and one partner to another; and globetrotters in search of interstices in which to settle, who voyeuristically resist as long as possible. The female point of view has greater autonomy and is more recognizable; and there is a decisively larger geographic range, which means that the canonical places of the New York area can be impulsively bypassed. It seems to me further symptomatic that traces of this isolated, intensely individualistic condition of the new Italian American appear even in a popular Anglo-American writer like Oliver Sacks.[19]

The profile of our relationship with American culture, itself in continuous movement, has been undoubtedly revived by it, even beyond individual results (it is indisputable that while the titles of De Carlo and Celati have rightfully entered the ranks of contemporary Italian writers who count, the others appear much more perishable). The choice of generational stories can involve the adoption of a deliberately stripped down language that goes along with an indifference to plot and the consequent incapacity to enter convincingly into the motivations of the new Italian Americans. The thin, unstructured narrative corresponds to the precariousness of the alternative lifestyles that are described. The uncertainties, which are at times real limits, originate in a liberal and full adhesion to the present. Meanwhile, however, the atmosphere has changed: our writers, including, significantly, some who are highly visible on the public scene, have noticed and have undertaken to recount the lives of the new Italians across the ocean, displaying an unmistakable sensibility that at its finest finds original words and images to express the fascination and the anguish of the New World. Here is the final passage of *Treno di panna* [The Cream Train]:

> I looked down, and suddenly there was the city, like an immense black lake full of luminous plankton, extending to the ends of the horizon. I looked at the points of light that vibrated in the distance: those that formed a subtle framework of landscape, fragile, trembling; those in movement along waving courses, along semicircular trajectories, along intersecting lines. There were points that left ropy traces, slime of liquid light; points that gathered in intense concentrations, until they drew the outlines of a fragment of the city and then broke up again, to separate

and move apart and disappear further and further into the darkness. I watched them furrow the completely black spaces that, motionless, filled the void, waiting to absorb some reflection in the humid night.[20]

Liquid lights, big city, one is tempted to say, paraphrasing a title that captured the Zeitgeist of the eighties. De Carlo, an acute and prolific author, consistently elaborated on similar themes and images in the following twenty years or more. The most perceptive among contemporary Italian writers have been well aware of the existence of these new, sometimes temporary Italian Americans, or Italo-Italians, as others call them. But then again Italy, *il bel Paese,* is a country where, in many ways, nothing ever, or hardly ever, changes. It tends to be stubbornly faithful and still in its attitudes, including its imagery and its ideological positions vis-à-vis America. Some—among them American visitors—find this comforting and at the same time an endless source of fascination. Italian Americans would probably have a different view. The trite Italian dichotomy between public anti-Americanism and private or aesthetic American dream, although understandable, has little to do with a century-long history of emigration, which is far more real than all the images that have originated within the sobering realms of the Italian intelligentsia. America as the ultimate threat: just what was perceived by a young man named Camillo Cavour when, after a bitter argument with his father, the marquis, he shrank at the idea of having to start a new life, perhaps in the wild continent across the Ocean. Or the New World as the fairy-land where Pinocchio might look for his lost dad. One might wonder what would have happened if Cavour had made America, not Italy, and Pinocchio had arrived at Castle Garden, instead of being captured after the fact by Disney, Wayne Shorter, Benigni, and so many others. But these are, precisely, pure fantasies: two examples of America untouched by experience, taken from the bottomless well of the Italian collective imagination. Things seem different when seen with our own eyes. Sergei Dovlatov, one of the greatest immigrant writers, observed, shortly after his arrival in the U.S., "Happiness is not of this world. Nor is peace." What I think still remains to be better examined and appreciated is the *vera storia* of a people, fragmented and diverse like all peoples, who left their land because of deprivation, and made a new one, with their own baggage. When the *paesani* first opened their mouths to tell their stories and invent new ones, they wrote and published, more or less, what you can read in the pages of this book.

# Notes

## INTRODUCTION

1. Francesco Durante, *Italoamericana. Storia e letteratura degli italiani negli Stati Uniti, 1776–1880* (Milan: Mondadori, 2001).

2. Rather than repeat yet another list of classic texts on the subject, I want to stress the importance of the work of these two young scholars, who have really opened new ground in their respective fields: Stefano Luconi, *From Paesani to White Ethnics: The Italian Experience in Philadelphia* (Albany: State University of New York Press, 2001); and Simone Cinotto, *Una famiglia che mangia insieme: Cibo ed etnicità nella comunità italoamericana di New York, 1920–1940* (Turin: Otto, 2001).

3. I am here thinking in particular of the contributions of Emilio Franzina and Sebastiano Martelli. And, as the book is going into print, I can only point out here an essay by Luigi Fontanella, *La parola transfuga. Scrittori italiani in America* (Fiesole: Cadmo, 2003).

4. Franco Ramella, "Reti sociali e mercato del lavoro in un caso di emigrazione. Gli operai italiani e gli altri a Paterson, New Jersey," in *Tra fabbrica e società. Mondi operai nell'Italia del Novecento,* ed. Stefano Musso (Milan: Fondazione Giangiacomo Feltrinelli, Annali, Year 33 [1997], 1999).

5. Ercole Sori, *L'emigrazione italiana dall'Unità alla seconda guerra mondiale* (Bologna: il Mulino, 1979).

6. Dana Gioia, "What Is Italian American Poetry?" in *Beyond "The Godfather": Italian American Writers on the Real Italian American Experience,* ed. A. Kenneth Ciongoli and Jay Parini (Hanover, N.H.: University Press of New England, 1997).

## CHAPTER 1. THE NOVEL OF THE ITALIAN IN AMERICA

1. Emilio Cecchi, "Pane al pane e vino al vino," *Corriere della Sera,* 30 March 1941; later in *Scrittori inglesi e americani,* vol. 2 (Milan: il Saggiatore, 1968), 330.

2. Besides the debut of the prose writers in those years that of the poet John Ciardi should at least be mentioned.

3. Important direct testimony on the wide success of *Reali di Francia,* of *Guerin Meschino,* of the novels of Sue, Ponson du Terrail, Montépin, Mastriani, Invernizio and company can be obtained in the articles by Amy Bernardy, in the catalogues for the use of Italian immigrants prepared in the 1910s by John Foster Carr and in the following decade by the librarian May Sweet, in extemporaneous notes of observers both internal (Zappulla) and external (Seabrook, in the context of the more engaging reportage on Little Italy), and in the regular and numerous advertisements of the omnipresent "book catalogues" promoted by the individual papers.

4. De Biasi and his review were recently studied by Cannistraro in the broader context of the Italo-American "black shirts."

5. The French original of the story, with the English in facing text, came out recently, with an important editor's note by Alide Cagidemetrio: Luigi Donato Ventura, *Peppino*, in *The Multilingual Anthology of American Literature: A Reader of Original Texts with English Translations*, ed. Marc Shell and Werner Sollors (New York: New York University Press, 2000).

6. Luigi Donato Ventura [with S. Shevitch], *Misfits and Remnants* (Boston: Ticknor and Company, 1886), 5.

7. This is further discussed in chapter 5, "Kneeling at the feet of a Negro."

8. "(La) Morte Improvvisa del Collega Cav. B. Ciambelli," *Il Progresso Italo-Americano*, 3 July 1931.

9. Contemporaneous with the New York novels there is, for example, one by Luigi Gualtieri, *I misteri di Buenos Aires*, published, significantly, by A. Bietti in both Milan and Buenos Aires.

10. Born in Turin (or, according to some sources, Milan), he moved to the United States in 1908–9, where, in New York, he worked for various publications, from *Il Progresso* to *Corriere d'America*, and including *Il Giornale Italiano*. In the early twenties, the publisher Ettore Patrizi called him to San Francisco to be the editor of *L'Italia*. In addition to novels, he wrote works for the theater and radio plays.

11. Paolo Pallavicini, *L'amante delle tre croci, seguito a Per le vie del mondo* (San Francisco: L'Italia Press Company, 1923), 200.

12. Two of the most important Italian American writers ended up living permanently in Scranton: the poet Efrem Bartoletti and the journalist Ludovico M. Caminita.

13. This is a different case from that of the more or less direct oral autobiographies recovered, and published, in recent years as a result of archival research and literary and social fieldwork; see the poignant example of a masterpiece like Marie Hall Ets, ed., *Rosa: The Life of an Italian Immigrant* (Minneapolis: University of Minnesota Press, 1970; reprint, Madison: University of Wisconsin Press, 1999).

14. On Cianfarra, see also chapter 5, "Labor Conditions and Plans in the Southern States."

15. For much of the biographical information on Caminita I gratefully acknowledge the help of my friend and colleague Salvatore Salerno. Later contact between Caminita and the American journalist Westbrook Pegler is revealing. See Caminita's last book, *Obici. Biografia* (New York: Tipografia Editrice Scarlino, 1943), and a few documents recently brought to my attention by Stefano Luconi, *La "diplomazia parallela." Il regime fascista e la mobilitazione politica degli italo-americani* (Milan: Franco Angeli, 2000), 68 and note.

16. Camillo Cianfarra, *Il diario di un emigrato* (New York: Tipografia dell'Araldo Italiano, 1904), 32.

17. Cianfarra, *Diario*, 99–100.

18. The most notable work of Alberico Molinari (1876–1948; in the United States from 1903 to 1921), the "doctor for the poor" (Vecoli), is the writing he did as the only contributor to a local paper, *L'Ascesa del Proletariato*, in Wilkes-Barre, Pennsylvania (1908–10), a biweekly that had limited objectives but which emerges, at a distance of decades, as one of the most lucid, mature, and, I would say, even intellectually elegant immigrant papers. Luigi Galleani (1861–1931; in the United States from 1901 to 1919), the *máximo* leader of anti-organizational anarchism, was able to gather around himself a group of faithful (and often monotonous) followers. Historiography has been generous with studies on him. Here it will suffice to mention the

elevated, archaizing flow that he regularly poured forth in the columns of his *Cronaca Sovversiva*, 1903–19: his disciples later collected his writings—he was expelled from the United States and in forced residence in Italy—in a series of volumes. In addition, obvious traces were left in the United States by the political fugitives Armando Borghi and Virgilia D'Andrea, the first a fiery rhetorician and anti-Mussolini pamphleteer, the second a grandiloquent, imagistic poet (*Torce nella Notte* [Torches in the Night] [New York: n.p., 1933]). A copious literature has flourished around Carlo Tresca (1879–1943; in the United States from 1904), especially because of the mystery surrounding his murder, which has fostered journalistic reconstructions and free, romantic interpretations; for a specimen in Italian of his hot-tempered and inventive eloquence one should read the editorials of *Il Martello* (1916–46)—the feared column *Martellate*—but also the anti-Fascist dramas imprinted with a sort of modernized and up-to-date Alfierism: *L'Attentato a Mussolini* [The Attempt on Mussolini], probably in more versions dating from the early twenties, is set at the Viminale and includes among its characters, besides Il Duce, Farinacci and the ex-socialist immigrant Rossoni; later and more demanding is *Il vendicatore* [The Avenger]. In general, the theater was cultivated with singular conviction by the anarchist writers (Borghi and others, less well known, such as Vincenzo Mortara, Virginio Della Vesa, Gigi Damiani, Paolina Breccia), who from time to time published, in short formats, humorous satires, tragedies, social-revolutionary dramas. Finally, Giuseppe Ciancabilla, another important name in libertarian radicalism, wrote short narrative in the early years of the century.

19. Journalist for the *Araldo Italiano*, political commentator in the twenties for Tresca's *Martello*, editor during the same period of the New York monthly *Zarathustra*, friend of the socialist Vacirca.

20. Later on, the name of the accused will appear often in the immigrant press; and in 1943 Ezio Taddei dedicated *Alberi e casolari* [Trees and Barns] to him.

21. In the late twenties, Vacirca already had to his credit—among various publications—several novels (the first significant for a certain extremely sweetened realism: *L'Apostata* [The Apostate], 1906) and works for the theater. In the United States he later wrote a romanticized biography of Mussolini (*Mussolini: Storia di un Cadavere* [New York: La Strada Publishing Co., 1942]; translated into English by Arturo Giovannitti, *Mussolini: History of a Corpse*, rejected by many publishers, finally published privately), which was recently discussed by Sergio Luzzatto (*Il Corpo del Duce. Un cadavere tra immaginazione, storia, e memoria* [Turin: Einaudi, 1998], 33–34). He was a central figure in Italian American journalism in those years, on the left but also moving between the milieu of the classic immigrants and that of those exiled by the regime (*La Notizia*, of Boston; *Il Nuovo Mondo*, an important voice of anti-Fascism; *La Stampa Libera;* and many others).

22. In Philadelphia, the Balch Institute for Ethnic Studies still retains some examples of his activity as a pedagogue. I note, for instance, the correspondence with the important school principal and intellectual Leonard Covello, and an unpublished typescript dated 1941: "Bridging the Gap between the Foreign Home and the School."

23. It was Giuseppe Prezzolini, in the pioneering if arguable *I trapiantati* [The Transplanted], who drew attention to this text (which had been mentioned years earlier in the biobibliographic volume of his student Olga Peragallo). The volume bears a significant dedication, to Migliaccio.

24. I confine myself to mentioning a couple of Migliaccio's eloquent titles, starting with the headline: *Bacilogia* [Kissology] and *Don Leopoldo. Annunciatore radiofonico, Chiaroveggente, Grafologo, Astrologo e altre sciocchezze* [Radio Announcer, Clair-

voyant, Graphologist, Astrologer and Other Nonsense], both of which appeared in *La Follia*.

25. I owe the information about the two films to the kindness of Giorgio Bertellini, who mentions them in a still unpublished work: Giorgio Bertellini, " 'Paradise Inhabited by Devils': Southern Italians, Modernity, and Cinema, from Italy to New York, up to 1920" (Ph.D. diss., New York University, 2001). For the magazine, see Carlotta Sgubbi, *Le figure del delitto. Il libro poliziesco in Italia dalle origini a oggi*, ed. Renzo Cremante (Bologna: Grafis, 1989), 127; and Giuliana Bruno, *Streetwalking on a Ruined Map: Cultural Theory and the City Films of Elvira Notari* (Princeton, N.J.: Princeton University Press, 1993), 132. For the information about Ciambelli's unpublished play, which consists of thirty-eight typewritten pages, in the Biblioteca Nazionale di Napoli, I thank the literary detective Francesco Durante.

26. The information available on this New York editor-in-chief of *Il Progresso* is incomplete: born in Aversa in 1897, in the United States from 1923 (he went immediately to *Il Progresso*, although his signature appears only irregularly in its columns), died in 1950. He is recalled as the author of some stories as well as comedies. His contribution to *Corriere della Sera*, in the immediate wake of the novel (in 1938), on the similar themes of the conjugal crisis and the tragicomic functioning of the American legal machine, was important.

27. Francescantonio Michele Daniele, native of Agnone (province of Isernia), emigrated, after receiving his medical degree in Naples, to Youngstown, Ohio (1905–11), where he began to practice his profession among numerous Agnonesi compatriots, but not only that. As he recounts in his autobiography, he quickly became interested, although a Catholic and a traditionalist, in the practice of birth control, struck by, among other things, the problems associated with clandestine abortions and infant mortality. From 1911 to 1919 he returned to Italy, but during the war, in which he took part as a medical captain in the reserves, he was captured by the Austrians and transferred to various prison camps, among them the terrible Mauthausen (1917–18). From 1919 he was again in the U.S.A.; soon afterward the move to Los Angeles.

## CHAPTER 2. STOWAWAY ON BOARD

1. *L'Adunata dei Refrattari* (1922–71), edited for decades by Raffaele Schiavina (very prolific himself under the pseudonym Max Sartin), was the paper that continued, with consistent, pure sectarianism, the antiorganizational anarchist tradition of the old leader Luigi Galleani. During most of its long existence, *L'Adunata* came out weekly on the "anarchist" bank of the Hudson, in Newark, New Jersey.

2. In that sense, the holdings of the Biblioteca di Studi Americani at the University of Florence (Fondo CNR) and of the Feltrinelli Foundation in Milan (among others, the Fondo Angelo Tasca) are essential.

3. Emilio Franzina, *Dall'Arcadia in America. Attività letteraria ed emigrazione transoceanica in Italia (1850–1940)* (Turin: Edizioni della Fondazione Giovanni Agnelli, 1996), 29 and note.

4. In connection with the murder of Tresca, besides the powerful accusatory speech made by Taddei in New York during a meeting on 14 February 1943, one should mention at least the novelistic treatment of a dean of Italian American letters, Jerre Mangione, *Night Search* (New York: Crown, 1965), and Joseph Arleo's *The Grand Street Collector* (New York: Walker & Co., 1969). Taddei's name also occurs frequently among the documents archived in the New York Public Library in the Special Collection of the Tresca Memorial Committee.

5. The fine biography of his friend Domenico Javarone draws generously on Taddei's written testimony. One curiosity: the Casellario Politico Centrale of the Archivio Centrale dello Stato (which I was able to consult thanks to the help of Salvatore Salerno) has a file headed Ezio Taddei, containing information gathered by the prefecture of Terni (a city where the writer had occasion to work in his youth). However, it turns out to be a singular case of homonymy.

6. The title refers, by antiphrasis, to one of the best-sellers of the Cold War, *I Chose Freedom* (New York: Scribner's, 1946), in which the ex-Soviet bureaucrat Victor A. Kravchenko denounced the repressive regime that was flourishing in the USSR.

7. The authors are Taddei's favorites, whom the writer sought to offer to his "people" as an example of reflection and inspiration to their own creation (the review did in fact publish some stories by readers): Pushkin, Turgenev, Chekhov, Maupassant, Jack London, Camillo Boito, Wilde, Zola, H. G. Wells, O. Henry, V. Kataev, Caldwell, etc.

8. For a brief list of his unpublished writings and works for theater (among which a tragedy, *Le Troiane* [The Trojan Women] was published posthumously), see Domenico Javarone, *Vita di scrittore (Ezio Taddei)* (Rome: Macchia, 1958), 190–92.

9. An exception is *Fra le tenebre* [In the Shadows], the penultimate story in *C'è posta per voi, Mr. Brown!*, a piece "written in internment, in 1935, in Bernalda (Matera)" (167), hence a sort of treasury of Taddei's writing, republished here after a first printing in the rare *Parole collettive*. *Fra le tenebre* recounts, less effectively in comparison with *Alberi e casolari*, a dark country tragedy (an infanticide), in lateveristic and hallucinatory tones.

10. On this theme, which in the first decade after the Second World War is intertwined with that of the "incipient Soviet mythology," Bruno Pischedda has carried out a valuable work of excavation and analysis, in *Due modernità: Le pagine culturali dell' "Unità": 1945–1956*, preface by Vittorio Spinazzola (Milan: Angeli, 1995), 193 ff.

## CHAPTER 3. THE NEW WORLD OF THE SECOND GENERATION

1. *Cristo fra i muratori* (Milan: Bompiani, 1941; translated by Eva Amendola—but the translator's name might have been used to cover up the work of an anti-Fascist intellectual). A "prophylactic" editor's note (attributable to Vittorini?) justifies the decision to publish by praising the presence of "a natural Italianness, which is overwhelmingly manifest [though] in the guise of another language: the conquered, not the conqueror." The encounter, twenty years afterward, between di Donato and Giose Rimanelli, an Italian American by choice, is interesting (*Il Giornale d'Italia*, 27–28 January 1960).

2. On the World's Fair, amid building activity, patriotic celebration, and presages of war, there is a valuable entry in the American diary of 1939 of Pier Antonio Quarantotti Gambini, *Neve a Manhattan* [Snowfall in Manhattan], edited by Raffaele Manica (Rome: Fazi, 1998), 151–57. A good point of departure is David Gelernter, *1939, The Lost World of the Fair* (New York: Avon, 1996).

3. Two testimonials of opposing implications: The school was "for a quarter of a century the purest banner of the most fervent Italian nationalism" (Filippo Fichera, *Letteratura italoamericana* [Milan: Editrice Convivio Letterario, 1958], 41–42); and yet in those same years, on the same street, between Tompkins Square Park and Third Avenue, "the citadel of Italo-American anti-fascism" would be found, concentrated

in the editorial offices of historic and glorious papers: *Il Nuovo Mondo*, edited by the socialists Bertelli and Vacirca; *Il Lavoratore:* and above all Carlo Tresca's *Il Martello* (Vanni B. Montana, *Amarostico: Testimonianze euro-americane* [Livorno: U. Bastogi, 1976], 98–102). On Ruotolo, see also chapter 4, "The 'harmonies and dissonances' of Ruotolo."

4. The story is not even mentioned in the two most recent monographs on the author: Matthew Diomede, *Pietro DiDonato: The Master Builder* (Lewisburg, Pa.: Bucknell University Press, 1995); and Louise Napolitano, *An American Story: Pietro DiDonato's Christ in Concrete* (New York: Peter Lang, 1995).

5. *Omnibus*, 10 December 1938. Even before Fante, another Italian American born in Denver was introduced, in a translation by Ester Danesi Traversari: Jo Pagano (*Il nonno di Napoli*, 23 July 1938).

6. For a discussion of the fertile scene of the Roman periodicals of the Fascist period, see Andrea Cortellessa, "Dalla torre d'avorio all'estetica del carro armato. Autonomia ed eteronomia del letterario sulle riviste romane, 1926–1944," in *La stampa periodica romana durante il fascismo (1927–1943)*, edited by Filippo Mazzonis, vol. 1 (Rome: Istituto Nazionale di Studi Romani, 1998).

7. *Oggi*, 17 June 1939. Pannunzio continued to publish Fante even after the Second World War, in *Il Mondo*.

8. In J. Fante, *Dago Red*, edited by Francesco Durante (Milan: Marcos y Marcos, 1997), who is the author of an indispensable *postfazione*. Another fine passage from *Dago Red* was published for the first time by Giuseppe Prezzolini, *I trapiantati* (Milan: Longanesi, 1963), 309–10.

9. *Oggi*, 18 November 1939.

10. In fact, Giorgio Monicelli's translation of *Wait until Spring, Bandini* (*Aspettiamo primavera, Bandini*), volume 207 of Mondadori's *Medusa*, published in 1948, differs from that presented in the excerpts in the magazine.

11. See for example, by way of a symptomatic anathema, "La lingua della 'giobba,'" *Lingua Nostra* 1, no. 4 (August 1939)—which reprints a longer article published in the *Bulletin* of the Casa Italiana of Columbia University, of which Prezzolini was then the director.

12. Mencken's voice is well represented in the Prezzolini Archive, thanks to a small but interesting correspondence and a series of press clippings and annotations on the sage of Baltimore (throughout a long essay by Edmund Wilson); certainly it was not a chance contact between two "irregular" conservatives.

13. Prezzolini, *I trapiantati*, 314–15.

14. Thus to his mother (presumably in the spring of 1943), informing her of his collaboration with the Italian department of the Office of War Information: "I am studying Italian, and in New York I will specialize in Italian, so that when I get to North Africa I will be able to speak the language well enough to deal with the big Italian population in Casablanca, or Tripoli, or wherever they propose to send me" (and a note from his wife, Joyce: "John never acquired enough fluency in the Italian language to take the assignment in North Africa. The plan was dropped") (*J. Fante, Selected Letters, 1932–1981*, edited by Seamus Cooney [Santa Rosa, Calif.: Black Sparrow, 1991], 201–2). Equally significant, for its historical and personal implications, is this passage from another letter to his mother (presumably dated June 1946): "Under separate cover I am sending Papa something that I think he will enjoy. It is the Italian translation of my novel, Ask the Dust. It was sent to me by a British soldier who saw it in a bookstore in Venice. I can't read it, but I think Papa will enjoy it" (215). More casual notes appear in the correspondence from Naples and Rome, during prolonged sojourns for work in 1957 and 1960.

15. *The Autobiography of Mother Jones,* edited by Mary Field Parton (Chicago: Charles H. Kerr & Company, 1972), 193.

16. *L'Italia Coloniale* 5, no. 1 (January–February 1904) gives detailed information on the miners' strike. A meeting with the community of Italian workers in Colorado is at the center of a remarkable letter (no. 19) of the journalist and government immigration official Adolfo Rossi, originally in "Per la tutela degli italiani negli Stati Uniti: Lettere dell'ispettore Cav. Adolfo Rossi, scritte al R. Commissariato dell'emigrazione nel corso di una sua missione negli Stati Uniti dell'America del Nord," *Bollettino dell'Emigrazione,* no. 16 (1904). Rossi left other recollections of the Italians in Colorado in *Un italiano in America* (Milan: Fratelli Treves, 1892).

17. On *Il Risveglio* one can read Ernesto Gerbi and Aluisius, *L'eterna lotta* (Milan: Nuova Editrice Internazionale, 1962), 124–25; and Bruno Cartosio, "La stampa operaia negli Stati Uniti (1900–1920)," in *Lavoratori negli Stati Uniti. Storia e culture politiche dalla schiavitù all'I.W.W.* (Milan: Arcipelago Edizioni, 1989), 296–97. For a general overview, see Giovanni Perilli, *Colorado and the Italians in Colorado* (n.p, 1922); and the entry "Press, Italian American," signed by Vincent A. Lapomarda, in *The Italian American Experience: An Encyclopedia,* ed. Salvatore J. LaGumina, Frank J. Cavaioli, Salvatore Primeggia, Joseph A. Varacalli (New York: Garland, 2000), 516.

## CHAPTER 4. POETRY OF THE ITALIAN AMERICANS

1. Giuseppe Prezzolini, *I trapiantati* (Milan: Longanesi, 1963), 328.

2. Giovannitti's case is well documented in the columns of *Avanti!* in October 1912.

3. See on this subject the first volume: *La parola difficile. Autobiografia di un italo-americano* (Fasano, Brindisi: Schena, 1988).

4. Born in Carpi, near Modena, in 1869, Righi was elected as a socialist to the city council of his home town in 1895. Personal and political troubles must have persuaded him to leave Italy within the next couple of years. (I want gratefully to acknowledge Gilberto Zacchè for his precious archival research.) An encounter with a "Dr. Saverio Righi," a late-nineteenth-century émigré, a socialist from Emilia in the old style and "of a humanistic culture," closes Mario Soldati's *Addio diletta Amelia* (Milan: Mondadori, 1979).

5. *I sonetti di Manhattan* (bearing a dedication "To Onorio Ruotolo" and flanked by a photograph of Columbus Circle) are subdivided into "Broadway," "The Subway," "Columbus Circle," "Greenwich Village," and "Little Italy."

6. See above: chapter 3, "Two Different Beginnings."

7. At the beginning of the century, the "ethnolinguistic" experiments of Thomas Augustine Daly, for example, had some success; he divided his *Carmina* (1914; but published in various journals, also in America, in the preceding years) into sections labelled "Italicè," "Hibernicè," and "Anglicè," using to sentimental or comic-realist effect a consistent mimetic and oral ability. The note of admiration with which Constantine Panunzio, one of the founding fathers of Italian American autobiography, introduces him in *The Soul of an Immigrant* (1922) is significant.

8. Quotation from envelope 368 of Casellario Politico Centrale, Archivio Centrale dello Stato, dedicated to the "subversive" Bartoletti. Particular thanks to Salvatore Salerno, who made it available to me.

A curious example of Bartoletti's literary activity in the course of the decade of repatriation is the poem in 650 free hendecasyllables *Un'escursione alla caverna di*

*Monte Cucco* [An Excursion to the Cave of Monte Cucco] (1924), a sort of "touristic-speleological" descent whose Dantism achieves a strong and obviously unintended effect of kitsch.

9. However, Bartoletti did dedicate a poem in eighteen octaves to the emblematic figure of the discoverer of the New World: *La Colombiade.*

10. Elsewhere, as in *Nel sogno d'oltretomba* [In the Dream of the Afterlife] (1931), praise of materialism, reason, and science is enigmatically intertwined with a false Gothic imagery, and, in addition to Monti, Dante and Lucretius are plundered with superficial facility.

11. The unpublished manuscripts preserve a long example of the latter, going back to the mid-teens, which is divided into four chapters: *L'asineide, o il parassita colo . . . d'America; La rassegna coloniale; L'irruzzione* [*sic*] *degli Indiani in Hibbing, Minn.; I prominenti coloniali* [The Donkeyad, or the Dumb . . . American Parasite; The Immigrants' Review; The Indian Uprising in Hibbing, Minn.; Bosses of the Immigrant Community].

12. Pier Paolo Pasolini, "La poesia dialettale del Novecento," *Passione e ideologia (1948–1958)*, in *Saggi sulla letteratura e sull'arte*. Vol. 1, ed. Walter Siti and Silvia De Laude (Milan: Mondadori, 1999), 731–32.

13. It is discussed, with regard to di Donato, in chapter 3.

14. In trying to put together a roughly chronological and incomplete list (I am indebted to the self-celebrating catalogues of Pucelli, Fichera, and, later, Alfonsi), I mention Cesare Crespi, Achille Almerini, Bellalma Forzato Spezia, Antonio Calitri, Salvatore Cutino, Severina Magni, Rosario Ingargiola and Giuseppe Zappulla (a particularly interesting couple for a study of the fortunes of the lyric language of D'Annunzio), Pietro Greco, the already mentioned Antonino Crivello, Liborio Lattoni, Germoglino Saggio, Nino Caradonna, the Calabrese Michele Pane (mentioned many times by Pasolini in his dialect study), F. Michele Daniele, and Giuseppe Incalicchio. The lyrics in dialect of the Abruzzese anarchist Umberto Postiglione should be noted, in addition to works for theater and political and social writings. The novelist Italo Stanco and the comedian and champion of the immigrant theater Eduardo Migliaccio (Farfariello) also wrote poems in Italian.

## CHAPTER 5. PROSE OF TESTIMONY

1. Mario Maffi, ed., *Voci di frontiera: Scritture dei Latinos negli Stati Uniti* (Milan: Feltrinelli, 1997).

2. A recurrent theme in the Italian American poetry of that period (often given a prominent position in the columns of the papers) is the highly rhetorical lament on the bloody defeats of Dogali and Adua, in Eritrea and in Ethiopia, corresponding to the tone of the Italian press.

3. Howard R. Marraro, *Relazioni fra l'Italia e gli Stati Uniti* (Rome: Edizioni dell'Ateneo, 1954), 145; and Pietro Russo, "La stampa periodica italo-americana," in *Gli italiani negli Stati Uniti. L'emigrazione e l'opera degli italiani negli Stati Uniti d'America. Atti del III Symposium di Studi Americani. Firenze, 27–29 Maggio 1969* (Florence: Istituto di Studi Americani—Università degli Studi di Firenze, 1972), 495–96 n. 13.

4. On Secchi De Casali and his journalistic activities, which were not limited to *L'Eco*, see Marraro, *Relazioni*, 141–45; Russo, "Stampa," 495–96 ff.; Mastro-Valerio, "Distribution of Certain Nationalities: A. Italians," *Reports of the Industrial Commission on Immigration and on Education*, vol. 15 (Washington: Government Printing Office [57th Congress, 1st Session, House of Representatives, doc. no. 184], 1901), 499–

500, where he calls him, however, a few years after his death in 1885, "a disciple of Mazzini"; and Francesco Durante, *Italoamericana. Storia e letteratura degli italiani negli Stati Uniti 1776–1880,* vol. 1 (Milan: Mondadori, 2001), 426–27.

5. Francesca Mazzariol, "La Capanna dello Zio Tom e la stampa italiana," *Il bianco e il nero* 2, no. 2 (1998): 123–29.

6. *L'Eco d'Italia,* 9 August 1862.

7. *L'Eco d'Italia,* 29 July 1865.

8. "L'Africa di Brooklyn" and "Situazione dei Negri," *L'Eco d'Italia,* 5 August 1865.

9. Dario Papa and Ferdinando Fontana, *New-York* (Milan: Giuseppe Galli, 1884), 243 (the quotation is by Fontana, a fairly well-known minor literary figure, in his early years a "young Turk," belonging to the radical school of the *Scapigliatura;* as for Papa, today less frequently mentioned than his colleague, see the study by Valerio Castronovo cited in the bibliography).

10. Papa and Fontana, *New-York,* 173–81.

11. The word "kneeling" is repeated seven times, deliberately, it seems, as if to mark the stations of a new *via crucis.*

12. On *Peppino* and Ventura see above: chapter 1, "Narrative and Press: The Ventura 'case.'" I refer here to the English version of the text.

13. Mario Maffi, "The Strange Case of Luigi Donato Ventura's *Peppino:* Some Speculations on the Beginnings of Italian-American Fiction," in *Multilingual America: Transnationalism, Ethnicity, and the Languages of American Literature,* ed. Werner Sollors (New York: New York University Press, 1998), 170.

14. A brief mention of "I Negri d'America" is in Arnaldo Testi, "L'immagine degli Stati Uniti nella stampa socialista italiana (1886–1914)," in *Italia e America dal Settecento all'età dell'imperialismo,* ed. Giorgio Spini et al. (n.p.: Marsilio, 1976).

15. Note that Ventura's article is part of a broader debate on "Races" (and in particular on "Despised Races") promoted by the review, whose participants included, in addition to the editor, Arcangelo Ghisleri, notable figures like Napoleone Colajanni, a principal in the debate on southernism, racism, and emigration (note only the essay "Gli italiani negli Stati Uniti" published by his *Rivista Popolare* in 1906).

16. The article gives a lot of space to quotations from a work by Henry A. Shepherd.

17. Thus in the "Editors' Note" that precedes the two articles by Ventura and Colajanni.

18. Mastro-Valerio, "Distribution," 503.

19. The tiny volume is the detailed diaristic account of two long journeys to the interior of the continent undertaken in the early years of the century.

20. Here and in the following citation I quote from Guido Rossati, "La colonizzazione negli Stati di Mississippi, Louisiana ed Alabama," *Bollettino dell'Emigrazione* 14 (1904): 12–14.

21. Compare the following passages: Adolfo Rossi, "Per la tutela degli Italiani negli Stati Uniti (Lettere dell'Ispettore cav. Adolfo Rossi, scritte al R. Commissariato dell'emigrazione nel corso di una sua missione negli Stati Uniti dell'America del Nord)," *Bollettino dell'Emigrazione* 16 (1904): 71–72 (from whom I take the other citations in the text): "Accomiatatici dal signor Sessions, ci recammo alla stazione di Coahoma con un carro guidato da un negro, attraverso boschi dagli alberi giganteschi. Mentre percorrevamo la strada appena tracciata e lunga otto chilometri, chiesi al negro: 'Come va che in queste piantagioni gli italiani risparmiano denaro e diventano poi proprietari di terre, mentre voialtri negri siete sempre senza un soldo?'" [Taking leave of Mr. Sessions, we went to the station at Coahoma in a cart

driven by a Negro, through woods with gigantic trees. As we traveled along the road, which was barely marked, and about eight kilometers long, I asked the Negro: 'How is it that in these plantations the Italians save money and then become owners of land, while you Negroes are always without a cent?'].

And W. E. B. Du Bois, *Of the Quest of the Golden Fleece,* in *The Souls of Black Folk* (New York: Library of America, 1986), 465: "I remember once meeting a little one-mule wagon on the River road. A young black fellow sat in it driving listlessly, his elbows on his knees. His dark-faced wife sat beside him, stolid, silent.

"'Hello!' cried my driver,—he has a most impudent way of addressing these people, though they seem used to it,—'what have you got there?'

"'Meat and meal,'" answered the man, stopping. The meat lay uncovered in the bottom of the wagon,—a great thin side of fat pork covered with salt; the meal was in a white bushed bag.

"'What did you pay for that meat?"

"'Ten cents a pound." It could have been bought for six or seven cents cash.'"

22. See also above: chapter 1, "Memoir and Commitment."

23. Camillo Cianfarra, *Il diario di un emigrato* (New York: Tipografia dell'Araldo Italiano, 1904), 99.

24. Cianfarra, *Diario,* 51.

25. Cianfarra, *Diario,* 143–44.

26. Guido Rossati, "Organizzazione ed opera dell'Ufficio di collocamento al lavoro in Nuova York per gli immigranti italiani," *Bollettino dell'Emigrazione* 3 (1907): 227.

27. Camillo Cianfarra, "La manodopera negra. Nel concetto degli Industriali del Sud degli Stati Uniti," *Gli Italiani e l'America—La Rassegna Nord Americana,* 16, no. 5 (November 1906). Cianfarra was a regular contributor of essays and short stories to the magazine. That same year *Il Proletario* advertised a new book by its former director: *Il movimento socialista in Europa ed in America.*

28. Emily Fogg Meade, "The Italian on the Land: A Study in Immigration," *Bulletin of the Bureau of Labor* 70 (May 1907): 479.

29. Cianfarra, "Manodopera," 6.

30. 1906 was also the year of *The Economic Future of the Negro,* by Du Bois, which can be read as a masterly refutation of the preceding analysis. (Reprinted in *W. E. B. Du Bois Speaks: Speeches and Addresses, 1890–1919,* ed. Philip S. Foner, with a tribute by Martin Luther King Jr. [New York: Pathfinder, 1970].) A century later, it is worth observing how, in authors so far apart, the articulation of ethnic consciousness manages to support results as divergent as the defense (Cianfarra) and, on the other side, the confutation of racism (Du Bois).

31. Francesco Durante informs me that there exist traces of Cianfarra's contributions to New York newspapers in 1911–13; he later became the director of the Rome office of the United Press, at least until 1925.

32. Guglielmo Di Palma Castiglione, "Relazione sull'attività spiegata dall'Ufficio del lavoro per gli immigranti italiani in New York durante l'anno 1908," *Bollettino dell'Emigrazione* 8 (1909): 736. A few years later, Gil, the correspondent for the Catholic *Italica Gens,* speaks precisely of this "liberation" from the "economic servitude that, without regard to color or race, oppresses Negroes and whites, including not a few Italian workers." An exhaustive bibliography on colonizing projects in the southern states can be found in the list of texts that ends the classic monograph by Grazia Dore, *La democrazia italiana e l'emigrazione in America* (Brescia: Morcelliana, 1964).

33. Allow me to mention here *Little America. Gli Stati Uniti e gli scrittori italiani del Novecento* (Milan: Marcos y Marcos, 1997). But also keep in mind the following paragraph.

34. Prezzolini, *I trapiantati* (Milano: Longanesi, 1963), 420.

## CHAPTER 6. AT ELLIS ISLAND

1. Quotation from Vittorio Sereni, "Lavori in corso. III" (a poem dated "New York, 1967"), in *Stella variabile* (Milan: Garzanti, 1981). See also a recent version in English: *Variable Star,* trans. Luigi Bonaffini (Toronto: Guernica, 1999). I limit myself to noting three other works that would require a thoughtful and precise comparison to bring out the different functions of the writing and different meaning attributed by each author to the topos of the return to a more and more demythologized America, and yet, for this very reason, again the landing place of inner freedom: from the pre-Museum visit of Georges Perec, in Georges Perec-Robert Bober, *Récits d'Ellis Island* (Paris: Institut national de l'audiovisuel, Sorbier, 1980), to the account in dialogue-memory of Sergio Campailla, "Album di famiglia," in *Romanzo americano* (Milano: Rusconi, 1994) and the passionate, multilingual remembrance of Nicola Gardini, first with a "fragmentary hymn" in ancient Greek and Italian, "Tempo straniero," *Testo a fronte* no. 17 (October 1997), then with a section and other poems in the surprising, beautiful book of verse *Atlas* (Milan: Crocetti, 1998). Through Ellis Island pass the characters of Ciambelli, Pellegrino, Stanco, Caminita (see chapter 1); and, with particular pathos, those of Tony Ardizzone, *In the Garden of Papa Santuzzu* (New York: Picador, 1999).

2. Corsi took on responsibilities there later as well, until the end of his life. Haarlem House had been founded in 1908, with the name of Home Garden, by the Protestant missionary Anna C. Ruddy, author of one of the first extensive accounts of life in the Italian American "ghetto": *The Heart of the Stranger: A Story of Little Italy* (New York: Fleming H. Revell Col, 1908).

3. Edward Corsi, "I miei novanta giorni a Washington" *Italiani nel Mondo* 11, no. 11 (10 June 1955): 8.

4. Stefano Luconi, *La "diplomazia parallela." Il regime fascista e la mobilitazione degli italoamericani* (Milan: Angeli, 2000), 70.

5. Amerigo Ruggiero, whose *Italiani in America* (Milan: Treves, 1937) was, according to Cecchi, one of his guidebooks in the horror of "bitter America," was in those years the most prolific and regular correspondent from the United States for *La Stampa,* from 1929 to 1939; and two decades later he was one of the most prestigious contributors to *Divagando,* the last Italian American weekly of real originality and breadth. Beniamino De Ritis, then working for the *Corriere della Sera* (from 1931–34), contributed from the States to many different major papers of the time, from *La Stampa* to *Critica Fascista,* from *Nuova Antologia* to *La Fiera Letteraria.* On him see Renato Romano, "Gli scritti di Beniamino De Ritis," in *Nei paesi dell'utopia. Identità e luoghi della letteratura abruzzese all'estero,* ed. Vito Moretti (Rome: Bulzoni, 1997); on the correspondents for the Italian press in New York, see Michel Beynet, *L'image de l'Amérique dans la culture italienne de l'entre-deux-guerres,* 3 vols. (Aix-en-Provence: Publications de l'Université de Provence, 1990). On Arbib-Costa I refer to Olga Ragusa, "A proposito di Arbib Costa," *Cartevive* 5, no. 1 (March 1994): 38. The educator Angelo Patri was one of the most active teachers in promoting Italian among the immigrants, a task that he undertook with particular effectiveness starting in 1913 as principal of P.S. 45 in the Bronx, where in the twenties a lively monthly was published, *Il Convito.*

6. On Corsi the pro-Fascist the exchange of opinions in 1942 between Salvemini and Max Ascoli should be seen, in two letters published by Maddalena Tirabassi: "La Mazzini Society (1940–1946): un'associazione degli antifascisti italiani negli Stati Uniti," in *Italia e America dalla Grande Guerra a oggi,* ed. Giorgio Spini, Gian Giacomo Migone, and Massimo Teodori (n.p.: Marsilio, 1976), 148–49.

7. The animating spirit of *La Follia,* Riccardo Cordiferro himself, had been

among the first reviewers of *In the Shadow of Liberty*, in the issue of 27 January 1935. As for the "anthology of the more important talks," it was published a year after the radio broadcasts: Eduardo Corsi, *Eduardo Corsi Speaks* (New York: Abruzzi Publishing Company, 1942).

8. Furthermore, Corsi had continued to work in immigration, as another volume of his testifies, *Paths to the New World: American Immigration, Yesterday, Today, and Tomorrow* (New York: Anti-Defamation League of B'nai B'rith, 1953).

9. On this subject I refer to Sandro Gerbi's wonderful essay, "Max Ascoli e Carlo Levi: il burbero e l'olimpico," *Belfagor* 52, no. 301 (31 January 1996).

10. On Corsi's life, besides the 1955 article on his "Ninety Days in Washington," the information given in *In the Shadow of Liberty*, and Prezzolini's "L'affare Corsi" (see below, note 16), I gathered my data from Alberto Cupelli, ed., *Gli Italiani di New York* (New York: Labor Press, 1939); Olga Peragallo, *Italian-American Authors and Their Contribution to American Literature*, ed. Anita Peragallo (New York: S.F. Vanni, 1949); Giovanni Schiavo, ed., *Italian-American Who's Who*, vol. 20, 1964–65, s.v. "Corsi" (El Paso, Tex.: Vigo Press, 1964); "Edoardo Corsi," *La Parola del Popolo* 16, no. 77 (February–March 1966); *Who Was Who in America with World Notables*, vol. 4, 1961–1968, s.v. "Corsi" (Chicago, Ill.: Marquis-Who's Who, Inc., 1968); Salvatore J. LaGumina, "The Immigrant and Politics: A Conservative or Liberal Influence: The Italo-Americans," in *Gli italiani negli Stati Uniti* (Florence: Istituto di Studi Americani—Università degli Studi di Firenze, 1972); John P. Diggins, *Mussolini and Fascism: The View from America* (Princeton, N.J.: Princeton University Press, 1972); Robert Anthony Orsi, *The Madonna of 115th Street: Faith and Community in Italian Harlem, 1880–1950* (New Haven: Yale University Press, 1985); Gerald Meyer, *Vito Marcantonio: Radical Politician, 1902–1954* (Albany: State University of New York Press, 1989); Stefano Luconi, *La "diplomazia parallela"* (see note 4).

11. Strictly speaking, responsibility for the translation of *Invasori* would also be confirmed, from the moment it is attributed to a "G." Prezzolini. Giuliano is the name of Prezzolini's second son (born in 1915), but was also the nom de plume of the father: see, among other works, a significant section of Giuseppe Prezzolini's *Diario, 1968–1982*, ed. Giuliano Prezzolini (Milan: Rusconi, 1999), 69.

12. Olga Ragusa, "Prezzolini's 'Transplanted' Italian-Americans," in *L'esilio come certezza. La ricerca d'identità culturale in Italia dalla Rivoluzione Francese ai nostri giorni*, ed. Andrea Ciccarelli and Paolo A. Giordano (West Lafayette, Ind.: Bordighera, 1998).

13. Leonard Covello, principal of Benjamin Franklin High School in East Harlem, is, among the "professionals of American assimilation," the only one mentioned by name, and with little admiration and sympathy, in Prezzolini, *Trapiantati*, 301; but the influence of his work and his writings cannot be hastily undervalued. See at least, for the similarities to *In the Shadow of Liberty*—with the long account of the departure from Italy and the trials of the little Leonard's adaptation—the autobiography written together with the novelist Guido D'Agostino: *The Heart Is the Teacher* (New York: McGraw-Hill Co., 1958); later republished under the title *The Teacher in the Urban Community: A Half Century in City Schools* (Totowa, N.J.: Littlefield and Adams, 1970).

Garibaldi Mario (misspelled as Marto) Lapolla, a teacher but above all the author of the most solid, vibrant, and dramatic novel on the Little Italy of East Harlem, *The Grand Gennaro*, published in the same year as Corsi's book (New York: Vanguard Press, 1935), is dismissed in *Trapiantati* as a "pseudonovelist" (299), but Prezzolini at least recognizes in it a certain literary value. Among the ample material in the archive preserved in Philadelphia at the Balch Institute for Ethnic Studies one finds also, not by chance, a slim correspondence between Lapolla and Covello. On the latter, see now Simone Cinotto, "Leonard Covello, la Collezione Covello e la storia alimentare degli immigrati italiani a New York." *Quaderni storici* 33, no. 111/3 (December 2002): 719–746; on Garibaldi Lapolla and *The Grand Gennaro*, see Martino Marazzi, "I due re di Harlem," *Belfagor* 58, no. 5 (347) (30 September 2003).

14. For example, *La Follia di New York* of 2 April 1939 (in the same period as the two translations) gives the news of a new, substantial arrival in Harlem of books from Italy. The library fund of the Aguilar Branch, unfortunately today untraceable, was in the care of the librarian Leonilda I. Sansone Gervasi, whose contacts with Prezzolini have been documented (Olga Ragusa, "Prezzolini e la diffusione del libro italiano," *Cartevive* 8, no. 1 [April 1997]).

15. A favorable mention by Prezzolini can be read in advance on the publication of the volume devoted to Ellis Island, in "Stati Uniti: autobiografia e romanzo," *Gazzetta del Popolo,* 19 December 1934.

16. *Trapiantati*, 376–77.

17. *Trapiantati*, 378.

## CHAPTER 7. ITALIAN AMERICANS AND ITALIAN WRITERS

1. In the last decade, there have been so many works on Italian emigration and its culture that it would not even be correct to talk of exceptions. I will just point out here such titles as Jean-Jacques Marchand (ed.), *Letteratura dell'emigrazione. Gli scrittori di lingua italiana nel mondo* (Turin: Edizioni della Fondazione Agnelli, 1991); Daniela Saresella's *Cattolicesimo italiano e sfida americana* (Brescia: Morcelliana, 2001); and especially *Storia dell'emigrazione italiana*, vol. 1, *Partenze* and vol. 2, *Arrivi*, Piero Bevilacqua, Andreina De Clementi, and Emilio Franzina (eds.) (Rome: Donzelli, 2001 and 2002), which host contributions by almost all the major scholars in the field. However, this scholarly bounty is not yet matched by a strong and reliable academic recognition, either in Italy or in the U.S. But this is another matter, although quite *pénible*.

2. See the issues of magazines and newspapers like *Il Foglio, Diario,* and *Poesia. Diario* selected 274 opinions by its readers, out of more than one thousand, responding to six basic questions dealing with the relationship between Italy and the U.S. Only about a dozen mentioned Italian Americans. Among twenty-seven poems by Italians, a special November 2001 issue of *Poesia* had only a beautiful one by Lucio Mariani (a contemporary Italian poet living in Rome), "Scacco matto": the voice of one of the victims of the attack on the Twin Towers, born in Rockaway, Long Island, reminding the "ill-hidden pride on the Italian face / of my father." The historian Massimo Teodori has produced a successful and documented overview of the Italian "antiamerican prejudice," which completely overlooks the history of immigration. And when, a year later, the opera *Ellis Island* premiered in Palermo's Teatro Massimo, of all places (with music by Giovanni Sollima and a libretto by Roberto Alajmo), a respected reviewer presented it as the story of "over 22 million desperadoes" (Carla Moreni, "Disoccupazione all'opera," *Il Sole—24 Ore,* 6 October 2002).

3. For this point, as well as for a discussion of a great number of the titles, the obligatory reference is to Sebastiano Martelli, "Letteratura ed emigrazione: congedo provvisorio," in *Il sogno italo-americano. Realtà e immaginario dell'emigrazione negli Stati Uniti,* ed. Sebastiano Martelli (Naples: Cuen, 1998), and to his "Dal vecchio mondo al sogno americano. Realtà e immaginario dell'emigrazione nella letteratura ita-

liana," in *Storia dell'emigrazione*. As for autobiographies, see Martelli, "Letteratura," 431–32 and its note for a list of texts (the volume by Maurino that I cite in the bibliography can be added; but also bear in mind Carlo Tresca's broad and incomplete autobiographical "torso" in English: chapter 1, "Memoir and Commitment").

4. Cited by Mario Soldati, *America primo amore* (Milan: Mondadori, 1981 [first edition, 1935]), 51.

5. Soldati, *America*, 54–55.

6. Mario Soldati, *Addio diletta Amelia* (Milan: Mondadori, 1979, 25).

7. Giuseppe Antonio Borgese, *Atlante americano* (Modena: Guanda, 1936), 59–60.

8. Pier Antonio Quarantotti Gambini, *Neve a Manhattan*, (ed.) Raffaele Manica (Rome: Fazi, 1998), 147–49.

9. Mario Maffi, *New York. L'isola delle colline* (Milan: il Saggiatore, 1995), 42–44. For a rapid foray into the Italian neighborhood of the Bronx (rather different from Soldati's), see Mario Maffi, *Sotto le torri di Manhattan. Mappe Nomi Storie Luoghi* (Milan: Rizzoli, 1998), 241.

10. It can be read in Prezzolini, *Tutta l'America* (Florence: Vallecchi, 1958).

11. For a historical-critical introduction I recommend Olga Ragusa, "Prezzolini's 'Transplanted' Italian-Americans," in *L'esilio come certezza. La ricerca d'identità culturale in Italia dalla Rivoluzione francese ai nostri giorni*, eds. Andrea Ciccarelli and Paolo Giordano (West Lafayette, Ind.: Bordighera Press, 1998).

12. Furio Colombo, *Da Kennedy a Watergate* (Turin: SEI, 1974), 11, 114. On the "unpleasant mystery" of the exclusion, in Italy, of Italian American history from the interest of specialists, Colombo expressed himself with authority and his usual *curiositas* in *La Repubblica* of 5 August 1999, ranging from *The Sopranos* to De Niro, from Spike Lee to Pascal D'Angelo.

13. Fausto Maria Martini, *Si sbarca a New York*, new ed., ed. by Giuseppe Farinelli (Milan: Istituto di Propaganda Libraria, n.d.), 254.

14. Aldo Rosselli, *La mia America e la tua* (Rome: Theoria, 1995), 27, 31.

15. A comment that is still valid on the subject is Massimo Teodori, *La fine del mito americano* (Milan: Feltrinelli, 1975).

16. The historical and critical work in this field is relevant. For the purposes of the discussion here keep in mind, for an overall perspective, Giorgio Bertellini, "New York City and the Representation of Italian Americans in the Cinema," in *The Italians of New York: Five Centuries of Struggle and Achievement*, ed. Philip V. Cannistraro (New York: New-York Historical Society, John D. Calandra Italian American Institute, 1999); for a militant reading, see Pasquale Verdicchio, *Bound by Distance: Rethinking Nationalism through the Italian Diaspora* (Madison, N.J.: Fairleigh Dickinson University Press, 1997), and "Unholy Manifestations: Cultural Transformations as Hereticism in the Films of De Michiel, Ferrara, Savoca, and Scorsese," in *Adjusting Sites: New Essays in Italian American Studies*, ed. William Boelhower and Rocco Pallone, *Forum Italicum-Filibrary Series*, 16 (1997 and 1999).

17. Campailla has given ample space to an erudite stereotyped painting in his essay "Little Italy" (in *Il sogno italo-americano. Realtà e immaginario dell'emigrazione negli Stati Uniti*, ed. Sebastiano Martelli [Naples: Cuen, 1998]); while in Gina Lagorio's novel (*L'arcadia americana* [Milan: Rizzoli, 1999]) there are also passages more easily ascribable to the traditional mode.

18. An affirmation readily viewed critically by Robert Viscusi, "La letteratura dell'emigrazione italiana negli Stati Uniti," in *La letteratura dell'emigrazione. Gli scrittori*

*di lingua italiana nel mondo,* ed. Jean-Jacques Marchand (Turin: Edizioni della Fondazione Agnelli, 1991), 132.

19. See the "case" of Franco Magnani examined by Oliver Sacks in *An Anthropologist on Mars* (New York: Knopf, 1995).

20. Andrea De Carlo, *Treno di panna* (Turin: Einaudi, 1981); American edition: *The Cream Train* (Berkeley, Calif.: Olive Press, 1987), 209–10.

# Bibliography

## CHAPTER 1.

*Primary Sources and Samples of Other Noteworthy Texts*

Altavilla, Corrado. *Gente lontana*. Milan: Medici Domus, 1938.

Avella, Caterina Maria. "La 'Flapper.'" *Il Carroccio* 18, no. 2 (August 1923).

———. "Patsy e Patricia." *Il Carroccio* 20, no. 4 (October 1924).

Borghi, Armando. *Mussolini in camicia*. New York: Edizioni Libertarie, 1927. American edition: *Mussolini Red and Black. With an Epilogue, Hitler: Mussolini's Disciple*. Trans. Dorothy Daudley. New York: Freie Arbeiter Stimme, 1938.

———. *Due bozzetti contro il fascismo. 1.o—Dante processato all'Inferno. 2.o—Italiani che ascoltano la radio dall'America*. Newark, N.J.: La Biblioteca de L'Adunata dei Refrattari, 1943.

Branchi, Eugenio Camillo. *Così parlò Mister Nature. Fatti e impressioni di un italiano in America*. Bologna: Licinio Cappelli, 1953.

———. "'Dagoes.'" In *Novelle Transatlantiche*. Bologna: Licinio Cappelli, 1927.

———. "Hold up!" *Il Carroccio* 24, no. 8 (August 1926).

———. "'Sarete mia, Laura.'" *Il Carroccio* 23, no. 1 (January 1926).

Caminita, Ludovico M. *Che cosa è la religione*. Preface by Guido Podrecca. Paterson, N.J.: Libreria sociologica, 1906.

———. *Free Country!* N.p., n.d.

———. *In Nuova York*. Scranton, Pa.: Il Minatore Publishing Co., 1936.

———. *Nell'isola delle lagrime: Ellis island*. New York: Stabilimento tipografico Italia, 1924.

———. *Obici. Biografia*. New York: Tipografia Editrice Scarlino, 1943.

———. *Sonata Elegiaca*. Brooklyn, N.Y.: Tartamella & Co., 1921 (and Paterson, N.J.: A. Fontanella, n.d.).

Ciambelli, Bernardino. *L'Aeroplano Fantasma. La Follia di New York* 24 September 1911–?

———. [Pin, pseud.]. "L'Arcibanchettone." *La Follia di New York*, 19 February 1911.

———. "La città nera ovvero i misteri di Chicago." *L'Italia* (Chicago) 15 July 1893–at least May 1894.

———. *Columbus Day*. In *Gli Italiani negli Stati Uniti d'America*. New York: Italian American Directory Co., 1906.

———. "Il delitto di Coney Island ovvero La vendetta della zingara." *La Follia di New York*, 1906?–26 July 1908.

———. *I drammi dell'emigrazione. (Seguito ai "Misteri di Mulberry.") Romanzo Contemporaneo.* New York: Frugone & Balletto, n.d.

———. *I misteri della polizia di New York. Il delitto di Water Street.* New York: Frugone & Balletto, 1895.

———. *I Misteri di Bleecker Street.* New York: Frugone & Balletto, 1899.

———. "I misteri di Harlem ovvero La bella di Elizabeth Street." *La Follia di New York,* 16 January 1910–17 September 1911.

———. *I misteri di Mulberry Street.* New York: Frugone & Balletto, 1893.

———. "Il Natale di Abele e quello di Caino." *La Follia di New York,* 18 December 1927.

———. "Il Natale di Caino." *La Follia di New York,* 19 December 1926.

———. "Il Natale di un eroe." *La Follia di New York,* 23 December 1928.

———. *I sotterranei di New York.* New York: Libraria Italiana, 1915.

———. "La strage degli Innocenti ossia I delitti di un medico." *La Follia di New York,* 30 August 1908–31 October 1909.

———. *Il terremoto in Sicilia e Calabria.* New York: Florence Publishing Company, 1909.

———. *La trovatella di Mulberry Street ovvero: La stella dei cinque punti.* New York: Società Libraria Italiana, 1919 [but probably earlier, circa 1915].

Cianfarra, Camillo. *Il diario di un emigrato.* New York: Tipografia dell'Araldo Italiano, 1904.

———. "Un'avventura di Natale." *La Follia di New York,* 18 December 1910.

———. "Io e la mia stenografa." *Gli italiani e l'America—La Rassegna Nord Americana* 16, no. 4 (October 1906).

Colonna, Dora. "'Common Clay.'" *Il Carroccio* 24, no. 8 (August 1926).

———. "Le due amiche." *Il Carroccio* 23, no. 4 (April 1926).

Damiani, Gigi. *La bottega. Scene della ricostruzione fascista.* Detroit, Mich.: Libreria Autonoma, 1927.

———. *Del delitto e delle pene nella Società di Domani.* Newark, N.J.: Biblioteca de L'Adunata dei Refrattari, 1928?

——— [Simplicio, pseud.]. *"Fecondità."* Newark, N.J.: Biblioteca de L'Adunata dei Refrattari, n.d. [circa 1938].

———. *Razzismo e Anarchismo.* Newark, N.J.: Biblioteca de L'Adunata dei Refrattari, circa 1938.

———. *Viva Rambolot! (Bozzetto in un atto).* Newark, N.J.: Biblioteca de L'Adunata dei Refrattari, 1929?

Daniele, F. Michele. *Calvario di guerra. Diario di prigionia da Faè di Longarone a Mauthausen.* Milan: Alpes, 1932.

———. *Signor Dottore: The Autobiography of F. Michele Daniele, Italian Immigrant Doctor (1879–1957).* Ed. Victor Rosen. New York: Exposition Press, 1959.

———. *Rime vecchie e nuove.* Bologna: Zanichelli, 1930.

———. *Yankee Faith and Other Stories.* New York: Greenberg, 1935.

Durante, Francesco. *Italoamericana. Storia e letteratura degli italiani negli Stati Uniti 1776–1880.* Vol. 1. Milan: Mondadori, 2001.

Fiaschetti, Michele [or Michael]. "Caccia grossa." *Corriere d'America,* 19–31 January 1926.

———. "Le due sorelle." Later retitled "La prova del fuoco." *Corriere d'America,* 19–27 February 1926.

———. *Gioco duro*. Ed. Martino Marazzi. Cava de' Tirreni (Salerno): Avagliano, 2003.

———. "La lotteria della morte." *Corriere d'America*, 6 March 1926.

———. "Il mistero della perla." *Corriere d'America*, 14 March 1928–?

———. "La scomparsa del sepolto." *Corriere d'America* 12–16 March 1926.

———. "Le spie e i confidenti." *Corriere d'America*, 5 May–14 June 1929.

———. "Le tre veglie." *Corriere d'America*, 10 February 1926.

———. *You Gotta Be Rough: The Adventures of Detective Fiaschetti of the Italian Squad as Told to Prosper Buranelli by Michael Fiaschetti*. Garden City, N.Y.: Doubleday, Doran & Company, 1930.

Migliaccio, Eduardo. "Bacilogia." *La Follia di New York*, 14 April 1945.

———. "Don Leopoldo. Annunciatore radiofonico, chiaroveggente, grafologo, astrologo e altre sciocchezze." *La Follia di New York*, 15 January 1946.

———. In "'Farfariello': Due 'macchiette coloniali.'" Ed. Francesco Durante. *Ácoma* 6, no. 16 (spring 1999).

Moro Gabelli, Maria. "Italo-Americani." *Il Carroccio* 8, no. 6 (December 1918).

Pallavicini, Paolo. *L'Amante delle tre croci, Seguito a Per le vie del mondo*. San Francisco: L'Italia Press Company, 1923.

———. *La carezza divina*. Milan: Sonzogno, 1939.

———. *La Guerra Italo-Austriaca (1915–1919)*. New York: Società Libraria Italiana, 1919.

———. *Nix, il figlio dell'Austriaco*. New York: Società Libraria Italiana—Italian Book Company, 1920.

———. *Per le vie del mondo*. Milan: Sonzogno, 1933.

———. *Tutto il dolore, tutto l'amore*. San Francisco: L'Italia Press Company, 1926 [Italian edition: Milan: Sonzogno, 1937].

———. *Il ventaglio di Aquileia*. Florence: Salani, 1917.

Pellegrino, Menotti. *I misteri di New York*. New York: Tipografia Italiana U. De Luca & Benedetti, 1903.

———. *I tre cavalieri di Trinacria*. New York: n.p., 1929.

Perotti, Ant. "Verso l'ideale. Scene vissute dall'emigrante italiano in America." *La Parola del Popolo*, 29 April–29 July 1922.

"Il Piccolo Genovese." *L'Eco d'Italia*, 14 May 1869. Now in *Italoamericana. Storia e letteratura degli italiani negli Stati Uniti 1776–1880*, ed. Francesco Durante, 1:442–46. Milan: Mondadori, 2001.

Seneca, Pasquale. *Il Presidente Scoppetta ovvero La Società della Madonna della Pace (dalla sua fondazione al suo scioglimento)*. Philadelphia: Artcraft Printing Company, 1927.

Stanco, Italo. "L'Amica del Kaiser." *La Follia di New York*, 22 December 1918–21 December 1919.

——— [J. Cansado]. "Lady Ryton, il diavolo biondo." *La Follia di New York*?–7 June 1914 [later in book form with the title *Il diavolo biondo*. New York: Nicoletti Bros. Press, Inc., 1916].

——— "Il nemico del bene." *La Follia di New York*, 5 July 1914–8 August 1915.

———. [Ettore Moffa, pseud.]. *La penna italiana. Paralipòmeni*. Naples: Stabilimento Tipografico degli Editori Fratelli Tornese, 1902.

———. "Le piovre di New York." *Corriere d'America* 1925?–1926? [later in *La Follia di New York*, 1 October 1944–1 November 1949].

——— [J. Cansado, pseud.]. "Il Re della Pampa." *La Follia di New York*, 24 September 1911–?

———. "Reginetta di fuoco." *Corriere d'America* 1931–? [later with the title *La figlia del dittatore* in *La Follia di New York,* 15 November 1949–1 March 1953].

——— "I rettili d'oro." *La Follia di New York,* 26 September 1915–9 December 1917 [later in *Divagando,* 2 July 1952–22 July 1953].

———. "Sull'oceano." *La Follia di New York,* 23 December 1917–3 November 1918.

Tresca, Carlo. *L'attentato a Mussolini ovvero Il segreto di Pulcinella.* New York: Casa Editrice "Il Martello," [1922? 1925?].

———. "Autobiography." Special Collections, New York Public Library.

———. *Il Vendicatore.* New York: Casa Editrice "Il Martello", n.d.

Tusiani, Joseph. *La parola antica. Autobiografia di un italo-americano (Parte III).* Fasano (Brindisi): Schena, 1992.

———. *La parola difficile. Autobiografia di un italo-americano.* Fasano (Brindisi): Schena, 1988.

———. *La parola nuova. Autobiografia di un italo-americano (Parte II).* Fasano (Brindisi): Schena, 1991.

Vacirca, Clara. *Cupido fra le Camicie Nere.* New York: La Strada Publishing Co., 1938.

Vacirca, Vincenzo. "Il rogo." *Il Solco,* 1, no. 1 (January 1927)–2, no. 5 (May 1928).

Valentini, Ernesto. *Il ricatto. Eccola, la giustizia! Rivelazioni e documenti.* Turin: Tipografia Silvestrelli & Cappelletto, 1924.

Ventura, Luigi Donato. *Biographical Reminiscences.* In *Memoirs and Artistic Studies,* ed. Adelaide Ristori. New York: Doubleday, Page & Company, 1907.

———. *Peppino.* In *The Multilingual Anthology of American Literature: A Reader of Original Texts with English Translations,* ed. Marc Shell and Werner Sollors. New York: New York University Press, 2000.

———. "Una prefazione americana al 'Testa' di P. Mantegazza." *Cuore e Critica* 2, no. 10 (September 1888).

———. "Le scrittrici italiane giudicate in America." *Cuore e Critica* 2, no. 14 (November 1888).

——— with S. Shevitch. *Misfits and Remnants.* Boston: Ticknor and Company, 1886.

## Works of Critical Reference

Accardi, Joseph J. "Giovanni De Rosalia: Playwright, Poet and 'Nofrio.'" *Italian Americana* 19, no. 2 (summer 2001).

Aleandri, Emelise. "A History of Italian-American Theatre: 1900 to 1905." Ph.D. diss. New York: City University of New York, 1983.

Basile Green, Rose. *The Italian-American Novel: A Document of the Interaction of Two Cultures.* Rutherford, N.J.: Fairleigh Dickinson University Press, 1974.

Bernabei, Franca. "Little Italy's Eugène Sue: The Novels of Bernardino Ciambelli." In *Adjusting Sites: New Essays in Italian American Studies,* ed. William Boelhower and Rocco Pallone. Vol. 16 of Forum Italicum-Filibrary Series. Stony Brook, N.Y.: Forum Italicum Publishing, 1999.

Bernardy, Amy A. *America vissuta.* Turin: Fratelli Bocca, 1911.

———. *Italia randagia attraverso gli Stati Uniti.* Turin: Fratelli Bocca, 1913.

Bertellini, Giorgio. "'Paradise Inhabited by Devils': Southern Italians, Modernity, and Cinema, from Italy to New York, up to 1920." Ph.D. diss., New York University, 2001.

BIBLIOGRAPHY

Boelhower, William. *Immigrant Autobiography in the United States (Four Versions of the Italian American Self)*. Verona: Essedue, 1982.

Bosi, Alfredo. *Cinquant'anni di vita italiana in America*. New York: Bagnasco Press, 1921.

Bruno, Giuliana. *Streetwalking on a Ruined Map: Cultural Theory and the City Films of Elvira Notari*. Princeton, N.J.: Princeton University Press, 1993.

Cacioppo, Marina. "Italian American Crime-Fiction from the 1890s to the 1930s: Bernardino Ciambelli, Prosper Buranelli and Louis Forgione." In *Holding Their Own Perspectives on the Multi-Ethnic Literatures of the United States*, ed. Dorothea Fischer-Hornung and Heike Raphael-Hernandez. Tübingen: Stauffenberg, 2000.

———. "'Se i marciapiedi di questa strada potessero parlare.' Space, Class, and Identity in Three Italian-American Autobiographies." In *Adjusting Sites. New Essays in Italian American Studies*. Eds. William Boelhower and Rocco Pallone. *Forum Italicum-Filibrary Series*, 16, 1999.

Cagidemetrio, Alide. *Peppino. 1885. Luigi Donato Ventura. French*. In *The Multilingual Anthology of American Literature: A Reader of Original Texts with English Translations*, ed. Marc Shell and Werner Sollors. New York: New York University Press, 2000.

Cannistraro, Philip V. *Blackshirts in Little Italy: Italian Americans and Fascism, 1921– 1929*. West Lafayette, Ind.: Bordighera Press, 1999.

Carr, John Foster. *Immigrant and Library: Italian Helps with List of Selected Books*. New York: Immigrant Education Society, 1914 [later in *Italians in the United States: A Repository of Rare Tracts and Miscellanea*. New York: Arno Press, 1975].

Cartosio, Bruno. *Lavoratori negli Stati Uniti. Storia e culture politiche dalla schiavitù all'I.W.W.* Milan: Arcipelago Edizioni, 1989.

Cecchi, Emilio. "Pane al pane e vino al vino." *Corriere della Sera*, 30 March 1941 [later in *Scrittori inglesi e americani*, Vol. 2. Milan: il Saggiatore, 1968].

Corsi, Edward. "'Homeward to America.'" *La Follia di New York*, 27 April 1941.

Deschamps, Bénédicte. *La letteratura d'appendice nei periodici italo-americani (1910– 1935)*. In *Il sogno italo-americano. Realtà e immaginario dell'emigrazione negli Stati Uniti*, ed. Sebastiano Martelli. Naples: Cuen, 1998.

———. *De la presse "coloniale" à la presse italo-américaine, le parcours de six périodiques italiens aux États-Unis (1910–1935)*. Thèse de doctorat. Paris: Université Paris VII— U.F.R. d'Études Anglophones, 1996.

Franzina, Emilio. *Dall'Arcadia in America. Attività letteraria ed emigrazione transoceanica in Italia (1850–1940)*. Turin: Edizioni della Fondazione Giovanni Agnelli, 1996.

———. *Gli italiani al Nuovo Mondo. L'emigrazione italiana in America, 1492–1942*. Milan: Mondadori, 1995.

Gardaphé, Fred L. *The Italian-American Writer: An Essay and an Annotated Checklist*. New York: Forkroads/Spencertown, 1995.

———. *Italian Signs, American Streets: The Evolution of Italian American Narrative*. Durham: Duke University Press, 1996.

Gardaphé, Fred, L., and James J. Periconi. *The Italian American Writers Association Bibliography of the Italian American Book*. Mount Vernon, N.Y.: Shea & Haarmann Publishing Company, 2000.

Haller, Hermann W. *Una lingua perduta e ritrovata. L'italiano degli italo-americani*. Scandicci (Florence): La Nuova Italia, 1993.

———. *Verso un nuovo italiano. L'esperienza linguistica dell'emigrazione negli Stati Uniti*. In *Il sogno italo-americano. Realtà e immaginario dell'emigrazione negli Stati Uniti*, ed. Sebastiano Martelli. Naples: Cuen, 1998.

Ingargiola, Rosario. "'Gente lontana' di Corrado Altavilla." *La Follia di New York*, 11 December 1938.

LaGumina, Salvatore J. *The Immigrants Speak: Italian Americans Tell Their Story*. New York: Center for Migration Studies, 1979.

Lentricchia, Frank. "Luigi Ventura and the Origins of Italian-American Fiction." *Italian Americana* 1, no. 2 (spring 1975).

Luconi, Stefano. *La "diplomazia parallela." Il regime fascista e la mobilitazione politica degli italo-americani*. Milan: Franco Angeli, 2000.

———. "Not Only 'A Tavola': Radio Broadcasting and Patterns of Ethnic Consumption among Italian Americans in the Interwar Years." In *A Tavola: Food, Tradition and Community among Italian Americans*, ed. Edvige Giunta and Samuel J. Patti. Staten Island, N.Y.: American Italian Historical Association, 1998.

Maffi, Mario. *Nel mosaico della città. Differenze etniche e nuove culture in un quartiere di New York*. Milan: Feltrinelli, 1992.

———. "The Strange Case of Luigi Donato Ventura's *Peppino:* Some Speculations on the Beginnings of Italian-American Fiction." In *Multilingual America: Transnationalism, Ethnicity, and the Languages of American Literature*, ed. Werner Sollors. New York: New York University Press, 1998.

"La morte improvvisa del Collega Cav. B. Ciambelli." *Il Progresso Italo-Americano*, 3 July 1931.

Peragallo, Olga. *Italian-American Authors and Their Contribution to American Literature*. Ed. Anita Peragallo. New York: S.F. Vanni, 1949.

Pernicone, Nunzio. "Luigi Galleani and Italian Anarchist Terrorism in the United States." *Studi Emigrazione* 30, no. 111 (September 1993).

Porcari, Serafino. "Italian American Fiction: A Selected Bibliography of Novels, Short Stories and Juvenile Fiction, 1950–1993." *Italian Americana* 12, no. 1 (fall/winter 1993).

Prezzolini, Giuseppe. *I trapiantati*. Milan: Longanesi, 1963.

Russo, Pietro. *Catalogo collettivo della stampa periodica italo americana (1836–1980)*. Rome: Centro Studi Emigrazione, 1983.

———. "La stampa periodica italo-americana." In *Gli italiani negli Stati Uniti. L'emigrazione e l'opera degli italiani negli Stati Uniti d'America. Atti del III Symposium di Studi Americani. Firenze, 27–29 Maggio 1969*. Florence: Istituto di Studi Americani— Università degli Studi di Firenze, 1972.

Seabrook, William. *These Foreigners*. New York: Harcourt, Brace and Company, 1938.

Sgubbi, Carlotta. [Undersigned articles from the catalogue] *Le figure del delitto. Il libro poliziesco in Italia dalle origini a oggi*. Ed. Renzo Cremante. Bologna: Grafis, 1989.

Sweet, May M. *Italian Books for American Libraries: A Supplement to The Italian Immigrant and His Reading*. Chicago: American Library Association, 1932.

———. *The Italian Immigrant and His Reading*. Chicago: American Library Association, 1925.

Traldi, Alberto. "La tematica dell'emigrazione nella narrativa italo-americana." *Comunità* 30 (August 1976).

Vecoli, Rudolph. "Alberico Molinari. Il medico dei poveri." *La Parola del Popolo* 29, no. 147 (November–December 1978).

Vezzosi, Elisabetta. *Carlo Tresca tra mito e realtà a 50 anni dalla morte*. In *Carlo Tresca. Vita e morte di un anarchico italiano in America*, ed. Italia Gualtieri. Chieti-Villamagna: Tinari, 1999.

———. *Il socialismo indifferente. Immigrati italiani e Socialist Party negli Stati Uniti del primo Novecento.* Rome: Edizioni Lavoro, 1991.

Zappulla, Giuseppe. "La coltura, la radio e la lingua italiana." *Il Carroccio* 37, no. 2 (February 1935).

———. "Panorama degl'italiani d'America." Unpublished manuscript dated 1966, deposited at the Center for Migration Studies, Staten Island, N.Y.

## CHAPTER 2.

### Works by Ezio Taddei

*Alberi e casolari.* New York: Edizioni in esilio, 1943.

*C'è posta per voi, Mr. Brown!* Rome: Edizioni di Cultura Sociale, 1953.

*La fabbrica parla.* Milan: Milano-Sera Editrice, 1950.

*Ho rinunciato alla libertà.* Milan: Le edizioni sociali, 1950.

"Michele Esposito." *Raccontanovelle* 2, nos. 8/9 (1955).

*Parole collettive.* New York: S.E.A., 1941 [American edition, *Hard as Stone.* Trans. Frances Keene. New York: New Writers, 1942].

*Il pino e la rufola.* New York: Edizioni in esilio, 1944 [American edition, *The Pine Tree and the Mole.* Trans. Samuel Putnam. New York: Dial Press, 1945; Italian edition, Rome: De Luigi, 1946].

*Le porte dell'inferno.* Rome: Mengarelli, n.d. [circa 1945].

"'Potente.'" *Il secondo Risorgimento d'Italia.* N.p.: Centro Editoriale d'Iniziativa, 1955.

*Il quinto Vangelo.* Rome: Mengarelli, 1950 [later Vicenza: La Locusta, 1970].

*Rotaia.* Turin: Einaudi, 1946 [The contemporary American edition in Italian could not be found; American edition in English, *The Sowing of the Seed.* Trans. Samuel Putnam. New York: Dial Press, 1946].

*L'uomo che cammina.* New York: Edizioni "L'Esule," 1940.

#### JOURNALISM AND PAMPHLETS

In *L'Adunata dei Refrattari* (Newark, N.J.), Taddei signed 19 pieces (articles and stories), from 8 January (*I due regimi*) to 17 September 1938 (*L'ebreo che cammina*).

"I crimini del titismo. Vittorio Poccecai. (Biografia d'un evaso dall'inferno di Tito)." *Il Lavoratore* (Trieste) [special issue], n.s., 8, no. 1048 (1952).

"De Gasperi consiglia gli italiani ad emigrare." *Propaganda* [Supplement to no. 47]. Rome: Ti.Co., n.d. [after October 1952].

*Hanno assassinato i Rosenberg!* N.p., 1953.

"Salviamo i Rosenberg." *Il Seme* 5, supplement to no. 1. Ed. Comitato italiano per la salvezza dei Rosenberg. Rome: n.d. [after November 1952].

*The Tresca Case.* New York: Allied Printing, 1943.

#### TEXT OF THE *INNO DELLE BARRICATE*

*E verrà il dì che innalzerem le barricate. (Inno di giovani libertari).* Music-CD *Quella sera a Milano era caldo . . . Antologia della canzone anarchica in Italia 2.* Modena: Ala

Bianca—Bella Ciao, 1996 [Text and notes to Taddei's song edited by Cesare Bermani, 1978].

## Works of Critical Reference

Bartolini, Ezio. "Ricordo di Ezio Taddei." *Il Paese,* 19 June 1956.

Belfiore, Umbrella. "Ricordo di Ezio Taddei." *La Parola del Popolo* 6, no. 83 (April–May 1967).

Bettini, Leonardo. *Bibliografia dell'anarchismo, volume I, tomo 2, periodici e numeri unici anarchici in lingua italiana pubblicati all'estero (1872–1971).* Florence: cp editrice, 1976.

"È morto Ezio Taddei." *L'Unità,* 17 May 1956.

"Ezio Taddei." *Il Dizionario degli italiani illustri e oscuri (Dal 1900 ad oggi). Il Borghese* 3, no. 21 (January 1960).

Franzina, Emilio. *Dall'Arcadia in America. Attività letteraria ed emigrazione transoceanica in Italia (1850–1940).* Turin: Edizioni della Fondazione Giovanni Agnelli, 1996.

Fusco, Giancarlo. *Gli indesiderabili.* Milan: Longanesi, 1962.

Gallagher, Dorothy. *All the Right Enemies: The Life and Murder of Carlo Tresca.* New Brunswick, N.J.: Rutgers University Press, 1988.

Javarone, Domenico. *Vita di scrittore (Ezio Taddei).* Rome: Macchia, 1958.

Lajolo, Davide. "Un libro su Taddei." *L'Unità,* 11 November 1958.

Montana, Vanni B. *Amarostico. Testimonianze euro-americane.* Livorno: Bastogi, 1976.

Peirce, Guglielmo. "Addio ad Ezio." *Il Borghese,* 26 and 28 June 1956.

## CHAPTER 4.

### *Primary Sources and Samples of Other Noteworthy Texts*

Bartoletti, Efrem. [Etrusco, pseud.]. ". . . ascoltando la radio." *Il Proletario,* 10 February 1940.

——— [Etrusco, pseud.]. "Il carme a Giacomo Leopardi. (Un'eco lontana del I centenario di sua morte)." *Il Proletario,* 22 April 1939.

———. *Documenti e poesie,* CD-ROM, privately edited and distributed by Romano Guerra. Bologna, 1999.

———. *Un'escursione alla caverna di Monte Cucco.* Fabriano: Premiata Tipografia Economica, 1924.

———. *Evocazioni e ricordi.* Bergamo: La Nuova Italia Letteraria, 1959.

——— *Nostalgie proletarie. Raccolta di canti poetici e di inni rivoluzionari di Efrem Bartoletti.* Brooklyn, N.Y.: Libreria Editrice dei Lavoratori Industriali del Mondo (Italian I.W.W. Publishing Bureau), 1919.

———. *Poesie. Alla scoperta delle nostre radici storiche.* Città di Castello: Alfagrafica-Comune di Costacciaro, 2001.

———. *Riflessioni poetiche.* Milan: Gastaldi, 1955.

——— [Etrusco, pseud.]. "Venticinque Luglio." *Il Proletario,* 25 August 1943.

Bertelli, Giuseppe. *Rime d'esilio—Il Bacio.* Chicago: Silvestri Printing Co., 1940.

Borgianini, Alfredo. *Sonetti e poesie romanesche.* Trenton, N.J.: White Eagle Printing Co., 1948.

Cordiferro, Riccardo. *Brindisi ed Augurii per ogni occasione.* New York: Società Libraria Italiana, 1917.

———. *Canzone d'a guerra: versi napoletani.* New York: Società Libraria Italiana, 1917.

———. *Gabriele D'Annunzio: nella vita e nell'arte.* New York: Cocce Bros., 1938.

———. *Gli stornelli della guerra.* New York: Società Libraria Italiana, 1917.

———. *Ode alla Calabria.* Buenos Aires: La Voce dei Calabresi, 1933.

———. *Poesie scelte.* Ed. Guido Massarelli. Campobasso: Pungolo Verde, 1967.

———. *Singhiozzi e sogghigni.* New York: L'Araldo Italiano, 1910.

Daly, Thomas Augustine. *Carmina.* New York: John Lane, 1914.

Giovannitti, Arturo. "Ammutiniamoci!" *Vita* (New York) 1, no. 2 (15 September 1915).

———. *The Collected Poems of Arturo Giovannitti.* Chicago: E. Clemente & Sons, 1962.

———. *Come era nel principio. (Tenebre rosse).* Brooklyn, N.Y.: Libreria Editrice dei Lavoratori Industriali del Mondo—Italian I.W.W. Publishing Bureau, 1918.

———. "Natale 1914." *La Parola del Popolo,* November/December 1978.

———. *Parole e sangue.* New York: The Labor Press, 1938.

———. *Quando canta il gallo.* Chicago: E. Clemente & Sons, 1957.

Mennella, Federico. *Canzoni de l'ora.* New York: Edizioni Sirena, 1945.

———. *Napule d'aiere.* New York: Cocce Press, 1944.

———. *Partenopea. Poesie napoletane.* Napoli: Ciro Russo, n.d. [after 1945].

———. *Rapsodia napoletana.* New York: Cocce Press, 1944.

Righi, Simplicio. "I sonetti di Manhattan." *Il Carroccio* 2 (February 1924).

——— [Rosina Vieni, pseud.]. "Vennero i bricchellieri. . . ." *Zarathustra* [1926]. In *The American Language: An Inquiry into the Development of English in the United States.* ed. Henry Louis Mencken. New York: Knopf, 1947.

Ruotolo, Onorio. *Accordi e dissonanze.* Milan: Convivio Letterario, 1958.

Sisca, Francesco. *Lu ciucciu.* Ed. Riccardo Cordiferro. Cosenza: Pellegrini, 1967.

Zappulla, Giuseppe. *Vette ed abissi. Liriche e poemi (1926–1936).* New York: V. Vecchioni Printing Co., 1936.

## Works of Critical Reference

Alfonsi, Ferdinando. *Dictionary of Italian-American Poets.* New York: Peter Lang, 1989.

———. *Poeti Italo-Americani. Italo-American Poets. Antologia bilingue—A Bilingual Anthology.* Catanzaro: Carello, 1985.

Cavaioli, Frank. "Ruotolo." *The Italian American Experience: An Encyclopedia.* Ed. Salvatore J. LaGumina, Frank J. Cavaioli, Salvatore Primeggia, and Joseph A. Varacalli. New York: Garland Publishing, Inc., 2000.

Cocchi, Raffaele. "In Search of Italian-American Poetry in the USA." *In Their Own Words* 2, no. 1 (winter 1984).

———. "Selected Bibliography of Italian American Poetry." *Italian Americana* 10, no. 2 (spring/summer 1992).

Durante, Francesco. *I poeti del "sottobosco" italo-americano.* In *Scritti di varia umanità in memoria di Benito Iezzi,* ed. Mario Capasso and Enzo Puglia. Sorrento (Naples): Franco Di Mauro, 1994.

Fichera, Filippo. *Letteratura italoamericana.* Milan: Convivio Letterario, 1958.

Fontanella, Luigi. "Poeti emigrati ed emigranti poeti negli Stati Uniti." In *Il sogno italo-americano. Realtà e immaginario dell'emigrazione negli Stati Uniti*, ed. Sebastiano Martelli. Naples: Cuen, 1998.

Galleani, Luigi. *Figure e Figuri*. Newark, N.J.: Biblioteca de L'Adunata dei Refrattari, 1930.

Gardaphé, Fred, and James J. Periconi. *The Italian American Writers Association Bibliography of the Italian American Book*. Mount Vernon, N.Y.: Shea & Haarmann Publishing Company, 2000.

Gioia, Dana. *What Is Italian American Poetry?* In *Beyond* The Godfather: *Italian American Writers on the Real Italian American Experience*, ed. A. Kenneth Ciongoli and Jay Parini. Hanover, N.H.: University Press of New England, 1997.

Marazzi, Martino. "Introduzione." In *Poesie. Alla scoperta delle nostre radici storiche* by Efrem Bartoletti. Città di Castello: Alfagrafica-Comune di Costacciaro, 2001.

———. "Poesia degli italoamericani." *Poesia* 14, nos. 149, 151, 154 (April, June, October 2001).

Pasolini, Pier Paolo. *La poesia dialettale del Novecento*, in *Passione e ideologia (1948–1958)*. In *Saggi sulla letteratura e sull'arte. Tomo primo*, ed. Walter Siti and Silvia De Laude. Milan: Mondadori, 1999.

Peragallo, Olga. *Italian-American Authors and Their Contribution to American Literature*. Ed. Anita Peragallo. New York: S.F. Vanni, 1949.

Prezzolini, Giuseppe. *I trapiantati*. Milan: Longanesi, 1963.

Pucelli, Rodolfo. ed. *Anthology of Italian and Italo-American Poetry*. Boston: Bruce Humphries, 1955.

——— "Poeti Americani d'Origine Italiana." *La Follia di New York*, 15 November 1944–15 January 1946.

———. "Il Tallone di Ferro. Vasto Poema di un Novantenne." *La Follia di New York*, 15 February 1946.

Sartarelli, Stephen. "Italian American Poets: A Chronological Survey." In *The Italian American Heritage: A Companion to Literature and Arts*, ed. Pellegrino D'Acierno. New York: Garland Publishing, Inc., 1999.

Vecoli, Rudolph. "Fare la Merica: sogno o incubo?" In *Il sogno italo-americano. Realtà e immaginario dell'emigrazione negli Stati Uniti*, ed. Sebastiano Martelli. Naples: Cuen, 1998.

Vezzosi, Elisabetta. *Il socialismo indifferente. Immigrati italiani e Socialist Party negli Stati Uniti del primo Novecento*. Rome: Edizioni Lavoro, 1991.

Zappulla, Giuseppe. *Panorama degl'italiani d'America*. Unpublished manuscript dated 1966, deposited at the Center for Migration Studies, Staten Island, N.Y.

## ON CORDIFERRO

Aleandri, Emelise. "Cordiferro." In *The Italian American Experience: An Encyclopedia*, ed. Salvatore J. LaGumina, Frank J. Cavaioli, Salvatore Primeggia, and Joseph A. Varacalli. New York: Garland Publishing, Inc., 2000.

———. "Italian-American Theatre." In *Il sogno italo-americano. Realtà e immaginario dell'emigrazione negli Stati Uniti*, ed. Sebastiano Martelli. Naples: Cuen, 1998.

———. "Riccardo Cordiferro and the Origins of La Follia." *Italian Americana* 15, no. 1 (winter 1997).

## ON GIOVANNITTI

Cavaioli, Frank, and Jerre Mangione. "Giovannitti." In *The Italian American Experience: An Encyclopedia*, ed. Salvatore J. LaGumina, Frank J. Cavaioli, Salvatore Primeggia, and Joseph A. Varacalli. New York: Garland Publishing, Inc., 2000.

D'Attilio, Robert. "Arturo Giovannitti." In *The American Radical*, ed. Mary Jo Buhle, Paul Buhle, and Harvey J. Kaye. New York: Routledge, 1994.

De Ciampis, Mario. "Arturo M. Giovannitti." *Controcorrente* (Boston, Mass.) 16, nos. 4–5, n.s. 16–17 (January–February and March–April 1960).

Lalli, Renato. *Arturo Giovannitti. Poesia, cristianesimo e socialismo tra le lotte operaie del primo Novecento americano.* Campobasso: Rufus, 1981.

Pernicone, Nunzio. "Arturo Giovannitti's 'Son of the Abyss' and the Westmoreland Strike of 1910–1911." *Italian Americana* 17, no. 2 (summer 1999).

Prezzolini, Giuseppe. "Elogio di un 'trapiantato' molisano bardo della libertà negli Stati Uniti." *Il Tempo*, 10 May 1963.

Tedeschini Lalli, Biancamaria. "La metapoesia di Arturo Giovannitti." *Letterature d'America—Tuttamerica* 2, nos. 9–10 (autumn 1981).

Tusiani, Joseph. "La poesia di Arturo Giovannitti." *La Parola del Popolo* (November/December 1978).

Zappulla, Giuseppe. "Arturo Giovannitti." *Italamerican* (February–May 1960).

## CHAPTER 5.

### Works Cited

Bertelli, Lidio. "Cultura di 'élite' e cultura di massa nell'emigrazione italiana negli Stati Uniti." In *Gli italiani negli Stati Uniti. L'emigrazione e l'opera degli italiani negli Stati Uniti d'America. Atti del III Symposium di Studi Americani. Firenze, 27–29 Maggio 1969.* Florence: Istituto di Studi Americani—Università degli Studi di Firenze, 1972.

Castronovo, Valerio. *La stampa italiana dall'unità al fascismo.* Rome: Laterza, 1973.

Cianfarra, Camillo. *Il diario di un emigrato.* New York: Tipografia dell'Araldo Italiano, 1904.

———. "La manodopera negra. Nel concetto degli Industriali del Sud degli Stati Uniti." *Gli Italiani e l'America—La Rassegna Nord Americana* 11, vol. 16, no. 5 (November 1906).

———. *Dell'unica protezione possibile al Nord-America.* Rome: Tipografia dell'Unione Cooperativa Editrice, 1909.

"Come nacque il 'Progresso.' " *Per la Mostra del Lavoro degl'Italiani all'Estero.* Turin: Esposizione Internazionale di Torino pel Cinquantenario dell'Unità Nazionale, 1911.

Di Palma Castiglione, Guglielmo. "Relazione sull'attività spiegata dall'Ufficio del lavoro per gli immigranti italiani in New York durante l'anno 1908." *Bollettino dell'Emigrazione* 8 (1909).

Durante, Francesco. *Italoamericana. Storia e letteratura degli italiani negli Stati Uniti 1776–1880.* Vol. 1. Milan: Mondadori, 2001.

Fogg Meade, Emily. "The Italian on the Land: A Study in Immigration." *Bulletin of the Bureau of Labor* 70 (May 1907).

Gil. "L'Ufficio Regionale dell'Italica Gens in New Orleans (Louisiana—Stati Uniti N.A.)." *Italica Gens* 5, nos. 1–2 (January–February 1914).

Maffi, Mario. "The Strange Case of Luigi Donato Ventura's *Peppino:* Some Speculations on the Beginnings of Italian-American Fiction." In *Multilingual America: Transnationalism, Ethnicity, and the Languages of American Literature,* ed. Werner Sollors. New York: New York University Press, 1998.

Marraro, Howard R. *Relazioni fra l'Italia e gli Stati Uniti.* Rome: Edizioni dell'Ateneo, 1954.

Mastro-Valerio. "Distribution of Certain Nationalities: A. Italians." *Reports of the Industrial Commission on Immigration and on Education.* Vol. 15. [57th Cong., 1st sess., House of Representatives, Doc. 184.] Washington, D.C.: Government Printing Office, 1901.

Mayor des Planches, E. *Attraverso gli Stati Uniti. Per l'emigrazione italiana.* Turin: Unione Tipografico-Editrice Torinese, 1913.

Mazzariol, Francesca. "La Capanna dello Zio Tom e la stampa italiana." *Il bianco e il nero* 2, no. 2 (1998).

Papa, Dario, and Ferdinando Fontana. *New-York.* Milan: Giuseppe Galli, 1884.

Prezzolini, Giuseppe. "Bianchi e negri: un'analisi del prof. Prezzolini." *Post-Gazette* (Boston), 1 September 1967.

———. *I trapiantati.* Milan: Longanesi, 1963.

Rossati, Guido. "La colonizzazione negli Stati di Mississippi, Louisiana ed Alabama." *Bollettino dell'Emigrazione* 14 (1904).

———. "Organizzazione ed opera dell'Ufficio di collocamento al lavoro in Nuova York per gli immigranti italiani." *Bollettino dell'Emigrazione* 3 (1907).

Rossi, Adolfo. "Per la tutela degli Italiani negli Stati Uniti (Lettere dell'Ispettore cav. Adolfo Rossi, scritte al R. Commissariato dell'emigrazione nel corso di una sua missione negli Stati Uniti dell'America del Nord)." *Bollettino dell'Emigrazione* 16 (1904).

Russo, Pietro. "La stampa periodica italo-americana." In *Gli italiani negli Stati Uniti. L'emigrazione e l'opera degli italiani negli Stati Uniti d'America. Atti del III Symposium di Studi Americani. Firenze, 27–29 Maggio 1969.* Florence: Istituto di Studi Americani—Università degli Studi di Firenze, 1972.

Testi, Arnaldo. "L'immagine degli Stati Uniti nella stampa socialista italiana (1886–1914)." In *Italia e America dal Settecento all'età dell'imperialismo,* eds. Giorgio Spini et al. Marsilio, 1976.

Ventura, Luigi Donato. "I Negri d'America." *Cuore e Critica* 3, no. 3 (20 February 1889).

———. "Peppino." In *Misfits and Remnants.* Boston: Ticknor and Company, 1886.

## CHAPTER 7.

*Primary Sources*

Arbasino, Alberto. *Fratelli d'Italia.* Milan: Adelphi, 1993.

———. *Grazie per le magnifiche rose.* Milan: Feltrinelli, 1965.

———. *Off-off.* Milan: Feltrinelli, 1968.

Barzini jr., Luigi. *Memories of Mistresses: Reflections from a Life.* New York: Collier-Macmillan, 1986.

334                  BIBLIOGRAPHY

———. *Nuova York.* Milan: Agnelli, 1931.

———. *O America!* Milan: Mondadori, 1978.

Bianchini, Angela. *Lungo equinozio.* Milan: Lerici, 1962.

Bonaviri, Giuseppe. *Silvinia.* Milan: Mondadori, 1997.

Borgese, Giuseppe Antonio. *Atlante americano.* Modena: Guanda, 1936.

Brolli, Daniele. *Chemical USA. Il viaggiatore assente.* Milan: Rizzoli, 2002.

Buzzolan, Dario. *Dall'altra parte degli occhi.* Milan: Mursia, 1999.

Calvino, Italo. *Saggi 1945–1985. Tomo secondo.* Ed. Mario Barenghi. Milan: Mondadori, 1995.

Campailla, Sergio. "Little Italy." In *Il sogno italo-americano. Realtà e immaginario dell'emigrazione negli Stati Uniti,* ed. Sebastiano Martelli. Naples: Cuen, 1998.

———. *Romanzo americano.* Milan: Rusconi, 1994.

Campo, Rossana. *L'attore americano.* Milan: Feltrinelli, 1997.

Cancogni, Manlio. *Lettere a Manhattan.* Rome: Fazi, 1997.

Cappelli, Gaetano. *Parenti lontani.* Milan: Mondadori, 2000.

Colombo, Furio. *Da Kennedy a Watergate.* Turin: SEI, 1974.

———. "Uno psichiatra a Little Italy." *La Repubblica* (5 August 1999).

De Carlo, Andrea. *Treno di panna.* Turin: Einaudi, 1981 [American edition: *The Cream Train.* Berkeley, Calif.: Olive Press, 1987].

*Diario* 6, no. 44 (2–8 November 2001).

Di Biasio, Rodolfo. *I quattro camminanti. Stampa d'epoca.* Florence: Sansoni, 1991.

Eco, Umberto. *Dalla periferia dell'Impero.* Milan: Bompiani, 1977.

Ferrarotti, Franco. *I grattacieli non hanno foglie.* Rome-Bari: Laterza, 1991.

Flaiano, Ennio. *Melampus.* Milan: Rizzoli, 1974.

*Il Foglio,* 10 November 2001.

Fontana, Pia. *Spokane.* Venice: Marsilio, 1988.

Grasso, Silvana. *Ninna nanna del lupo.* Turin: Einaudi, 1995.

Iannacce, Carmine Biagio. *La scoperta dell'America. Un'autobiografia—The Discovery of America: An Autobiography.* Trans. William Boelhower. West Lafayette, Ind.: Bordighera Press, 2000.

Lagorio, Gina. *L'arcadia americana.* Milan: Rizzoli, 1999.

Maffi, Mario. *New York. L'isola delle colline.* Milan: il Saggiatore, 1995.

———. *Sotto le torri di Manhattan. Mappe Nomi Storie Luoghi.* Milan: Rizzoli, 1998.

Mariani, Lucio. "Scacco matto." In *Poesia* 14 (special issue, *New York Anthology*), no. 155 (November 2001).

Martini, Fausto Maria. *Si sbarca a New York.* Milan: Mondadori, 1930 [new edition edited by Giuseppe Farinelli. Milan: Istituto di Propaganda Libraria, n.d.].

Maurino, Ferdinando. *Dal cavo delle mani. Pagine di vita attuale in Italia e in America.* Cosenza: Pellegrini, 1968.

Melega, Gianluigi. *Tempo lungo. III. Eravamo come piante.* Milan: Baldini & Castoldi, 1994.

Milano, Paolo. *Note in margine a una vita assente.* Ed. Laura Gonsalez. Milan: Adelphi, 1991.

———. *Racconto newyorchese.* Ed. Laura Gonsalez. Ripatransone, Ascoli Piceno: Sestante, 1993.

Morselli, Guido. *Il comunista*. Milan: Adelphi, 1976.

Parise, Goffredo. *Odore d'America*. Milan: Mondadori, 1990.

Piovene, Guido. *De America*. Milan: Garzanti, 1953.

Prezzolini, Giuseppe. *I trapiantati*. Milan: Longanesi, 1963.

———. *Tutta l'America*. Florence: Vallecchi, 1958.

Quarantotti Gambini, Pier Antonio. *Neve a Manhattan*. Ed. Raffaele Manica. Rome: Fazi, 1998.

Ravera, Lidia. *Viaggiare*. In *Un lungo inverno fiorito e altre storie*. Milan: La Tartaruga, 2001.

Rigoni Stern, Mario. *Uomini, boschi e api*. Turin: Einaudi, 1980.

———. "Vecchia America." In *Il bosco degli urogalli*. Turin: Einaudi, 1974.

Rimanelli, Giose. *Biglietto di terza*. Milan: Mondadori, 1958.

———. *Peccato originale*. Milan: Mondadori, 1954.

———. *La stanza grande*. Cava dei Tirreni: Avagliano, 1996 [first edition as *Una posizione sociale*. Florence: Vallecchi, 1959].

Rosselli, Aldo. *La mia America e la tua*. Rome: Theoria, 1995.

Ruggiero, Amerigo. *Italiani in America*. Milan: Treves, 1937.

Settembrini, Luigi. *A New York non si muore di vecchiaia. Quattro storie americane*. Milan: Rizzoli, 1990.

Soldati, Mario. *Addio diletta Amelia*. Milan: Mondadori, 1979.

———. *America primo amore*. 1935. Reprint, Milan: Mondadori, 1981.

Tresca, Carlo. "Autobiography." Special Collections, New York Public Library.

## Works of Critical Reference

Bertellini, Giorgio. "New York City and the Representation of Italian Americans in the Cinema." In *The Italians of New York: Five Centuries of Struggle and Achievement*, ed. Philip V. Cannistraro. New York: The New York Historical Society—The John D. Calandra Italian American Institute, 1999.

Ciccarelli, Andrea. "La letteratura dell'emigrazione oggi in Italia: definizioni e correnti." *Intersezioni* 19, no. 1 (April 1999).

De Nicola, Francesco. "Gli scrittori italiani dell'emigrazione." In *Studi di filologia e letteratura offerti a Franco Croce*. Rome: Bulzoni, 1997.

Fallaci, Oriana. *La rabbia e l'orgoglio*. Milan: Rizzoli, 2001 [American edition: *The Rage and the Pride*. New York: Rizzoli, 2002].

Gabaccia, Donna R. *Italy's Many Diasporas*. London: UCL Press, 2000.

Gardaphé, Fred L. *Dagoes Read: Tradition and the Italian American Writer*. Toronto: Guernica, 1995.

———. "The Evolution of Italian American Autobiography." In *The Italian American Heritage: A Companion to Literature and Arts*, ed. Pellegrino D'Acierno. New York: Garland, 1999.

Marazzi, Martino. "America." In *Alberto Arbasino*, ed. Marco Belpoliti and Elio Grazioli. Milan: Marcos y Marcos, 2001.

———. *Little America. Gli Stati Uniti e gli scrittori italiani del Novecento*. Milan: Marcos y Marcos, 1997.

Martelli, Sebastiano, "Dal vecchio mondo al sogno americano. Realtà e immaginario dell'emigrazione nella letteratura italiana." In *Storia dell'emigrazione italiana*, eds.

Piero Bevilacqua, Andreina De Clementi, and Emilio Franzina. Rome: Donzelli, 2001.

———. *Letteratura contaminata. Storie parole immagini tra Ottocento e Novecento.* Salerno: Pietro Laveglia, 1994.

———. "Letteratura ed emigrazione: congedo provvisorio." In *Il sogno italo-americano. Realtà e immaginario dell'emigrazione negli Stati Uniti*, ed. Sebastiano Martelli. Naples: Cuen, 1998.

———, ed. *Rimanelliana. Studi su Giose Rimanelli. Studies on Giose Rimanelli.* Stony Brook, N.Y.: Forum Italicum Publishing, 2000.

Nacci, Michela. *La barbarie del comfort. Il modello di vita americano nella cultura francese del '900.* Milan: Guerini e Associati—Istituto per gli Studi Filosofici, 1996.

Parrino, Maria. "Breaking the Silence: Autobiographies of Italian Immigrant Women." *Storia Nordamericana* 5, no. 2 (1988).

Portelli, Alessandro. *America, dopo. Immaginario e immaginazione.* Rome: Donzelli, 2002.

Sanfilippo, Matteo. "Le professioni dei viaggiatori italiani negli Stati Uniti, 1860–1992." *Il Veltro* 36, nos. 1–2 (January–April 1992).

Saresella, Daniela. *Cattolicesimo italiano e sfida americana.* Brescia: Morcelliana, 2001.

Shell, Marc, and Werner Sollors, eds. *The Multilingual Anthology of American Literature: A Reader of Original Texts with English Translations.* New York: New York University Press, 2000.

Teodori, Massimo. *La fine del mito americano.* Milan: Feltrinelli, 1975.

———. *Maledetti americani. Destra, sinistra e cattolici: storia del pregiudizio antiamericano.* Milan: Mondadori, 2002.

Verdicchio, Pasquale. *Bound by Distance: Rethinking Nationalism through the Italian Diaspora.* Madison, N.J.: Fairleigh Dickinson University Press, 1997.

———. "Unholy Manifestations: Cultural Transformations as Hereticism in the Films of De Michiel, Ferrara, Savoca, and Scorsese." In *Adjusting Sites: New Essays in Italian American Studies*, ed. William Boelhower and Rocco Pallone. Vol. 16 of Forum Italicum-Filibrary Series. Stony Brook, N.Y.: Forum Italicum, 1999.

Viscusi, Robert. "La letteratura dell'emigrazione italiana negli Stati Uniti." In *La letteratura dell'emigrazione. Gli scrittori di lingua italiana nel mondo*, ed. Jean-Jacques Marchand. Turin: Edizioni della Fondazione Agnelli, 1991.

# Index